AMERICAN POETRY

Reader's Bookshelf of American Literature

American Drama, edited by Alan S. Downer

American Literary Essays, edited by Lewis Leary

American Poetry, edited by Karl Shapiro

American Short Novels, edited by R. P. Blackmur

American Short Stories, edited by Ray B. West, Jr.

GENERAL EDITOR: WILLIAM VAN O'CONNOR

American Poetry

✳ *Edited by Karl Shapiro*

Thomas Y. Crowell Company · New York · Established 1834

Acknowledgments

Acknowledgment is gratefully made as follows on pages iv to viii for permission to reprint copyrighted material:

Conrad Aiken: "Morning Song of Senlin" from *Collected Poems* by Conrad Aiken. Copyright 1953 by Conrad Aiken. Reprinted by permission of Oxford University Press, Inc.

Stephen Vincent Benét: "American Names" from *Selected Works of Stephen Vincent Benét*, Rinehart & Company, Inc. Copyright, 1927, by Stephen Vincent Benét; copyright renewed, 1945, by Rosemary Carr Benét. "The Song of the Breath" from *John Brown's Body*, Rinehart & Company, Inc. Copyright 1927, 1928, by Stephen Vincent Benét; copyright renewed, 1955, 1956, by Rosemary Carr Benét.

John Berryman: "Homage to Mistress Bradstreet" from *Homage to Mistress Bradstreet*, by John Berryman, copyright 1956 by John Berryman. Used by permission of the publishers, Farrar, Straus and Cudahy, Inc.

Elizabeth Bishop: "A Miracle for Breakfast," "Wading at Wellfleet," and "Florida" are reprinted by permission of and arrangement with Houghton Mifflin Company, the authorized publishers.

John Ciardi: "Mystic River" reprinted by permission of the author.

Hart Crane: From *The Bridge:* "Praise for an Urn," "The Hurricane," "The Broken Tower," "Proem: To Brooklyn Bridge," "The Harbor Dawn," "Van Winkle," "The River," "National Winter Garden," "The Tunnel" from: *The Collected Poems of Hart Crane*. By permission of Liveright, Publishers, New York, N.Y. Copyright, Liveright, Inc., 1933.

Stephen Crane: "I Stood upon a High Place," "A Man Saw a Ball of Gold in the Sky," "It Was Wrong to Do This,

Said the Angel," "I Explain," "The Black Riders," "The Blades of Grass," "A Newspaper," "The Peaks," "A Slant of Sun" reprinted from *The Collected Poems of Stephen Crane* by Stephen Crane, by permission of Alfred A. Knopf, Inc. Copyright 1930 by Alfred A. Knopf, Inc.

E. E. Cummings: For "i Sing of Olaf glad and big" Copyright, 1931, 1958, by E. E. Cummings. Reprinted from *Poems 1923–1954* by E. E. Cummings by permission of Harcourt, Brace and Company, Inc. For "POEM, OR BEAUTY HURTS, MR. VINAL" and "next to of course god america i" Copyright, 1926, by Horace Liveright, renewed, 1953, by E. E. Cummings. Reprinted from *Poems 1923–1954* by E. E. Cummings by permission of Harcourt, Brace and Company, Inc. For "pity this busy monster,manunkind" and "a salesman is an it that stinks Excuse" Copyright, 1944, by E. E. Cummings. Reprinted from *Poems 1923–1954* by E. E. Cummings by permission of Harcourt, Brace and Company, Inc. For "the way to hump a cow is not" and "my father moved through dooms of love" Copyright, 1940, by E. E. Cummings. Reprinted from *Poems 1923–1954* by E. E. Cummings by permission of Harcourt, Brace and Company, Inc.

Emily Dickinson: Poems 67, 76, 89, 126, 189, 210, 214, 249, 254, 258, 265, 303, 609, 632, 640, 701, 712, 739, 1100, 1176, 1207, 1463, and 1510 reprinted by permission of the publishers from Thomas H. Johnson, Editor, *The Poems of Emily Dickinson*. Cambridge, Mass.: The Belknap Press of Harvard University Press, Copyright, 1951, 55, by The President and Fellows of Harvard College.

Richard Eberhart: "The Groundhog," "The Soul Longs to Return Whence It Came" "The Fury of Aerial Bombardment" from *Selected Poems* by Richard Eberhart. 1951. Reprinted by permission of Oxford University Press, Inc.

T. S. Eliot: "Preludes," "Rhapsody on a Windy Night," "Journey of the Magi," and "Marina" from *Collected Poems 1909–1935* by T. S. Eliot, copyright, 1936, by Harcourt, Brace and Company, Inc. and reprinted with their permission. Reprinted for the Canadian market by permission of Faber and Faber Limited.

Kenneth Fearing: "Dirge" and "SOS" from *New and Selected Poems* by Kenneth Fearing, published by Indiana University Press, copyright 1956 by Kenneth Fearing.

John Gould Fletcher: "Elegy on an Empty Skyscraper" from *Selected Poems* by John Gould Fletcher. Copyright, 1938, by John Gould Fletcher. Reprinted by permission of Rinehart & Company, Inc., New York, publishers.

Robert Frost: "Mending Wall," "The Wood-Pile," "After Apple-Picking," "The Witch of Coös," "The Tuft of Flowers," "Stopping by Woods on a Snowy Evening," "The Onset," "West-running Brook," "Acquainted with the Night," "Provide, Provide," "The Gift Outright," "Neither Out Far nor In Deep," "Departmental," "The Bear," "The Lovely Shall Be Choosers," "A Considerable Speck" from *Complete Poems of Robert Frost*. Copyright, 1930, 1949, by Henry Holt and Company, Inc.

Allen Ginsberg: "Howl," from *Howl and Other Poems*, by Allen Ginsberg. Reprinted by permission of City Lights Books.

Randall Jarrell: "The Orient Express" from *The Seven-League Crutches* by Randall Jarrell, copyright, 1951, by Randall Jarrell. Reprinted by permission of Harcourt, Brace and Company, Inc.

Robinson Jeffers: "To the Stone-Cutters" from *The Selected Poetry of Robinson Jeffers*. Copyright 1924 and renewed 1951 by Robinson Jeffers. Reprinted by permission of Random House, Inc. "Apology for Bad Dreams" and "Shine, Perishing Republic" from *The Selected Poetry of Robinson Jeffers.* Copyright 1925 and renewed 1953 by Robinson Jeffers. Reprinted by permission of Random House, Inc. "Hurt Hawks" from *The Selected Poetry of Robinson Jeffers.* Copyright 1928 and renewed 1956 by Robinson Jeffers. Reprinted by permission of Random House, Inc.

Vachel Lindsay: "The Congo" and "The Eagle That Is Forgotten" from *Collected Poems* by Vachel Lindsay. Copyright 1929 by The Macmillan Company. Reprinted by permission of The Macmillan Company.

Robert Lowell: "Mr. Edwards and the Spider," "Where the Rainbow Ends," and "The Drunken Fisherman" from *Lord Weary's Castle,* copyright, 1944, 1946, by Robert Lowell. Reprinted by permission of Harcourt, Brace and Company, Inc.

Archibald MacLeish: "Ars Poetica," "The Too-Late Born," "Empire Builders," and "You, Andrew Marvell" are reprinted by permission of and arrangement with Houghton Mifflin Company, the authorized publishers. "Brave New World" from *Active and Other Poems* by Archibald MacLeish. Copyright 1946 by Archibald MacLeish. Reprinted by permission of Random House, Inc.

Edgar Lee Masters: "Fiddler Jones," "The Village Atheist," "Carl Hamblin," "Anne Rutledge," "The Hill," "Henry C. Calhoun" from *The Spoon River Anthology* by Edgar Lee Masters, The Macmillan Company. Reprinted by permission of Mrs. Edgar Lee Masters.

Edna St. Vincent Millay: "First Fig," "Second Fig," and from "Epitaph for the Race of Man," from *Collected Poems* Edna St. Vincent Millay, Harper & Brothers. By permission of Norma Millay Ellis. Copyright 1922, 1934, 1950 by Edna St. Vincent Millay.

Marianne Moore: "Poetry" and "What Are Years?" from *Collected Poems* by Marianne Moore. Copyright 1951 by Marianne Moore. Reprinted by permission of The Macmillan Company.

Ezra Pound: "Sestina: Altaforte," "The River-Merchant's Wife: A Letter," "The Seafarer: From the Anglo-Saxon," "The Rest," "In a Station of the Metro" from *Personae.* Copyright 1926 by Ezra Pound. Reprinted by permission of New Directions.

John Crowe Ransom: "Bells for John Whiteside's Daughter," "Philomela," "The Equilibrists," "Janet Waking," "Blue Girls" reprinted from *Selected Poems* by John Crowe Ransom, by permission of Alfred A. Knopf, Inc. Copyright 1924, 1927, 1945 by Alfred A. Knopf, Inc.

Edwin Arlington Robinson: "Mr. Flood's Party," "The Mill," "New England" from *Collected Poems* by Edwin Arlington Robinson. Copyright 1937 by The Macmillan Company. Reprinted by permission of The Macmillan Company. "How Annandale Went Out" and "The Master" reprinted with the permission of Charles Scribner's Sons from *The Town Down the River* by Edwin Arlington Robinson, copyright 1910 Charles Scribner's Sons; renewal copyright 1938 Ruth Nivison. "Luke Havergal," "Richard Cory," "Cliff Klingenhagen," "Reuben Bright," and "Walt Whitman" are also published by Charles Scribner's Sons.

Selden Rodman: From the Introduction to *A New Anthology of Modern Poetry* ed. by Selden Rodman. Copyright 1938 by Random House, Inc. Reprinted by permission.

Theodore Roethke: "Dolor" from *The Lost Son & Other Poems,* by Theodore Roethke. Copyright 1947 by Theodore Roethke. Reprinted by permission of Doubleday & Company, Inc. "My Papa's

Waltz" from *The Lost Son & Other Poems,* by Theodore Roethke. Copyright 1942 Hearst Magazines, Inc. Reprinted by permission of Doubleday & Company, Inc. "Night Crow" from *The Lost Son & Other Poems,* by Theodore Roethke. Copyright 1947 by Theodore Roethke. Reprinted by permission of Doubleday & Company, Inc. "Elegy for Jane" from *The Waking,* by Theodore Roethke. Copyright 1950 by Theodore Roethke. Reprinted by permission of Doubleday & Company, Inc. "The Dream" from *Words for the Wind,* by Theodore Roethke. Copyright © 1955 Theodore Roethke. Reprinted by permission of Doubleday & Co., Inc. "The Shape of the Fire" from *Praise to the End,* by Theodore Roethke. Copyright 1950 by Theodore Roethke. Reprinted by permission of Doubleday & Company, Inc.

Carl Sandburg: "Gone," "A Fence," and "Limited" from *Cornhuskers* by Carl Sandburg. Copyright, 1918, by Henry Holt and Company, Inc. Copyright, 1946, by Carl Sandburg. "Cool Tombs" and "Bricklayer Love" from *Chicago Poems* by Carl Sandburg. Copyright, 1916, by Henry Holt and Company, Inc. Copyright, 1944, by Carl Sandburg. By permission of Henry Holt and Company, Inc.

Delmore Schwartz: "A Dog Named Ego," poem X from "The Repetitive Heart," from *In Dreams Begin Responsibilities.* Copyright 1938 by Delmore Schwartz. Reprinted by permission of New Directions. "Starlight like Intuition Pierced the Twelve" from *Vaudeville for a Princess,* copyright 1950 by New Directions. Reprinted by permission of New Directions.

Karl Shapiro: "Adam and Eve," from *Poems 1940–1953,* by Karl Shapiro. Copyright 1951 by Karl Shapiro. Reprinted by permission of Random House, Inc.

Wallace Stevens: "Sunday Morning," "Disillusionment of Ten O'Clock," "The Emperor of Ice-Cream," "The Idea of Order in Key West," "Mozart, 1935," "Of Modern Poetry," "No Possums, No Sop, No Taters," "The Poems of Our Climate" reprinted from *The Collected Poems of Wallace Stevens* by Wallace Stevens, by permission of Alfred A. Knopf, Inc. Copyright 1923, 1931, 1935, 1936, 1937, 1942, 1947, 1952, 1954 by Wallace Stevens.

Allen Tate: "The Mediterranean" copyright 1933 Yale University Press. Reprinted from *Poems 1922–1947* by Allen Tate with the permission of Charles Scribner's Sons. "Last Days of Alice" reprinted with the permission of Charles Scribner's Sons from *Poems: 1928–1931* by Allen Tate, copyright 1932 Charles Scribner's Sons. "Sonnets at Christmas" copyright 1934 New Republic, Inc. Reprinted from *Poems 1922–1947* by Allen Tate with the permission of Charles Scribner's Sons.

Edward Taylor: "Huswifery," "Upon a Spider Catching a Fly," "Meditation Eight," "The Joy of Church Fellowship," "The Ebb and Flow" from *The Poetical Works of Edward Taylor,* edited by Thomas H. Johnson, Copyright, 1939 Rockland Edition, copyright 1953, Princeton University Press.

Peter Viereck: "The Day's No Rounder Than Its Angles Are." This poem is from Peter Viereck's first book of poems, *Terror and Decorum,* New York, Charles Scribner's Sons, 1948.

Robert Penn Warren: "Original Sin: A Short Story," "Bearded Oaks," "Crime" from *Selected Poems 1923–1943* by Robert Penn Warren, copyright, 1944, by Robert Penn Warren.

Richard Wilbur: "The Death of a Toad" and "Juggler" from *Ceremony and Other Poems,* copyright, 1950, by Richard Wilbur. Reprinted by permission of Harcourt, Brace and Company, Inc.

William Carlos Williams: "Tract," "Classic Scene," "The Botticellian Trees," "This Is Just to Say" from *The Collected Earlier Poems of William Carlos Williams*. Copyright 1938, 1951 by William Carlos Williams. "The Dance" from *The Collected Later Poems of William Carlos Williams*. Copyright 1944, 1948, and 1950 by William Carlos Williams. Reprinted by permission of New Directions.

Edmund Wilson: Letter to Van Wyck Brooks from *Shock of Recognition*, Doubleday & Company, Inc., 1943; *Letters of Sherwood Anderson*, edited by Howard Mumford Jones and published by Little, Brown & Company.

Elinor Wylie: "Wild Peaches" Sonnets one through four of "Wild Peaches," by Elinor Wylie, reprinted by permission of Alfred A. Knopf, Inc. Copyright 1921, 1932 by Alfred A. Knopf, Inc.

"Losses" and "The Angels at Hamburg" by Randall Jarrell, reprinted by permission of the author.

Contents

AMERICAN POETRY

What Is American Poetry?

When I think of American poetry, the first thing that comes to my mind is the witticism of a modern British poet: "American poetry is a very easy subject to discuss for the simple reason that it does not exist." Nowadays, when American poets feel so sure of themselves, the malice of this epigram has a kind of charm. American poets repeat it and even use it in their writings. Not very long ago —a generation or two—such a quip would have been met with indignation.

To say that American poetry does not exist is simply a roundabout way of saying that our poetry still belongs to English literature. On the face of it this seems a likely argument. We still use the English language to the exclusion of any other, and despite the radically new idiom of American speech, ours is obviously a not too distant version of the mother tongue. When we consider the amazing linguistic and racial mixtures of the American people it is surprising that our language has remained as "English" as it has; for there is scarcely a corner in the United States where people speak anything else. The English writer naturally feels a proprietary interest in American literature, though it cannot be said that our poetry has been well understood in England.

The use of the same language for English and for American poetry is misleading to the student of our literature unless he bears in mind that the contents of the two poetries are quite unlike. Or rather, it is the struggle to free itself from English convention which has given our poetry its character. It is no exaggeration to say that any discussion of American poetry resolves itself into a search for the meaning of "American." This quest for self-definition may be said to be the main theme of all American literature. It is a unique theme: we do not find the Roman or the French or the British writer debating the question What is a Roman, What is a Frenchman, or What is an Englishman. But few American novelists and poets have been able to resist the theme What is an American.

At the risk of emphasizing the obvious let us look at the language situation for the American writer and poet. At the time of the founding of the United States our white population was of 90 per cent British stock (the blacks were not counted in the population). A generation after independence the Germans and the Irish began to arrive in large numbers on our shores. From the midcentury on, hordes of Irish, Dutch, Danes, Swedes, Norwegians, Swiss, and Jews entered America as homesteaders and factory laborers. Toward the end of the century still larger waves of Italians, Russians, Poles, Austrians, Bohemians, and Hungarians entered the new land. All of these people, almost without exception, were foreign-speaking or dialect-speaking peoples. And though the Englishman proper was the least represented in these grand influxes of refugees, English remained the language of education, government, and literature in the United States. The vast majority of these stocks were white Europeans, the Asiatic races having been excluded by law and by prejudice. By 1900 we were no longer what had once been

1

known as New England; we were New Europe.

Generally speaking, the New World immigrants did not belong to the lettered classes to begin with, and during the century of heavy immigration literature was left to the "Anglo-Saxon" minority, as in the early years it was left to the governing classes and the clergy. The nineteenth-century refugees from famine, political oppression, and military conscription did not come to the United States to write novels or poems nor, for that matter, to read them. A fair part of our political or semipolitical writing was done by the newcomers but almost none of the pure literature. It is not until the twentieth century that "foreign" names begin to decorate the literary anthology.

One of the most extraordinary facts about the new America was and is the rapid disappearance of Old World traits and the evolution of a common American personality. Writers have from time to time appeared shocked at this cultural amnesia and have frequently interpreted it as "materialism," "isolationism," or just an ordinary lapse into frontier barbarism. American folklore, with its love for the shooting cowboy, the gangster, and the boy who goes from rags to riches, tends to corroborate the image of the American without a past. The image is repeated in serious American literature as well with the heroic Huck Finn lighting out for the frontier to escape civilization, and the martyred Billy Budd who cannot comprehend the mores of organized society. Only among antiquarians do we find any considerable nostalgia for the home country or for the cultural past.

American poetry is a poetry of departure from the past. It is a poetry still struggling for freedom from the past and from its own enemies, the American "expatriates." It has thus far only partly succeeded in creating the appropriate poetry of the New World. The high point of our literature was reached a century ago with *Leaves of Grass.* Whitman's book was a part of a renaissance that included Emerson's *Representative Men* and Thoreau's *Walden.* Emerson, Whitman, and Thoreau have a great deal in common. Hawthorne and Melville were a part of that renaissance also and they too, in their preoccupation with innocence and newness, have a kinship with these other three writers. But there is a darker side to Hawthorne and Melville which casts shadows over the sunny landscape and on occasion caused them to be satiric at the expense of their contemporaries who were insufficiently aware of the inevitable limitations in any human situation, American or otherwise. By and large, the modernist poets, those in the Pound-Eliot line, have overstressed this darker side, and caused the waste land image to dominate not only twentieth-century poetry but all of twentieth-century literature.

Our cultural amnesia is held in contempt by most Europeans and by our noisy handful of expatriate writers, but on the whole our insistent forgetfulness of the past is the first characteristic of the American. To break loose from the grip of the old religions, the old forms of government, the old manners and morality, is still the American aim. It is no accident that America has been used from the beginning as an experimental station for every conceivable kind of utopia, religious, political, scientific, and even literary. What dream or crackpot plan has not been tried, or is not still being put into action in the U.S.? And compare the American sense of social pioneering with that of our neighbors—the Canadians to the north and the Spanish-Americans to the south. How are we to account for the mysterious dynamism of the Middle Americans, almost all of them refugees from Europe?

Our poetry is very new, raw, full of the clumsiest trials and errors and yet it has become one of the most vital in the world. Is ours a vital and influential poetry because it is great poetry in itself, or because it is the poetry of a people upon whom the eyes of the world are constantly focused for other reasons? Have we produced a "poetry for the ages" or a mere challenge to the past? American poetry is no more than a century old (a century and a half at a liberal estimate) yet it has attracted more attention in that time than literatures ten times older. Beyond a doubt it is the label "American" that accounts for the bulk of this interest.

The reader will find this anthology top-heavy on the modern side. We have included only a few poets from the seventeenth century and only one from the eighteenth! The bulk of the poetry that is more American than English comes toward the middle of the nineteenth century and thereafter. As this is not an historical survey it appeared useless to reprint the usual poets whom we remember for some historical reason rather than for literary merit. The tendency to repeat is the vice of the anthologist, and in this collection we are attempting to recast the list of American poets, emphasizing the American element. Many, if not most, of our poets have followed the literary fashions of England unthinkingly. In the seventeenth century we had our Metaphysical poets; in the eighteenth our Neo-Classical wits; in the nineteenth century our Romantics. Imitation was the rule up to the time of Poe, Emerson, and Whitman. A fair amount of competent American verse, for example Bryant and Longfellow, is mostly poetry *à la mode*, poetry that has nothing fundamentally American about it, even when it talks about honeysuckle or Hiawatha. Longfellow has always been more respected by English writers than by Americans.

Our seventeenth-century literature, by and large, is a theology-centered literature. Our eighteenth-century literature is a politics-centered literature. But in the nineteenth century there is a flowering of literary consciousness which takes two forms, one led by the intellectualizing Poe, the other by the humanizing Whitman. And twentieth-century poetry is either a "Poe" poetry or a "Whitman" poetry, with the Whitman being very much out of favor in the first half of our century.

SEVENTEENTH CENTURY

The dark determinism of the Puritan, with his bitter vengeful God and his fanatical devotion to hardship and hard work, set the tone of our early poetry, which we can still detect in some of our moderns. The New England child was taught his letters and his theology in the same breath with the baleful words:

> In Adam's fall
> We sinned all.

This was the opening of the famous *New England Primer,* also called "The Little Bible of New England." And it is typical of New England poetry that the first book published on this side of the ocean was a versified translation of the Psalms. Poetry, in other words, was tolerated if it could be made useful. The preacher Michael Wigglesworth celebrated the Calvinist hell fire in an endless series of couplets which New Englanders committed to memory by the page. It is doggerel poetry and we do not include it here, except for this sample:

> The mountains smoke, the hills are shook,
>   the earth is rent and torn
> As if she should be clear dissolved or from
>   her center borne.
> The sea doth roar, forsakes the shore, and
>   shrinks away for fear;
> The wild beasts flee into the sea, so soon
>   as He draws near . . .

> It's vain moreover for men to cover the least
>   iniquity;
> The Judge hath seen, and privy been to all
>   their villainy.

He unto light and open sight the work of
    darkness brings;
He doth unfold both new and old, both
    known and hidden things.

Thus he doth find of all mankind that stand
    at His left hand,
No mother's son but hath misdone, and
    broken God's command.
All have transgressed, even the best, and
    merited God's wrath,
Unto their own perdition and everlasting
    scath.

This kind of naive verse is somewhat re-
deemed by other New England writers.
Nearly every American anthology of
poetry begins with Anne Bradstreet, a
very competent and frequently charming
poetess, a Puritan of a more sophisticated
type. She is still read today, if only by
poets and scholars, and a twentieth-
century American poet (John Berryman)
has rediscovered Mistress Bradstreet for
himself and has written what in effect
is a love poem to his three-hundred-year-
old sweetheart. Both Anne Bradstreet
and Edward Taylor, who is the best of
our seventeenth-century poets, are very
conscious of our religious dogma. Taylor
even left a request at his death that his
poems be left unpublished, and it is only
recently that they have come to light. In
their richness of imagery and attention to
worldly beauty there may be something
that points to the death of the God-
ridden Puritan world.

EIGHTEENTH CENTURY

As English-speaking and English-read-
ing people (Americans are notorious for
their lack of interest in languages), we
tend to overlook our deep relationship
to France. Our great political visions and
ideals have more to do with French so-
cial visionary thinking than with English.
Our law is basically derived from English
law but not our sense of liberty. Herman
Melville wrote an attack on the Articles

of War of the U.S. Navy which we had
swallowed whole from English maritime
law. His account of our naval discipline
in *White Jacket* was a deciding factor in
humanizing our military regulations and
turning them away from the authoritarian
practices of the past. English law remains
the foundation of our legal thinking, but
our idealism comes from elsewhere.
Rousseau, Chateaubriand, Crèvecoeur are
as Americanized as Lafayette, and
whether their ideals were good or bad,
true or false, they are part and parcel of
American social thought. It is no accident
that the literary genius of America in its
early years went not into poetry but into
political writing. Pamphleteers like Tom
Paine (if we can claim him) were men
of journalistic genius, to say the least;
Franklin, John Adams, and Jefferson bent
their literary gifts toward shaping the
documents upon which the democratic
world would stand. The *Declaration of
Independence* was Jefferson's proudest
accomplishment and one of the most
sweeping revolutionary writings in hu-
man history. In effect, the *Declaration,*
with its premise that the "laws of nature
and nature's God" entitled us to separa-
tion from the past, called for a new hu-
man order throughout the world, the
rule of man rather than the rule of God
and the God-anointed kings.

The American poets of the eighteenth
century are weak. There is something
frivolous and irrelevant about our eight-
eenth-century poets, especially the so-
called Hartford Wits. They imitate the
fashions of eighteenth-century English
wit and satire; they do not appear to un-
derstand the magnitude of the drama
taking place before them, and on the
whole they are more sympathetic with
England than with America. The general
mediocrity of their verse detracts from
whatever position they may occupy even
in a purely historical scheme of things.

The only poet we represent from this
period is Philip Freneau, the critic and

opponent of the Hartford Wits, revolutionary, sea captain, and the first American poet who tried in poetry to write without benefit of the British example.

NINETEENTH CENTURY

It is the habit of modern anthologists, editors, and poets to tell their readers that American poetry reaches its high point in the twentieth century. This is a mistaken view of our poetry, in my opinion. In the nineteenth century we produced the one American poet who is a world poet, Walt Whitman. In the nineteenth century we produced also the school of Moderns who derive from Poe, and who are the antithesis of Whitman. The immense poetic activity of our time is probably a reflection of statistical literacy more than it is a spontaneous growth of poetic consciousness. We must not be misled by the size and the cleverness of the contemporary anthology.

One of the best critics of American literature is D. H. Lawrence. Speaking of the rhythm of American art-activity Lawrence says that there are two forces at work:

1. A disintegrating and sloughing of the old consciousness.
2. The forming of a new consciousness underneath.

And Edgar Allan Poe, says Lawrence, had only the first disintegrative force in his work. This makes Poe almost more a scientist than a poet. Poe is a man who must reduce everything to knowledge; he must *know* even at the expense of killing in order to know. Poe is credited with inventing the "whodunit," the modern detective story; he is also the father of *ratiocinative* criticism, the "scientific" criticism which is the fashion in the twentieth century.

Walt Whitman, on the other hand, celebrates the new consciousness of man, the American consciousness. To Poe, God is a great and terrifying Will. To Whitman, man and the universe are divine. All of Poe is dressed in mourning for the terrible funeral of the old consciousness; while Whitman clothes the world and everything in the world with light.

Walt Whitman is one of the most misinterpreted writers in all literary history, and he has been less understood in America than in any other country. The most common error about Whitman which we find in textbooks is that *Leaves of Grass* is primarily a political document celebrating the size and the glorious might of these States. He is thus mistakenly considered a kind of historical poet, or a self-styled Poet Laureate of America. Among modern critics, T. S. Eliot and Ezra Pound have done much to encourage this distorted view of Whitman. But even our scholars have misled us about Whitman to a large degree. The tradition of rationalism which pervades our scholarship has led scholars to overlook the central meaning of Whitman, which is *mystical and irreligious.* It is in this significant respect that Whitman is related to Emerson, Thoreau, the primitivist Melville, and the whole tradition of mystical literature from the *Bhagavad-Gita* up through Blake. This literature is taboo to the Modernist critic and scholar, who see in it the destruction of institutions and a threat to civilization itself. Whitman and the "Transcendentalists" are in fact enemies of society and of organized religion and of all that is left over from the historical lumber-room of Europe, as Hegel called it. They are the carriers of the American dream of the new free race of men.

Beyond question the poem "Song of Myself" records an actual mystical experience of the author. The modern critic, who is embarrassed at any mention of a "mystical experience," turns away from the poem and its meaning. In so doing he departs from that element in our thinking and writing which is perhaps the most authentic American element. The underlying idealism of equality, freedom from the past, and the sense of "nature's law" are extended in Whitman's poetry to a vision of the universal America and to the cosmic harmony of all things. The Modernist, who sees everything in terms of historical struggle and inherent evil, naturally disdains Whitman's Americanism. The Modernist turns rather to Poe.

Poe's reputation as poet and critic has always been higher in Europe than in this country. Because of Charles Baudelaire's fascination with Poe, Poe may be considered the godfather of Symbolist poetry and thus one of the godfathers of twentieth-century poetry. The morbidity of Poe's poems and tales was very attractive to the author of *Flowers of Evil,* who found in them a reflection of his own despair. The somewhat phony aristocratic pose of Poe also attracted the democracy-hating Baudelaire. And the cold rationalism of the American lent a kind of Faustian "scientific" glamour to the analysis of society which the Symbolists were to make one of their fields of interest. But above all, it was Poe's discovery of the "effect" in poetry which was to influence Symbolist and Modern poetry and to turn it into the most obscure poetry in history. The modern idea that the thing is not as important in a work of art as the effect of the thing is a doctrine of Poe's which has led to many grotesque forms of poetry in our age. Add to this the psychological nostalgia of Poe for the splendors and vulgarities of the past, and his worship of the perverse in human nature, and we have all the trappings for the founding of a new school of poetry. It was easy for the French poet Baudelaire to turn Poe's images into a replica of man's fall from grace and from civilization. Modern civilization especially was to be the enemy of the new poetry; the villain was Progress.

TWENTIETH CENTURY

Twentieth-century poetry (the first half of it certainly) belongs to the Modernists or, as they shrewdly call themselves, the Modern Classicists. These Classicists are led by Ezra Pound and his disciple T. S. Eliot, both of whom follow a kind of esthetic-political-religious platform laid down by an English essayist named T. E. Hulme. The planks of this platform are these: a belief in Original Sin or in the natural brutality of man; a belief in aristocratic institutions and in the leadership principle; a belief in the poet or artist as a priest of civilized culture and the interpreter of history.

The anti-Americanism of Eliot and Pound manifests itself in various ways in contemporary American verse. In E. E. Cummings, for example, the salesman, the politician, the soldier, the business man, and the scientist are all mercilessly lampooned. Nobody in modern America, in fact, is left unscathed by this satirical poet except the poet himself, members of his family, and a few isolated individuals who have never been drawn into the "system." Following the lead of Eliot and Pound, many other modern poets write out of their contempt for modern life. Most of these poets, also following the lead of Eliot and Pound, consider Whitman a provincial flag-waving rustic who never learned how to write a respectable line of verse.

But this snobbish and expatriate brand of anti-Americanism is not the only kind in the modern anthology. There is a more native variety which we see in poets like Edwin Arlington Robinson and Edgar Lee Masters. Masters describes in his *Spoon River* portraits the degeneration of the pioneer spirit in the Middle West into the petty self-centered and vicious lives of villagers. Robinson takes a somewhat similar view of New England men, though with a good deal more subtlety.

And Robinson Jeffers, following the intellectual fads of the early twentieth century (Freud and Spengler with their sexual and historical pessimism) condemns not only America but all the works of man. Jeffers dreams of a world in which man himself is no more—the not uncommon nihilistic image in so much popular writing of our day.

There are virtually no poets of the twentieth century who carry on the Whitman-Emerson-Thoreau view of American man. A poet like Robert Frost, for all his genius and control, is really more of an English than an American poet, more of a Victorian than a contemporary. The New England mask which he wears and which becomes him perfectly is, after all, only a literary device for talking about man in general philosophical terms. There is nothing of the visionary or the seer in Frost, nor of the revolutionary, nor even of the idealist. Frost has discovered the balance of man in the New England landscape, yet it is a specialized man—the white, Protestant, small farmer of Anglo-Saxon stock. Frost is without words when it comes to, say, the Bostonian or New Yorker, the New England Irish Catholic, or the Negro, or the Middle Western farmer. In symbolizing the American through his New England countryman he does not so much oversimplify our situation as to ignore the twentieth-century world. Frost really sees America through the eyes of the nineteenth-century rural New Englander.

Whitman has a minor following in poets like Sandburg, Fletcher and Lindsay, though these men seem to miss the real import of *Leaves of Grass.* They are fascinated by imagery and the rhythms of American speech. Sandburg celebrates the free immigrant but in rather heavy-handed journalistic poetry; Lindsay is virtually the only American poet to date who has seriously adopted the rhythms of the Negro and the Midwest hymnal.

The most respected though probably least read of the modern followers of Eliot and Pound are Marianne Moore, Wallace Stevens, and Archibald MacLeish. Stevens is the nearest thing to the French Symbolists we have and thereby shares a relationship with Eliot. Marianne Moore has stuck to the dry prose statement and the image which Eliot early recommended to her. MacLeish has followed Eliot, Pound, and the contemporary French poet St. John Perse in the use of "mythic method"; his beliefs, however, are hard to ascertain, though it is clear that he takes the aristocratic view of Poe, Baudelaire, and Eliot, without somehow completely violating his interest in democracy.

Every attempt to revive the Whitman influence in our time has thus far been defeated by the "new criticism," an immense collection of writings embodying the Pound-Eliot-Hulme esthetic and politick. An example in passing is Hart Crane's *The Bridge,* an epic work which has been consistently denigrated by the new critics and Classicists. The Hart Crane influence is therefore considered by the Eliot faction to be a weakening, undisciplined, "Romantic" influence. At the same time Hart Crane, more than other twentieth-century poets, except perhaps D. H. Lawrence, is a symbolic figure for the modern visionary and the poet who sees beyond civilizations and history into the great significance of man.

But perhaps it is an exaggeration to say that the Whitman vision has been defeated by the New Criticism. The fact is that we have had no poets, other than Crane and William Carlos Williams, who have been successful in re-establishing the Whitman influence.

It appears possible that the remaining years of the twentieth century will manifest an increasing reaction against the Europeanism of twentieth-century American poetry, and a return to the mystique of the American vision as it is expressed in "Song of Myself." The definition of *American* is given us in varied works from our own brief past and not merely in poems. We find its nature and essence in Whitman above all, but also in the political documents of the founding fathers, in *Huckleberry Finn,* in Melville's islanders, in Thoreau, in Hawthorne's *The House of the Seven Gables,* in the poetry of Crane and William Carlos Williams. These writers, and their works, are only beginning to assume their proper importance for us. Each of these writers has attempted a partial definition of what it is to be American.

Anne Bradstreet

✳ 1612(?)–1672

The Flesh and the Spirit

In secret place where once I stood
Close by the banks of lacrim flood,
I heard two sisters reason on
Things that are past and things to come.
One Flesh was called, who had her eye
On worldly wealth and vanity;
The other Spirit, who did rear
Her thoughts unto a higher sphere.
"Sister," quoth Flesh, "what liv'st thou
   on—
Nothing but meditation?   10
Doth Contemplation feed thee, so
Regardlessly to let earth go?
Can Speculation satisfy
Notion without Reality?
Dost dream of things beyond the moon,
And dost thou hope to dwell there soon?
Hast treasures there laid up in store,
That all in th' world thou count'st but
   poor?
Art fancy sick, or turned a sot,
To catch at shadows which are not?   20
Come, come, I'll show unto thy sense
Industry hath its recompense.
What canst desire but thou mayst see
True substance in variety?
Dost honor like? Acquire the same,
As some to their immortal fame;
And trophies to thy name erect
Which wearing time shall ne'er deject.
For riches dost thou long full sore?
Behold enough of precious store.   30
Earth hath more silver, pearls, and gold
Than eyes can see or hands can hold.
Affect'st thou pleasure? Take thy fill,
Earth hath enough of what you will.
Then let not go, what thou mayst find,
For things unknown, only in mind."
Spirit: "Be still, thou unregenerate part;
Disturb no more my settled heart,
For I have vowed (and so will do)
Thee as a foe, still to pursue,   40
And combat with thee will and must
Until I see thee laid in th' dust.
Sisters we are, yea, twins we be,
Yet deadly feud 'twixt thee and me;
For from one father are we not:
Thou by old Adam wast begot,
But my arise is from above,
Whence my dear Father I do love.
Thou speak'st me fair but hat'st me sore;
Thy flattering shows I'll trust no more.
How oft thy slave hast thou me made
When I believed what thou hast said,
And never had more cause of woe   53
Than when I did what thou bad'st do.
I'll stop mine ears at these thy charms
And count them for my deadly harms.
Thy sinful pleasures I do hate,
Thy riches are to me no bait,
Thine honors do nor will I love;
For my ambition lies above.   60
My greatest honor it shall be
When I am victor over thee
And triumph shall, with laurel head,
When thou my captive shalt be led.
How I do live thou need'st not scoff,
For I have meat thou know'st not of;
The hidden manna I do eat,
The word of life it is my meat.
My thoughts do yield me more content
Than can thy hours in pleasure spent.
Nor are they shadows which I catch,   71
Nor fancies vain at which I snatch;
But reach at things that are so high,
Beyond thy dull capacity,
Eternal substance I do see,

With which enriched I would be;
Mine eye doth pierce the heavens, and
    see
What is invisible to thee.
My garments are not silk nor gold
Nor such like trash which earth doth
    hold,   80
But royal robes I shall have on
More glorious than the glist'ring sun.
My crown not diamonds, pearls, and
    gold,
But such as angels' heads infold.
The City where I hope to dwell
There's none on earth can parallel;
The stately walls both high and strong
Are made of precious jasper stone;
The gates of pearl both rich and clear;
And angels are for porters there;   90
The streets thereof transparent gold,
Such as no eye did e'er behold;
A crystal river there doth run,
Which doth proceed from the Lamb's
    throne;
Of life there are the waters sure,
Which shall remain forever pure;
Nor sun nor moon they have no need,
For glory doth from God proceed;
No candle there, nor yet torchlight,
For there shall be no darksome night.
From sickness and infirmity   101
For evermore they shall be free,
Nor withering age shall e'er come there,
But beauty shall be bright and clear.
This City pure is not for thee,
For things unclean there shall not be.
If I of heaven may have my fill,
Take thou the world, and all that will."

Upon the Burning of Our House

JULY 10TH, 1666

In silent night when rest I took,
For sorrow near I did not look,
I waken'd was with thund'ring noise
And piteous shrieks of dreadful voice.

That fearful sound of fire and fire,
Let no man know is my desire.

I, starting up, the light did spy,
And to my God my heart did cry
To strengthen me in my distress
And not to leave me succourless.   10
Then coming out beheld a space,
The flame consume my dwelling place.

And, when I could no longer look,
I blest his Name that gave and took,
That laid my goods now in the dust:
Yea so it was, and so 'twas just.
It was his own: it was not mine;
Far be it that I should repine.

He might of all justly bereft,
But yet sufficient for us left.   20
When by the ruins oft I past,
My sorrowing eyes aside did cast,
And here and there the places spy
Where oft I sat, and long did lie.

Here stood that trunk, and there that
    chest;
There lay that store I counted best:
My pleasant things in ashes lie,
And them behold no more shall I.
Under thy roof no guest shall sit,
Nor at thy table eat a bit.   30

No pleasant tale shall e'er be told,
Nor things recounted done of old.
No candle e'er shall shine in thee,
Nor bridegroom's voice e'er heard shall
    be.
In silence ever shalt thou lie;
Adieu, adieu; all's vanity.

Then straight I gin my heart to chide,
And did thy wealth on earth abide?
Didst fix thy hope on mould'ring dust,
The arm of flesh didst make thy trust?
Raise up thy thoughts above the sky   41
That dunghill mists away may fly.

Thou hast an house on high erect,
Fram'd by that mighty Architect,
With glory richly furnished,
Stands permanent tho' this be fled.

It's purchased, and paid for too
By him who hath enough to do.

A prize so vast as is unknown,
Yet, by his gift, is made thine own.   50
There's wealth enough, I need no more;
Farewell my pelf, farewell my store.
The world no longer let me love,
My hope and treasure lies above.

A Letter to Her Husband

Phoebus, make haste, the day's too long,
   be gone;
The silent night's the fittest time for
   moan.
But stay this once, unto my suit give ear,
And tell my griefs in either hemisphere;
And if the whirling of thy wheels don't
   drown'd
The woful accents of my doleful sound,
If in thy swift carrier thou canst make
   stay,
I crave this boon, this errand by the way:
Commend me to the man more loved
   than life,
Shew him the sorrows of his widowed
   wife,   10
My dumpish thoughts, my groans, my
   brakish tears,
My sobs, my longing hopes, my doubt-
   ing fears,
And if he love, how can he there abide?
My interest's more than all the world
   beside.
He that can tell the stars or ocean sand,
Or all the grass that in the meads do
   stand,
The leaves in the woods, the hail or drops
   of rain,
Or in a cornfield number every grain,
Or every mote that in the sunshine hops,
May count my sighs and number all my
   drops.   20
Tell him the countless steps that thou
   dost trace,

That once a day thy spouse thou mayst
   embrace;
And when thou canst not treat by loving
   mouth,
Thy rays afar salute her from the south.
But for one month I see no day, poor
   soul,
Like those far situate under the pole,
Which day by day long wait for thy
   arise:
O how they joy when thou dost light the
   skys.
O Phoebus, hadst thou but thus long
   from thine
Restrained the beams of thy beloved
   shine,   30
At thy return, if so thou could'st or durst,
Behold a Chaos blacker than the first.
Tell him here's worse than a confused
   matter—
His little world's a fathom under water;
Nought but the fervor of his ardent
   beams
Hath power to dry the torrent of these
   streams.
Tell him I would say more, but cannot
   well:
Oppressed minds abruptest tales do tell.
Now post with double speed, mark what
   I say;   39
By all our loves conjure him not to stay.

To My Dear and
Loving Husband

If ever two were one, then surely we.
If ever man were loved by wife, then
   thee;
If ever wife was happy in a man,
Compare with me ye women if you can.
I prize thy love more than whole mines
   of gold,
Or all the riches that the East doth hold.
My love is such that rivers cannot
   quench,

Nor ought but love from thee give recompense.
Thy love is such I can no way repay;
The heavens reward thee manifold, I pray. 10
Then while we live, in love let's so persever,
That when we live no more we may live ever.

Edward Taylor

✳ 1645?–1729

Huswifery

Make me, O Lord, thy Spin[n]ing Wheele compleat;
    Thy Holy Worde my Distaff make for mee.
Make mine Affections thy Swift Flyers neate,
    And make my Soule thy holy Spoole to bee.
    My Conversation make to be thy Reele,
    And reele the yarn thereon spun of thy Wheele.

Make me thy Loome then, knit therein this Twine:
    And make thy Holy Spirit, Lord, winde quills:
Then weave the Web thyselfe. The yarn is fine.
    Thine Ordinances make my Fulling Mills. 10
    Then dy the same in Heavenly Colours Choice,
    All pinkt with Varnish't Flowers of Paradise.

Then cloath therewith mine Understanding, Will,
    Affections, Judgment, Conscience, Memory;

My Words and Actions, that their shine may fill
My wayes with glory and thee glorify.
Then mine apparell shall display before yee
That I am Cloathd in Holy robes for glory.

Upon a Spider Catching a Fly

Thou sorrow, venom Elfe:
    Is this thy play,
To spin a web out of thyselfe
    To Catch a Fly?
    For why?

I saw a pettish wasp
    Fall foule therein:
Whom yet thy whorle pins did no[t hasp]
    Lest he should fling
    His sting. 10

But as afraid, remote
    Didst stand hereat,
And with thy little fingers stroke
    And gently tap
    His back.

Thus gently him didst treate
    Lest he should pet,
And in a froppish, aspish heate
    Should greatly fret
    Thy net. 20

Whereas the silly Fly,
    Caught by its leg,
Thou by the throate took'st hastily,
    And 'hinde the head
    Bite Dead.

This goes to pot, that not
    Nature doth call.
Strive not above what strength hath got,
    Lest in the brawle
    Thou fall. 30

This Fray seems thus to us:
    Hells Spider gets

His intrails spun to whip Cords thus,
  And wove to nets,
    And sets.

To tangle Adams race
  In's stratagems
To their Destructions, Spoil'd, made base
  By venom things,
    Damn'd Sins.   40

But mighty, Gracious Lord,
  Communicate
Thy Grace to breake the Cord; afford
  Us Glorys Gate
    And State.

We'l Nightingaile sing like,
  When pearcht on high
In Glories Cage, thy glory, bright:
  [Yea,] thankfully,
    For joy.   50

Meditation Eight

  John VI: 51. I am the living bread.

I kenning through Astronomy Divine
  The Worlds bright Battlement, where-
    in I spy
A Golden Path my Pensill cannot line
  From that bright Throne unto my
    Threshold ly.
  And while my puzzled thoughts about
    it pore,
  I find the Bread of Life in't at my
    doore.

When that this Bird of Paradise put in
  The Wicker Cage (my Corps) to
    tweedle praise
Had peckt the Fruit forbid: and so did
    fling
  Away its Food, and lost its golden
    dayes,   10
  It fell into Celestiall Famine sore,
  And never could attain a morsell more.

Alas! alas! Poore Bird, what wilt thou
    doe?
  This Creatures field no food for Souls
    e're gave:
And if thou knock at Angells dores, they
    show
  An Empty Barrell: they no soul bread
    have.
  Alas! Poore Bird, the Worlds White
    Loafe is done,
  And cannot yield thee here the small-
    est Crumb.

In this sad state, Gods Tender Bowells
    run
  Out streams of Grace: and he to end
    all strife,   20
The Purest Wheate in Heaven, his deare-
    dear Son
  Grinds, and kneads up into this Bread
    of Life:
  Which Bread of Life from Heaven
    down came and stands
  Disht on thy Table up by Angells
    Hands.

Did God mould up this Bread in Heaven,
    and bake,
  Which from his Table came, and to
    thine goeth?
Doth he bespeake thee thus: This Soule
    Bread take;
  Come, Eate thy fill of this, thy Gods
    White Loafe?
  Its Food too fine for Angells; yet come,
    take
  And Eate thy fill! Its Heavens Sugar
    Cake.   30

What Grace is this knead in this Loafe?
    This thing
  Souls are but petty things it to admire.
Yee Angells, help: This fill would to
    the brim
  Heav'ns   whelm'd-down   Chrystall
    meele Bowle, yea and higher.
  This Bread of Life dropt in thy mouth
    doth Cry:
  Eate, Eate me, Soul, and thou shalt
    never dy.

The Joy of Church Fellowship

In heaven soaring up I dropt an ear
  On earth, and, oh! sweet melody!
And listening found it was the saints who
    were
    Encoached for heaven that sang for
    joy.
  For in Christ's coach they sweetly sing
As they to glory ride therein.

Oh, joyous hearts! Enfired with holy
    flame!
  Is speech thus tasselèd with praise?
Will not your inward fire of joy contain,
  That it in open flames doth blaze?   10
  For in Christ's coach saints sweetly
    sing
As they to glory ride therein.

And if a string do slip by chance, they
    soon
  Do screw it up again, whereby
They set it in a more melodious tune
  And a diviner harmony.
  For in Christ's coach they sweetly sing
As they to glory ride therein.

In all their acts public and private, nay
  And secret too, they praise impart;   20
But in their acts divine and worship, they
  With hymns do offer up their heart.
  Thus in Christ's coach they sweetly
    sing
As they to glory ride therein.

Some few not in; and some, whose time
    and place
  Block up this coach's way, do go
As travellers afoot, and so do trace
  The road that gives them right thereto.
  While in this coach these sweetly sing
As they to glory ride therein.   30

The Ebb and Flow

When first Thou on me, Lord, wrought-
    est Thy sweet print,

My heart was made Thy tinder box.
My 'ffections were Thy tinder in't,
  Where fell Thy sparks by drops.
These holy sparks of heavenly fire that
    came
Did ever catch and often out would
    flame.

But now my heart is made Thy censer
    trim,
  Full of Thy golden altar's fire,
  To offer up sweet incense in
    Unto Thyself entire: 10
I find my tinder scarce Thy sparks can
    feel
That drop out from Thy holy flint and
    steel.

Hence doubts out-bud for fear Thy fire in
    me
  Is a mocking ignis fatuus;
  Or lest Thine altar's fire out be
    It's hid in ashes thus.
Yet when the bellows of Thy spirit blow
Away mine ashes, then Thy fire doth
    glow.

Philip Freneau
✳ 1752–1832

To the Memory of the
Brave Americans

UNDER GENERAL GREENE, IN SOUTH CARO-
LINA, WHO FELL IN THE ACTION OF SEP-
TEMBER 8, 1781

At Eutaw Springs the valiant died;
  Their limbs with dust are covered
    o'er—
Weep on, ye springs, your tearful tide;
  How many heroes are no more!

If in this wreck of ruin, they
  Can yet be thought to claim a tear,

O smite your gentle breast, and say
  The friends of freedom slumber here!

Thou, who shalt trace this bloody plain,
  If goodness rules thy generous breast,
Sigh for the wasted rural reign;   11
  Sigh for the shepherds, sunk to rest!

Stranger, their humble graves adorn;
  You too may fall, and ask a tear;
'Tis not the beauty of the morn
  That proves the evening shall be
    clear.—

They saw their injured country's woe;
  The flaming town, the wasted field;
Then rushed to meet the insulting foe;
  They took the spear—but left the
    shield.   20

Led by thy conquering genius, Greene,
  The Britons they compelled to fly;
None distant viewed the fatal plain,
  None grieved, in such a cause to die—

But, like the Parthian, famed of old,
  Who, flying, still their arrows threw,
These routed Britons, full as bold,
  Retreated, and retreating slew.

Now rest in peace, our patriot band;
  Though far from nature's limits thrown,
We trust they find a happier land,   31
  A brighter sunshine of their own.

The Parting Glass

The man that joins in life's career
And hopes to find some comfort here,
To rise above this earthly mass,—
The only way's to drink his glass.

But still, on this uncertain stage
Where hopes and fears the soul engage,
And while, amid the joyous band,
Unheeded flows the measured sand,
Forget not as the moments pass
That time shall bring the parting glass!

In spite of all the mirth I've heard,   11
This is the glass I always feared,

The glass that would the rest destroy,
The farewell cup, the close of joy!

With you, whom reason taught to think,
I could for ages sit and drink;
But with the fool, the sot, the ass,
I haste to take the parting glass.

The luckless wight, that still delays
His draught of joys to future days,   20
Delays too long—for then, alas!
Old age steps up, and—breaks the glass!

The nymph who boasts no borrowed
    charms,
Whose sprightly wit my fancy warms,—
What though she tends this country inn,
And mixes wine and deals out gin?
With such a kind, obliging lass,
I sigh to take the parting glass.

With him who always talks of gain
(Dull Momus, of the plodding train),   30
The wretch who thrives by others' woes,
And carries grief where'er he goes,—
With people of this knavish class
The first is still my parting glass,

With those that drink before they dine,
With him that apes the grunting swine,
Who fills his page with low abuse,
And strives to act the gabbling goose
Turned out by fate to feed on grass—
Boy, give me quick, the parting glass.   40

The man whose friendship is sincere,
Who knows no guilt, and feels no fear,—
It would require a heart of brass
With him to take the parting glass!

With him who quaffs his pot of ale,
Who holds to all an even scale,
Who hates a knave in each disguise,
And fears him not—whate'er his size—
With him, well pleased my days to pass,
May   Heaven   forbid   the   Parting
    Glass!   50

The Indian Burying Ground

In spite of all the learned have said,
  I still my old opinion keep;

The posture, that we give the dead,
  Points out the soul's eternal sleep.

Not so the ancients of these lands—
  The Indian, when from life released,
Again is seated with his friends,
  And shares again the joyous feast.

His imaged birds, and painted bowl,
  And venison, for a journey dressed,   10
Bespeak the nature of the soul,
  Activity, that knows no rest.

His bow, for action ready bent,
  And arrows, with a head of stone,
Can only mean that life is spent,
  And not the old ideas gone.

Thou, stranger, that shalt come this way,
  No fraud upon the dead commit—
Observe the swelling turf, and say
  They do not lie, but here they sit.   20

Here still a lofty rock remains,
  On which the curious eye may trace
(Now wasted, half, by wearing rains)
  The fancies of a ruder race.

Here still an aged elm aspires,
  Beneath whose far-projecting shade
(And which the shepherd still admires)
  The children of the forest played!

There oft a restless Indian queen
  (Pale Shebah, with her braided hair)
And many a barbarous form is seen   31
  To chide the man that lingers there.

By midnight moons, o'er moistening
    dews;
  In habit for the chase arrayed,
The hunter still the deer pursues,
  The hunter and the deer, a shade!

And long shall timorous fancy see
  The painted chief, and pointed spear,
And Reason's self shall bow the knee
  To shadows and delusions here.   40

The Wild Honey Suckle

Fair flower, that dost so comely grow,
Hid in this silent, dull retreat,

Untouched thy honied blossoms blow,
Unseen thy little branches greet:
  No roving foot shall crush thee here,
  No busy hand provoke a tear.

By Nature's self in white arrayed,
She bade thee shun the vulgar eye,
And planted here the guardian shade,
And sent soft waters murmuring by;   10
  Thus quietly thy summer goes,
  Thy days declining to repose.

Smit with those charms, that must decay,
I grieve to see your future doom;
They died—nor were those flowers more
    gay,
The flowers that did in Eden bloom;
  Unpitying frosts, and Autumn's power
  Shall leave no vestige of this flower.

From morning suns and evening dews
At first thy little being came: 20
If nothing once, you nothing lose,
For when you die you are the same;
  The space between, is but an hour,
  The frail duration of a flower.

On the Universality and Other Attributes of the God of Nature

All that we see, about, abroad,
What is it all, but nature's God?
In meaner works discovered here
No less than in the starry sphere.

In seas, on earth, this God is seen;
All that exist, upon him lean;
He lives in all, and never strayed
A moment from the works he made:

His system fixed on general laws
Bespeaks a wise creating cause;   10
Impartially he rules mankind
And all that on this globe we find.

Unchanged in all that seems to change,
Unbounded space is his great range;
To one vast purpose always true,
No time, with him, is old or new.

In all the attributes divine
Unlimited perfectings shine;

In these enwrapt, in these complete,
All virtues in that centre meet.   20

This power doth all powers transcend,
To all intelligence a friend,
Exists, the greatest and the best
Throughout all the worlds, to make them
    blest.

All that he did he first approved,
He all things into being loved;
O'er all he made he still presides,
For them in life, or death provides.

To a Caty-did

In a branch of willow hid
Sings the evening Caty-did:
From the lofty locust bough
Feeding on a drop of dew,
In her suit of green arrayed
Hear her singing in the shade
    Caty-did, Caty-did, Caty-did!

While upon a leaf you tread,
Or repose your little head,
On your sheet of shadows laid,   10
All the day you nothing said:
Half the night your cheery tongue
Reveled out its little song,
    Nothing else but Caty-did.

From your lodgings on the leaf
Did you utter joy or grief?—
Did you only mean to say,
I have had my summer's day,
And am passing, soon, away
To the grave of Caty-did:—   20
    Poor, unhappy Caty-did!

But you would have uttered more
Had you known of nature's power—
From the world when you retreat,
And a leaf's your winding sheet,
Long before your spirit fled,
Who can tell but nature said,
Live again, my Caty-did!
    Live and chatter, Caty-did.

Tell me, what did Caty do?   30
Did she mean to trouble you?

Why was Caty not forbid
To trouble little Caty-did?
Wrong indeed at you to fling,
Hurting no one while you sing
    Caty-did! Caty-did! Caty-did!

Why continue to complain?
Caty tells me, she again
Will not give you plague or pain:—
Caty says you may be hid   40
Caty will not go to bed
While you sing us Caty-did.
    Caty-did! Caty-did! Caty-did!

But while singing, you forgot
To tell us what did Caty not:
Caty did not think of cold,
Flocks retiring to the fold,
Winter, with his wrinkles old,
Winter, that yourself foretold
    When you gave us Caty-did.   50

Stay securely in your nest;
Caty now, will do her best,
All she can to make you blest;
But, you want no human aid—
Nature, when she formed you, said,
"Independent you are made,
My dear little Caty-did:
Soon yourself must disappear
With the verdure of the year,—"
And to go, we know not where,   60
    With your song of Caty-did.

William Cullen Bryant
✳ 1794–1878

Thanatopsis

To him who in the love of Nature holds
Communion with her visible forms, she
        speaks
A various language; for his gayer hours
She has a voice of gladness, and a smile
And eloquence of beauty, and she glides
Into his darker musings, with a mild

And healing sympathy, that steals away
Their sharpness, ere he is aware. When
    thoughts
Of the last bitter hour come like a blight
Over thy spirit, and sad images   10
Of the stern agony, and shroud, and pall,
And breathless darkness, and the narrow
    house,
Make thee to shudder, and grow sick at
    heart,—
Go forth, under the open sky, and list
To Nature's teachings, while from all
    around—
Earth and her waters, and the depths of
    air,—
Comes a still voice—
             Yet a few days, and thee
The all-beholding sun shall see no more
In all his course; nor yet in the cold
    ground,
Where thy pale form was laid, with many
    tears,   20
Nor in the embrace of ocean, shall exist
Thy image. Earth, that nourished thee,
    shall claim
Thy growth, to be resolved to earth again,
And, lost each human trace, surrendering
    up
Thine individual being, shalt thou go
To mix forever with the elements,
To be a brother to the insensible rock
And to the sluggish clod, which the rude
    swain
Turns with his share, and treads upon.
    The oak
Shall send his roots abroad, and pierce
    thy mould.   30

    Yet not to thine eternal resting-place
Shalt thou retire alone, nor couldst thou
    wish
Couch more magnificent. Thou shalt lie
    down
With patriarchs of the infant world, with
    kings,
The powerful of the earth, the wise, the
    good,
Fair forms, and hoary seers of ages past,
All in one mighty sepulchre. The hills

Rock-ribbed and ancient as the sun, the
    vales
Stretching in pensive quietness between;
The venerable woods—rivers that move
In majesty, and the complaining brooks
That make the meadows green; and,
    poured round all,   42
Old Ocean's gray and melancholy
    waste,—
Are but the solemn decorations all
Of the great tomb of man. The golden
    sun,
The planets, all the infinite host of
    heaven,
Are shining on the sad abodes of death,
Through the still lapse of ages. All that
    tread
The globe are but a handful to the tribes
That slumber in its bosom.—Take the
    wings   50
Of morning, pierce the Barcan wilder-
    ness,
Or lose thyself in the continuous woods
Where rolls the Oregon, and hears no
    sound,
Save his own dashings—yet the dead are
    there:
And millions in those solitudes, since first
The flight of years began, have laid them
    down
In their last sleep—the dead reign there
    alone.
So shalt thou rest, and what if thou with-
    draw
In silence from the living, and no friend
Take note of thy departure? All that
    breathe   60
Will share thy destiny. The gay will laugh
When thou art gone, the solemn brood of
    care
Plod on, and each one as before will
    chase
His favorite phantom; yet all these shall
    leave
Their mirth and their employments, and
    shall come
And make their bed with thee. As the
    long train
Of ages glide away, the sons of men,

The youth in life's green spring, and he
     who goes
In the full strength of years, matron and
     maid,
The speechless babe, and the gray-
     headed man—   70
Shall one by one be gathered to thy side,
By those, who in their turn shall follow
     them.

     So live, that when thy summons comes
          to join
The innumerable caravan, which moves
To that mysterious realm, where each
     shall take
His chamber in the silent halls of death,
Thou go not, like the quarry-slave at
     night,
Scourged to his dungeon, but, sustained
     and soothed
By an unfaltering trust, approach thy
     grave,
Like one who wraps the drapery of his
     couch   80
About him, and lies down to pleasant
     dreams.

*Inscription for the Entrance
to a Wood*

Stranger, if thou hast learned a truth
     which needs
No school of long experience, that the
     world
Is full of guilt and misery, and hast seen
Enough of all its sorrows, crimes, and
     cares
To tire thee of it, enter this wild wood
And view the haunts of Nature. The calm
     shade
Shall bring a kindred calm; and the sweet
     breeze,
That makes the green leaves dance, shall
     waft a balm
To thy sick heart. Thou wilt find nothing
     here

Of all that pained thee in the haunts of
     men   10
And made thee loathe thy life. The
     primal curse
Fell, it is true, upon the unsinning earth,
But not in vengeance. God hath yoked to
     guilt
Her pale tormentor, misery. Hence these
     shades
Are still the abodes of gladness: the thick
     roof
Of green and stirring branches is alive
And musical with birds, that sing and
     sport
In wantonness of spirit; while, below,
The squirrel, with raised paws and form
     erect,
Chirps merrily. Throngs of insects in the
     shade   20
Try their thin wings and dance in the
     warm beam
That waked them into life. Even the
     green trees
Partake the deep contentment; as they
     bend
To the soft winds, the sun from the blue
     sky
Looks in and sheds a blessing on the
     scene.
Scarce less the cleft-born wild-flower
     seems to enjoy
Existence than the wingèd plunderer
That sucks its sweets. The mossy rocks
     themselves,
And the old and ponderous trunks of
     prostrate trees
That lead from knoll to knoll a causey
     rude   30
Or bridge the sunken brook, and their
     dark roots,
With all their earth upon them, twisting
     high,
Breathe fixed tranquillity. The rivulet
Sends forth glad sounds, and, tripping
     o'er its bed
Of pebbly sands or leaping down the
     rocks,
Seems with continuous laughter to rejoice
In its own being. Softly tread the marge,

Lest from her midway perch thou scare
 the wren
That dips her bill in water. The cool
 wind,
That stirs the stream in play, shall come
 to thee,   40
Like one that loves thee nor will let thee
 pass
Ungreeted, and shall give its light em-
 brace.

To a Waterfowl

 Whither, midst falling dew,
While glow the heavens with the last
 steps of day,
Far through their rosy depths dost thou
 pursue
 Thy solitary way?

 Vainly the fowler's eye
Might mark thy distant flight, to do thee
 wrong,
As, darkly seen against the crimson sky,
 Thy figure floats along.

 Seek'st thou the plashy brink 9
Of weedy lake, or marge of river wide,
Or where the rocking billows rise and sink
 On the chafed ocean side?

 There is a Power, whose care
Teaches thy way along that pathless
 coast,—
The desert and illimitable air,
 Lone wandering, but not lost.

 All day thy wings have fann'd,
At that far height, the cold thin atmos-
 phere;
Yet stoop not, weary, to the welcome
 land,
 Though the dark night is near. 20

 And soon that toil shall end,
Soon shalt thou find a summer home, and
 rest,
And scream among thy fellows; reeds
 shall bend,
 Soon, o'er thy sheltered nest.

Thou'rt gone, the abyss of heaven
Hath swallowed up thy form, yet, on my
 heart
Deeply hath sunk the lesson thou hast
 given,
 And shall not soon depart.

 He, who, from zone to zone,
Guides through the boundless sky thy
 certain flight, 30
In the long way that I must trace alone,
 Will lead my steps aright.

To the Fringed Gentian

Thou blossom bright with autumn dew,
And colored with the heaven's own blue,
That openest when the quiet light
Succeeds the keen and frosty night—

Thou comest not when violets lean
O'er wandering brooks and springs un-
 seen,
Or columbines, in purple dressed,
Nod o'er the ground-bird's hidden nest.

Thou waitest late and com'st alone,
When woods are bare and birds are
 flown, 10
And frosts and shortening days portend
The aged year is near his end.

Then doth thy sweet and quiet eye
Look through its fringes to the sky,
Blue—blue—as if that sky let fall
A flower from its cerulean wall.

I would that thus, when I shall see
The hour of death draw near to me,
Hope, blossoming within my heart,
May look to heaven as I depart. 20

The Prairies

These are the gardens of the Desert,
 these

The unshorn fields, boundless and beauti-
ful,
For which the speech of England has no
name—
The Prairies. I behold them for the first,
And my heart swells, while the dilated
sight
Takes in the encircling vastness. Lo! they
stretch
In airy undulations, far away,
As if the Ocean, in his gentlest swell,
Stood still, with all his rounded billows
fixed,
And motionless forever. Motionless?—
No—they are all unchained again. The
clouds   11
Sweep over with their shadows, and, be-
neath,
The surface rolls and fluctuates to the
eye;
Dark hollows seem to glide along and
chase
The sunny ridges. Breezes of the South!
Who toss the golden and the flame-like
flowers,
And pass the prairie-hawk that, poised on
high,
Flaps his broad wings, yet moves not—
ye have played
Among the palms of Mexico and vines
Of Texas, and have crisped the limpid
brooks   20
That from the fountains of Sonora glide
Into the calm Pacific—have ye fanned
A nobler or a lovelier scene than this?
Man hath no part in all this glorious
work:
The hand that built the firmament hath
heaved
And smoothed these verdant swells, and
sown their slopes
With herbage, planted them with island-
groves,
And hedged them round with forests.
Fitting floor
For this magnificent temple of the sky—
With flowers whose glory and whose mul-
titude   30

Rival the constellations! The great
heavens
Seem to stoop down upon the scene in
love,—
A nearer vault, and of a tenderer blue,
Than that which bends above our East-
ern hills.

As o'er the verdant waste I guide my
steed,
Among the high rank grass that sweeps
his sides
The hollow beating of his footstep seems
A sacrilegious sound. I think of those
Upon whose rest he tramples. Are they
here—
The dead of other days?—and did the
dust   40
Of these fair solitudes once stir with life
And burn with passion? Let the mighty
mounds
That overlook the rivers, or that rise
In the dim forest crowded with old oaks,
Answer. A race, that long has passed
away,
Built them; a disciplined and populous
race
Heaped, with long toil, the earth, while
yet the Greek
Was hewing the Pentelicus to forms
Of symmetry, and rearing on its rock
The glittering Parthenon. These ample
fields   50
Nourished their harvests, here their herds
were fed,
When haply by their stalls the bison
lowed,
And bowed his manèd shoulder to the
yoke.
All day this desert murmured with their
toils,
Till twilight blushed, and lovers walked,
and wooed
In a forgotten language, and old tunes,
From instruments of unremembered
form,
Gave the soft winds a voice. The red-
man came—

The roaming hunter-tribes, warlike and
  fierce,
And the mound-builders vanished from
  the earth.   60
The solitude of centuries untold
Has settled where they dwelt. The
  prairie-wolf
Hunts in their meadows, and his fresh-
  dug den
Yawns by my path. The gopher mines the
  ground
Where stood their swarming cities. All is
  gone;
All—save the piles of earth that hold
  their bones,
The platforms where they worshipped
  unknown gods,
The barriers which they builded from the
  soil
To keep the foe at bay—till o'er the walls
The wild beleaguerers broke, and, one by
  one,   70
The strongholds of the plain were forced,
  and heaped
With corpses. The brown vultures of the
  wood
Flocked to those vast uncovered sepul-
  chres,
And sat, unscared and silent, at their
  feast.
Haply some solitary fugitive,
Lurking in marsh and forest, till the sense
Of desolation and of fear became
Bitterer than death, yielded himself to
  die.
Man's better nature triumphed then.
  Kind words
Welcomed and soothed him; the rude
  conquerors   80
Seated the captive with their chiefs; he
  chose
A bride among their maidens, and at
  length
Seemed to forget—yet ne'er forgot—the
  wife
Of his first love, and her sweet little
  ones,
Butchered, amid their shrieks, with all his
  race.

Thus change the forms of being. Thus
  arise
Races of living things, glorious in
  strength,
And perish, as the quickening breath of
  God
Fills them, or is withdrawn. The red-man,
  too,
Has left the blooming wilds he ranged so
  long,   90
And, nearer to the Rocky Mountains,
  sought
A wilder hunting-ground. The beaver
  builds
No longer by these streams, but far away,
On waters whose blue surface ne'er gave
  back
The white man's face—among Missouri's
  springs,
And pools whose issues swell the Ore-
  gon—
He rears his little Venice. In these plains
The bison feeds no more. Twice twenty
  leagues
Beyond remotest smoke of hunter's camp,
Roams the majestic brute, in herds that
  shake   100
The earth with thundering steps—yet
  here I meet
His ancient footprints stamped beside the
  pool.

  Still this great solitude is quick with
    life.
Myriads of insects, gaudy as the flowers
They flutter over, gentle quadrupeds,
And birds, that scarce have learned the
  fear of man,
Are here, and sliding reptiles of the
  ground,
Startlingly beautiful. The graceful deer
Bounds to the wood at my approach. The
  bee,   109
A more adventurous colonist than man,
With whom he came across the eastern
  deep,
Fills the savannas with his murmurings,
And hides his sweets, as in the golden
  age,

Within the hollow oak. I listen long
To his domestic hum, and think I hear
The sound of that advancing multitude
Which soon shall fill these deserts. From
    the ground
Comes up the laugh of children, the soft
    voice
Of maidens, and the sweet and solemn
    hymn
Of Sabbath worshippers. The low of
    herds   120
Blends with the rustling of the heavy
    grain
Over the dark brown furrows. All at once
A fresher wind sweeps by, and breaks my
    dream,
And I am in the wilderness alone.

A Forest Hymn

The groves were God's first temples.
    Ere man learned
To hew the shaft, and lay the architrave,
And spread the roof above them—ere he
    framed
The lofty vault, to gather and roll back
The sound of anthems; in the darkling
    wood,
Amid the cool and silence, he knelt down,
And offered to the Mightiest solemn
    thanks
And supplication. For his simple heart
Might not resist the sacred influences
Which, from the stilly twilight of the
    place,   10
And from the gray old trunks that high in
    heaven
Mingled their mossy boughs, and from
    the sound
Of the invisible breath that swayed at
    once
All their green tops, stole over him, and
    bowed
His spirit with the thought of boundless
    power
And inaccessible majesty. Ah, why

Should we, in the world's riper years,
    neglect
God's ancient sanctuaries, and adore
Only among the crowd, and under roofs
That our frail hands have raised? Let me,
    at least,   20
Here, in the shadow of this aged wood,
Offer one hymn—thrice happy, if it find
Acceptance in His ear.

                    Father, thy hand
Hath reared these venerable columns,
    thou
Didst weave this verdant roof. Thou didst
    look down
Upon the naked earth, and, forthwith,
    rose
All these fair ranks of trees. They, in thy
    sun,
Budded, and shook their green leaves in
    thy breeze,
And shot toward heaven. The century-
    living crow
Whose birth was in their tops, grew old
    and died   30
Among their branches, till, at last, they
    stood,
As now they stand, massy, and tall, and
    dark,
Fit shrine for humble worshipper to hold
Communion with his Maker. These dim
    vaults,
These winding aisles, of human pomp or
    pride
Report not. No fantastic carvings show
The boast of our vain race to change the
    form
Of thy fair works. But thou art here—
    thou fill'st
The solitude. Thou art in the soft winds
That run along the summit of these
    trees
In music; thou art in the cooler breath
That from the inmost darkness of the
    place   42
Comes, scarcely felt; the barky trunks,
    the ground,
The fresh moist ground, are all instinct
    with thee.

Here is continual worship;—Nature,
here,
In the tranquillity that thou dost love,
Enjoys thy presence. Noiselessly, around,
From perch to perch, the solitary bird
Passes; and yon clear spring, that, midst
its herbs,
Wells softly forth and wandering steeps
the roots   50
Of half the mighty forest, tells no tale
Of all the good it does. Thou hast not left
Thyself without a witness, in the shades,
Of thy perfections. Grandeur, strength,
and grace
Are here to speak of thee. This mighty
oak—
By whose immovable stem I stand and
seem
Almost annihilated—not a prince,
In all that proud old world beyond the
deep,
E'er wore his crown as loftily as he
Wears the green coronal of leaves with
which   60
Thy hand had graced him. Nestled at his
root
Is beauty, such as blooms not in the glare
Of the broad sun. That delicate forest
flower,
With scented breath and look so like a
smile,
Seems, as it issues from the shapeless
mould,
An emanation of the indwelling Life.
A visible token of the upholding Love,
That are the soul of this great universe.

My heart is awed within me when I
think   69
Of the great miracle that still goes on,
In silence, round me—the perpetual work
Of thy creation, finished, yet renewed
Forever. Written on thy works I read
The lesson of thy own eternity.
Lo! all grow old and die—but see again,
How on the faltering footsteps of decay
Youth presses—ever gay and beautiful
youth
In all its beautiful forms. These lofty
trees

Wave not less proudly that their ances-
tors
Moulder beneath them. Oh, there is not
lost   80
One of earth's charms: upon her bosom
yet,
After the flight of untold centuries,
The freshness of her far beginning lies
And yet shall lie. Life mocks the idle hate
Of his arch-enemy Death—yea, seats
himself
Upon the tyrant's throne—the sepulchre,
And of the triumphs of his ghastly foe
Makes his own nourishment. For he came
forth
From thine own bosom, and shall have no
end.

There have been holy men who hid
themselves   90
Deep in the woody wilderness, and gave
Their lives to thought and prayer, till
they outlived
The generation born with them, nor
seemed
Less aged than the hoary trees and rocks
Around them;—and there have been holy
men
Who deemed it were not well to pass life
thus.
But let me often to these solitudes
Retire, and in thy presence reassure
My feeble virtue. Here its enemies,
The passions, at thy plainer footsteps
shrink   100
And tremble and are still. O God! when
thou
Dost scare the world with tempests, set
on fire
The heavens with falling thunderbolts, or
fill,
With all the waters of the firmament,
The swift dark whirlwind that uproots
the woods
And drowns the villages; when, at thy
call,
Uprises the great deep and throws him-
self
Upon the continent, and overwhelms
Its cities—who forgets not, at the sight

Of these tremendous tokens of thy
    power,   110
His pride, and lays his strifes and follies
    by?
Oh, from these sterner aspects of thy face
Spare me and mine, nor let us need the
    wrath
Of the mad unchained elements to teach
Who rules them. Be it ours to meditate,
In these calm shades, thy milder majesty,
And to the beautiful order of thy works
Learn to conform the order of our lives.

The Death of Lincoln

Oh, slow to smite and swift to spare,
    Gentle and merciful and just!
Who, in the fear of God, didst bear
    The sword of power, a nation's trust!

In sorrow by thy bier we stand,
    Amid the awe that hushes all,
And speak the anguish of a land
    That shook with horror at thy fall.

Thy task is done; the bond are free:
    We bear thee to an honored grave,   10
Whose proudest monument shall be
    The broken fetters of the slave.

Pure was thy life; its bloody close
    Hath placed thee with the sons of light,
Among the noble host of those
    Who perished in the cause of Right.

Ralph Waldo Emerson

✳ 1803–1882

Concord Hymn

SUNG AT THE COMPLETION OF THE
BATTLE MONUMENT, JULY 4, 1837

By the rude bridge that arched the flood,
    Their flag to April's breeze unfurled,

Here once the embattled farmers stood
    And fired the shot heard round the
    world.

The foe long since in silence slept;
    Alike the conqueror silent sleeps;
And Time the ruined bridge has swept
    Down the dark stream which seaward
    creeps.

On this green bank, by this soft stream,
    We set to-day a votive stone;   10
That memory may their deed redeem,
    When, like our sires, our sons are gone.

Spirit, that made those heroes dare
    To die, and leave their children free,
Bid Time and Nature gently spare
    The shaft we raise to them and thee.

Each and All

Little thinks, in the field, yon red-cloaked
    clown
Of thee from the hill-top looking down;
The heifer that lows in the upland farm,
Far-heard, lows not thine ear to charm;
The sexton, tolling his bell at noon,
Deems not that great Napoleon
Stops his horse, and lists with delight,
Whilst his files sweep round yon Alpine
    height;
Nor knowest thou what argument
Thy life to thy neighbor's creed has lent.
All are needed by each one;   11
Nothing is fair or good alone.
I thought the sparrow's note from heaven,
Singing at dawn on the alder bough;
I brought him home, in his nest, at even;
He sings the song, but it cheers not now,
For I did not bring home the river and
    sky;—
He sang to my ear,—they sang to my eye.
The delicate shells lay on the shore;
The bubbles of the latest wave   20
Fresh pearls to their enamel gave,
And the bellowing of the savage sea
Greeted their safe escape to me.
I wiped away the weeds and foam,
I fetched my sea-born treasures home;

But the poor, unsightly, noisome things
Had left their beauty on the shore
With the sun and the sand and the wild
uproar.
The lover watched his graceful maid,
As 'mid the virgin train she strayed,   30
Nor knew her beauty's best attire
Was woven still by the snow-white choir.
At last she came to his hermitage,
Like the bird from the woodlands to the
cage:—
The gay enchantment was undone,
A gentle wife, but fairy none.
Then I said, "I covet truth;
Beauty is unripe childhood's cheat;
I leave it behind with the games of
youth:"—
As I spoke, beneath my feet   40
The ground-pine curled its pretty wreath,
Running over the club-moss burrs;
I inhaled the violet's breath;
Around me stood the oaks and firs;
Pine-cones and acorns lay on the ground;
Over me soared the eternal sky,
Full of light and of deity;
Again I saw, again I heard,
The rolling river, the morning bird;—
Beauty through my senses stole;   50
I yielded myself to the perfect whole.

Come see the north wind's masonry.
Out of an unseen quarry evermore   11
Furnished with tile, the fierce artificer
Curves his white bastions with projected
roof
Round every windward stake, or tree, or
door.
Speeding the myriad-handed, his wild
work
So fanciful, so savage, nought cares he
For number or proportion. Mockingly,
On coop or kennel he hangs Parian
wreaths;
A swan-like form invests the hidden
thorn;
Fills up the farmer's lane from wall to
wall,   20
Maugre the farmer's sighs; and at the
gate
A tapering turret overtops the work.
And when his hours are numbered, and
the world
Is all his own, retiring, as he were not,
Leaves, when the sun appears, astonished
Art
To mimic in slow structures, stone by
stone,
Built in an age, the mad wind's night-
work,
The frolic architecture of the snow.

The Snow-Storm

Announced by all the trumpets of the sky,
Arrives the snow, and, driving o'er the
fields,
Seems nowhere to alight: the whited air
Hides hills and woods, the river, and the
heaven,
And veils the farm-house at the garden's
end.
The sled and traveller stopped, the cour-
ier's feet
Delayed, all friends shut out, the house-
mates sit
Around the radiant fireplace, enclosed
In a tumultuous privacy of storm.

The Problem

I like a church; I like a cowl;
I love a prophet of the soul;
And on my heart monastic aisles
Fall like sweet strains, or pensive smiles;
Yet not for all his faith can see
Would I that cowled churchman be.

Why should the vest on him allure,
Which I could not on me endure?

Not from a vain or shallow thought
His awful Jove young Phidias brought,
Never from lips of cunning fell   11
The thrilling Delphic oracle;

Out from the heart of nature rolled
The burdens of the Bible old;
The litanies of nations came,
Like the volcano's tongue of flame,
Up from the burning core below,—
The canticles of love and woe;
The hand that rounded Peter's dome
And groined the aisles of Christian Rome
Wrought in a sad sincerity;   21
Himself from God he could not free;
He builded better than he knew;—
The conscious stone to beauty grew.

Know'st thou what wove yon woodbird's
          nest
Of leaves, and feathers from her breast?
Or how the fish outbuilt her shell,
Painting with morn each annual cell?
Or how the sacred pine-tree adds
To her old leaves new myriads?   30
Such and so grew these holy piles,
Whilst love and terror laid the tiles.
Earth proudly wears the Parthenon,
As the best gem upon her zone;
And Morning opes with haste her lids,
To gaze upon the Pyramids;
O'er England's abbeys bends the sky,
As on its friends, with kindred eye;
For out of Thought's interior sphere,
These wonders rose to upper air;   40
And Nature gladly gave them place,
Adopted them into her race,
And granted them an equal date
With Andes and with Ararat.

These temples grew as grows the grass;
Art might obey, but not surpass.
The passive Master lent his hand
To the vast soul that o'er him planned;
And the same power that reared the
          shrine
Bestrode the tribes that knelt within.   50
Ever the fiery Pentecost
Girds with one flame the countless host,
Trances the heart through chanting
          choirs,
And through the priest the mind inspires.
The word unto the prophet spoken
Was writ on tables yet unbroken;
The word by seers or sibyls told,

In groves of oak, or fanes of gold,
Still floats upon the morning wind,
Still whispers to the willing mind.   60
One accent of the Holy Ghost
The heedless world hath never lost.
I know what say the fathers wise,—
The Book itself before me lies,
Old Crysostom, best Augustine,
And he who blent both in his line,
The younger *Golden Lips* or mines,
Taylor, the Shakspeare of divines.
His words are music in my ear,
I see his cowled portrait dear;   70
And yet, for all his faith could see,
I would not the good bishop be.

Fable

The mountain and the squirrel
Had a quarrel,
And the former called the latter "Little
          Prig";
Bun replied,
"You are doubtless very big;
But all sorts of things and weather
Must be taken in together,
To make up a year
And a sphere.
And I think it no disgrace   10
To occupy my place.
If I'm not so large as you,
You are not so small as I,
And not half so spry.
I'll not deny you make
A very pretty squirrel track;
Talents differ; all is well and wisely put;
If I cannot carry forests on my back,
Neither can you crack a nut."

Bacchus

Bring me wine, but wine which never
          grew
In the belly of the grape,
Or grew on vine whose tap-roots, reach-
          ing through

Under the Andes to the Cape,
Suffered no savor of the earth to scape.

Let its grapes the morn salute
From a nocturnal root,
Which feels the acrid juice
Of Styx and Erebus;
And turns the woe of Night,   10
By its own craft, to a more rich delight.

We buy ashes for bread;
We buy diluted wine;
Give me of the true,—
Whose ample leaves and tendrils curled
Among the silver hills of heaven,
Draw everlasting dew;
Wine of wine,
Blood of the world,
Form of forms, and mould of statures,
That I intoxicated,   21
And by the draught assimilated,
May float at pleasure through all natures;
The bird-language rightly spell,
And that which roses say so well.
Wine that is shed
Like the torrents of the sun
Up the horizon walls,
Or like the Atlantic streams, which run
When the South Sea calls.   30

Water and bread,
Food which needs no transmuting,
Rainbow-flowering, wisdom-fruiting
Wine which is already man,
Food which teach and reason can.

Wine which Music is,—
Music and wine are one,—
That I, drinking this,
Shall hear far Chaos talk with me;
Kings unborn shall walk with me;   40
And the poor grass shall plot and plan
What it will do when it is man.
Quickened so, will I unlock
Every crypt of every rock.

I thank the joyful juice
For all I know;—
Winds of remembering
Of the ancient being blow,

And seeming-solid walls of use
Open and flow.   50

Pour, Bacchus! the remembering wine;
Retrieve the loss of me and mine!
Vine for vine be antidote,
And the grape requite the lote!

Haste to cure the old despair,—
Reason in Nature's lotus drenched,
The memory of ages quenched;
Give them again to shine;
Let wine repair what this undid;

And where the infection slid,   60
A dazzling memory revive;
Refresh the faded tints,
Recut the aged prints,
And write my old adventures with the
    pen
Which on the first day drew,
Upon the tablets blue,
The dancing Pleiads and eternal men.

Saadi

Trees in groves,
Kine in droves,
In ocean sport the scaly herds,
Wedge-like cleave the air the birds,
To northern lakes fly wind-borne ducks,
Browse the mountain sheep in flocks,
Men consort in camp and town,
But the poet dwells alone.

God, who gave to him the lyre,
Of all mortals the desire,   10
For all breathing men's behoof,
Straitly charged him, "Sit aloof;"
Annexed a warning, poets say,
To the bright premium,—
Ever, when twain together play,
Shall the harp be dumb.

Many may come,
But one shall sing;
Two touch the string,
The harp is dumb.   20

Though there come a million,
Wise Saadi dwells alone.

Yet Saadi loved the race of men,—
No churl, immured in cave or den;
In bower and hall
He wants them all,
Who in their pride forgive not ours.
Thus the sad-eyed Fakirs preach:
"Bard, when thee would Allah teach,
And lift thee to his holy mount,   30
He sends thee from his bitter fount
Wormwood,—saying 'Go thy ways;
Drink not the Malaga of praise,
But do the deed thy fellows hate,
And compromise thy peaceful state;
Smite the white breasts which thee fed,
Stuff sharp thorns beneath the head
Of them thou shouldst have comforted;
For out of woe and out of crime
Draws the heart a lore sublime.' "   40
And yet it seemeth not to me
That the high gods love tragedy;
For Saadi sat in the sun,
And thanks was his contrition;
For haircloth and for bloody whips,
Had active hands and smiling lips;
And yet his runes he rightly read,
And to his folk his message sped.
Sunshine in his heart transferred
Lighted each transparent word,   50
And well could honoring Persia learn
What Saadi wished to say;
For Saadi's nightly stars did burn
Brighter than Jami's day.

Whispered the Muse in Saadi's cot:
"O gentle Saadi, listen not,
Tempted by thy praise of wit,
Or by thirst and appetite
His tongue can paint as bright, as keen;
And what his tender heart hath felt   60
With equal fire thy heart shalt melt.
For, whom the Muses smile upon,
And touch with soft persuasion,
His words like a storm-wind can bring
Terror and beauty on their wing;
In his every syllable

Lurketh Nature veritable;
And though he speak in midnight
    dark,—
In heaven no star, on earth no spark,—
Yet before the listener's eye   70
Swims the world in ecstasy,
The forest waves, the morning breaks,
The pastures sleep, ripple the lakes,
Leaves twinkle, flowers like persons be,
And life pulsates in rock or tree.
Saadi, so far thy words shall reach:
Suns rise and set in Saadi's speech!"

And thus to Saadi said the Muse:
"Eat thou the bread which men refuse;
Flee from the goods which from thee
    flee;   80
Seek nothing,—Fortune seeketh thee.
Nor mount, nor dive; all good things keep
The midway of the eternal deep.
Wish not to fill the isles with eyes
To fetch thee birds of paradise:
On thine orchard's edge belong
All the brags of plume and song;
Wise Ali's sunbright sayings pass
For proverbs in the market-place:
Through mountains bored by regal art,
Toil whistles as he drives the cart.   91
Nor scour the seas, nor sift mankind,
A poet or a friend to find:
Behold, he watches at the door!
Behold his shadow on the floor!
Open innumerable doors
The heaven where unveiled Allah pours
The flood of truth, the flood of good,
The Seraph's and the Cherub's food:
Those doors are men: the Pariah hind
Admits thee to the perfect Mind.   101
Seek not beyond thy cottage wall
Redeemers that can yield thee all:
While thou sittest at thy door
On the desert's yellow floor,
Listening to the gray-haired crones,
Foolish gossips, ancient drones,
Saadi, see! They rise in stature
To the height of mighty Nature,
And the secret stands revealed   110
Fraudulent Time in vain concealed,—

That blessed gods in servile masks
Plied for thee thy household tasks."

Hamatreya

Bulkeley, Hunt, Willard, Hosmer, Mer-
  iam, Flint,
Possessed the land which rendered to
  their toil
Hay, corn, roots, hemp, flax, apples, wool
  and wood.
Each of these landlords walked amidst his
  farm,
Saying, " 'Tis mine, my children's and my
  name's.
How sweet the west wind sounds in my
  own trees!
How graceful climb those shadows on my
  hill!
I fancy these pure waters and the flags
Know me, as does my dog: we sympa-
  thize;
And, I affirm, my actions smack of the
  soil."   10

Where are these men? Asleep beneath
  their grounds:
And strangers, fond as they, their furrows
  plough.
Earth laughs in flowers, to see her boast-
  ful boys
Earth-proud, proud of the earth which is
  not theirs;
Who steer the plough, but cannot steer
  their feet
Clear of the grave.
They added ridge to valley, brook to
  pond,
And sighed for all that bounded their
  domain;
"This suits me for a pasture; that's my
  park;
We must have clay, lime, gravel, granite-
  ledge,   20
And misty lowland, where to go for peat.
The land is well,—lies fairly to the south.
'Tis good, when you have crossed the sea
  and back,
To find the sitfast acres where you left
  them."
Ah! the hot owner sees not Death, who
  adds
Him to his land, a lump of mould the
  more.
Hear what the Earth says:—

Earth-Song

Mine and yours;
Mine, not yours.
Earth endures;   30
Stars abide—
Shine down in the old sea;
Old are the shores;
But where are old men?
I who have seen much,
Such have I never seen.

The lawyer's deed
Ran sure,
In tail,
To them, and to their heirs   40
Who shall succeed,
Without fail,
Forevermore.

Here is the land,
Shaggy with wood,
With its old valley,
Mound and flood.
But the heritors?—
Fled like the flood's foam.
The lawyer, and the laws,   50
And the kingdom,
Clean swept herefrom.

They called me theirs,
Who so controlled me;
Yet every one
Wished to stay, and is gone,
How am I theirs,
If they cannot hold me,
But I hold them?

When I heard the Earth-song,   60
I was no longer brave;
My avarice cooled
Like lust in the chill of the grave.

Ode

INSCRIBED TO W. H. CHANNING

Though loath to grieve
The evil time's sole patriot,
I cannot leave
My honied thought
For the priest's cant,
Or statesman's rant.

If I refuse
My study for their politique,
Which at the best is trick,
The angry Muse   10
Puts confusion in my brain.

But who is he that prates
Of the culture of mankind,
Of better arts and life?
Go, blindworm, go,
Behold the famous States
Harrying Mexico
With rifle and with knife!

Or who, with accent bolder,
Dare praise the freedom-loving moun-
    taineer?   20
I found by thee, O rushing Contoocook!
And in thy valleys, Agiochook!
The jackals of the negro-holder.

The God who made New Hampshire
Taunted the lofty land
With little men;—
Small bat and wren
House in the oak:—
If earth-fire cleave
The upheaved land, and bury the folk,
The southern crocodile would grieve.   31
Virtue palters; Right is hence;
Freedom praised, but hid;
Funeral eloquence
Rattles the coffin-lid.

What boots thy zeal,
O glowing friend,
That would indignant rend
The northland from the south?

Wherefore? to what good end?   40
Boston Bay and Bunker Hill
Would serve things still;—
Things are of the snake.

The horseman serves the horse,
The neatherd serves the neat,
The merchant serves the purse,
The eater serves his meat;
'Tis the day of the chattel,
Web to weave, and corn to grind;
Things are in the saddle,   50
And ride mankind.

There are two laws discrete,
Not reconciled,—
Law for man, and law for things;
The last builds town and fleet,
But it runs wild,
And doth the man unking.

'Tis fit the forest fall,
The steep be graded,
The mountain tunnelled,   60
The sand shaded,
The orchard planted,
The glebe tilled,
The prairie granted,
The steamer built.

Let man serve law for man;
Live for friendship, live for love,
For truth's and harmony's behoof;
The state may follow how it can,
As Olympus follows Jove.   70

    Yet do not I implore
The wrinkled shopman to my sounding
    woods,
Nor bid the unwilling senator
Ask votes of thrushes in the solitudes.
Every one to his chosen work;—
Foolish hands may mix and mar;
Wise and sure the issues are.
Round they roll till dark is light,
Sex to sex, and even to odd;—
The over-god   80
Who marries Right to Might,
Who peoples, unpeoples,—
He who exterminates
Races by stronger races,

Black by white faces,—
Knows to bring honey
Out of the lion;
Grafts gentlest scion
On pirate and Turk.

The Cossack eats Poland,   90
Like stolen fruit;
Her last noble is ruined,
Her last poet mute:
Straight, into double band
The victors divide;
Half for freedom strike and stand;—
The astonished Muse finds thousands at
    her side.

Give All to Love

Give all to love;
Obey thy heart;
Friends, kindred, days,
Estate, good-fame,
Plans, credit and the Muse,—
Nothing refuse.

'Tis a brave master;
Let it have scope:
Follow it utterly,
Hope beyond hope: 10
High and more high
It dives into noon,
With wing unspent,
Untold intent;
But it is a god,
Knows its own path
And the outlets of the sky.

It was never for the mean;
It requireth courage stout.
Souls above doubt,   20
Valor unbending,
It will reward,—
They shall return
More than they were,
And ever ascending.

Leave all for love;
Yet, hear me, yet,
One word more thy heart behoved,

One pulse more of firm endeavor,—
Keep thee to-day,   30
To-morrow, forever,
Free as an Arab
Of thy beloved.

Cling with life to the maid;
But when the surprise,
First vague shadow of surmise
Flits across her bosom young,
Of a joy apart from thee,
Free be she, fancy-free;
Nor thou detain her vesture's hem,   40
Nor the palest rose she flung
From her summer diadem.

Though thou loved her as thyself,
As a self of purer clay,
Though her parting dims the day,
Stealing grace from all alive;
Heartily know,
When half-gods go,
The gods arrive.

Merlin

1

Thy trivial harp will never please
Or fill my craving ear;
Its chords should ring as blows the
    breeze,
Free, peremptory, clear.
No jingling serenader's art,
Nor tinkle of piano strings,
Can make the wild blood start
In its mystic springs.
The kingly bard
Must smite the chords rudely and hard,
As with hammer or with mace;   11
That they may render back
Artful thunder, which conveys
Secrets of the solar track,
Sparks of the supersolar blaze.
Merlin's blows are strokes of fate,
Chiming with the forest tone,
When boughs buffet boughs in the wood;
Chiming with the gasp and moan
Of the ice-imprisoned flood;   20

With the pulse of manly hearts;
With the voice of orators;
With the din of city arts;
With the cannonade of wars;
With the marches of the brave;
And prayers of might from martyrs' cave.

Great is the art,
Great be the manners, of the bard.
He shall not his brain encumber
With the coil of rhythm and number;   30
But, leaving rule and pale forethought,
He shall aye climb
For his rime.
"Pass in, pass in," the angels say,
"In to the upper doors,
Nor count compartments of the floors.
But mount to paradise
By the stairway of surprise."

Blameless master of the games,
King of sport that never shames,   40
He shall daily joy dispense
Hid in song's sweet influence.
Things more cheerly live and go.
What time the subtle mind
Sings aloud the tune whereto
Their pulses beat,
And march their feet,
And their members are combined.

By Sybarites beguiled,
He shall no task decline;   50
Merlin's mighty line
Extremes of nature reconciled,—
Bereaved a tyrant of his will,
And made the lion mild.
Songs can the tempest still,
Scattered on the stormy air,
Mold the year to fair increase
And bring in poetic peace.

He shall not seek to weave,
In weak, unhappy times,   60
Efficacious rimes;
Wait his returning strength.
Bird, that from the nadir's floor
To the zenith's top can soar,
The soaring orbit of the muse exceeds
     that journey's length.
Nor profane affect to hit

Or compass that, by meddling wit,
Which only the propitious mind
Publishes when 'tis inclined.
There are open hours   70
When the God's will sallies free,
And the dull idiot might see
The flowing fortunes of a thousand
     years;—
Sudden, at unawares,
Self-moved, fly-to the doors,
Nor sword of angels could reveal
What they conceal.

2

The rime of the poet
Modulates the king's affairs;
Balance-loving Nature   80
Made all things in pairs.
To every foot its antipode;
Each color with its counter glowed;
To every tone beat answering tones,
Higher or graver;
Flavor gladly blends with flavor;
Leaf answers leaf upon the bough;
And match the paired cotyledons.
Hands to hands, and feet to feet,
In one body grooms and brides;   90
Eldest rite, two married sides
In every mortal meet.
Light's far furnace shines,
Smelting balls and bars,
Forging double stars,
Glittering twins and trines.
The animals are sick with love,
Lovesick with rime;
Each with all propitious time
Into chorus wove.   100

Like the dancer's ordered band,
Thoughts come also hand in hand;
In equal couples mated,
Or else alternated;
Adding by their mutual gage,
One to other, health and age.
Solitary fancies go
Short-lived wandering to and fro,
Most like to bachelors,
Or an ungiven maid,   110
Not ancestors,

With no posterity to make the lie afraid,
Or keep truth undecayed.
Perfect-paired as eagle's wings,
Justice is the rime of things;
Trade and counting use
The self-same tuneful muse;
And Nemesis,
Who with even matches odd,
Who athwart space redresses   120
The partial wrong,
Fills the just period,
And finishes the song.

Subtle rimes, with ruin rife,
Murmur in the house of life,
Sung by the Sisters as they spin;
In perfect time and measure they
Build and unbuild our echoing clay,
As the two twilights of the day
Fold us music-drunken in.   130

The Furies laid,
The plague is stayed,
All fortunes made;
Turn the key and bolt the door,
Sweet is death forevermore.
Nor haughty hope, nor swart chagrin,
Nor murdering hate, can enter in.
All is now secure and fast;   10
Nor the gods can shake the Past;
Flies-to the adamantine door
Bolted down forevermore.
None can re-enter there,—
No thief so politic,
No Satan with a royal trick
Steal in by window, chink, or hole,
To bind or unbind, add what lacked,
Insert a leaf, or forge a name,
New-face or finish what is packed,   20
Alter or mend eternal Fact.

Brahma

If the red slayer think he slays,
    Or if the slain think he is slain,
They know not well the subtle ways
    I keep, and pass, and turn again.

Far or forgot to me is near;
    Shadow and sunlight are the same;
The vanished gods to me appear;
    And one to me are shame and fame.

They reckon ill who leave me out;
    When me they fly, I am the wings;   10
I am the doubter and the doubt,
    And I the hymn the Brahmin sings.

The strong gods pine for my abode,
    And pine in vain the sacred Seven,
But thou, meek lover of the good!
    Find me, and turn thy back on heaven.

The Past

The debt is paid,
The verdict said,

Henry Wadsworth Longfellow

❋ 1807–1882

The Jewish Cemetery at Newport

How strange it seems! These Hebrews in
    their graves,
    Close by the street of this fair seaport
    town,
Silent beside the never-silent waves,
    At rest in all this moving up and
    down!

The trees are white with dust, that o'er
    their sleep
    Wave their broad curtains in the
    southwind's breath,
While underneath these leafy tents they
    keep
    The long, mysterious Exodus of Death.

And these sepulchral stones, so old and
   brown,
    That pave with level flags their burial-
     place,   10
Seem like the tablets of the Law, thrown
   down
    And broken by Moses at the moun-
     tain's base.

The very names recorded here are
   strange,
    Of foreign accent, and of different
     climes;
Alvares and Rivera interchange
    With Abraham and Jacob of old times.

"Blessed be God! for he created Death!"
    The mourners said, "and Death is rest
     and peace;"
Then added, in the certainty of faith,
    "And giveth Life that nevermore shall
     cease."   20

Closed are the portals of their Syna-
   gogue,
    No Psalms of David now the silence
     break,
No Rabbi reads the ancient Decalogue
    In the grand dialect the Prophets
     spake.

Gone are the living, but the dead remain,
   And not neglected; for a hand unseen,
Scattering its bounty, like a summer rain,
    Still keeps their graves and their re-
     membrance green.

How came they here? What burst of
   Christian hate,   29
    What persecution, merciless and blind,
Drove o'er the sea—that desert deso-
   late—
    These Ishmaels and Hagars of man-
     kind?

They lived in narrow streets and lanes
   obscure,
    Ghetto and Judenstrass, in mirk and
     mire;
Taught in the school of patience to en-
   dure

The life of anguish and the death of
   fire.

All their lives long, with the unleavened
   bread
    And bitter herbs of exile and its fears,
The wasting famine of the heart they fed,
    And slaked its thirst with marah of
     their tears.   40

Anathema maranatha! was the cry
    That rang from town to town, from
     street to street;
At every gate the accursed Mordecai
    Was mocked and jeered, and spurned
     by Christian feet.

Pride and humiliation hand in hand
    Walked with them through the world
     where'er they went;
Trampled and beaten were they as the
   sand,
    And yet unshaken as the continent.

For in the background figures vague and
   vast
    Of patriarchs and of prophets rose sub-
     lime,   50
And all the great traditions of the Past
    They saw reflected in the coming time.

And thus forever with reverted look
    The mystic volume of the world they
     read,
Spelling it backward, like a Hebrew
   book,
    Till life became a Legend of the Dead.

But ah! what once has been shall be no
   more!
    The groaning earth in travail and in
     pain
Brings forth its races, but does not re-
   store,   59
    And the dead nations never rise again.

Hymn to the Night

I heard the trailing garments of the Night
    Sweep through her marble halls!

I saw her sable skirts all fringed with
  light
  From the celestial walls!

I felt her presence, by its spell of might,
  Stoop o'er me from above;
The calm, majestic presence of the
  Night,
  As of the one I love.

I heard the sounds of sorrow and delight,
  The manifold, soft chimes,   10
That fill the haunted chambers of the
  Night,
  Like some old poet's rhymes.

From the cool cisterns of the midnight air
  My spirit drank repose;
The fountain of perpetual peace flows
  there,—
  From those deep cisterns flows.

O holy Night! from thee I learn to bear
  What man has borne before!
Thou layest thy finger on the lips of Care,
  And they complain no more.   20

Peace! Peace! Orestes-like I breathe this
  prayer!
  Descend with broad-winged flight,
The welcome, the thrice-prayed for, the
  most fair,
  The best-beloved Night!

Divina Commedia

1

Oft have I seen at some cathedral door
  A laborer, pausing in the dust and
    heat,
  Lay down his burden, and with rever-
    ent feet
  Enter, and cross himself, and on the
    floor
Kneel to repeat his paternoster o'er;
  Far off the noises of the world retreat;
  The loud vociferations of the street
  Become an undistinguishable roar.
So, as I enter here from day to day,

And leave my burden at this minster
  gate,   10
Kneeling in prayer, and not ashamed
  to pray,
The tumult of the time disconsolate
  To inarticulate murmurs dies away,
  While the eternal ages watch and wait.

2

How strange the sculptures that adorn
  these towers!
  This crowd of statues, in whose folded
    sleeves
  Birds build their nests; while canopied
    with leaves
  Parvis and portal bloom like trellised
    bowers,
And the vast minster seems a cross of
  flowers!
  But fiends and dragons on the gar-
    goyled eaves
  Watch the dead Christ between the
    living thieves,
  And, underneath, the traitor Judas
    lowers!
Ah! from what agonies of heart and
  brain,
  What exultations trampling on de-
    spair,   10
  What tenderness, what tears, what
    hate of wrong,
What passionate outcry of a soul in pain,
  Uprose this poem of the earth and air,
  This mediæval miracle of song!

3

I enter, and I see thee in the gloom
  Of the long aisles, O poet saturnine!
  And strive to make my steps keep pace
    with thine.
  The air is filled wth some unknown
    perfume;
The congregation of the dead make room
  For thee to pass; the votive tapers
    shine;
  Like rooks that haunt Ravenna's groves
    of pine
  The hovering echoes fly from tomb to
    tomb.

From the confessionals I hear arise
  Rehearsals of forgotten tragedies,   10
  And lamentations from the crypts be-
    low;
And then a voice celestial that begins
  With the pathetic words, "Although
    your sins
  As scarlet be," and ends with "as the
    snow."

4

With snow-white veil and garments as of
    flame,
  She stands before thee, who so long
    ago
  Filled thy young heart with passion
    and the woe
  From which thy song and all its splen-
    dors came;
And while with stern rebuke she speaks
    thy name,
  The ice about thy heart melts as the
    snow
  On mountain heights, and in swift
    overflow
  Comes gushing from thy lips in sobs of
    shame.
Thou makest full confession; and a
    gleam,
  As of the dawn on some dark forest
    cast,   10
  Seems on thy lifted forehead to in-
    crease;
Lethe and Eunoë—the remembered
    dream
  And the forgotten sorrow—bring at
    last
  That perfect pardon which is perfect
    peace.

5

I lift mine eyes, and all the windows
    blaze
  With forms of Saints and holy men
    who died,
  Here martyred and hereafter glorified;
  And the great Rose upon its leaves dis-
    plays

Christ's Triumph, and the angelic roun-
    delays,
  With splendor upon splendor multi-
    plied;
  And Beatrice again at Dante's side
  No more rebukes, but smiles her words
    of praise.
And then the organ sounds, and unseen
    choirs
  Sing the old Latin hymns of peace and
    love   10
  And benedictions of the Holy Ghost;
And the melodious bells among the spires
  O'er all the house-tops and through
    heaven above
  Proclaim the elevation of the Host!

6

O star of morning and of liberty!
  O bringer of the light, whose splendor
    shines
  Above the darkness of the Apennines,
  Forerunner of the day that is to be!
The voices of the city and the sea,
  The voices of the mountains and the
    pines,
  Repeat thy song, till the familiar lines
  Are footpaths for the thought of Italy!
Thy flame is blown abroad from all the
    heights,
  Through all the nations, and a sound is
    heard,   10
  As of a mighty wind, and men devout,
Strangers of Rome, and the new prose-
    lytes,
  In their own language hear thy won-
    drous word,
  And many are amazed and many
    doubt.

The Children's Hour

Between the dark and the daylight,
  When the night is beginning to lower,
Comes a pause in the day's occupations,
  That is known as the Children's Hour.

I hear in the chamber above me
　The patter of little feet,
The sound of a door that is opened,
　And voices soft and sweet.

From my study I see in the lamplight,
　Descending the broad hall stair.   10
Grave Alice, and laughing Allegra,
　And Edith with golden hair.

A whisper, and then a silence:
　Yet I know by their merry eyes
They are plotting and planning together
　To take me by surprise.

A sudden rush from the stairway,
　A sudden raid from the hall!
By three doors left unguarded
　They enter my castle wall!   20

They climb up into my turret
　O'er the arms and back of my chair;
If I try to escape, they surround me;
　They seem to be everywhere.

They almost devour me with kisses,
　Their arms about me entwine,
Till I think of the Bishop of Bingen
　In his Mouse-Tower on the Rhine!

Do you think, O blue-eyed banditti,
　Because you have scaled the wall,   30
Such an old mustache as I am
　Is not a match for you all!

I have you fast in my fortress,
　And will not let you depart,
But put you down into the dungeon
　In the round-tower of my heart.

And there will I keep you forever,
　Yes, forever and a day,
Till the walls shall crumble to ruin,
　And moulder in dust away!   40

The Bells of San Blas

What say the Bells of San Blas
To the ships that southward pass
　From the harbor of Mazatlan?
To them it is nothing more

Than the sound of surf on the shore.—
　Nothing more to master or man.

But to me, a dreamer of dreams,
To whom what is and what seems,
　Are often one and the same,—
The Bells of San Blas to me   10
Have a strange, wild melody,
　And are something more than a
　name.

For bells are the voice of the church;
They have tones that touch and search
　The hearts of young and old;
One sound to all, yet each
Lends a meaning to their speech,
　And the meaning is manifold.

They are a voice of the Past,
Of an age that is fading fast,   20
　Of a power austere and grand;
When the flag of Spain unfurled
Its folds o'er this western world,
　And the Priest was lord of the land.

The chapel that once looked down
On the little seaport town
　Has crumbled into the dust;
And on oaken beams below
The bells swing to and fro,
　And are green with mould and rust.

"Is, then, the old faith dead,"   31
They say, "and in its stead
　Is some new faith proclaimed,
That we are forced to remain
Naked to sun and rain,
　Unsheltered and ashamed?

"Once in our tower aloof
We rang over wall and roof
　Our warnings and our complaints;
And round about us there   40
The white doves filled the air,
　Like the white souls of the saints.

"The saints! Ah, have they grown
Forgetful of their own?
　Are they asleep, or dead,
That open to the sky
Their ruined Missions lie,
　No longer tenanted?

"Oh, bring us back once more
The vanished days of yore,   50
    When the world with faith was
    filled;
Bring back the fervid zeal,
The hearts of fire and steel,
    The hands that believe and build.

"Then from our tower again
We will send over land and main
    Our voices of command,
Like exiled kings who return
To their thrones, and the people learn
    That the Priest is lord of the land"
O Bells of San Blas, in vain   61
Ye call back the Past again!
    The Past is deaf to your prayer;
Out of the shadows of night
The world rolls into light;
    It is daybreak everywhere.

Chaucer

An old man in a lodge within a park;
    The chamber walls depicted all around
    With portraitures of huntsman, hawk,
    and hound,
    And the hurt deer. He listeneth to the
    lark,
Whose song comes with the sunshine
    through the dark
    Of painted glass in leaden lattice
    bound;
    He listeneth and he laugheth at the
    sound,
    Then writeth in a book like any clerk.
He is the poet of the dawn, who wrote
    The Canterbury Tales, and his old
    age   ·   10
    Made beautiful with song; and as I
    read
I hear the crowing cock, I hear the note
    Of lark and linnet, and from every
    page
    Rise odors of ploughed field or flowery
    mead.

Milton

I pace the sounding sea-beach and be-
    hold
    How the voluminous billows roll and
    run,
    Upheaving and subsiding, while the
    sun
    Shines through their sheeted emerald
    far unrolled
And the ninth wave, slow gathering
    fold by fold
    All its loose-flowing garments into one,
    Plunges upon the shore, and floods the
    dun
    Pale reach of sands, and changes them
    to gold.
So in majestic cadence rise and fall
    The mighty undulations of thy song,
    O sightless Bard, England's Mæonides!
And ever and anon, high over all   12
    Uplifted, a ninth wave superb and
    strong,
    Floods all the soul with its melodious
    seas.

Keats

The young Endymion sleeps Endymion's
    sleep;
    The Shepherd-boy whose tale was left
    half told!
    The solemn grove uplifts its shield of
    gold
    To the red rising moon, and loud and
    deep
The nightingale is singing from the
    steep;
    It is midsummer, but the air is cold;
    Can it be death? Alas, beside the fold
    A shepherd's pipe lies shattered near
    his sheep.
Lo! in the moonlight gleams a marble
    white,
    On which I read: "Here lieth one
    whose name   10

Was writ in water." And was this the
    meed
Of his sweet singing? Rather let me
    write:
"The smoking flax before it burst to
    flame
Was quenched by death, and broken
    the bruised reed."

The Cross of Snow

In the long, sleepless watches of the
    night,
    A gentle face—the face of one long
        dead—
Looks at me from the wall, where
    round its head
The night-lamp casts a halo of pale
    light.
Here in this room she died; and soul
    more white
    Never through martyrdom of fire was
        led
To its repose; nor can in books be read
The legend of a life more benedight.
There is a mountain in the distant West
    That, sun-defying, in its deep ravines
Displays a cross of snow upon its
    side.   11
Such is the cross I wear upon my breast
    These eighteen years, through all the
        changing scenes
And seasons, changeless since the day
    she died.

John Greenleaf Whittier
✳ 1807–1892

Ichabod

So fallen! so lost! the light withdrawn
    Which once he wore!
The glory from his gray hairs gone
    Forevermore!

Revile him not, the Tempter hath
    A snare for all;
And pitying tears, not scorn and wrath,
    Befit his fall!

Oh, dumb be passion's stormy rage,
    When he who might   10
Have lighted up and led his age,
    Falls back in night.

Scorn! would the angels laugh, to mark
    A bright soul driven,
Fiend-goaded, down the endless dark,
    From hope and heaven!

Let not the land once proud of him
    Insult him now,
Nor brand with deeper shame his dim,
    Dishonored brow.   20

But let its humbled sons, instead,
    From sea to lake,
A long lament, as for the dead,
    In sadness make.

Of all we loved and honored, naught
    Save power remains;
A fallen angel's pride of thought,
    Still strong in chains.

All else is gone; from those great eyes
    The soul has fled: 30
When faith is lost, when honor dies,
    The man is dead!

Then pay the reverence of old days
    To his dead fame;
Walk backward, with averted gaze,
    And hide the shame!

Skipper Ireson's Ride

Of all the rides since the birth of time,
Told in story or sung in rhyme,—
On Apuleius's Golden Ass,
Or one-eyed Calender's horse of brass,
Witch astride of a human back,
Islam's prophet on Al-Borák,—
The strangest ride that ever was sped
Was Ireson's, out from Marblehead!
    Old Floyd Ireson, for his hard heart,

Tarred and feathered and carried in a
    cart   10
  By the women of Marblehead!

Body of turkey, head of owl,
Wings a-droop like a rained-on fowl,
Feathered and ruffled in every part,
Skipper Ireson stood in the cart.
Scores of women, old and young,
Strong of muscle, and glib of tongue,
Pushed and pulled up the rocky lane,
Shouting and singing the shrill refrain:
  "Here's Flud Oirson, fur his horrd
    horrt,   20
  Torr'd an' futherr'd an' corr'd in a corrt
  By the women o' Morble'ead!"

Wrinkled scolds with hands on hips,
Girls in bloom of cheek and lips,
Wild-eyed, free-limbed, such as chase
Bacchus round some antique vase,
Brief of skirt, with ankles bare,
Loose of kerchief and loose of hair,
With conch-shells blowing and fish-horns'
    twang,
Over and over the Maenads sang: 30
  "Here's Flud Oirson, fur his horrd
    horrt,
  Torr'd an' futherr'd an' corr'd in a corrt
  By the women o' Morble'ead!"

Small pity for him!—He sailed away
From a leaking ship in Chaleur Bay,—
Sailed away from a sinking wreck,
With his own town's-people on her deck!
"Lay by! lay by!" they called to him.
Back he answered, "Sink or swim!
Brag of your catch of fish again!"   40
And off he sailed through the fog and
    rain!
  Old Floyd Ireson, for his hard heart,
  Tarred and feathered and carried in a
    cart
  By the women of Marblehead!

Fathoms deep in dark Chaleur
That wreck shall lie forevermore.
Mother and sister, wife and maid,
Looked from the rocks of Marblehead
Over the moaning and rainy sea,—
Looked for the coming that might not
    be!   50

What did the winds and the sea-birds say
Of the cruel captain who sailed away—?
  Old Floyd Ireson, for his hard heart,
  Tarred and feathered and carried in a
    cart
  By the women of Marblehead!

Through the street, on either side,
Up flew windows, doors swung wide;
Sharp-tongued spinsters, old wives gray,
Treble lent the fish-horn's bray.
Sea-worn grandsires, cripple-bound,   60
Hulks of old sailors run aground,
Shook head, and fist, and hat, and cane,
And cracked with curses the hoarse re-
    frain:
  "Here's Flud Oirson, fur his horrd
    horrt,
  Torr'd an' futherr'd an' corr'd in a
    corrt
  By the women o' Morble'ead!"

Sweetly along the Salem road
Bloom of orchard and lilac showed.
Little the wicked skipper knew
Of the fields so green and the sky so
    blue.   71 70
Riding there in his sorry trim,
Like an Indian idol glum and grim,
Scarcely he seemed the sound to hear
Of voices shouting, far and near:
  "Here's Flud Oirson, fur his horrd
    horrt,
  Torr'd an' futherr'd an' corr'd in a
    corrt
  By the women o' Morble'ead!"

"Hear me, neighbors!" at last he cried,—
"What to me is this noisy ride?
What is the shame that clothes the
    skin   80
To the nameless horror that lives within?
Waking or sleeping, I see a wreck,
And hear a cry from a reeling deck!
Hate me and curse me,—I only dread
The hand of God and the face of the
    dead!"
  Said old Floyd Ireson, for his hard
    heart,
  Tarred and feathered and carried in a
    cart
  By the women of Marblehead!

Then the wife of the skipper lost at sea
Said, "God has touched him! why should
    we!"   90
Said an old wife mourning her only son,
"Cut the rogue's tether and let him run!"
So with soft relentings and rude excuse,
Half scorn, half pity, they cut him loose,
And gave him a cloak to hide him in,
And left him alone with his shame and
    sin.
    Poor Floyd Ireson, for his hard heart,
    Tarred and feathered and carried in a
    cart
    By the women of Marblehead!

Laus Deo

    It is done!
    Clang of bell and roar of gun
Send the tidings up and down.
    How the belfries rock and reel!
    How the great guns, peal on peal,
Fling the joy from town to town!

    Ring, O bells!
    Every stroke exulting tells
Of the burial hour of crime.
    Loud and long, that all may hear,   10
    Ring for every listening ear
Of Eternity and Time!

    Let us kneel:
    God's own voice is in that peal,
And this spot is holy ground.
    Lord, forgive us! What are we,
    That our eyes this glory see,
That our ears have heard this sound!

    For the Lord
    On the whirlwind is abroad;   20
In the earthquake He has spoken;
    He has smitten with His thunder
    The iron walls asunder,
And the gates of brass are broken!

    Loud and long
    Lift the old exulting song;
Sing with Miriam by the sea,
    He has cast the mighty down;
    Horse and rider sink and drown;
"He hath triumphed gloriously!"   30

    Did we dare,
    In our agony of prayer,
Ask for more than He has done?
    When was ever his right hand
    Over any time or land
Stretched as now beneath the sun?

    How they pale,
    Ancient myth and song and tale,
In this wonder of our days,
    When the cruel rod of war   40
    Blossoms white with righteous law,
And the wrath of man is praise!

    Blotted out!
    All within and all about
Shall a fresher life begin;
    Freer breathe the universe
    As it rolls its heavy curse
On the dead and buried sin!

    It is done!
    In the circuit of the sun   50
Shall the sound thereof go forth.
    It shall bid the sad rejoice,
    It shall give the dumb a voice,
It shall belt with joy the earth!

    Ring and swing,
    Bells of joy! On morning's wing
Sound the song of praise abroad!
    With a sound of broken chains
    Tell the nations that He reigns,
Who alone is Lord and God!   60

Edgar Allan Poe
✳ 1809–1849

Tamerlane

Kind solace in a dying hour!
    Such, father, is not (now) my theme—
I will not madly deem that power
    Of Earth may shrive me of the sin
    Unearthly pride hath revell'd in—
I have no time to dote or dream:
You call it hope—that fire of fire!

It is but agony of desire:
  If I *can* hope—oh, God! I can—
    Its fount is holier—more divine—   10
I would not call thee fool, old man,
  But such is not a gift of thine.

Know thou the secret of a spirit
  Bow'd from its wild pride into shame.
O yearning heart! I did inherit
  Thy withering portion with the fame,
The searing glory which hath shone
Amid the jewels of my throne,
Halo of Hell! and with a pain
Not Hell shall make me fear again—   20
O craving heart, for the lost flowers
And sunshine of my summer hours!
The undying voice of that dead time,
With its interminable chime,
Rings, in the spirit of a spell,
Upon thy emptiness—a knell.

I have not always been as now:
The fever'd diadem on my brow
I claim'd and won usurpingly—
Hath not the same fierce heirdom given
  Rome to the Caesar—this to me?   31
    The heritage of a kingly mind,
And a proud spirit which hath striven
    Triumphantly with human kind.

On mountain soil I first drew life:
  The mists of the Taglay have shed
  Nightly their dews upon my head,
And, I believe, the winged strife
And tumult of the headlong air
Have nestled in my very hair.   40

So late from Heaven—that dew—it fell
  ('Mid dreams of an unholy night)
Upon me with a touch of Hell,
  While the red flashing of the light
From clouds that hung, like banners, o'er,
  Appeared to my half-closing eye
  The pageantry of monarchy,
And the deep trumpet-thunder's roar
  Came hurriedly upon me, telling
    Of human battle, where my voice,
My own voice, silly child!—was swell-
      ing   51
      (O! how my spirit would rejoice,
And leap within me at the cry)
The battle-cry of Victory!

The rain came down upon my head
  Unshelter'd—and the heavy wind
  Rendered me mad and deaf and blind.
It was but man, I thought, who shed
  Laurels upon me: and the rush—
  The torrent of the chilly air   60
Gurgled within my ear the crush
  Of   empires—with   the   captive's
      prayer—
The hum of suitors—and the tone
Of flattery 'round a sovereign's throne.

My passions, from that hapless hour,
  Usurp'd a tyranny which men
Have deem'd, since I have reach'd to
      power,
  My innate nature—be it so:
But, father, there liv'd one who, then,
Then—in my boyhood—when their fire
  Burn'd with a still intenser glow   71
(For passion must, with youth, expire)
  E'en *then* who knew this iron heart
In woman's weakness had a part.

I have no words—alas!—to tell
The loveliness of loving well!
Nor would I now attempt to trace
The more than beauty of a face
Whose lineaments, upon my mind,
Are—shadows on th' unstable wind: 80
Thus I remember having dwelt
  Some page of early lore upon,
With loitering eye, till I have felt
The letters—with their meaning—melt
  To fantasies—with none.

O, she was worthy of all love!
  Love—as in infancy was mine—
'Twas such as angel minds above
  Might envy; her young heart the shrine
On which my every hope and thought
  Were incense—then a goodly gift,   91
    For they were childish and up-
      right—
Pure—as her young example taught:
  Why did I leave it, and, adrift,
    Trust to the fire within, for light?

We grew in age—and love—together—
  Roaming the forest, and the wild;
My breast her shield in wintry weather—

And, when the friendly sunshine smil'd,
And she would mark the opening skies,
I saw no Heaven—but in her eyes.   101

Young Love's first lesson is—the heart:
    For 'mid that sunshine, and those smiles,
When, from our little cares apart,
    And laughing at her girlish wiles,
I'd throw me on her throbbing breast,
    And pour my spirit out in tears—
There was no need to speak the rest—
    No need to quiet any fears
Of her—who ask'd no reason why,   110
But turn'd on me her quiet eye!

Yet *more* than worthy of the love
My spirit struggled with, and strove,
When, on the mountain peak, alone,
Ambition lent it a new tone—
I had no being—but in thee:
    The world, and all it did contain
In the earth—the air—the sea—
    Its joy—its little lot of pain
That was new pleasure—the ideal,   120
    Dim, vanities of dreams by night—
And dimmer nothings which were real—
    (Shadows—and a more shadowy light!)
Parted upon their misty wings,
    And, so, confusedly, became
        Thine image and—a name—a name!
Two separate—yet most intimate things.

I was ambitious—have you known
    The passion, father? You have not:
A cottager, I mark'd a throne   130
Of half the world as all my own,
    And murmur'd at such lowly lot—
But, just like any other dream,
    Upon the vapor of the dew
My own had past, did not the beam
    Of beauty which did while it thro'
The minute—the hour—the day—oppress
My mind with double loveliness.

We walk'd together on the crown
Of a high mountain which look'd down
Afar from its proud natural towers   141

Of rock and forest, on the hills—
The dwindled hills! begirt with bowers
    And shouting with a thousand rills.

I spoke to her of power and pride,
    But mystically—in such guise
That she might deem it nought beside
    The moment's converse; in her eyes
I read, perhaps too carelessly,
    A mingled feeling with my own—   150
The flush on her bright cheek, to me
    Seem'd to become a queenly throne
Too well that I should let it be
    Light in the wilderness alone.

I wrapp'd myself in grandeur then
    And donn'd a visionary crown—
        Yet it was not that Fantasy
            Had thrown her mantle over me—
But that, among the rabble—men,
    Lion ambition is chain'd down—   160
And crouches to a keeper's hand—
Not so in deserts where the grand—
The wild—the terrible conspire
With their own breath to fan his fire.

Look 'round thee now on Samarcand!—
    Is she not queen of Earth? her pride
Above all cities? in her hand
    Their destinies? in all beside
Of glory which the world hath known
Stands she not nobly and alone?   170
Falling—her veriest stepping-stone
Shall form the pedestal of a throne—
And who her sovereign? Timour—he
    Whom the astonished people saw
Striding o'er empires haughtily
    A diadem'd outlaw!

O, human love! thou spirit given,
On Earth, of all we hope in Heaven!
Which fall'st into the soul like rain
Upon the Siroc-wither'd plain,   180
And, failing in thy power to bless,
But leav'st the heart a wilderness!
Idea! which bindest life around
With music of so strange a sound
And beauty of so wild a birth—
Farewell! for I have won the Earth.

When Hope, the eagle that tower'd, could see

No cliff beyond him in the sky,
His pinions were bent droopingly—   189
   And homeward turn'd his soften'd eye.
'Twas sunset: when the sun will part
There comes a sullenness of heart
To him who still would look upon
The glory of the summer sun.
That soul will hate the ev'ning mist
So often lovely, and will list
To the sound of the coming darkness
     (known
To those whose spirits harken) as one
Who, in a dream of night, *would* fly
But *cannot* from a danger nigh.   200

What tho' the moon—the white moon—
Shed all the splendor of her noon,
Her smile is chilly—and *her* beam,
In that time of dreariness, will seem
(So like you gather in your breath)
A portrait taken after death.
And boyhood is a summer sun
Whose waning is the dreariest one.
For all we live to know is known,
And all we seek to keep hath flown.   210
Let life, then, as the day-flower, fall
With the noon-day beauty—which is all.

I reach'd my home—my home no more—
   For all had flown who made it so.
I pass'd from out its mossy door,
   And, tho' my tread was soft and low,
A voice came from the threshold stone
Of one whom I had earlier known—
   O, I defy thee, Hell, to show
   On beds of fire that burn below,   220
   An humbler heart—a deeper wo.

Father, I firmly do believe—
   I *know*—for Death who comes for me
   From regions of the blest afar,
Where there is nothing to deceive,
   Hath left his iron gate ajar,
   And rays of truth you cannot see
   Are flashing thro' Eternity—
I do believe that Eblis hath
A snare in every human path—   230
Else how, when in the holy grove
I wandered of the idol, Love,
Who daily scents his snowy wings

With incense of burnt offerings
From the most unpolluted things,
Whose pleasant bowers are yet so riven
Above with trellis'd rays from Heaven
No mote may shun—no tiniest fly—
The light'ning of his eagle eye—
How was it that Ambition crept,   240
   Unseen, amid the revels there,
Till growing bold, he laughed and leapt
   In the tangles of Love's very hair?

The Lake: To ————

In spring of youth it was my lot
To haunt of the wide world a spot
The which I could not love the less—
So lovely was the loneliness
Of a wild lake, with black rock bound,
And the tall pines that towered around.

But when the Night had thrown her pall
Upon that spot, as upon all,
And the mystic wind went by
Murmuring in melody,   10
Then—ah, then—I would awake
To the terror of the lone lake.

Yet that terror was not fright,
But a tremulous delight—
A feeling not the jewelled mine
Could teach or bribe me to define—
Nor Love—although the Love were
    thine.

Death was in that poisonous wave,
And in its gulf a fitting grave
For him who thence could solace bring
To his lone imagining,   21
Whose solitary soul could make
An Eden of that dim lake.

Evening Star

'Twas noontide of summer,
   And mid-time of night;
And stars, in their orbits,
   Shone pale, thro' the light

Of the brighter, cold moon,
  'Mid planets her slaves,
Herself in the Heavens,
  Her beam on the waves.
  I gaz'd a while
  On her cold smile;   10
Too cold—too cold for me.
  There pass'd as a shroud,
  A fleecy cloud,
And I turn'd away to thee,
  Proud Evening Star,
  In thy glory afar,
And dearer thy beam shall be;
  For joy to my heart
  Is the proud part
Thou bearest in Heav'n at night,   20
  And more I admire
  Thy distant fire
Than that colder, lowly light.

Sonnet—To Science

Science! true daughter of Old Time thou
    art!
  Who alterest all things with thy peer-
    ing eyes.
Why preyest thou thus upon the poet's
    heart,
  Vulture, whose wings are dull realities?
How should he love thee? or how deem
    thee wise,
  Who wouldst not leave him in his wan-
    dering
To seek for treasure in the jewelled skies,
  Albeit he soared with an undaunted
    wing?
Hast thou not dragged Diana from her
    car?
  And driven the Hamadryad from the
    wood   10
To seek a shelter in some happier star?
  Hast thou not torn the Naiad from her
    flood,
The Elfin from the green grass, and from
    me
The summer dream beneath the tamarind
    tree?

Al Aaraaf

Part 1

O! Nothing earthly save the ray
(Thrown back from flowers) of Beauty's
    eye,
As in those gardens where the day
Springs from the gems of Circassy—
O! nothing earthly save the thrill
Of melody in woodland rill—
Or (music of the passion-hearted)
Joy's voice so peacefully departed
That, like the murmur in the shell,
Its echo dwelleth and will dwell—   10
Oh, nothing of the dross of ours—
Yet all the beauty—all the flowers
That list our Love, and deck our
    bowers—
Adorn yon world afar, afar—
The wandering star.

  'Twas a sweet time for Nesace—for
    there
Her world lay lolling on the golden air,
Near four bright suns—a temporary
    rest—
An oasis in desert of the blest.   19
Away—away—'mid seas of rays that roll
Empyrean splendor o'er th' unchained
    soul—
The soul that scarce (the billows are so
    dense)
Can struggle to its destin'd eminence—
To distant spheres, from time to time, she
    rode,
And late to ours, the favor'd one of
    God—
But, now, the ruler of an anchor'd realm,
She throws aside the sceptre—leaves the
    helm,
And, amid incense and high spiritual
    hymns,
Laves in quadruple light her angel limbs.

  Now happiest, loveliest in yon lovely
    Earth,   30

Whence sprang the "Idea of Beauty" into
    birth
(Falling in wreaths thro' many a startled
    star,
Like woman's hair 'mid pearls, until, afar,
It lit on hills Achaian, and there dwelt),
She look'd into Infinity—and knelt.
Rich clouds, for canopies, about her
    curled—
Fit emblems of the model of her world—
Seen but in beauty—not impeding sight
Of other beauty glittering thro' the
    light—
A wreath that twined each starry form
    around,   40
And all the opal'd air in color bound.

All hurriedly she knelt upon a bed
Of flowers: of lilies such as rear'd the
    head
On the fair Capo Deucato, and sprang
So eagerly around about to hang
Upon the flying footsteps of—deep
    pride—
Of her who lov'd a mortal—and so died.
The Sephalica, budding with young bees,
Uprear'd its purple stem around her
    knees:
And gemmy flower, of Trebizond mis-
    nam'd—   50
Inmate of highest stars, where erst it
    sham'd
All other loveliness: its honied dew
(The fabled nectar that the heathen
    knew)
Deliriously sweet, was dropp'd from
    Heaven,
And fell on gardens of the unforgiven
In Trebizond—and on a sunny flower
So like its own above, that, to this hour,
It still remaineth, torturing the bee
With madness, and unwonted reverie:
In Heaven, and all its environs, the leaf
And blossom of the fairy plant, in grief
Disconsolate linger—grief that hangs her
    head,   62
Repenting follies that full long have fled,
Heaving her white breast to the balmy
    air,

Like guilty beauty, chasten'd, and more
    fair:
Nyctanthes too, as sacred as the light
She fears to perfume, perfuming the
    night:
And Clytia pondering between many a
    sun,
While pettish tears adown her petals run:
And that aspiring flower that sprang on
    Earth—   70
And died, ere scarce exalted into birth,
Bursting its odorous heart in spirit to
    wing
Its way to Heaven, from garden of a
    king:
And Valisnerian lotus thither flown
From struggling with the waters of the
    Rhone:
And thy most lovely purple perfume,
    Zante!
Isola d'oro!—Fior di Levante!
And the Nelumbo bud that floats for ever
With Indian Cupid down the holy river—
Fair flowers, and fairy! to whose care is
    given   80
To bear the Goddess' song, in odors, up
    to Heaven:

    "Spirit! that dwellest where,
        In the deep sky,
    The terrible and fair,
        In beauty vie!
    Beyond the line of blue—
        The boundary of the star
    Which turneth at the view
        Of thy barrier and thy bar—
    Of the barrier overgone   90
        By the comets who were cast
    From their pride, and from their
        throne
        To be drudges till the last—
    To be carriers of fire
        (The red fire of their heart)
    With speed that may not tire
        And with pain that shall not
        part—
    Who livest—*that* we know—
        In Eternity—we feel—
    But the shadow of whose brow   100

What spirit shall reveal?
Tho' the beings whom thy Nesace,
    Thy messenger, hath known,
Have dream'd for thy Infinity
    A model of their own—
Thy will is done, oh, God!
    The star hath ridden high
Thro' many a tempest, but she rode
    Beneath thy burning eye;
And here, in thought, to thee—   110
    In thought that can alone
Ascend thy empire and so be
    A partner of thy throne—
By winged Fantasy,
    My embassy is given,
Till secrecy shall knowledge be
    In the environs of Heaven."

She ceas'd—and buried then her burn-
        ing cheek
Abash'd, amid the lilies there, to seek
A shelter from the fervour of His eye;
For the stars trembled at the Deity.   121
She stirr'd not—breath'd not—for a voice
        was there
How solemnly pervading the calm air!
A sound of silence on the startled ear
Which dreamy poets name "the music of
        the sphere."
Ours is a world of words: Quiet we call
"Silence"—which is the merest word of
        all.
All Nature speaks, and ev'n ideal things
Flap shadowy sounds from visionary
        wings—
But ah! not so when, thus, in realms on
        high   130
The eternal voice of God is passing by,
And the red winds are withering in the
        sky!

"What tho' in worlds which sightless
        cycles run,
Link'd to a little system, and one sun—
Where all my love is folly, and the crowd
Still think my terrors but the thunder
        cloud,
The storm, the earthquake, and the
        ocean-wrath—

(Ah! will they cross me in my angrier
        path?)
What tho' in worlds which own a single
        sun
The sands of Time grow dimmer as they
        run,   140
Yet thine is my resplendency, so given
To bear my secrets thro' the upper
        Heaven.
Leave tenantless thy crystal home, and
        fly,
With all thy train, athwart the moony
        sky—
Apart—like fire-flies in Sicilian night,
And wing to other worlds another light!
Divulge the secrets of thy embassy
To the proud orbs that twinkle—and so
        be
To ev'ry heart a barrier and a ban   149
Lest the stars totter in the guilt of man!"

Up rose the maiden in the yellow
        night,
The single-mooned eve!—on Earth we
        plight
Our faith to one love—and one moon
        adore—
The birth-place of young Beauty had no
        more.
As sprang that yellow star from downy
        hours
Up rose the maiden from her shrine of
        flowers,
And bent o'er sheeny mountain and dim
        plain
Her way—but left not yet her Thera-
        saean reign.

Part 2

High on a mountain of enamell'd head—
Such as the drowsy shepherd on his bed
Of giant pasturage lying at his ease,   161
Raising his heavy eyelid, starts and sees
With many a mutter'd "hope to be for-
        given,"
What time the moon is quadrated in
        Heaven—
Of rosy head, that towering far away
Into the sunlit ether, caught the ray

Of sunken suns at eve—at noon of night,
While the moon danc'd with the fair
    stranger light—
Uprear'd upon such height arose a pile
Of gorgeous columns on th' unburthen'd
    air,   170
Flashing from Parian marble that twin
    smile
Far down upon the wave that sparkled
    there,
And nursled the young mountain in its
    lair.
Of molten stars their pavement, such as
    fall
Thro' the ebon air, besilvering the pall
Of their own dissolution, while they die—
Adorning then the dwellings of the sky.
A dome, by linked light from Heaven let
    down,
Sat gently on these columns as a crown—
A window of one circular diamond, there,
Look'd out above into the purple air,   181
And rays from God shot down that me-
    teor chain
And hallow'd all the beauty twice again,
Save when, between th' Empyrean and
    that ring,
Some eager spirit flapp'd his dusky wing.
But on the pillars Seraph eyes have seen
The dimness of this world: that greyish
    green
That Nature loves the best for Beauty's
    grave
Lurk'd in each cornice, round each archi-
    trave—   189
And every sculptur'd cherub thereabout
That from his marble dwelling peeréd
    out,
Seem'd earthly in the shadow of his
    niche—
Achaian statues in a world so rich!
Friezes from Tadmor and Persepolis—
From Balbec, and the stilly, clear abyss
Of beautiful Gomorrah! O, the wave
Is now upon thee—but too late to save!

Sound loves to revel in a summer
    night:
Witness the murmur of the grey twilight

That stole upon the ear, in Eyraco,   200
Of many a wild star-gazer long ago—
That stealeth ever on the ear of him
Who, musing, gazeth on the distance
    dim,
And sees the darkness coming as a
    cloud—
Is not its form—its voice—most palpable
    and loud?

But what is this?—it cometh—and it
    brings
A music with it—'tis the rush of wings—
A pause—and then a sweeping, falling
    strain,
And Nesace is in her halls again.
From the wild energy of wanton haste
    Her cheeks were flushing, and her lips
        apart;   211
And zone that clung around her gentle
    waist
    Had burst beneath the heaving of her
        heart.
Within the centre of that hall to breathe
She paus'd and panted, Zanthe! all be-
    neath,
The fairy light that kiss'd her golden hair
And long'd to rest, yet could but sparkle
    there!

    Young flowers were whispering in
        melody
To happy flowers that night—and tree to
    tree;
Fountains were gushing music as they
    fell   220
In many a star-lit grove, or moon-lit dell;
Yet silence came upon material things—
Fair flowers, bright waterfalls and angel
    wings—
And sound alone, that from the spirit
    sprang,
Bore burthen to the charm the maiden
    sang:

    " 'Neath blue-bell or streamer—
      Or tufted wild spray
    That keeps from the dreamer
      The moonbeam away—
    Bright beings! that ponder,   230

With half closing eyes,
On the stars which your wonder
    Hath drawn from the skies,
Till they glance thro' the shade, and
    Come down to your brow
Like—eyes of the maiden
    Who calls on you now—
Arise! from your dreaming
    In violet bowers,
To duty beseeming   240
    These star-litten hours—
And shake from your tresses,
    Encumber'd with dew,
The breath of those kisses
    That cumber them too
(O, how, without you, Love!
    Could angels be blest?)—
Those kisses of true love
    That lull'd ye to rest!
Up!—shake from your wing   250
    Each hindering thing:
The dew of the night—
    It would weigh down your
        flight;
And true love caresses—
    O! leave them apart:
They are light on the tresses,
    But lead on the heart.

"Ligeia! Ligeia!
    My beautiful one!
Whose harshest idea   260
    Will to melody run,
O! is it thy will
    On the breezes to toss?
Or, capriciously still,
    Like the lone Albatross,
Incumbent on night
    (As she on the air)
To keep watch with delight
    On the harmony there?

"Ligeia! wherever   270
    Thy image may be,
No magic shall sever
    Thy music from thee.
Thou hast bound many eyes
    In a dreamy sleep—
But the strains shall arise

Which *thy* vigilance keep:
The sound of the rain
    Which leaps down to the
        flower,
And dances again   280
    In the rhythm of the shower—
The murmur that springs
    From the growing of grass
Are the music of things—
    But are modell'd, alas!—
Away, then, my dearest,
    O! hie thee away
To springs that lie clearest
    Beneath the moon-ray—
To lone lake that smiles,   290
    In its dream of deep rest,
At the many star-isles
    That enjewel its breast—
Where wild flowers, creeping,
    Have mingled their shade,
On its margin is sleeping
    Full many a maid—
Some have left the cool glade, and
    Have slept with the bee—
Arouse them, my maiden,   300
    On moorland and lea—
Go! breathe on their slumber,
    All softly in ear,
The musical number
    They slumber'd to hear—
For what can awaken
    An angel so soon,
Whose sleep hath been taken
    Beneath the cold moon,
As the spell which no slumber   310
    Of witchery may test,
The rhythmical number
    Which lull'd him to rest?"

Spirits in wing, and angels to the view,
A thousand seraphs burst th' Empyrean
    thro',
Young dreams still hovering on their
    drowsy flight—
Seraphs in all but "Knowledge," the keen
    light
That fell, refracted, thro' thy bounds,
    afar
O Death! from eye of God upon that star:

Sweet was that error—sweeter still that
    death—   320
Sweet was that error—ev'n with *us* the
    breath
Of Science dims the mirror of our joy—
To them 'twere the Simoom, and would
    destroy—
For what (to them) availeth it to know
That Truth is Falsehood—or that Bliss is
    Woe?
Sweet was their death—with them to die
    was rife
With the last ecstasy of satiate life—
Beyond that death no immortality—
But sleep that pondereth and is not "to
    be"—
And there—oh! may my weary spirit
    dwell—   330
Apart from Heaven's Eternity—and yet
    how far from Hell!

What guilty spirit, in what shrubbery
    dim,
Heard not the stirring summons of that
    hymn?
But two: they fell: for Heaven no grace
    imparts
To those who hear not for their beating
    hearts.
A maiden-angel and her seraph-lover—
O! where (and ye may seek the wide
    skies over)
Was Love, the blind, near sober Duty
    known?
Unguided Love hath fallen—'mid "tears
    of perfect moan."   339

He was a goodly spirit—he who fell:
A wanderer by moss-y-mantled well—
A gazer on the lights that shine above—
A dreamer in the moonbeam by his love:
What wonder? for each star is eye-like
    there,
And looks so sweetly down on Beauty's
    hair;
And they, and ev'ry mossy spring were
    holy
To his love-haunted heart and melan-
    choly.

The night had found (to him a night of
    wo)
Upon a mountain crag, young Angelo—
Beetling it bends athwart the solemn sky,
And scowls on starry worlds that down
    beneath it lie.   351
Here sate he with his love—his dark eye
    bent
With eagle gaze along the firmament:
Now turn'd it upon her—but ever then
It trembled to the orb of EARTH again.

    "Ianthe, dearest, see! how dim that
    ray!
How lovely 'tis to look so far away!
She seem'd not thus upon that autumn
    eve
I left her gorgeous halls—nor mourn'd to
    leave.
That eve—that eve—I should remember
    well—   360
The sun-ray dropp'd in Lemnos, with a
    spell
On th' Arabesque carving of a gilded hall
Wherein I sate, and on the draperied
    wall—
And on my eyelids—O the heavy light!
How drowsily it weigh'd them into night!
On flowers, before, and mist, and love
    they ran
With Persian Saadi in his Gulistan:
But O that light!—I slumber'd—Death,
    the while,
Stole o'er my senses in that lovely isle
So softly that no single silken hair   370
Awoke that slept—or knew that he was
    there.

    "The last spot of Earth's orb I trod
    upon
Was a proud temple call'd the Parthenon.
More beauty clung around her column'd
    wall
Than ev'n thy glowing bosom beats
    withal,
And when old Time my wing did disen-
    thral—
Thence sprang I—as the eagle from his
    tower,

And years I left behind me in an hour.
What time upon her airy bounds I hung,
One half the garden of her globe was
    flung,   380
Unrolling as a chart unto my view—
Tenantless cities of the desert too!
Ianthe, beauty crowded on me then,
And half I wish'd to be again of men."

    "My Angelo! and why of them to be?
A brighter dwelling-place is here for
    thee—
And greener fields than in yon world
    above,
And woman's loveliness—and passionate
    love."

    "But, list, Ianthe! when the air so
    soft
Fail'd, as my pennon'd spirit leapt aloft,
Perhaps my brain grew dizzy—but the
    world   391
I left so late was into chaos hurl'd—
Sprang from her station, on the winds
    apart,
And roll'd, a flame, the fiery Heaven
    athwart.
Methought, my sweet one, then I ceased
    to soar,
And fell—not swiftly as I rose before,
But with a downward, tremulous motion
    thro'
Light, brazen rays, this golden star unto!
Nor long the measure of my falling hours,
For nearest of all stars was thine to
    ours—   400

Dread star! that came, amid a night of
    mirth,
A red Daedalion on the timid Earth."

    "We came—and to thy Earth—but
    not to us
Be given our lady's bidding to discuss:
We came, my love; around, above, below,
Gay fire-fly of the night we come and
    go,
Nor ask a reason save the angel-nod
She grants to us, as granted by her God—
But, Angelo, than thine grey Time un-
    furl'd   409
Never his fairy wing o'er fairier world!
Dim was its little disk, and angel eyes
Alone could see the phantom in the skies,
When first Al Aaraaf knew her course to
    be
Headlong thitherward o'er the starry
    sea—
But when its glory swell'd upon the sky,
As glowing Beauty's bust beneath man's
    eye,
We paus'd before the heritage of men,
And thy star trembled—as doth Beauty
    then!"

    Thus, in discourse, the lovers whiled
    away
The night that waned and waned and
    brought no day.   420
They fell: for Heaven to them no hope
    imparts
Who hear not for the beating of their
    hearts.

Lenore

Ah, broken is the golden bowl!—the spirit flown forever!
Let the bell toll!—a saintly soul floats on the Stygian river:—
And, Guy de Vere, hast *thou* no tear?—weep now or never more!
See! on yon drear and rigid bier low lies thy love, Lenore!
Come, let the burial rite be read—the funeral song be sung!—
An anthem for the queenliest dead that ever died so young—
A dirge for her the doubly dead in that she died so young.

"Wretches! ye loved her for her wealth, and ye hated her for her pride;
And, when she fell in feeble health, ye blessed her—that she died:—

How *shall* the ritual, then, be read—the requiem how be sung   10
By you—by yours, the evil eye,—by yours, the slanderous tongue
That did to death the innocence that died, and died so young?"

Peccavimus; yet rave not thus! but let a Sabbath song
Go up to God so solemnly the dead may feel no wrong!
The sweet Lenore hath gone before, with Hope that flew beside,
Leaving thee wild for the dear child that should have been thy bride—
For her, the fair and debonair, that now so lowly lies,
The life upon her yellow hair, but not within her eyes—
The life still there upon her hair, the death upon her eyes.

"Avaunt!—avaunt! to friends from fiends the indignant ghost is riven—   20
From Hell unto a high estate within the utmost Heaven—
From moan and groan to a golden throne beside the king of Heaven:—
Let *no* bell toll, then, lest her soul, amid its hallowed mirth,
Should catch the note as it doth float up from the damnéd Earth!
And I—tonight my heart is light:—no dirge will I upraise,
But waft the angel on her flight with a Paean of old days!"

To Helen

Helen, thy beauty is to me
    Like those Nicéan barks of yore,
That gently, o'er a perfumed sea,
    The weary, way-worn wanderer bore
    To his own native shore.

On desperate seas long wont to roam,
    Thy hyacinth hair, thy classic face,
Thy Naiad airs have brought me home
    To the glory that was Greece,
And the grandeur that was Rome.   10

Lo! in yon brilliant window-niche
    How statue-like I see thee stand,
    The agate lamp within thy hand!
Ah, Psyche, from the regions which
    Are Holy-Land!

The City in the Sea

Lo! Death has reared himself a throne
In a strange city lying alone
Far down within the dim West,
Where the good and the bad and the
    worst and the best

Have gone to their eternal rest.
There shrines and palaces and towers
(Time-eaten towers that tremble not!)
Resemble nothing that is ours.
Around, by lifting winds forgot,
Resignedly beneath the sky   10
The melancholy waters lie.

No rays from the holy heaven come down
On the long night-time of that town;
But light from out the lurid sea
Streams up the turrets silently—
Gleams up the pinnacles far and free—
Up domes—up spires—up kingly halls—
Up fanes—up Babylon-like walls—
Up shadowy long-forgotten bowers   19
Of sculptured ivy and stone flowers—
Up many and many a marvellous shrine
Whose wreathéd friezes intertwine
The viol, the violet, and the vine.

Resignedly beneath the sky
The melancholy waters lie.
So blend the turrets and shadows there
That all seem pendulous in air,
While from a proud tower in the town
Death looks gigantically down.

There open fanes and gaping graves   30
Yawn level with the luminous waves;

But not the riches there that lie
In each idol's diamond eye—
Not the gaily-jewelled dead
Tempt the waters from their bed;
For no ripples curl, alas!
Along that wilderness of glass—
No swellings tell that winds may be
Upon some far-off happier sea—
No heavings hint that winds have been
On seas less hideously serene.   41

But lo, a stir is in the air!
The wave—there is a movement there!
As if the towers had thrust aside,
In slightly sinking, the dull tide—
As if their tops had feebly given
A void within the filmy Heaven.
The waves have now a redder glow—
The hours are breathing faint and low—
And when, amid no earthly moans,   50
Down, down that town shall settle hence,
Hell, rising from a thousand thrones,
Shall do it reverence.

Israfel

> And the angel Israfel, whose heart-
> strings are a lute, and who has the
> sweetest voice of all God's creatures.
> *Koran*

In Heaven a spirit doth dwell
  "Whose heart-strings are a lute;"
None sing so wildly well
As the angel Israfel,
And the giddy stars (so legends tell),
Ceasing their hymns, attend the spell
  Of his voice, all mute.

Tottering above
  In her highest noon,
  The enamoured moon   10
Blushes with love,
  While, to listen, the red levin
  (With the rapid Pleiads, even,
  Which were seven,)
  Pauses in Heaven.

And they say (the starry choir
  And the other listening things)
That Israfeli's fire
Is owing to that lyre
  By which he sits and sings—   20
The trembling living wire
  Of those unusual strings.

But the skies that angel trod,
  Where deep thoughts are a duty—
Where Love's a grown-up God—
  Where the Houri glances are
Imbued with all the beauty
  Which we worship in a star.

Therefore, thou are not wrong,
  Israfeli, who despisest   30
An unimpassioned song;
To thee the laurels belong,
  Best bard, because the wisest!
Merrily live, and long!

The ecstasies above
  With thy burning measures suit—
Thy grief, thy joy, thy hate, thy love,
  With the fervour of thy lute—
  Well may the stars be mute!

Yes, Heaven is thine; but this   40
  Is a world of sweets and sours;
  Our flowers are merely—flowers,
And the shadow of thy perfect bliss
  Is the sunshine of ours.

If I could dwell
Where Israfel
  Hath dwelt, and he where I,
He might not sing so wildly well
  A mortal melody,
While a bolder note than this might swell
From my lyre within the sky.   51

The Haunted Palace

In the greenest of our valleys,
  By good angels tenanted,
Once a fair and stately palace—

Radiant palace—reared its head.
In the monarch Thought's dominion—
  It stood there!
Never seraph spread a pinion
  Over fabric half so fair!

Banners yellow, glorious, golden,
  On its roof did float and flow,   10
(This—all this—was in the olden
  Time long ago,)
And every gentle air that dallied,
  In that sweet day,
Along the ramparts plumed and pallid,
  A wingéd odor went away.

Wanderers in that happy valley,
  Through two luminous windows, saw
Spirits moving musically
  To a lute's well-tunéd law,   20
Round about a throne, where sitting,
  Porphyrogene!
In state his glory well befitting,
  The ruler of the realm was seen.

And all with pearl and ruby glowing
  Was the fair palace door,
Through which came flowing, flowing,
    flowing,
  And sparkling evermore,
A troop of Echoes, whose sweet duty
  Was but to sing,   30
In voices of surpassing beauty,
  The wit and wisdom of their king.

But evil things, in robes of sorrow,
  Assailed the monarch's high estate.
(Ah, let us mourn!—for never morrow
  Shall dawn upon him, desolate!)
And round about his home the glory
  That blushed and bloomed,
Is but a dim-remembered story
  Of the old time entombed.   40

And travellers, now, within that valley,
  Through the red-litten windows see
Vast forms that move fantastically
  To a discordant melody,
While, like a ghastly rapid river,
  Through the pale door
A hideous throng rush out forever,
  And laugh—but smile no more.

The Conqueror Worm

Lo! 'tis a gala night
  Within the lonesome latter years!
An angel throng, bewinged, bedight
  In veils, and drowned in tears,
Sit in a theatre, to see
  A play of hopes and fears,
While the orchestra breathes fitfully
  The music of the spheres.

Mimes, in the form of God on high,
  Mutter and mumble low,   10
And hither and thither fly—
  Mere puppets they, who come and go
At bidding of vast formless things
  That shift the scenery to and fro,
Flapping from out their Condor wings
  Invisible Wo!

That motley drama—oh, be sure
  It shall not be forgot!
With its Phantom chased for evermore
  By a crowd that seize it not,   20
Through a circle that ever returneth in
  To the self-same spot,
And much of Madness, and more of Sin,
  And Horror the soul of the plot.

But see, amid the mimic rout,
  A crawling shape intrude!
A blood-red thing that writhes from out
  The scenic solitude!
It writhes!—it writhes!—with mortal
    pangs
  The mimes become its food,   30
And seraphs sob at vermin fangs
  In human gore imbued.

Out—out are the lights—out all!
  And, over each quivering form,
The curtain, a funeral pall,
  Comes down with the rush of a storm,
While the angels, all pallid and wan,
  Uprising, unveiling, affirm
That the play is the tragedy, "Man,"   39
  And its hero, the Conqueror Worm.

Dream-Land

By a route obscure and lonely,
Haunted by ill angels only,
Where an Eidolon, named NIGHT,
On a black throne reigns upright,
I have reached these lands but newly
From an ultimate dim Thule—
From a wild weird clime that lieth, sub-
    lime,
    Out of SPACE—out of TIME.

Bottomless vales and boundless floods,
And chasms, and caves, and Titan
    woods,   10
With forms that no man can discover
For the tears that drip all over;
Mountains toppling evermore
Into seas without a shore;
Seas that restlessly aspire,
Surging, unto skies of fire;
Lakes that endlessly outspread
Their lone waters—lone and dead,—
Their still waters—still and chilly
With the snows of the lolling lily.   20

By the lakes that thus outspread
Their lone waters, lone and dead,—
Their sad waters, sad and chilly
With the snows of the lolling lily—
By the mountains—near the river
Murmuring lowly, murmuring ever,—
By the grey woods,—by the swamp
Where the toad and the newt en-
    camp,—
By the dismal tarns and pools
    Where dwell the Ghouls,—   30
By each spot the most unholy—
In each nook most melancholy,—
There the traveller meets, aghast,
Sheeted Memories of the Past—
Shrouded forms that start and sigh
As they pass the wanderer by—
White-robed forms of friends long
    given,
In agony, to the Earth—and Heaven.

For the heart whose woes are legion
'Tis a peaceful, soothing region—   40

For the spirit that walks in shadow
'Tis—oh, 'tis an Eldorado!
But the traveller, travelling through it,
May not—dare not openly view it;
Never its mysteries are exposed
To the weak human eye unclosed;
So wills its King, who hath forbid
The uplifting of the fringéd lid;
And thus the sad Soul that here passes
Beholds it but through darkened
    glasses.   50

By a route obscure and lonely,
Haunted by ill angels only,
Where an Eidolon, named NIGHT,
On a black throne reigns upright,
I have wandered home but newly
From this ultimate dim Thule.

The Raven

Once upon a midnight dreary, while I
    pondered, weak and weary,
Over many a quaint and curious volume
    of forgotten lore—
While I nodded, nearly napping, sud-
    denly there came a tapping,
As of some one gently rapping, rapping
    at my chamber door.
" 'Tis some visitor," I muttered, "tapping
    at my chamber door—
    Only this and nothing more."

Ah, distinctly I remember it was in the
    bleak December;
And each separate dying ember wrought
    its ghost upon the floor.
Eagerly I wished the morrow;—vainly I
    had sought to borrow
From my books surcease of sorrow—sor-
    row for the lost Lenore—   10
For the rare and radiant maiden whom
    the angels name Lenore—
    Nameless *here* for evermore.

And the silken, sad, uncertain rustling of
    each purple curtain
Thrilled me—filled me with fantastic ter-
    rors never felt before;

So that now, to still the beating of my
  heart, I stood repeating,
" 'Tis some visitor entreating entrance at
  my chamber door—
Some late visitor entreating entrance at
  my chamber door;—
    This it is and nothing more."

Presently my soul grew stronger; hesitat-
  ing then no longer,
"Sir," said I, "or Madam, truly your for-
  giveness I implore;   20
But the fact is I was napping, and so
  gently you came rapping,
And so faintly you came tapping, tapping
  at my chamber door,
That I scarce was sure I heard you"—
  here I opened wide the door;—
    Darkness there and nothing more.

Deep into that darkness peering, long I
  stood there wondering, fearing,
Doubting, dreaming dreams no mortal
  ever dared to dream before;
But the silence was unbroken, and the
  stillness gave no token,
And the only word there spoken was the
  whispered word, "Lenore?"
This I whispered, and an echo murmured
  back the word "Lenore!"
    Merely this and nothing more.   30

Back into the chamber turning, all my
  soul within me burning,
Soon again I heard a tapping somewhat
  louder than before.
"Surely," said I, "surely that is something
  at my window lattice;
Let me see, then, what thereat is, and
  this mystery explore—
Let my heart be still a moment and this
  mystery explore;—
    'Tis the wind and nothing more!"

Open here I flung the shutter, when,
  with many a flirt and flutter,
In there stepped a stately Raven of the
  saintly days of yore;
Not the least obeisance made he; not a
  minute stopped or stayed he;

But, with mien of lord or lady, perched
  above my chamber door—   40
Perched upon a bust of Pallas just above
  my chamber door—
    Perched, and sat, and nothing more.

Then this ebony bird beguiling my sad
  fancy into smiling,
By the grave and stern decorum of the
  countenance it wore,
"Though thy crest be shorn and shaven,
  thou," I said, "art sure no craven,
Ghastly grim and ancient Raven wander-
  ing from the Nightly shore—
Tell me what thy lordly name is on the
  Night's Plutonian shore!"
    Quoth the Raven, "Nevermore."

Much I marvelled this ungainly fowl to
  hear discourse so plainly,
Though its answer little meaning—little
  relevancy bore;   50
For we cannot help agreeing that no
  living human being
Ever yet was blessed with seeing bird
  above his chamber door—
Bird or beast upon the sculptured bust
  above his chamber door,
    With such name as "Nevermore."

But the Raven, sitting lonely on the
  placid busts spoke only
That one word, as if his soul in that one
  word he did outpour.
Nothing farther then he uttered—not a
  feather then he fluttered—
Till I scarcely more than muttered "Other
  friends have flown before—
On the morrow *he* will leave me, as my
  hopes have flown before."
    Then the bird said "Nevermore."

Startled at the stillness broken by reply
  so aptly spoken,   61
"Doubtless," said I, "what it utters is its
  only stock and store
Caught from some unhappy master
  whom unmerciful Disaster
Followed fast and followed faster till his
  songs one burden bore—

Till the dirges of his Hope that melan-
choly burden bore
Of 'Never—nevermore.' "

But the Raven still beguiling all my fancy
into smiling,
Straight I wheeled a cushioned seat in
front of bird, and bust and door;
Then, upon the velvet sinking, I betook
myself to linking
Fancy unto fancy, thinking what this
ominous bird of yore—   70
What this grim, ungainly, ghastly, gaunt,
and ominous bird of yore
Meant in croaking "Nevermore."

This I sat engaged in guessing, but no
syllable expressing
To the fowl whose fiery eyes now burned
into my bosom's core;
This and more I sat divining, with my
head at ease reclining
On the cushion's velvet lining that the
lamp-light gloated o'er,
But whose velvet-violet lining with the
lamp-light gloating o'er,
She shall press, ah, nevermore!

Then, methought, the air grew denser,
perfumed from an unseen censer
Swung by Seraphim whose foot-falls tin-
kled on the tufted floor.   80
"Wretch," I cried, "thy God hath lent
thee—by these angels he hath
sent thee
Respite—respite and nepenthe from thy
memories of Lenore;
Quaff, oh, quaff this kind nepenthe and
forget this lost Lenore!"
Quoth the Raven, "Nevermore."

"Prophet!" said I, "thing of evil!—prophet
still, if bird or devil!—
Whether Tempter sent, or whether
tempest tossed thee here ashore,
Desolate yet all undaunted, on this desert
land enchanted—
On this home by Horror haunted—tell
me truly, I implore—

Is there—*is* there balm in Gilead?—tell
me—tell me, I implore!"
Quoth the Raven, "Nevermore."

"Prophet!" said I, "thing of evil!—
prophet still, if bird or devil!   91
By that Heaven that bends above us—by
that God we both adore—
Tell this soul with sorrow laden if, within
the distant Aidenn,
It shall clasp a sainted maiden whom the
angels name Lenore—
Clasp a rare and radiant maiden whom
the angels name Lenore."
Quoth the Raven, "Nevermore."

"Be that word our sign of parting, bird or
fiend!" I shrieked, upstarting—
"Get thee back into the tempest and the
Night's Plutonian shore!
Leave no black plume as a token of that
lie thy shoul hath spoken!
Leave my loneliness unbroken!—quit the
bust above my door!   100
Take thy beak from out my heart, and
take thy form from off my door!"
Quoth the Raven, "Nevermore."

And the Raven, never flitting, still is sit-
ting, *still* is sitting
On the pallid bust of Pallas just above my
chamber door;
And his eyes have all the seeming of a
demon's that is dreaming,
And the lamp-light o'er him streaming
throws his shadow on the floor;
And my soul from out that shadow that
lies floating on the floor
Shall be lifted—nevermore!

Ulalume—A Ballad

The skies they were ashen and sober;
   The leaves they were crispéd and
   sere—
   The leaves they were withering and
   sere:
It was night, in the lonesome October
   Of my most immemorial year:

It was hard by the dim lake of Auber,
    In the misty mid region of Weir—
It was down by the dank tarn of Auber,
    In the ghoul-haunted woodland of
      Weir.

Here once, through an alley Titanic,   10
    Of cypress, I roamed with my
      Soul—
    Of cypress, with Psyche, my soul.
These were days when my heart was vol-
      canic
    As the scoriac rivers that roll—
    As the lavas that restlessly roll
Their sulphurous currents down Yaanek
    In the ultimate climes of the Pole—
That groan as they roll down Mount
      Yaanek
    In the realms of the Boreal Pole.

Our talk had been serious and sober,   20
    But our thoughts they were palsied
      and sere—
    Our memories were treacherous and
      and sere—
For we knew not the month was October,
    And we marked not the night of the
      year
    (Ah, night of all nights in the
      year!)—
We noted not the dim lake of Auber
    (Though once we had journeyed
      down here)—
We remembered not the dank tarn of
      Auber,
    Nor the ghoul-haunted woodland of
      Weir.

And now, as the night was senescent   30
    And star-dials pointed to morn—
    As the star-dials hinted of morn—
At the end of our path a liquescent
    And nebulous lustre was born,
Out of which a miraculous crescent
    Arose with a duplicate horn—
Astarte's bediamonded crescent
    Distinct with its duplicate horn.

And I said: "She is warmer than Dian;
    She rolls through an ether of sighs—
    She revels in a region of sighs.   41

She has seen that the tears are not dry on
    These cheeks, where the worm never
      dies,
And has come past the stars of the Lion,
    To point us the path to the skies—
    To the Lethean peace of the skies—
Come up, in despite of the Lion,
    To shine on us with her bright
      eyes—
Come up through the lair of the Lion,
    With love in her luminous eyes."

But Psyche, uplifting her finger,   51
    Said: "Sadly this star I mistrust—
    Her pallor I strangely mistrust:
Ah, hasten!—ah, let us not linger!
    Ah, fly!—let us fly!—for we must."
In terror she spoke, letting sink her
    Wings until they trailed in the
      dust—
In agony sobbed, letting sink her
    Plumes till they trailed in the dust—
    Till they sorrowfully trailed in the
      dust.   60

I replied: "This is nothing but dreaming:
    Let us on by this tremulous light!
    Let us bathe in this crystalline light!
Its Sibyllic splendor is beaming
    With Hope and in Beauty to-
      night:—
    See!—it flickers up the sky through
      the night!
Ah, we safely may trust to its gleaming,
    And be sure it will lead us aright—
We surely may trust to a gleaming
    That cannot but guide us aright,   70
    Since it flickers up to Heaven
      through the night."

Thus I pacified Psyche and kissed her,
    And tempted her out of her gloom—
    And conquered her scruples and
      gloom;
And we passed to the end of the vista,
    But were stopped by the door of a
      tomb—
    By the door of a legended tomb;
And I said—"What is written, sweet sis-
    ter,

On the door of this legended tomb?"
She replied: "Ulalume—Ulalume!—
'Tis the vault of thy lost Ulalume!"

Then my heart it grew ashen and sober
  As the leaves that were crispéd and
    sere—   83
  As the leaves that were withering
    and sere;
And I cried: "It was surely October
  On *this* very night of last year
  That I journeyed—I journeyed
    down here!—
  That I brought a dread burden
    down here—
  On this night of all nights in the
    year,
  Ah, what demon has tempted me
    here?   90
Well I know, now, this dim lake of Au-
  ber—
  This misty mild region of Weir—
Well I know, now, this dank tarn of Au-
  ber,
  This ghoul-haunted woodland of
    Weir."

Said we, then,—the two, then: "Ah, can
  it
  Have been that the woodlandish
    ghouls—
  The pitiful, the merciful ghouls—
To bar up our way and to ban it
  From the secret that lies in these
    wolds—
  From the thing that lies hidden in
    these wolds—   100
Have drawn up the spectre of a planet
  From the limbo of lunary souls—
This sinfully scintillant planet
  From the Hell of the planetary
    souls?"

A Dream within a Dream

Take this kiss upon the brow!
And, in parting from you now,
Thus much let me avow—

You are not wrong, who deem
That my days have been a dream;
Yet if hope has flown away
In a night, or in a day,
In a vision, or in none,
Is it therefore the less *gone*?
All that we see or seem   10
Is but a dream within a dream.

I stand amid the roar
Of a surf-tormented shore,
And I hold within my hand
Grains of the golden sand—
How few! yet how they creep
Through my fingers to the deep,
While I weep—while I weep!
O God! can I not grasp
Them with a tighter clasp?   20
O God! can I not save
One from the pitiless wave?
Is *all* that we see or seem
But a dream within a dream?

For Annie

Thank Heaven! the crisis,
  The danger, is past,
And the lingering illness
  Is over at last—
And the fever called "Living"
  Is conquered at last.

Sadly, I know
  I am shorn of my strength,
And no muscle I move
  As I lie at full length—   10
But no matter!—I feel
  I am better at length.

And I rest so composedly,
  Now, in my bed,
That any beholder
  Might fancy me dead—
Might start at beholding me,
  Thinking me dead.

The moaning and groaning,
  The sighing and sobbing,   20
Are quieted now,

With that horrible throbbing
At heart:—ah, that horrible,
    Horrible throbbing!

The sickness—the nausea—
    The pitiless pain—
Have ceased, with the fever
    That maddened my brain—
With the fever called "Living"
    That burned in my brain.   30

And oh! of all tortures
    That torture the worst
Has abated—the terrible
    Torture of thirst
For the naphthaline river
    Of Passion accurst:—
I have drank of a water
    That quenches all thirst:—

Of a water that flows,
    With a lullaby sound,   40
From a spring but a very few
    Feet under ground—
From a cavern not very far
    Down under ground.

And ah! let it never
    Be foolishly said
That my room it is gloomy
    And narrow my bed;
For man never slept
    In a different bed—   50
And, to *sleep*, you must slumber
    In just such a bed.

My tantalized spirit
    Here blandly reposes,
Forgetting, or never
    Regretting, its roses—
Its old agitations
    Of myrtles and roses:

For now, while so quietly
    Lying, it fancies   60
A holier odor
    About it, of pansies—
A rosemary odor,
    Commingled with pansies—
With rue and the beautiful
    Puritan pansies.

And so it lies happily,
    Bathing in many
A dream of the truth
    And the beauty of Annie—   70
Drowned in a bath
    Of the tresses of Annie.

She tenderly kissed me,
    She fondly caressed,
And then I fell gently
    To sleep on her breast—
Deeply to sleep
    From the heaven of her breast.

When the light was extinguished,
    She covered me warm,   80
And she prayed to the angels
    To keep me from harm—
To the queen of the angels
    To shield me from harm.

And I lie so composedly,
    Now, in my bed,
(Knowing her love),
    That you fancy me dead—
And I rest so contentedly,
    Now, in my bed   90
(With her love at my breast),
    That you fancy me dead—
That you shudder to look at me,
    Thinking me dead:—

But my heart it is brighter
    Than all of the many
Stars of the sky,
    For it sparkles with Annie—
It glows with the light
    Of the love of my Annie—   100
With the thought of the light
    Of the eyes of my Annie.

Annabel Lee

It was many and many a year ago,
    In a kingdom by the sea,
That a maiden there lived whom you may
    know
    By the name of ANNABEL LEE;

And this maiden she lived with no other
    thought
    Than to love and be loved by me.

I was a child and *she* was a child,
    In this kingdom by the sea,
But we loved with a love that was more
    than love—
    I and my ANNABEL LEE—   10
With a love that the wingéd seraphs of
    Heaven
    Coveted her and me.

And this was the reason that, long ago,
    In this kingdom by the sea,
A wind blew out of a cloud, chilling
    My beautiful ANNABEL LEE;
So that her highborn kinsmen came
    And bore her away from me,
To shut her up in a sepulchre
    In this kingdom by the sea.   20

The angels, not half so happy in Heaven,
    Went envying her and me:—
Yes!—that was the reason (as all men
    know,
    In this kingdom by the sea)
That the wind came out of the cloud by
    night,
    Chilling and killing my ANNABEL
    LEE.

But our love it was stronger by far than
    the love
    Of those who were older than we—
    Of many far wiser than we—
And neither the angels in Heaven above,
    Nor the demons down under the
    sea,   31
Can ever dissever my soul from the soul
    Of the beautiful ANNABEL LEE:—

For the moon never beams, without
    bringing me dreams
    Of the beautiful ANNABEL LEE;
And the stars never rise, but I feel the
    bright eyes
    Of the beautiful ANNABEL LEE:
And so, all the night-tide, I lie down by
    the side

Of my darling—my darling—my life and
    my bride,   39
    In the sepulchre there by the sea—
    In her tomb by the sounding sea.

Oliver Wendell Holmes
✳ 1809–1894

My Aunt

My aunt! my dear unmarried aunt!
    Long years have o'er her flown;
Yet still she strains the aching clasp
    That binds her virgin zone;
I know it hurts her,—though she looks
    As cheerful as she can;
Her waist is ampler than her life,
    For life is but a span.

My aunt! my poor deluded aunt!
    Her hair is almost gray;   10
Why will she train that winter curl
    In such a spring-like way?
How can she lay her glasses down,
    And say she reads as well,
When through a double convex lens
    She just makes out to spell?

Her father—grandpa! forgive
    This erring lip its smiles—
Vowed she should make the finest girl
    Within a hundred miles;   20
He sent her to a stylish school;
    'Twas in her thirteenth June;
And with her, as the rules required,
    "Two towels and a spoon."

They braced my aunt against a board,
    To make her straight and tall;
They laced her up, they starved her
    down,
    To make her light and small;
They pinched her feet, they singed her
    hair,
    They screwed it up with pins;—   30

Oh, never mortal suffered more
    In penance for her sins.

So, when my precious aunt was done,
    My grandsire brought her back
(By daylight, lest some rabid youth
    Might follow on the track);
"Ah!" said my grandsire, as he shook
    Some powder in his pan,
"What could this lovely creature do
    Against a desperate man!"   40

Alas! nor chariot, nor barouche,
    Nor bandit cavalcade,
Tore from the trembling father's arms
    His all-accomplished maid.
For her how happy had it been!
    And Heaven had spared to me
To see one sad, ungathered rose
    On my ancestral tree.

The Chambered Nautilus

This is the ship of pearl, which, poets
        feign,
    Sails the unshadowed main,—
    The venturous bark that flings
On the sweet summer wind its purpled
        wings
In gulfs enchanted, where the Siren
        sings,
    And coral reefs lie bare,
Where the cold sea-maids rise to sun
        their streaming hair.

Its webs of living gauze no more unfurl;
    Wrecked is the ship of pearl!
    And every chambered cell,   10
Where its dim dreaming life was wont to
        dwell,
As the frail tenant shaped his growing
        shell,
    Before thee lies revealed,—
Its irised ceiling rent, its sunless crypt
        unsealed!

Year after year beheld the silent toil
    That spread his lustrous coil;
    Still, as the spiral grew,

He left the past year's dwelling for the
        new,
Stole with soft step its shining archway
        through,
    Built up its idle door,   20
Stretched in his last-found home, and
        knew the old no more.

Thanks for the heavenly message brought
        by thee,
    Child of the wandering sea,
    Cast from her lap, forlorn!
From thy dead lips a clearer note is born
Than ever Triton blew from wreathèd
        horn!
    While on mine ear it rings,
Through the deep caves of thought I hear
        a voice that sings:—

Build thee more stately mansions, O my
        soul,
    As the swift seasons roll!   30
    Leave thy low-vaulted past!
Let each new temple, nobler than the
        last,
Shut thee from heaven with a dome more
        vast,
    Till thou at length art free,
Leaving thine outgrown shell by life's
        unresting sea!

The Deacon's Masterpiece
OR, THE WONDERFUL "ONE-HOSS SHAY"
A LOGICAL STORY

Have you heard of the wonderful one-
        hoss shay,
That was built in such a logical way
It ran a hundred years to a day,
And then, of a sudden, it—ah, but stay,
I'll tell you what happened without de-
        lay,
Scaring the parson into fits,
Frightening people out of their wits,—
Have you ever heard of that, I say?

Seventeen hundred and fifty-five.
Georgius Secundus was then alive,—   10
Snuffy old drone from the German hive.

That was the year when Lisbon-town
Saw the earth open and gulp her down,
And Braddock's army was done so
    brown,
Left without a scalp to its crown.
It was on the terrible Earthquake-day
That the Deacon finished the one-hoss
    shay.

Now in building of chaises, I tell you
    what,
There is always *somewhere* a weakest
    spot,—
In hub, tire, felloe, in spring or thill,   20
In panel, or crossbar, or floor, or sill,
In screw, bolt, thoroughbrace,—lurking
    still,
Find it somewhere you must and will,—
Above or below, or within or without,—
And that's the reason, beyond a doubt,
That a chaise *breaks down*, but doesn't
    wear out.

But the Deacon swore (as deacons do,
With an "I dew vum," or an "I tell
    yeou")
He would build one shay to beat the
    taown
'N' the keounty 'n' all the kentry raoun';
It should be so built that it *could n'*
    break daown: 31
"Fur," said the Deacon, "'t 's mighty
    plain
Thut the weakes' place mus' stan' the
    strain;
'N' the way t' fix it, uz I maintain,
            Is only jest
T' make that place uz strong uz the rest."

So the Deacon inquired of the village folk
Where he could find the strongest oak,
That couldn't be split nor bent nor
    broke,—
That was for spokes and floor and sills;
He sent for lancewood to make the thills;
The crossbars were ash, from the straight-
    est trees,   42
The panels of white-wood, that cuts like
    cheese,
But lasts like iron for things like these;

The hubs of logs from the "Settler's el-
    lum,"—
Last of its timber,—they couldn't sell 'em,
Never an axe had seen their chips,
And the wedges flew from between their
    lips,
Their blunt ends frizzled like celery-tips;
Step and prop-iron, bolt and screw,   50
Spring, tire, axle, and linchpin too,
Steel of the finest, bright and blue;
Thoroughbrace bison-skin, thick and
    wide;
Boot, top, dasher, from tough old hide
Found in the pit when the tanner died.
That was the way he "put her through."
"There!" said the Deacon, "naow she'll
    dew!"

Do! I tell you, I rather guess
She was a wonder, and nothing less!
Colts grew horses, beards turned gray,
Deacon and deaconess dropped away,
Children and grandchildren—where were
    they?   62
But there stood the stout old one-hoss
    shay
As fresh as on Lisbon-earthquake-day!

EIGHTEEN HUNDRED;—it came and found
The Deacon's masterpiece strong and
    sound.
Eighteen hundred increased by ten;—
"Hahnsum kerridge" they called it then.
Eighteen hundred and twenty came;—
Running as usual; much the same.   70
Thirty and forty at last arrive,
And then come fifty, and FIFTY-FIVE.

Little of all we value here
Wakes on the morn of its hundredth year
Without both feeling and looking queer.
In fact, there's nothing that keeps its
    youth,
So far as I know, but a tree and truth.
(This is a moral that runs at large;
Take it.—You're welcome.—No extra
    charge.)

FIRST OF NOVEMBER,—the earthquake-
    day,—   80

There are traces of age in the one-hoss
shay,
A general flavor of mild decay,
But nothing local, as one may say.
There couldn't be,—for the Deacon's art
Had made it so like in every part
That there wasn't a chance for one to
start.
For the wheels were just as strong as the
thills,
And the floor was just as strong as the
sills,
And the panels just as strong as the floor,
And the whipple-tree neither less nor
more,   90
And the back crossbar as strong as the
fore,
And spring and axle and hub *encore*.
And yet, *as a whole*, it is past a doubt
In another hour it will be *worn out!*

First of November, 'Fifty-five!
This morning the parson takes a drive.
Now, small boys, get out of the way!
Here comes the wonderful one-hoss
shay,
Drawn by a rat-tailed, ewe-necked bay.
"Huddup!" said the parson.—Off went
they.   100
The parson was working his Sunday's
text,—
Had got to *fifthly*, and stopped perplexed
At what the—Moses—was coming next.
All at once the horse stood still,
Close by the meet'n'-house on the hill.
First a shiver, and then a thrill,
Then something decidedly like a spill,—
And the parson was sitting upon a rock,
At half past nine by the meet'n'-house
clock,—   109
Just the hour of the Earthquake shock!
What do you think the parson found,
When he got up and stared around?
The poor old chaise in a heap or mound,
As if it had been to the mill and ground!
You see, of course, if you're not a dunce,
How it went to pieces all at once,—
All at once, and nothing first,—
Just as bubbles do when they burst.

End of the wonderful one-hoss shay.
Logic is logic. That's all I say.   120

Jones Very
✳ 1813–1880

The Latter Rain

The latter rain,—it falls in anxious haste
Upon the sun-dried fields and branches
bare,
Loosening with searching drops the rigid
waste,
As if it would each root's lost strength
repair;
But not a blade grows green as in the
spring,
No swelling twig puts forth its thickening
leaves;
The robins only mid the harvests sing,
Pecking the grain that scatters from the
sheaves:
The rain falls still,—the fruit all ripened
drops,
It pierces chestnut burr and walnut shell,
The furrowed fields disclose the yellowed
crops,   11
Each bursting pod of talents used can
tell,
And all that once received the early rain
Declare to man it was not sent in vain.

The Earth

I would lie low—the ground on which
men tread—
Swept by thy Spirit like the wind of
heaven;
An earth, where gushing springs and corn
for bread
By me at every season should be given;
Yet not the water or the bread that now

Supplies their tables with its daily food,
But they should gather fruit from every
   bough,
Such as Thou givest me, and call it good;
And water from the stream of life should
   flow
By every dwelling that thy love has
   built,   10
Whose taste the ransomed of thy Son
   shall know,
Whose robes are washed from every stain
   of guilt;
And men would own it was thy hand that
   blest,
And from thy bosom find a surer rest.

The Garden

I saw the spot where our first parents
   dwelt;
And yet it wore to me no face of change,
For while amid its fields and groves, I
   felt
As if I had not sinned, nor thought it
   strange;
My eye seemed but a part of every sight,
My ear heard music in each sound that
   rose;
Each sense forever found a new delight,
Such as the spirit's vision only knows;
Each act some new and ever-varying joy
Did by my Father's love for me pre-
   pare;   10
To dress the spot my ever fresh employ,
And in the glorious whole with Him to
   share;
No more without the flaming gate to
   stray,
No more for sin's dark stain the debt of
   death to pay.

In Him We Live

Father! I bless thy name that I do live,
And in each motion am made rich with
   Thee,

That when a glance is all that I can give,
It is a kingdom's wealth, if I but see;
This stately body cannot move, save I
Will to its nobleness my little bring;
My voice its measured cadence will not
   try,
Save I with every note consent to sing;
I cannot raise my hands to hurt or bless,
But I with every action must con-
   spire   10
To show me there how little I possess,
And yet that little more than I desire;
May each new act my new allegiance
   prove,
Till in thy perfect love I ever live and
   move.

The Created

There is naught for thee by thy haste to
   gain;
'Tis not the swift with me that win the
   race;
Through long endurance of delaying
   pain,
Thine open eye shall see thy Father's
   face;
Nor here nor there, where now thy feet
   would turn,
Thou wilt find Him who ever waits for
   thee;
But let obedience quench desires that
   burn,
And where thou art thy Father too will
   be.
Behold! as day by day the spirit grows,
Thou see'st by inward light things hid
   before;   10
Till what God is, thyself, His image
   shows;
And thou wilt wear the robe that first
   thou wore,
When bright with radiance from his
   forming hand,
He saw the lord of all His creatures
   stand.

The harbingers of summer heats
Which from afar he bears.

Henry David Thoreau

✳ 1817–1862

The Summer Rain

The Inward Morning

Packed in my mind lie all the clothes
    Which outward nature wears,
And in its fashion's hourly change
    It all things else repairs.

In vain I look for change abroad,
    And can no difference find,
Till some new ray of peace uncalled
    Illumes my inmost mind.

What is it gilds the trees and clouds,
    And paints the heavens so gay,   10
But yonder fast-abiding light
    With its unchanging ray?

Lo, when the sun streams through the
    wood,
    Upon a winter's morn,
Where'er his silent beams intrude
    The murky night is gone.

How could the patient pine have known
    The morning breeze would come,
Or humble flowers anticipate
    The insect's noonday hum,—   20

Till the new light with morning cheer
    From far streamed through the aisles,
And nimbly told the forest trees
    For many stretching miles?

I've heard within my inmost soul
    Such cheerful morning news,
In the horizon of my mind
    Have seen such orient hues,

As in the twilight of the dawn,
    When the first birds awake,   30
Are heard within some silent wood,
    Where they the small twigs break,

Or in the eastern skies are seen,
    Before the sun appears,

The Summer Rain

My books I'd fain cast off, I cannot read;
    'Twixt every page my thoughts go stray
        at large
Down in the meadow, where is richer
    feed,
And will not mind to hit their proper
    targe.

Plutarch was good, and so was Homer
    too,
Our Shakespeare's life were rich to live
    again;
What Plutarch read, that was not good
    nor true,
Nor Shakespeare's books, unless his books
    were men.

Here while I lie beneath this walnut
    bough,
What care I for the Greeks or for Troy
    town,   10
If juster battles are enacted now
Between the ants upon this hummock's
    crown?

Bid Homer wait till I the issue learn,
If red or black the gods will favor most,
Or yonder Ajax will the phalanx turn,
Struggling to heave some rock against the
    host.

Tell Shakespeare to attend some leisure
    hour,
For now I've business with this drop of
    dew,
And see you not, the clouds prepare a
    shower,—
I'll meet him shortly when the sky is
    blue.   20

This bed of herd's-grass and wild oats
    was spread
Last year with nicer skill than monarchs
    use,

A clover tuft is pillow for my head,
And violets quite overtop my shoes.

And now the cordial clouds have shut
    all in,
And gently swells the wind to say all's
    well,
The scattered drops are falling fast and
    thin,
Some in the pool, some in the flower-bell.

I am well drenched upon my bed of oats;
But see that globe come rolling down its
    stem;   30
Now like a lonely planet there it floats,
And now it sinks into my garment's hem.

Drip, drip the trees for all the country
    round,
And richness rare distills from every
    bough,
The wind alone it is makes every sound,
Shaking down crystals on the leaves be-
    low.

For shame the sun will never show him-
    self,
Who could not with his beams e'er melt
    me so,
My dripping locks,—they would become
    an elf,
Who in a beaded coat does gayly go.   40

The Fall of the Leaf

Thank God who seasons thus the year,
And sometimes kindly slants his rays;
For in his winter he's most near
And plainest seen upon the shortest days.

Who gently tempers now his heats,
And then his harsher cold, lest we
Should surfeit on the summer's sweets,
Or pine upon the winter's crudity.

A sober mind will walk alone,
Apart from nature, if need be,   10
And only its own seasons own;
For nature leaving its humanity.

Sometimes a late autumnal thought
Has crossed my mind in green July,
And to its early freshness brought
Late ripened fruits, and an autumnal sky.

The evening of the year draws on,
The fields a later aspect wear;
Since Summer's garishness is gone,
Some grains of night tincture the noon-
    tide air.   20

Behold! the shadows of the trees
Now circle wider 'bout their stem,
Like sentries that by slow degrees
Perform their rounds, gently protecting
    them.

And as the year doth decline,
The sun allows a scantier light;
Behind each needle of the pine
There lurks a small auxiliar to the night.

I hear the cricket's slumbrous lay
Around, beneath me, and on high;   30
It rocks the night, it soothes the day,
And everywhere is Nature's lullaby.

But most he chirps beneath the sod,
When he has made his winter bed;
His creak grown fainter but more broad,
A film of autumn o'er the summer spread.

Small birds, in fleets migrating by,
Now beat across some meadow's bay,
And as they tack and veer on high,
With faint and hurried click beguile the
    way.   40

Far in the woods, these golden days,
Some leaf obeys its Maker's call;
And through their hollow aisles it plays
With delicate touch the prelude of the
    Fall.

Gently withdrawing from its stem,
It lightly lays itself along
Where the same hand hath pillowed
    them,
Resigned to sleep upon the old year's
    throng.

The loneliest birch is brown and sere,
The furthest pool is strewn with leaves,

Which float upon their watery bier,   51
Where is no eye that sees, no heart that
   grieves.

The jay screams through the chestnut
   wood;
The crisped and yellow leaves around
Are hue and texture of my mood—
And these rough burrs my heirlooms on
   the ground.

The threadbare trees, so poor and thin—
They are no wealthier than I;
But with as brave a core within
They rear their boughs to the October
   sky.   60

Poor knights they are which bravely wait
The charge of Winter's cavalry,
Keeping a simple Roman state,
Discumbered of their Persian luxury.

Walt Whitman

✳ 1819–1892

Song of Myself

1

I celebrate myself, and sing myself,
And what I assume you shall assume,
For every atom belonging to me as good belongs to you.

I loafe and invite my soul,
I lean and loafe at my ease observing a spear of summer grass.

My tongue, every atom of my blood, form'd from this soil, this air,
Born here of parents born here from parents the same, and their parents the same,
I, now thirty-seven years old in perfect health begin,
Hoping to cease not till death.

Creeds and schools in abeyance,   10
Retiring back a while sufficed at what they are, but never forgotten,
I harbor for good or bad, I permit to speak at every hazard,
Nature without check with original energy.

2

Houses and rooms are full of perfumes, the shelves are crowded with perfumes,
I breathe the fragance myself and know it and like it,
The distillation would intoxicate me also, but I shall not let it.

The atmosphere is not a perfume, it has no taste of the distillation, it is odorless,
It is for my mouth forever, I am in love with it,
I will go to the bank by the wood and become undisguised and naked,
I am mad for it to be in contact with me.   20

The smoke of my own breath,
Echoes, ripples, buzz'd whispers, love-root, silk-thread, crotch and vine,

My respiration and inspiration, the beating of my heart, the passing of blood and air
    through my lungs,
The sniff of green leaves and dry leaves, and of the shore and dark-color'd sea-rocks,
    and of hay in the barn,
The sound of the belch'd words of my voice loos'd to the eddies of the wind,
A few light kisses, a few embraces, a reaching around of arms,
The play of shine and shade on the trees as the supple boughs wag,
The delight alone or in the rush of the streets, or along the fields and hill-sides,
The feeling of health, the full-noon trill, the song of me rising from bed and meeting
    the sun.

Have you reckon'd a thousand acres much? have you reckon'd the earth much?   30
Have you practis'd so long to learn to read?
Have you felt so proud to get at the meaning of poems?

Stop this day and night with me and you shall possess the origin of all poems,
You shall possess the good of the earth and sun, (there are millions of suns left,)
You shall no longer take things at second or third hand, nor look through the eyes of
    the dead, nor feed on the spectres in books,
You shall not look through my eyes either, nor take things from me,
You shall listen to all sides and filter them from your self.

3

I have heard what the talkers were talking, the talk of the beginning and the end,
But I do not talk of the beginning or the end.

There was never any more inception than there is now,   40
Nor any more youth or age than there is now,
And will never be any more perfection than there is now,
Nor any more heaven or hell than there is now.

Urge and urge and urge,
Always the procreant urge of the world.

Out of the dimness opposite equals advance, always substance and increase, always
    sex,
Always a knit of identity, always distinction, always a breed of life.

To elaborate is no avail, learn'd and unlearn'd feel that it is so.

Sure as the most certain sure, plumb in the uprights, well entretied, braced in the
    beams,
Stout as a horse, affectionate, haughty, electrical,   50
I and this mystery here we stand.

Clear and sweet is my soul, and clear and sweet is all that is not my soul.

Lack one lacks both, and the unseen is proved by the seen,
Till that becomes unseen and receives proof in its turn.

Showing the best and dividing it from the worst age vexes age,
Knowing the perfect fitness and equanimity of things, while they discuss I am silent,
    and go bathe and admire myself.

Welcome is every organ and attribute of me, and of any man hearty and clean,
Not an inch nor a particle of an inch is vile, and none shall be less familiar than the
rest.

I am satisfied—I see, dance, laugh, sing;
As the hugging and loving bed-fellow sleeps at my side through the night, and
withdraws at the peep of the day with stealthy tread,   60
Leaving me baskets cover'd with white towels swelling the house with their plenty,
Shall I postpone my acceptation and realization and scream at my eyes,
That they turn from gazing after and down the road,
And forthwith cipher and show to me a cent,
Exactly the value of one and exactly the value of two, and which is ahead?

4

Trippers and askers surround me,
People I meet, the effect upon me of my early life or the ward and city I live in, or
the nation,
The latest dates, discoveries, inventions, societies, authors old and new,
My dinner, dress, associates, looks, compliments, dues,
The real or fancied indifference of some man or woman I love,   70
The sickness of one of my folks or of myself, or ill-doing or loss or lack of money,
or depressions or exaltations,
Battles, the horrors of fratricidal war, the fever of doutbful news, the fitful events;
These come to me days and nights and go from me again,
But they are not the Me myself.

Apart from the pulling and hauling stands what I am,
Stands amused, complacent, compassionating, idle, unitary,
Looks down, is erect, or bends an arm on an impalpable certain rest,
Looking with side-curved head curious what will come next,
Both in and out of the game and watching and wondering at it.

Backward I see in my own days where I sweated through fog with linguists and
contenders,   80
I have no mockings or arguments, I witness and wait.

5

I believe in you my soul, the other I am must not abase itself to you,
And you must not be abased to the other.

Loafe with me on the grass, loose the stop from your throat,
Not words, not music or rhyme I want, not custom or lecture, not even the best,
Only the lull I like, the hum of your valvèd voice.

I mind how once we lay such a transparent summer morning,
How you settled your head athwart my hips and gently turn'd over upon me,
And parted the shirt from my bosom-bone, and plunged your tongue to my bare-
stript heart,
And reach'd till you felt my beard, and reach'd till you held my feet.   90

Swiftly arose and spread around me the peace and knowledge that pass all the
argument of the earth,

And I know that the hand of God is the promise of my own,
And I know that the spirit of God is the brother of my own,
And that all the men ever born are also my brothers, and the women my sisters and
    lovers,
And that a kelson of the creation is love,
And limitless are leaves stiff or drooping in the fields,
And brown ants in the little wells beneath them,
And mossy scabs of the worm fence, heap'd stones, elder, mullein and poke-weed.

6

A child said *What is the grass?* fetching it to me with full hands,
How could I answer the child? I do not know what it is any more than he.   100

I guess it must be the flag of my disposition, out of hopeful green stuff woven.

Or I guess it is the handkerchief of the Lord,
A scented gift and remembrancer designedly dropt,
Bearing the owner's name someway in the corners, that we may see and remark, and
    say *Whose?*

Or I guess the grass is itself a child, the produced babe of the vegetation.

Or I guess it is a uniform hieroglyphic,
And it means, Sprouting alike in broad zones and narrow zones,
Growing among black folks as among white,
Kanuck, Tuckahoe, Congressman, Cuff, I give them the same, I receive them the
    same.

And now it seems to me the beautiful uncut hair of graves.   110

Tenderly will I use you curling grass,
It may be you transpire from the breasts of young men,
It may be if I had known them I would have loved them,
It may be you are from old people, or from offspring taken soon out of their
    mothers' laps,
And here you are the mothers' laps.

This grass is very dark to be from the white heads of old mothers,
Darker than the colorless beards of old men,
Dark to come from under the faint red roofs of mouths.

O I perceive after all so many uttering tongues,
And I perceive they do not come from the roofs of mouths for nothing.   120

I wish I could translate the hints about the dead young men and women,
And the hints about old men and mothers, and the offspring taken soon out of their
    laps.

What do you think has become of the young and old men?
And what do you think has become of the women and children?

They are alive and well somewhere,
The smallest sprout shows there is really no death,
And if ever there was it led forward life, and does not wait at the end to arrest it,
And ceas'd the moment life appear'd.

All goes onward and outward, nothing collapses,
And to die is different from what any one supposed, and luckier.   130

7

Has any one supposed it lucky to be born?
I hasten to inform him or her it is just as lucky to die, and I know it.

I pass death with the dying and birth with the new-wash'd babe, and am not
    contain'd between my hat and boots,
And peruse manifold objects, no two alike and every one good,
The earth good and the stars good, and their adjuncts all good.

I am not an earth nor an adjunct of an earth,
I am the mate and companion of people, all just as immortal and fathomless as
    myself,
(They do not know how immortal, but I know.)

Every kind for itself and its own, for me mine male and female,
For me those that have been boys and that love women,   140
For me the man that is proud and feels how it stings to be slighted,
For me the sweet-heart and the old maid, for me mothers and the mothers of
    mothers,
For me lips that have smiled, eyes that have shed tears,
For me children and the begetters of children.

Undrape! you are not guilty to me, nor stale nor discarded,
I see through the broadcloth and gingham whether or no,
And am around, tenacious, acquisitive, tireless, and cannot be shaken away.

8

The little one sleeps in its cradle,
I lift the gauze and look a long time, and silently brush away flies with my hand.

The youngster and the red-faced girl turn aside up the bushy hill,   150
I peeringly view them from the top.

The suicide sprawls on the bloody floor of the bedroom,
I witness the corpse with its dabbled hair, I note where the pistol has fallen.

The blab of the pave, tires of carts, sluff of boot-soles, talk of the promenaders,
The heavy omnibus, the driver with his interrogating thumb, the clank of the shod
    horses on the granite floor,
The snow-sleighs, clinking, shouted jokes, pelts of snowballs,
The hurrahs for popular favorites, the fury of rous'd mobs,
The flap of the curtain'd litter, a sick man inside borne to the hospital,
The meeting of enemies, the sudden oath, the blows and fall,
The excited crowd, the policeman with his star quickly working his passage to the
    centre of the crowd,   160
The impassive stones that receive and return so many echoes,
What groans of over-fed or half-starv'd who fall sunstruck or in fits,
What exclamations of women taken suddenly who hurry home and give birth to
    babes,

What living and buried speech is always vibrating here, what howls restrain'd by
decorum,
Arrests of criminals, slights, adulterous offers made, acceptances, rejections with
convex lips,
I mind them or the show of resonance of them—I come and I depart.

9

The big doors of the country barn stand open and ready,
The dried grass of the harvest-time loads the slow-drawn wagon,
The clear light plays on the brown gray and green intertinged,   170
The armfuls are pack'd to the sagging mow.

I am there, I help, I came stretch'd atop of the load,
I felt its soft jolts, one leg reclined on the other,
I jump from the cross-beams and seize the clover and timothy,
And roll head over heels and tangle my hair full of wisps.

10

Alone far in the wilds and mountains I hunt,
Wandering amazed at my own lightness and glee,
In the late afternoon choosing a safe spot to pass the night,
Kindling a fire and broiling the fresh-kill'd game,
Falling asleep on the gather'd leaves with my dog and gun by my side.

The Yankee clipper is under her sky-sails, she cuts the sparkle and scud,   180
My eyes settle the land, I bend at her prow or shout joyously from the deck.

The boatmen and clam-diggers arose early and stopt for me,
I tuck'd my trowser-ends in my boots and went and had a good time;
You should have been with us that day round the chowder-kettle.

I saw the marriage of the trapper in the open air in the far west, the bride was a red
girl,
Her father and his friends sat near cross-legged and dumbly smoking, they had
moccasins to their feet and large thick blankets hanging from their shoulders,
On a bank lounged the trapper, he was drest mostly in skins, his luxuriant beard and
curls protected his neck, he held his bride by the hand,
She had long eyelashes, her head was bare, her coarse straight locks descended upon
her voluptuous limbs and reach'd to her feet.

The runaway slave came to my house and stopt outside,   190
I heard his motions crackling the twigs of the woodpile,
Through the swung half-door of the kitchen I saw him limpsy and weak,
And went where he sat on a log and led him in and assured him,
And brought water and fill'd a tub for his sweated body and bruis'd feet,
And gave him a room that enter'd from my own, and gave him some coarse clean
clothes,
And remember perfectly well his revolving eyes and his awkwardness,
And remember putting plasters on the galls of his neck and ankles;
He staid with me a week before he was recuperated and pass'd north,
I had him sit next to me at table, my fire-lock lean'd in the corner.

11

Twenty-eight young men bathe by the shore,
Twenty-eight young men and all so friendly;   200
Twenty-eight years of womanly life and all so lonesome.

She owns the fine house by the rise of the bank,
She hides handsome and richly drest aft the blinds of the window.

Which of the young men does she like the best?
Ah the homeliest of them is beautiful to her.

Where are you off to, lady? for I see you,
You splash in the water there, yet stay stock still in your room.

Dancing and laughing along the beach came the twenty-ninth bather,
The rest did not see her, but she saw them and loved them.

The beards of the young men glisten'd with wet, it ran from their long hair,   210
Little streams pass'd all over their bodies.

An unseen hand also pass'd over their bodies,
It descended tremblingly from their temples and ribs.

The young men float on their backs, their white bellies bulge to the sun, they do not
    ask who seizes fast to them,
They do not know who puffs and declines with pendant and bending arch,
They do not think whom they souse with spray.

12

The butcher-boy puts off his killing-clothes, or sharpens his knife at the stall in the
    market,
I loiter enjoying his repartee and his shuffle and breakdown.

Blacksmiths with grimed and hairy chests environ the anvil,
Each has his main-sledge, they are all out, there is a great heat in the fire.   220

From the cinder-strew'd threshold I follow their movements,
The lithe sheer of their waists plays even with their massive arms,
Overhand the hammers swing, overhand so slow, overhand so sure,
They do not hasten, each man hits in his place.

13

The negro holds firmly the reins of his four horses, the block swags underneath on its
    tied-over chain,
The negro that drives the long dray of the stone-yard, steady and tall he stands pois'd
    on one leg on the string-piece,
His blue shirt exposes his ample neck and breast and loosens over his hip-band,
His glance is calm and commanding, he tosses the slouch of his hat away from his
    forehead,
The sun falls on his crispy hair and mustache, falls on the black of his polish'd and
    perfect limbs.

I behold the picturesque giant and love him, and I do not stop there,   230
I go with the team also.

In me the caresser of life wherever moving, backward as well as forward sluing,
To niches aside and junior bending, not a person or object missing,
Absorbing all to myself and for this song.

Oxen that rattle the yoke and chain or halt in the leafy shade, what is that you ex-
      press in your eyes?
It seems to me more than all the print I have read in my life.

My tread scares the wood-drake and wood-duck on my distant and day-long ramble,
They rise together, they slowly circle around.

I believe in those wing'd purposes,   240
And acknowledge red, yellow, white, playing within me,
And consider green and violet and the tufted crown intentional,
And do not call the tortoise unworthy because she is not something else,
And the jay in the woods never studied the gamut, yet trills pretty well to me,
And the look of the bay mare shames silliness out of me.

14

The wild gander leads his flock through the cool night,
Ya-honk he says, and sounds it down to me like an invitation,
The pert may suppose it meaningless, but I listening close,
Find its purpose and place up there toward the wintry sky.

The sharp-hoof'd moose of the north, the cat on the house-sill, the chickadee, the
      prairie-dog,
The litter of the grunting sow as they tug at her teats,   250
The brood of the turkey-hen and she with her half-spread wings,
I see in them and myself the same old law.

The press of my foot to the earth springs a hundred affections,
They scorn the best I can do to relate them.

I am enamour'd of growing out-doors,
Of men that live among cattle or taste of the ocean or woods,
Of the builders and steerers of ships and the wielders of axes and mauls, and the
      drivers of horses,
I can eat and sleep with them week in and week out.

What is commonest, cheapest, nearest, easiest, is Me,   260
Me going in for my chances, spending for vast returns,
Adorning myself to bestow myself on the first that will take me,
Not asking the sky to come down to my good will,
Scattering it freely forever.

15

The pure contralto sings in the organ loft,
The carpenter dresses his plank, the tongue of his foreplane whistles its wild ascend-
      ing lisp,

The married and unmarried children ride home to their Thanksgiving dinner,
The pilot seizes the king-pin, he heaves down with a strong arm,
The mate stands braced in the whale-boat, lace and harpoon are ready,
The duck-shooter walks by silent and cautious stretches,
The deacons are ordain'd with cross'd hands at the altar, 270
The spinning-girl retreats and advances to the hum of the big wheel,
The farmer stops by the bars as he walks on a First-day loafe and looks at the oats
and rye,
The lunatic is carried at last to the asylum a confirm'd case,
(He will never sleep any more as he did in the cot in his mother's bed-room;)
The jour printer with gray head and gaunt jaws works at his case,
He turns his quid of tobacco while his eyes blurr with the manuscript;
The malform'd limbs are tied to the surgeon's table,
What is removed drops horribly in a pail;
The quadroon girl is sold at the auction-stand, the drunkard nods by the bar-room
stove,
The machinist rolls up his sleeves, the policeman travels his beat, the gate-keeper
marks who pass, 280
The young fellow drives the express-wagon, (I love him though I do not know him;)
The half-breed straps on his light boots to compete in the race,
The western turkey-shooting draws old and young, some lean on their rifles, some sit
on logs,
Out from the crowd steps the marksman, takes his position, levels his piece;
The groups of newly-come immigrants cover the wharf or levee,
As the woolly-pates hoe in the sugar-field, the overseer views them from his saddle,
The bugle calls in the ball-room, the gentlemen run for their partners, the dancers
bow to each other,
The youth lies awake in the cedar-roof'd garret and harks to the musical rain,
The Wolverine sets traps on the creek that helps fill the Huron,
The squaw wrapt in her yellow-hemm'd cloth is offering moccasins and bead-bags for
sale, 290
The connoisseur peers along the exhibition-gallery with half-shut eyes bent sideways,
As the deck-hands make fast the steamboat the plank is thrown for the shore-going
passengers,
The young sister holds out the skein while the elder sister winds it off in a ball, and
stops now and then for the knots,
The one-year wife is recovering and happy having a week ago borne her first child,
The clean-hair'd Yankee girl works with her sewing-machine or in the factory or mill,
The paving-man leans on his two-handed rammer, the reporter's lead flies swiftly over
the note-book, the sign-painter is lettering with blue and gold,
The canal boy trots on the tow-path, the book-keeper counts at his desk, the shoe-
maker waxes his thread,
The conductor beats time for the band and all the performers follow him,
The child is baptized, the convert is making his first professions,
The regatta is spread on the bay, the race is begun, (how the white sails sparkle!)
The drover watching his drove sings out to them that would stray, 301
The pedler sweats with his pack on his back, (the purchaser higgling about the odd
cent;)
The bride unrumples her white dress, the minute-hand of the clock moves slowly,

The opium-eater reclines with rigid head and just-open'd lips,
The prostitute draggles her shawl, her bonnet bobs on her tipsy and pimpled neck,
The crowd laugh at her blackguard oaths, the men jeer and wink to each other,
(Miserable! I do not laugh at your oaths nor jeer you;)
The President holding a cabinet council is surrounded by the great Secretaries,
On the piazza walk three matrons stately and friendly with twined arms,
The crew of the fish-smack pack repeated layers of halibut in the hold,   310
The Missourian crosses the plains toting his wares and his cattle,
As the fare-collector goes through the train he gives notice by the jingling of loose
    change,
The floor-men are laying the floor, the tinners are tinning the roof, the masons are
    calling for mortar,
In single file each shouldering his hod pass onward the laborers;
Seasons pursuing each other the indescribable crowd is gather'd, it is the fourth of
    Seventh-month, (what salutes of cannon and small arms!)
Seasons pursuing each other the plougher ploughs, the mower mows, and the winter-
    grain falls in the ground;
Off on the lakes the pike-fisher watches and waits by the hole in the frozen surface,
The stumps stand thick round the clearing, the squatter strikes deep with his axe,
Flatboatmen make fast towards dusk near the cotton-wood or pecan-trees,
Coon-seekers go through the regions of the Red river or through those drain'd by the
    Tennessee, or through those of the Arkansas,   320
Torches shine in the dark that hangs on the Chattahooche or Altamahaw,
Patriarchs sit at supper with sons and grandsons and great-grandsons around them,
In walls of adobie, in canvas tents, rest hunters and trappers after their day's sport,
The city sleeps and the country sleeps,
The living sleep for their time, the dead sleep for their time,
The old husband sleeps by his wife and the young husband sleeps by his wife;
And these tend inward to me, and I tend outward to them,
And such as it is to be of these more or less I am,
And of these one and all I weave the song of myself.

16

                                                                                          330
I am of old and young, of the foolish as much as the wise,
Regardless of others, ever regardful of others,
Maternal as well as paternal, a child as well as a man,
Stuff'd with the stuff that is coarse and stuff'd with the stuff that is fine,
One of the Nation of many nations, the smallest the same and the largest the same,
A Southerner soon as a Northerner, a planter nonchalant and hospitable down by the
    Oconee I live,
A Yankee bound my own way ready for trade, my joints the limberest joints on earth
    and the sternest joints on earth,
A Kentuckian walking the vale of the Elkhorn in my deerskin leggings, a Louisianian
    or Georgian,
A boatman over lakes or bays or along coasts, a Hoosier, Badger, Buckeye;
At home on Kanadian snow-shoes or up in the bush, or with fishermen off Newfound-
    land,
At home in the fleet of ice-boats, sailing with the rest and tacking,   340
At home on the hills of Vermont or in the woods of Maine, or the Texan ranch,

Comrade of Californians, comrade of free North-Westerners, (loving their big pro-
     portions,)
Comrade of raftsmen and coalmen, comrade of all who shake hands and welcome to
     drink and meat,
A learner with the simplest, a teacher of the thoughtfullest,
A novice beginning yet experient of myriads of seasons,
Of every hue and caste am I, of every rank and religion,
A farmer, mechanic, artist, gentleman, sailor, quaker,
Prisoner, fancy-man, rowdy, lawyer, physician, priest.

I resist any thing better than my own diversity,
Breathe the air but leave plenty after me,   350
And am not stuck up, and am in my place.

(The moth and the fish-eggs are in their place,
The bright suns I see and the dark suns I cannot see are in their place,
The palpable is in its place and the impalpable is in its place.)

17

These are really the thoughts of all men in all ages and lands, they are not original
     with me,
If they are not yours as much as mine they are nothing, or next to nothing,
If they are not the riddle and the untying of the riddle they are nothing,
If they are not just as close as they are distant they are nothing.

This is the grass that grows wherever the land is and the water is,
This the common air that bathes the globe.   360

18

With music strong I come, with my cornets and my drums,
I play not marches for accepted victors only, I play marches for conquer'd and slain
     persons.

Have you heard that it was good to gain the day?
I also say it is good to fall, battles are lost in the same spirit in which they are won.

I beat and pound for the dead,
I blow through my embouchures my loudest and gayest for them.

Vivas to those who have fail'd!
And to those whose war-vessels sank in the sea!
And to those themselves who sank in the sea!
And to all generals that lost engagements, and all overcome heroes!   370
And the numberless unknown heroes equal to the greatest heroes known!

19

This is the meal equally set, this the meat for natural hunger,
It is for the wicked just the same as the righteous, I make appointments with all,
I will not have a single person slighted or left away,
The kept-woman, sponger, thief, are hereby invited,
The heavy-lipp'd slave is invited, the venerealee is invited;
There shall be no difference between them and the rest.

This is the press of a bashful hand, this the float and odor of hair,
This the touch of my lips to yours, this the murmur of yearning,
This the far-off depth and height reflecting my own face,   380
This the thoughtful merge of myself, and the outlet again.

Do you guess I have some intricate purpose?
Well I have, for the Fourth-month showers have, and the mica on the side of a rock
    has.

Do you take it I would astonish?
Does the daylight astonish? does the early redstart twittering through the woods?
Do I astonish more than they?

This hour I tell things in confidence,
I might not tell everybody, but I will tell you.

    20

Who goes there? hankering, gross, mystical, nude;
How is it I extract strength from the beef I eat?   390

What is a man anyhow? what am I? what are you?

All I mark as my own you shall offset it with your own,
Else it were time lost listening to me.

I do not snivel that snivel the world over,
That months are vacuums and the ground but wallow and filth.

Whimpering and truckling fold with powders for invalids, conformity goes to the
    fourth-remov'd,
I wear my hat as I please indoors or out.

Why should I pray? why should I venerate and be ceremonious?

Having pried through the strata, analyzed to a hair, counsel'd with doctors and calcu-
    lated close,
I find no sweeter fat than sticks to my own bones.   400

In all people I see myself, none more and not one a barley-corn less,
And the good or bad I say of myself I say of them.

I know I am solid and sound,
To me the converging objects of the universe perpetually flow,
All are written to me, and I must get what the writing means.

I know I am deathless,
I know this orbit of mine cannot be swept by a carpenter's compass,
I know I shall not pass like a child's carlacue cut with a burnt stick at night.

I know I am august,
I do not trouble my spirit to vindicate itself or be understood,   410
I see that the elementary laws never apologize,
(I reckon I behave no prouder than the level I plant my house by, after all.)

I exist as I am, that is enough,
If no other in the world be aware I sit content,
And if each and all be aware I sit content.

One world is aware and by far the largest to me, and that is myself,
And whether I come to my own to-day or in ten thousand or ten million years,
I can cheerfully take it now, or with equal cheerfulness I can wait.

My foothold is tenon'd and mortis'd in granite,
I laugh at what you call dissolution,
And I know the amplitude of time.

420

21

I am the poet of the Body and I am the poet of the Soul,
The pleasures of heaven are with me and the pains of hell are with me,
The first I graft and increase upon myself, the latter I translate into a new tongue.

I am the poet of the woman the same as the man,
And I say it is as great to be a woman as to be a man,
And I say there is nothing greater than the mother of men.

I chant the chant of dilation or pride,
We have had ducking and deprecating about enough,
I show that size is only development.

430

Have you outstript the rest? are you the President?
It is a trifle, they will more than arrive there every one, and still pass on.

I am he that walks with the tender and growing night,
I call to the earth and sea half-held by the night.

Press close bare-bosom'd night—press close magnetic nourishing night!
Night of south winds—night of the large few stars!
Still nodding night—mad naked summer night.

Smile O voluptuous cool-breath'd earth!
Earth of the slumbering and liquid trees!
Earth of departed sunset—earth of the mountains misty-topt!
Earth of the vitreous pour of the full moon just tinged with blue!
Earth of shine and dark mottling the tide of the river!
Earth of the limpid gray of clouds brighter and clearer for my sake!
Far-swooping elbow'd earth—rich apple-blossom'd earth!
Smile, for your lover comes.

440

Prodigal, you have given me love—therefore I to you give love!
O unspeakable passionate love.

22

You sea! I resign myself to you also—I guess what you mean,
I behold from the beach your crooked inviting fingers,
I believe you refuse to go back without feeling of me,
We must have a turn together, I undress, hurry me out of sight of the land,
Cushion me soft, rock me in billowy drowse,
Dash me with amorous wet, I can repay you.

450

Sea of stretch'd ground-swells,
Sea breathing broad and convulsive breaths,
Sea of the brine of life and of unshovell'd yet always-ready graves,

Howler and scooper of storms, capricious and dainty sea,
I am integral with you, I too am of one phase and of all phases.

Partaker of influx and efflux I, extoller of hate and conciliation,
Extoller of amies and those that sleep in each others' arms.   460

I am he attesting sympathy,
(Shall I make my list of things in the house and skip the house that supports them?)

I am not the poet of goodness only, I do not decline to be the poet of wickedness also.

What blurt is this about virtue and about vice?
Evil propels me and reform of evil propels me, I stand indifferent,
My gait is no fault-finder's or rejecter's gait,
I moisten the roots of all that has grown.

Did you fear some scrofula out of the unflagging pregnancy?
Did you guess the celestial laws are yet to be work'd over and rectified?

I find one side a balance and the antipodal side a balance,   470
Soft doctrine as steady help as stable doctrine,
Thoughts and deeds of the present our rouse and early start.

This minute that comes to me over the past decillions,
There is no better than it and now.

What behaved well in the past or behaves well to-day is not such a wonder,
The wonder is always and always how there can be a mean man or an infidel.

23

Endless unfolding of words of ages!
And mine a word of the modern, the word En-Masse.

A word of the faith that never balks,
Here or henceforward it is all the same to me, I accept Time absolutely.   480

It alone is without flaw, it alone rounds and completes all,
That mystic baffling wonder alone completes all.

I accept Reality and dare not question it,
Materialism first and last imbuing.

Hurrah for positive science! long live exact demonstration!
Fetch stonecrop mixt with cedar and branches of lilac,
This is the lexicographer, this the chemist, this made a grammar of the old cartouches,
These mariners put the ship through dangerous unknown seas,
This is the geologist, this works with the scalpel, and this is a mathematician.

Gentlemen, to you the first honors always!   490
Your facts are useful, and yet they are not my dwelling,
I but enter by them to an area of my dwelling.

Less the reminders of properties told my words,
And more the reminders they of life untold, and of freedom and extrication,

And make short account of neuters and geldings, and favor men and women fully
    equipt,
And beat the gong of revolt, and stop with fugitives and them that plot and conspire.

24

Walt Whitman, a kosmos, of Manhattan the son,
Turbulent, fleshy, sensual, eating, drinking and breeding,
No sentimentalist, no stander above men and women or apart from them,
No more modest than immodest.   500

Unscrew the locks from the doors!
Unscrew the doors themselves from their jambs!

Whoever degrades another degrades me,
And whatever is done or said returns at last to me.

Through me the afflatus surging and surging, through me the current and index.

I speak the pass-word primeval, I give the sign of democracy,
By God! I will accept nothing which all cannot have their counterpart of on the same
    terms.

Through me many long dumb voices,
Voices of the interminable generations of prisoners and slaves,
Voices of the diseas'd and despairing and of thieves and dwarfs,   510
Voices of cycles of preparation and accretion,
And of the threads that connect the stars, and of wombs and of the father-stuff,
And of the rights of them the others are down upon,
Of the deform'd, trivial, flat, foolish, despised,
Fog in the air, beetles rolling balls of dung.

Through me forbidden voices,
Voices of sexes and lusts, voices veil'd and I remove the veil,
Voices indecent by me clarified and transfigur'd.

I do not press my fingers across my mouth,
I keep as delicate around the bowels as around the head and heart,   520
Copulation is no more rank to me than death is.

I believe in the flesh and the appetites,
Seeing, hearing, feeling, are miracles, and each part and tag of me is a miracle.

Divine am I inside and out, and I make holy whatever I touch or am touch'd from,
The scent of these arm-pits aroma finer than prayer,
This head more than churches, bibles, and all the creeds.

If I worship one thing more than another it shall be the spread of my own body, or
    any part of it,
Translucent mould of me it shall be you!
Shaded ledges and rests it shall be you!
Firm masculine colter it shall be you!   530
Whatever goes to the tilth of me it shall be you!
You my rich blood! your milky stream pale strippings of my life!

Breast that presses against other breasts it shall be you!
My brain it shall be your occult convolutions!
Root of wash'd sweet-flag! timorous pond-snipe! nest of guarded duplicate eggs! it
    shall be you!
Mix'd tussled hay of head, beard, brawn, it shall be you!
Trickling sap of maple, fibre of manly wheat, it shall be you!
Sun so generous it shall be you!
Vapors lighting and shading my face it shall be you!
You sweaty brooks and dews it shall be you!   540
Winds whose soft-tickling genitals rub against me it shall be you!
Broad muscular fields, branches of live oak, loving lounger in my winding paths, it
    shall be you!
Hands I have taken, face I have kiss'd, mortal I have ever touch'd, it shall be you.

I dote on myself, there is that lot of me and all so luscious,
Each moment and whatever happens thrills me with joy,
I cannot tell how my ankles bend, nor whence the cause of my faintest wish,
Nor the cause of the friendship I emit, nor the cause of the friendship I take again.

That I walk up my stoop, I pause to consider if it really be,
A morning-glory at my window satisfies me more than the metaphysics of books.

To behold the day-break!   550
The little light fades the immense and diaphanous shadows,
The air tastes good to my palate.

Hefts of the moving world at innocent gambols silently rising, freshly exuding,
Scooting obliquely high and low.

Something I cannot see puts upward libidinous prongs,
Seas of bright juice suffuse heaven.

The earth by the sky staid with, the daily close of their junction,
The heav'd challenge from the east that moment over my head,
The mocking taunt, See then whether you shall be master!

25

Dazzling and tremendous how quick the sun-rise would kill me,   560
If I could not now and always send sun-rise out of me.

We also ascend dazzling and tremendous as the sun,
We found our own O my soul in the calm and cool of the daybreak.

My voice goes after what my eyes cannot reach,
With the twirl of my tongue I encompass worlds and volumes of worlds.

Speech is the twin of my vision, it is unequal to measure itself,
It provokes me forever, it says sarcastically,
Walt you contain enough, why don't you let it out then?

Come now I will not be tantalized, you conceive too much of articulation,
Do you not know O speech how the buds beneath you are folded?   570
Waiting in gloom, protected by frost,

The dirt receding before my prophetical screams,
I underlying causes to balance them at last,
My knowledge my live parts, it keeping tally with the meaning of all things,
Happiness, (which whoever hears me let him or her set out in search of this day.)

My final merit I refuse you, I refuse putting from me what I really am,
Encompass worlds, but never try to encompass me,
I crowd your sleekest and best by simply looking toward you.

Writing and talk do not prove me,
I carry the plenum of proof and every thing else in my face,   580
With the hush of my lips I wholly confound the skeptic.

26

Now I will do nothing but listen,
To accrue what I hear into this song, to let sounds contribute toward it.

I hear bravuras of birds, bustle of growing wheat, gossip of flames, clack of sticks
    cooking my meals,
I hear the sound I love, the sound of the human voice,
I hear all sounds running together, combined, fused or following,
Sounds of the city and sounds out of the city, sounds of the day and night,
Talkative young ones to those that like them, the loud laugh of work-people at their
    meals,
The angry base of disjointed friendship, the faint tones of the sick,
The judge with hands tight to the desk, his pallid lips pronouncing a death-sentence,
The heave'e'yo of stevedores unlading ships by the wharves, the refrain of the anchor-
    lifters,   591
The ring of alarm-bells, the cry of fire, the whirr of swift-streaking engines and hose-
    carts with premonitory tinkles and color'd lights,
The steam-whistle, the solid roll of the train of approaching cars,
The slow march play'd at the head of the association marching two and two,
(They go to guard some corpse, the flag-tops are draped with black muslin.)

I hear the violoncello, ('tis the young man's heart's complaint,)
I hear the key'd cornet, it glides quickly in through my ears,
It shakes mad-sweet pangs through my belly and breast.

I hear the chorus, it is a grand opera,
Ah this indeed is music—this suits me.   600

A tenor large and fresh as the creation fills me,
The orbic flex of his mouth is pouring and filling me full.

I hear the train'd soprano (what work with hers is this?)
The orchestra whirls me wider than Uranus flies,
It wrenches such ardors from me I did not know I possess'd them,
It sails me, I dab with bare feet, they are lick'd by the indolent waves,
I am cut by bitter and angry hail, I lose my breath,
Steep'd amid honey'd morphine, m/ windpipe throttled in fakes of death,
At length let up again to feel the puzzle of puzzles,
And that we call Being.   610

27

To be in any form, what is that?
(Round and round we go, all of us, and ever come back thither,)
If nothing lay more develop'd the quahaug in its callous shell were enough.

Mine is no callous shell,
I have instant conductors all over me whether I pass or stop,
They seize every object and lead it harmlessly through me.

I merely stir, press, feel with my fingers, and am happy,
To touch my person to some one else's is about as much as I can stand.

28

Is this then a touch? quivering me to a new identity,
Flames and ether making a rush for my veins,   620
Treacherous tip of me reaching and crowding to help them,
My flesh and blood playing out lightning to strike what is hardly different from my-
    self,
On all sides prurient provokers stiffening my limbs,
Straining the udder of my heart for its withheld drip,
Behaving licentious toward me, taking no denial,
Depriving me of my best as for a purpose,
Unbuttoning my clothes, holding me by the bare waist,
Deluding my confusion with the calm of the sunlight and pasture-fields,
Immodesty sliding the fellow-senses away,
They bribed to swap off with touch and go and graze at the edges of me,   630
No consideration, no regard for my draining strength or my anger,
Fetching the rest of the herd around to enjoy them a while,
Then all uniting to stand on a headland and worry me.

The sentries desert every other part of me,
They have left me helpless to a red marauder,
They all come to the headland to witness and assist against me.

I am given up by traitors,
I talk wildly, I have lost my wits, I and nobody else am the greatest traitor,
I went myself first to the headland, my own hands carried me there.

You villain touch! what are you doing? my breath is tight in its throat,   640
Unclench your floodgates, you are too much for me.

29

Blind loving wrestling touch, sheath'd hooded sharp-tooth'd touch!
Did it make you ache so, leaving me?

Parting track'd by arriving, perpetual payment of perpetual loan,
Rich showering rain, and recompense richer afterward.

Sprouts take and accumulate, stand by the curb prolific and vital,
Landscapes projected masculine, full-sized and golden.

30

All truths wait in all things,
They neither hasten their own delivery nor resist it,
They do not need the obstetric forceps of the surgeon, 650
The insignificant is as big to me as any,
(What is less or more than a touch?)

Logic and sermons never convince,
The damp of the night drives deeper into my soul.

(Only what proves itself to every man and woman is so,
Only what nobody denies is so.)

A minute and a drop of me settle my brain,
I believe the soggy clods shall become lovers and lamps,
And a compend of compends is the meat of a man or woman,
And a summit and flower there is the feeling they have for each other, 660
And they are to branch boundlessly out of that lesson until it becomes omnific,
And until one and all shall delight us, and we them.

31

I believe a leaf of grass is no less than the journey-work of the stars,
And the pismire is equally perfect, and a grain of sand, and the egg of the wren,
And the tree-toad is a chef-d'oeuvre for the highest,
And the running blackberry would adorn the parlors of heaven,
And the narrowest hinge in my hand puts to scorn all machinery,
And the cow crunching with depress'd head surpasses any statue,
And a mouse is miracle enough to stagger sextillions of infidels.

I find I incorporate gneiss, coal, long-threaded moss, fruits, grains, esculent roots,
And am stucco'd with quadrupeds and birds all over, 671
And have distanced what is behind me for good reasons,
But call any thing back again when I desire it.

In vain the speeding or shyness,
In vain the plutonic rocks send their old heat against my approach,
In vain the mastodon retreats beneath its own powder'd bones,
In vain objects stand leagues off and assume manifold shapes,
In vain the ocean settling in hollows and the great monsters lying low,
In vain the buzzard houses herself with the sky,
In vain the snake slides through the creepers and logs, 680
In vain the elk takes to the inner passes of the woods,
In vain the razor-bill'd aux sails far north to Labrador,
I follow quickly, I ascend to the nest in the fissure of the cliff.

32

I think I could turn and live with animals, they're so placid and self-contain'd,
I stand and look at them long and long.

They do not sweat and whine about their condition,
They do not lie awake in the dark and weep for their sins,

They do not make me sick discussing their duty to God,
Not one is dissatisfied, not one is demented with the mania of owning things,
Not one kneels to another, nor to his kind that lived thousands of years ago,   690
Not one is respectable or unhappy over the whole earth.

So they show their relations to me and I accept them,
They bring me tokens of myself, they evince them plainly in their possession.

I wonder where they get those tokens,
Did I pass that way huge times ago and negligently drop them?

Myself moving forward then and now and forever,
Gathering and showing more always and with velocity,
Infinite and omnigenous, and the like of these among them,
Not too exclusive toward the reachers of my remembrancers,
Picking out here one that I love, and now go with him on brotherly terms.

A gigantic beauty of a stallion, fresh and responsive to my caresses,   700
Head high in the forehead, wide between the ears,
Limbs glossy and supple, tail dusting the ground,
Eyes full of sparkling wickedness, ears finely cut, flexibly moving.

His nostrils dilate as my heels embrace him,
His well-built limbs tremble with pleasure as we race around and return.
I but use you a minute, then I resign you, stallion,
Why do I need your paces when I myself out-gallop them?
Even as I stand or sit passing faster than you.

33

Space and Time! now I see it is true, what I guessed at,
What I guess'd when I loaf'd on the grass,   710
What I guess'd while I lay alone in my bed,
And again as I walk'd the beach under the paling stars of the morning.

My ties and ballasts leave me, my elbows rest in sea-gaps,
I skirt sierras, my palms cover continents,
I am afoot with my vision.

By the city's quadrangular houses—in log huts, camping with lumbermen,
Along the ruts of the turnpike, along the dry gulch and rivulet bed,
Weeding my onion-patch or hoeing rows of carrots and parsnips, crossing savannas,
    trailing in forests,
Prospecting, gold-digging, girdling the trees of a new purchase,
Scorch'd ankle-deep by the hot sand, hauling my boat down the shallow river,   720
Where the panther walks to and fro on a limb overhead, where the buck turns furi-
    ously at the hunter,
Where the rattlesnake suns his flabby length on a rock, where the otter is feeding on
    fish,
Where the alligator in his tough pimples sleeps by the bayou,
Where the black bear is searching for roots or honey, where the beaver pats the mud
    with his paddle-shaped tail;

Over the growing sugar, over the yellow-flower'd cotton plant, over the rice in its low
    moist field,
Over the sharp-peak'd farm house, with its scallop'd scum and slender shoots from
    the gutters,
Over the western persimmon, over the long-leav'd corn, over the delicate blue-flower
    flax,
Over the white and brown buckwheat, a hummer and buzzer there with the rest,
Over the dusky green of the rye as it ripples and shades in the breeze;
Scaling mountains, pulling myself cautiously up, holding on by low scragged limbs,
Walking the path worn in the grass and beat through the leaves of the brush,   731
Where the quail is whistling betwixt the woods and the wheat-lot,
Where the bat flies in the Seventh-month eve, where the great gold-bug drops
    through the dark,
Where the brook puts out of the roots of the old tree and flows to the meadow,
Where cattle stand and shake away flies with the tremulous shuddering of their hides,
Where the cheese-cloth hangs in the kitchen, where andirons straddle the hearth-slab,
    where cobwebs fall in festoons from the rafters;
Where trip-hammers crash, where the press is whirling its cylinders,
Wherever the human heart beats with terrible throes under its ribs,
Where the pear-shaped balloon is floating aloft, (floating in it myself and looking
    composedly down,)
Where the life-car is drawn on the slip-noose, where the heat hatches pale-green eggs
    in the dented sand,   740
Where the she-whale swims with her calf and never forsakes it,
Where the steam-ship trails hind-ways its long pennant of smoke,
Where the fin of the shark cuts like a black chip out of the water,
Where the half-burn'd brig is riding on unknown currents,
Where shells grow to her slimy deck, where the dead are corrupting below;
Where the dense-starr'd flag is borne at the head of the regiments,
Approaching Manhattan up by the long-stretching island,
Under Niagara, the cataract falling like a veil over my countenance,
Upon a door-step, upon the horse-block of hard wood outside,
Upon the race-course, or enjoying pictures of jigs or a good game of base-ball,   750
At he-festivals, with blackguard gibes, ironical license, bull-dances, drinking, laugh-
    ter,
At the cider-mill tasting the sweets of the brown mash, sucking the juice through a
    straw,
At apple-peelings wanting kisses for all the red fruit I find,
At musters, beach-parties, friendly bees, huskings, house-raisings;
Where the mocking-bird sounds his delicious gurgles, cackles, screams, weeps,
Where the hay-rick stands in the barn-yard, where the dry-stalks are scatter'd, where
    the brood-cow waits in the hovel,
Where the bull advances to do his masculine work, where the stud to the mare,
    where the cock is treading the hen,
Where the heifers browse, where geese nip their food with short jerks,
Where sun-down shadows lengthen over the limitless and lonesome prairie,
Where herds of buffalo make a crawling spread of the square miles far and near,
Where the humming-bird shimmers, where the neck of the long-lived swan is curving
    and winding,   761

Where the laughing-gull scoots by the shore, where she laughs her near-human
    laugh,
Where bee-hives range on a gray bench in the garden half hid by the high weeds,
Where band-neck'd partridges roost in a ring on the ground with their heads out,
Where burial coaches enter the arch'd gates of a cemetery,
Where winter wolves bark amid wastes of snow and icicled trees,
Where the yellow-crown'd heron comes to the edge of the marsh at night and feeds
    upon small crabs,
Where the splash of swimmers and divers cools the warm noon,
Where the katy-did works her chromatic reed on the walnut-tree over the well,
Through patches of citrons and cucumbers with silver-wired leaves,   770
Through the salt-lick or orange glade, or under conical firs,
Through the gymnasium, through the curtain'd saloon, through the office or public
    hall;
Pleas'd with the native and pleas'd with the foreign, pleas'd with the new and old,
Pleas'd with the homely woman as well as the handsome,
Pleas'd with the quakeress as she puts off her bonnet and talks melodiously,
Pleas'd with the tune of the choir of the whitewash'd church,
Pleas'd with the earnest words of the sweating Methodist preacher, impress'd seri-
    ously at the camp-meeting;
Looking in at the shop-windows of Broadway the whole forenoon, flatting the flesh
    of my nose on the thick plate glass,
Wandering the same afternoon with my face turn'd up to the clouds, or down a lane
    or along the beach,
My right and left arms round the sides of two friends, and I in the middle;   780
Coming home with the silent and dark-cheek'd bush-boy, (behind me he rides at the
    drape of the day,)
Far from the settlements studying the print of animals' feet, or the moccasin print,
By the cot in the hospital reaching lemonade to a feverish patient,
Night the coffin'd corpse when all is still, examining with a candle;
Voyaging to every port to dicker and adventure,
Hurrying with the modern crowd as eager and fickle as any,
Hot toward one I hate, ready in my madness to knife him,
Solitary at midnight in my back yard, my thoughts gone from me a long while,
Walking the old hills of Judaea with the beautiful gentle God by my side,
Speeding through space, speeding through heaven and the stars,   790
Speeding amid the seven satellites and the broad ring, and the diameter of eighty
    thousand miles,
Speeding with tail'd meteors, throwing fire-balls like the rest,
Carrying the crescent child that carries its own full mother in its belly,
Storming, enjoying, planning, loving, cautioning,
Backing and filling, appearing and disappearing,
I tread day and night such roads.

I visit the orchards of spheres and look at the product,
And look at quintillions ripen'd and look at quintillions green.

I fly those flights of a fluid and swallowing soul,
My course runs below the soundings of plummets.   800

I help myself to material and immaterial,
No guard can shut me off, no law prevent me.

I anchor my ship for a little while only,
My messengers continually cruise away or bring their returns to me.

I go hunting polar furs and the seal, leaping chasms with a pike-pointed staff, clinging to topples of brittle and blue.

I ascend to the foretruck,
I take my place late at night in the crow's-nest,
We sail the arctic sea, it is plenty light enough,
Through the clear atmosphere I stretch around on the wonderful beauty,
The enormous masses of ice pass me and I pass them, the scenery is plain in all directions, 810
The white-topt mountains show in the distance, I fling out my fancies toward them,
We are approaching some great battle-field in which we are soon to be engaged,
We pass the colossal outposts of the encampment, we pass with still feet and caution,
Or we are entering by the suburbs some vast and ruin'd city,
The blocks and fallen architecture more than all the living cities of the globe.

I am a free companion, I bivouac by invading watchfires,
I turn the bridegroom out of bed and stay with the bride myself,
I tighten her all night to my thighs and lips.

My voice is the wife's voice, the screech by the rail of the stairs,
They fetch my man's body up dripping and drown'd.

I understand the large hearts of heroes, 820
The courage of present times and all times,
How the skipper saw the crowded and rudderless wreck of the steam-ship, and Death chasing it up and down the storm,
How he knuckled tight and gave not back an inch, and was faithful of days and faithful of nights,
And chalk'd in large letters on a board, *Be of good cheer, we will not desert you;*
How he follow'd with them and tack'd with them three days and would not give it up,
How he saved the drifting company at last,
How the lank loose-gown'd women look'd when boated from the side of their prepared graves,
How the silent old-faced infants and the lifted sick, and the sharp-lipp'd unshaved men;
All this I swallow, it tastes good, I like it well, it becomes mine,
I am the man, I suffer'd, I was there. 830

The disdain and calmness of martyrs,
The mother of old, condemn'd for a witch, burnt with dry wood, her children gazing on,
The hounded slave that flags in the race, leans by the fence, blowing, cover'd with sweat,

The twinges that sting like needles his legs and neck, the murderous buckshot and
    the bullets,
All these I feel or am.

I am the hounded slave, I wince at the bite of the dogs,
Hell and despair are upon me, crack and again crack the marksmen,
I clutch the rails of the fence, my gore dribs, thinn'd with the ooze of my skin,
I fall on the weeds and stones,
The riders spur their unwilling horses, haul close,   840
Taunt my dizzy ears and beat me violently over the head with whip-stocks.

Agonies are one of my changes of garments,
I do not ask the wounded person how he feels, I myself become the wounded person,
My hurts turn livid upon me as I lean on a cane and observe.

I am the mash'd fireman with breast-bone broken,
Tumbling walls buried me in their debris,
Heat and smoke I inspired, I heard the yelling shouts of my comrades,
I heard the distant click of their picks and shovels,
They have clear'd the beams away, they tenderly lift me forth.

I lie in the night air in my red shirt, the pervading hush is for my sake,   850
Painless after all I lie exhausted but not so unhappy,
White and beautiful are the faces around me, the heads are bared of their fire-caps,
The kneeling crowd fades with the light of the torches.

Distant and dead resuscitate,
They show as the dial or move as the hands of me, I am the clock myself.

I am an old artillerist, I tell of my fort's bombardment,
I am there again.

Again the long roll of the drummers,
Again the attacking cannon, mortars,
Again to my listening ears the cannon responsive.   860

I take part, I see and hear the whole,
The cries, curses, roar, the plaudits for well-aim'd shots,
The ambulanza slowly passing trailing its red drip,
Workmen searching after damages, making indispensable repairs,
The fall of grenades through the rent roof, the fan-shaped explosion,
The whizz of limbs, heads, stone, wood, iron, high in the air.

Again gurgles the mouth of my dying general, he furiously waves with his hand,
He gasps through the clot *Mind not me—mind—the entrenchments.*

34

Now I tell what I knew in Texas in my early youth,
(I tell not the fall of Alamo,   870
Not one escaped to tell the fall of Alamo,
The hundred and fifty are dumb yet at Alamo,)
'Tis the tale of the murder in cold blood of four hundred and twelve young men.

Retreating they had form'd in a hollow square with their baggage for breastworks,
Nine hundred lives out of the surrounding enemy's, nine times their number, was the
    price they took in advance,
Their colonel was wounded and their ammunition gone,
They treated for an honorable capitulation, receiv'd writing and seal, gave up their
    arms and march'd back prisoners of war.

They were the glory of the race of rangers,
Matchless with horse, rifle, song, supper, courtship,
Large, turbulent, generous, handsome, proud, and affectionate,   880
Bearded, sunburnt, drest in the free costume of hunters,
Not a single one over thirty years of age.

The second First-day morning they were brought out in squads and massacred, it
    was beautiful early summer,
The work commenced about five o'clock and was over by eight.

None obey'd the command to kneel,
Some made a mad and helpless rush, some stood stark and straight,
A few fell at once, shot in the temple or heart, the living and dead lay together,
The maim'd and mangled dug in the dirt, the new-comers saw them there,
Some half-kill'd attempted to crawl away,
These were dispatch'd with bayonets or batter'd with the blunts of muskets.   890
A youth not seventeen years old seiz'd his assassin till two more came to release him,
The three were all torn and cover'd with the boy's blood.

At eleven o'clock began the burning of the bodies;
That is the tale of the murder of the four hundred and twelve young men.

   35

Would you hear of an old-time sea-fight?
Would you learn who won by the light of the moon and stars?
List to the yarn, as my grandmother's father the sailor told it to me.

Our foe was no skulk in his ship I tell you, (said he,)
His was the surly English pluck, and there is no tougher or truer, and never was, and
    never will be;
Along the lower'd eve he came horribly raking us.   900

We closed with him, the yards entangled, the cannon touch'd,
My captain lash'd fast with his own hands.

We had receiv'd some eighteen pound shots under the water,
On our lower-gun-deck two large pieces had burst at the first fire, killing all around
    and blowing up overhead.

Fighting at sun-down, fighting at dark,
Ten o'clock at night, the full moon well up, our leaks on the gain, and five feet of
    water reported,
The master-at-arms loosing the prisoners confined in the after-hold to give them a
    chance for themselves.

The transit to and from the magazine is now stopt by the sentinels,
They see so many strange faces they do not know whom to trust.

Our frigate takes fire,   910
The other asks if we demand quarter?
If our colors are struck and the fighting done?

Now I laugh content, for I hear the voice of my little captain,
We have not struck, he composedly cries, *we have just begun our part of the fighting.*

Only three guns are in use,
One is directed by the captain himself against the enemy's main-mast,
Two well serv'd with grape and canister silence his musketry and clear his decks.

The tops alone second the fire of this little battery, especially the main-top,
They hold out bravely during the whole of the action.

Not a moment's cease,   920
The leaks gain fast on the pumps, the fire eats toward the powder-magazine.
One of the pumps has been shot away, it is generally thought we are sinking.

Serene stands the little captain,
He is not hurried, his voice is neither high nor low,
His eyes give more light to us than our battle-lanterns.

Toward twelve there in the beams of the moon they surrender to us.

36

Stretch'd and still lies the midnight,
Two great hulls motionless on the breast of the darkness,
Our vessel riddled and slowly sinking, preparations to pass to the one we have conquer'd,
The captain on the quarter-deck coldly giving his orders through a countenance white as a sheet,   930
Near by the corpse of the child that serv'd in the cabin,
The dead face of an old salt with long white hair and carefully curl'd whiskers,
The flames spite of all that can be done flickering aloft and below,
The husky voices of the two or three officers yet fit for duty,
Formless stacks of bodies and bodies by themselves, dabs of flesh upon the masts and spars,
Cut of cordage, dangle of rigging, slight shock of the soothe of waves,
Black and impassive guns, litter of powder-parcels, strong scent,
A few large stars overhead, silent and mournful shining,
Delicate sniffs of sea-breeze, smells of sedgy grass and fields by the shore, death-messages given in charge to survivors,
The hiss of the surgeon's knife, the gnawing teeth of his saw,   940
Wheeze, cluck, swash of falling blood, short wild scream, and long, dull, tapering groan,
These so, these irretrievable.

37

You laggards there on guard! look to your arms!
In at the conquer'd doors they crowd! I am possess'd!

Embody all presences outlaw'd or suffering,
See myself in prison shaped like another man,
And feel the dull unintermitted pain,
For me the keepers of convicts shoulder their carbines and keep watch,
It is I let out in the morning and barr'd at night.

Not a mutineer walks handcuff'd to jail but I am handcuff'd to him and walk by his
    side,   950
(I am less the jolly one there, and more the silent one with sweat on my twitching
    lips.)

Not a youngster is taken for larceny but I go up too, and am tried and sentenced.

Not a cholera patient lies at the last gasp but I also lie at the last gasp,
My face is ash-color'd, my sinews gnarl, away from me people retreat.

Askers embody themselves in me and I am embodied in them,
I project my hat, sit shame-faced, and beg.

38

Enough! enough! enough!
Somehow I have been stunn'd. Stand back!
Give me a little time beyond my cuff'd head, slumbers, dreams, gaping,
I discover myself on the verge of a usual mistake.   960

That I could forget the mockers and insults!
That I could forget the trickling tears and the blows of the bludgeons and hammers!
That I could look with a separate look on my own crucifixion and bloody crowning!

I remember now,
I resume the overstaid fraction,
The grave of rock multiplies what has been confided to it, or to any graves,
Corpses rise, gashes heal, fastenings roll from me.

I troop forth replenish'd with supreme power, one of an average unending procession,
Inland and sea-coast we go, and pass all boundary lines,
Our swift ordinances on their way over the whole earth,   970
The blossoms we wear in our hats the growth of thousands of years.

Eleves, I salute you! come forward!
Continue your annotations, continue your questionings.

39

The friendly and flowing savage, who is he?
Is he waiting for civilization, or past it and mastering it?

Is he some Southwesterner rais'd out-doors? is he Kanadian?
Is he from the Mississippi country? Iowa, Oregon, California?
The mountains? prairie-life, bush-life? or sailor from the sea?

Wherever he goes men and women accept and desire him,
They desire he should like them, touch them, speak to them, stay with them.   980

Behavior lawless as snow-flakes, words simple as grass, uncomb'd head, laughter,
    and naiveté,

Slow-stepping feet, common features, common modes and emanations,
They descend in new forms from the tips of his fingers,
They are wafted with the odor of his body or breath, they fly out of the glance of
    his eyes.

40

Flaunt of the sunshine I need not your bask—lie over!
You light surfaces only, I force surfaces and depths also.

Earth! you seem to look for something at my hands,
Say, old top-knot, what do you want?

Man or woman, I might tell how I like you, but cannot,
And might tell what it is in me and what it is in you, but cannot,   990
And might tell that pining I have, that pulse of my nights and days.

Behold, I do not give lectures or a little charity,
When I give I give myself.

You there, impotent, loose in the knees,
Open your scarf'd chops till I blow grit within you,
Spread your palms and lift the flaps of your pockets,
I am not to be denied, I compel, I have stores plenty and to spare,
And any thing I have I bestow.

I do not ask who you are, that is not important to me,
You can do nothing and be nothing but what I will infold you.   1000

To cotton-field drudge or cleaner of privies I lean,
On his right cheek I put the family kiss,
And in my soul I swear I never will deny him.

On women fit for conception I start bigger and nimbler babes,
(This day I am jetting the stuff of far more arrogant republics.)

To any one dying, thither I speed and twist the knob of the door,
Turn the bed-clothes toward the foot of the bed,
Let the physician and the priest go home.

I seize the descending man and raise him with resistless will,
O despairer, here is my neck,   1010
By God, you shall not go down! hang your whole weight upon me.

I dilate you with tremendous breath, I buoy you up,
Every room of the house do I fill with an arm'd force,
Lovers of me, bafflers of graves.

Sleep—I and they keep guard all night,
Not doubt, not disease shall dare to lay finger upon you,
I have embraced you, and henceforth possess you to myself,
And when you rise in the morning you will find what I tell you is so.

41

I am he bringing help for the sick as they pant on their backs,
And for strong upright men I bring yet more needed help.   1020

I heard what was said of the universe,
Heard it and heard it of several thousand years;
It is middling well as far as it goes—but is that all?

Magnifying and applying come I,
Outbidding at the start the old cautious hucksters,
Taking myself the exact dimensions of Jehovah,
Lithographing Kronos, Zeus his son, and Hercules his grandson,
Buying drafts of Osiris, Isis, Belus, Brahma, Buddha,
In my portfolio placing Manito loose, Allah on a leaf, the crucifix engraved,
With Odin and the hideous-faced Mexitli and every idol and image,   1030
Taking them all for what they are worth and not a cent more,
Admitting they were alive and did the work of their days,
(They bore mites as for unfledg'd birds who have now to rise and fly and sing for
   themselves,)
Accepting the rough deific sketches to fill out better in myself, bestowing them freely
   on each man and woman I see,
Discovering as much or more in a framer framing a house,
Putting higher claims for him there with his roll'd-up sleeves driving the mallet and
   chisel,
Not objecting to special revelations, considering a curl of smoke or a hair on the back
   of my hand just as curious as any revelation,
Lads ahold of fire-engines and hook-and-ladder ropes no less to me than the gods of
   the antique wars,
Minding their voices peal through the crash of destruction,
Their brawny limbs passing safe over charr'd laths, their white foreheads whole and
   unhurt out of the flames;   1040
By the mechanic's wife with her babe at her nipple interceding for every person
   born,
Three scythes at harvest whizzing in a row from three lusty angels with shirts bagg'd
   out at their waists,
The snag-tooth'd hostler with red hair redeeming sins past and to come,
Selling all he possesses, traveling on foot to fee lawyers for his brother and sit by
   him while he is tried for forgery;
What was strewn in the amplest strewing the square rod about me, and not filling
   the square rod then,
The bull and the bug never worshipp'd half enough,
Dung and dirt more admirable than was dream'd,
The supernatural of no account, myself waiting my time to be one of the supremes,
The day getting ready for me when I shall do as much good as the best, and be as
   prodigious;
But my life-lumps! becoming already a creator,   1050
Putting myself here and now to the ambush'd womb of the shadows.

42

A call in the midst of the crowd,
My own voice, orotund sweeping and final.

Come my children,
Come my boys and girls, my women, household and intimates,

Now the performer launches his nerve, he has pass'd his prelude on the reeds within.

Easily written loose-finger'd chords—I feel the thrum of your climax and close.

My head slues round on my neck,
Music rolls, but not from the organ,
Folks are around me, but they are no household of mine.   1060

Ever the hard unsunk ground,
Ever the eaters and drinkers, ever the upward and downward sun, ever the air and
    the ceaseless tides,
Ever myself and my neighbors, refreshing, wicked, real,
Ever the old inexplicable query, ever that thorn'd thumb, that breath of itches and
    thirsts,
Ever the vexer's *hoot! hoot!* till we find where the sly one hides and bring him forth,
Ever love, ever the sobbing liquid of life,
Ever the bandage under the chin, ever the trestles of death.

Here and there with dimes on the eyes walking,
To feed the greed of the belly the brains liberally spooning,
Tickets buying, taking, selling, but in to the feast never once going,   1070
Many sweating, ploughing, thrashing, and then the chaff for payment receiving,
A few idly owning, and they the wheat continually claiming.

This is the city and I am one of the citizens,
Whatever interests the rest interests me, politics, wars, markets, newspapers, schools,
The mayor and councils, banks, tariffs, steamships, factories, stocks, stores, real estate
    and personal estate.

The little plentiful manikins skipping around in collars and tail'd coats,
I am aware who they are, (they are positively not worms or fleas,)
I acknowledge the duplicates of myself, the weakest and shallowest is deathless with
    me,
What I do and say the same waits for them,
Every thought that flounders in me the same flounders in them.   1080

I know perfectly well my own egotism,
Know my omnivorous lines and must not write any less,
And would fetch you whoever you are flush with myself.

Not words of routine this song of mine,
But abruptly to question, to leap beyond yet nearer bring;
This printed and bound book—but the printer and the printing-office boy?
The well-taken photographs—but your wife or friend close and solid in your arms?
The black ship mail'd with iron, her mighty guns in her turrets—but the pluck of
    the captain and engineers?
In the houses the dishes and fare and furniture—but the host and hostess, and the
    look out of their eyes?
The sky up there—yet here or next door, or across the way?   1090
The saints and sages in history—but you yourself?
Sermons, creeds, theology—but the fathomless human brain,
And what is reason? and what is love? and what is life?

43

I do not despise you priests, all time, the world over,
My faith is the greatest of faiths and the least of faiths,
Enclosing worship ancient and modern and all between ancient and modern,
Believing I shall come again upon the earth after five thousand years,
Waiting responses from oracles, honoring the gods, saluting the sun,
Making a fetich of the first rock or stump, powowing with sticks in the circle of obis,
Helping the lama or brahmin as he trims the lamps of the idols,   1100
Dancing yet through the streets in a phallic procession, rapt and austere in the woods
    a gymnosophist,
Drinking mead from the skull-cup, to Shastas and Vedas admirant, minding the
    Koran,
Walking the teokallis, spotted with gore from the stone and knife, beating the
    serpent-skin drum,
Accepting the Gospels, accepting him that was crucified, knowing assuredly that he
    is divine,
To the mass kneeling or the puritan's prayer rising, or sitting patiently in a pew,
Ranting and frothing in my insane crisis, or waiting dead-like till my spirit arouses
    me,
Looking forth on pavement and land, or outside of pavement and land,
Belonging to the winders of the circuit of circuits.

One of that centripetal and centrifugal gang I turn and talk like a man leaving
    charges before a journey.

Down-hearted doubters dull and excluded,   1110
Frivolous, sullen, moping, angry, affected, dishearten'd, atheistical,
I know every one of you, I know the sea of torment, doubt, despair and unbelief.

How the flukes splash!
How they contort rapid as lightning, with spasms and spouts of blood!

Be at peace bloody flukes of doubters and sullen mopers,
I take my place among you as much as among any,
The past is the push of you, me, all, precisely the same,
And what is yet untried and afterward is for you, me, all, precisely the same.

I do not know what is untried and afterward,
But I know it will in its turn prove sufficient, and cannot fail.   1120

Each who passes is consider'd, each who stops is consider'd, not a single one can it
    fail.

It cannot fail the young man who died and was buried,
Nor the young woman who died and was put by his side,
Nor the little child that peep'd in at the door, and then drew back and was never
    seen again,
Nor the old man who has lived without purpose, and feels it with bitterness worse
    than gall,
Nor him in the poor house tubercled by rum and the bad disorder,

Nor the numberless slaughter'd and wreck'd, nor the brutish koboo call'd the ordure
    of humanity,
Nor the sacs merely floating with open mouths for food to slip in,
Nor any thing in the earth, or down in the oldest graves of the earth,
Nor any thing in the myriads of spheres, nor the myriads of myriads that inhabit
    them,   1130
Nor the present, nor the least wisp that is known.

44

It is time to explain myself—let us stand up.

What is known I strip away,
I launch all men and women forward with me into the Unknown.

The clock indicates the moment—but what does eternity indicate?

We have thus far exhausted trillions of winters and summers,
There are trillions ahead, and trillions ahead of them.

Births have brought us richness and variety,
And other births will bring us richness and variety.

I do not call one greater and one smaller,   1140
That which fills its period and place is equal to any.

Were mankind murderous or jealous upon you, my brother, my sister?
I am sorry for you, they are not murderous or jealous upon me,
All has been gentle with me, I keep no account with lamentation,
(What have I to do with lamentation?)

I am an acme of things accomplish'd, and I am encloser of things to be.

My feet strike an apex of the apices of the stairs,
On every step bunches of ages, and larger bunches between the steps,
All below duly travel'd, and still I mount and mount.

Rise after rise bow the phantoms behind me,   1150
Afar down I see the huge first Nothing, I know I was even there,
I waited unseen and always, and slept through the lethargic mist,
And took my time, and took no hurt from the fetid carbon.

Long I was hugg'd close—long and long.

Immense have been the preparations for me,
Faithful and friendly the arms that have help'd me.

Cycles ferried my cradle, rowing and rowing like cheerful boatmen,
For room to me stars kept aside in their own rings,
They sent influences to look after what was to hold me.

Before I was born out of my mother generations guided me,   1160
My embryo has never been torpid, nothing could overlay it.

For it the nebula cohered to an orb,
The long slow strata piled to rest it on,

Vast vegetables gave it sustenance,
Monstrous sauroids transported it in their mouths and deposited it with care.

All forces have been steadily employ'd to complete and delight me,
Now on this spot I stand with my robust soul.

45

O span of youth! ever-push'd elasticity!
O manhood, balanced, florid and full.

My lovers suffocate me,   1170
Crowding my lips, thick in the pores of my skin,
Jostling me through streets and public halls, coming naked to me at night,
Crying by day *Ahoy!* from the rocks of the river, swinging and chirping over my
    head,
Calling my name from flower-beds, vines, tangled underbrush,
Lighting on every moment of my life,
Bussing my body with soft balsamic busses,
Noiselessly passing handfuls out of their hearts and giving them to be mine.

Old age superbly rising! O welcome, ineffable grace of dying days!

Every condition promulges not only itself, it promulges what grows after and out of
    itself,
And the dark hush promulges as much as any.   1180

I open my scuttle at night and see the far-sprinkled systems,
And all I see multiplied as high as I can cipher edge but the rim of the farther sys-
    tems.

Wider and wider they spread, expanding, always expanding,
Outward and outward and forever outward.

My sun has his sun and round him obediently wheels,
He joins with his partners a group of superior circuit,
And greater sets follow, making specks of the greatest inside them.

There is no stoppage and never can be stoppage,
If I, you, and the worlds, and all beneath or upon their surfaces, were this moment
    reduced back to a pallid float, it would not avail in the long run,
We should surely bring up again where we now stand,   1190
And surely go as much farther, and then farther and farther.

A few quadrillions of eras, a few octillions of cubic leagues, do not hazard the span
    or make it impatient,
They are but parts, any thing is but a part.

See ever so far, there is limitless space outside of that,
Count ever so much, there is limitless time around that.

My rendezvous is appointed, it is certain,
The Lord will be there and wait till I come on perfect terms,
The great Camerado, the lover true for whom I pine will be there.

46

I know I have the best of time and space, and was never measured and never will
be measured.

I tramp a perpetual journey, (come listen all!)   1200
My signs are a rain-proof coat, good shoes, and a staff cut from the woods,
No friend of mine takes his ease in my chair,
I have no chair, no church, no philosophy,
I lead no man to a dinner-table, library, exchange,
But each man and each woman of you I lead upon a knoll,
My left hand hooking you round the waist,
My right hand pointing to landscapes of continents and the public road.

Not I, not any one else can travel that road for you,
You must travel it for yourself.

It is not far, it is within reach,   1210
Perhaps you have been on it since you were born and did not know,
Perhaps it is everywhere on water and on land.

Shoulder your duds dear son, and I will mine, and let us hasten forth,
Wonderful cities and free nations we shall fetch as we go.

If you tire, give me both burdens, and rest the chuff of your hand on my hip,
And in due time you shall repay the same service to me,
For after we start we never lie by again.

This day before dawn I ascended a hill and look'd at the crowded heaven,
And I said to my spirit *When we become the enfolders of those orbs, and the pleas-
ure and knowledge of every thing in them, shall we be fill'd and satisfied then?*
And my spirit said *No, we but level that lift to pass and continue beyond.*   1220

You are also asking me questions and I hear you,
I answer that I cannot answer, you must find out for yourself.

Sit a while dear son,
Here are biscuits to eat and here is milk to drink,
But as soon as you sleep and renew yourself in sweet clothes, I kiss you with a
good-by kiss and open the gate for your egress hence.

Long enough have you dream'd contemptible dreams,
Now I wash the gum from your eyes,
You must habit yourself to the dazzle of the light and of every moment of your life.

Long have you timidly waded holding a plank by the shore,
Now I will you to be a bold swimmer,   1230
To jump off in the midst of the sea, rise again, nod to me, shout, and laughingly
dash with your hair.

47

I am the teacher of athletes,
He that by me spreads a wider breast than my own proves the width of my own,
He most honors my style who learns under it to destroy the teacher.

The boy I love, the same becomes a man not through derived power, but in his own
    right,
Wicked rather than virtuous out of conformity or fear,
Fond of his sweetheart, relishing well his steak,
Unrequited love or a slight cutting him worse than sharp steel cuts,
First-rate to ride, to fight, to hit the bull's eye, to sail a skiff, to sing a song or play
    on the banjo,
Preferring scars and the beard and faces pitted with small-pox over all latherers,
And those well-tann'd to those that keep out of the sun.   1241

I teach straying from me, yet who can stray from me?
I follow you whoever you are from the present hour,
My words itch at your ears till you understand them.

I do not say these things for a dollar or to fill up the time while I wait for a boat,
(It is you talking just as much as myself, I act as the tongue of you,
Tied in your mouth, in mine it begins to be loosen'd.)

I swear I will never again mention love or death inside a house,
And I swear I will never translate myself at all, only to him or her who privately stays
    with me in the open air.

If you would understand me go to the heights or water-shore,   1250
The nearest gnat is an explanation, and a drop or motion of waves a key,
The maul, the oar, the hand-saw, second my words.

No shutter'd room or school can commune with me,
But roughs and little children better than they.

The young mechanic is closest to me, he knows me well,
The woodman that takes his axe and jug with him shall take me with him all day,
The farm-boy ploughing in the field feels good at the sound of my voice,
In vessels that sail my words sail, I go with fishermen and seamen and love them.

The soldier camp'd or upon the march is mine,
On the night ere the pending battle many seek me, and I do not fail them,   1260
On that solemn night (it may be their last) those that know me seek me.

My face rubs to the hunter's face when he lies down alone in his blanket,
The driver thinking of me does not mind the jolt of his wagon,
The young mother and old mother comprehend me,
The girl and the wife rest the needle a moment and forget where they are,
They and all would resume what I have told them.

48

I have said that the soul is not more than the body,
And I have said that the body is not more than the soul,
And nothing, not God, is greater to one than one's self is,
And whoever walks a furlong without sympathy walks to his own funeral drest in his
    shroud,   1270
And I or you pocketless of a dime may purchase the pick of the earth,
And to glance with an eye or show a bean in its pod confounds the learning of all
    times,

And there is no trade or employment but the young man following it may become a
  hero,
And there is no object so soft but it makes a hub for the wheel'd universe,
And I say to any man or woman, Let your soul stand cool and composed before a
  million universes.

And I say to mankind, Be not curious about God,
For I who am curious about each am not curious about God,
(No array of terms can say how much I am at peace about God and about death.)

I hear and behold God in every object, yet understand God not in the least,
Nor do I understand who there can be more wonderful than myself.   1280

Why should I wish to see God better than this day?
I see something of God each hour of the twenty-four, and each moment then,
In the faces of men and women I see God, and in my own face in the glass,
I find letters from God dropt in the street, and every one is sign'd by God's name,
And I leave them where they are, for I know that wheresoe'er I go,
Others will punctually come for ever and ever.

49

And as to you Death, and you bitter hug of mortality, it is idle to try to alarm me.

To his work without flinching the accoucheur comes,
I see the elder-hand pressing receiving supporting,
I recline by the sills of the exquisite flexible doors,   1290
And mark the outlet, and mark the relief and escape.

And as to you Corpse I think you are good manure, but that does not offend me,
I smell the white roses sweet-scented and growing,
I reach to the leafy lips, I reach to the polish'd breasts of melons.

And as to you Life I reckon you are the leavings of many deaths,
(No doubt I have died myself ten thousand times before.)

I hear you whispering there O stars of heaven,
O suns—O grass of graves—O perpetual transfers and promotions,
If you do not say any thing how can I say any thing?

Of the turbid pool that lies in the autumn forest,   1300
Of the moon that descends the steeps of the soughing twilight,
Toss, sparkles of day and dusk—toss on the black stems that decay in the muck,
Toss to the moaning gibberish of the dry limbs.

I ascend from the moon, I ascend from the night,
I perceive that the ghastly glimmer is noonday and sunbeams reflected,
And debouch to the steady and central from the offspring great or small.

50

There is that in me—I do not know what it is—but I know it is in me.

Wrench'd and sweaty—calm and cool then my body becomes,
I sleep—I sleep long.

I do not know it—it is without name—it is a word unsaid, 1310
It is not in any dictionary, utterance, symbol.

Something it swings on more than the earth I swing on,
To it the creation is the friend whose embracing awakes me.

Perhaps I might tell more. Outlines! I plead for my brothers and sisters.

Do you see O my brothers and sisters?
It is not chaos or death—it is form, union, plan—it is eternal life—it is Happiness.

51

The past and present wilt—I have fill'd them, emptied them,
And proceed to fill my next fold of the future.

Listener up there! what have you to confide to me?
Look in my face while I snuff the sidle of evening, 1320
(Talk honestly, no one else hears you, and I stay only a minute longer.)

Do I contradict myself?
Very well then I contradict myself,
(I am large, I contain multitudes.)

I concentrate toward them that are nigh, I wait on the door-slab.

Who has done his day's work? who will soonest be through with his supper?
Who wishes to walk with me?

Will you speak before I am gone? will you prove already too late?

52

The spotted hawk swoops by and accuses me, he complains of my gab and my
loitering.

I too am not a bit tamed, I too am untranslatable, 1330
I sound my barbaric yawp over the roofs of the world.

The last scud of days holds back for me,
It flings my likeness after the rest and true as any on the shadow'd wilds,
It coaxes me to the vapor and the dusk.

I depart as air, I shake my white locks at the runaway sun,
I effuse my flesh in eddies, and drift it in lacy jags.

I bequeath myself to the dirt to grow from the grass I love,
If you want me again look for me under your boot-soles.

You will hardly know who I am or what I mean,
But I shall be good health to you nevertheless, 1340
And filter and fibre your blood.

Failing to fetch me at first keep encouraged,
Missing me one place search another,
I stop somewhere waiting for you.

The Sleepers

I wander all night in my vision,
Stepping with light feet, swiftly and noiselessly stepping and stopping,
Bending with open eyes over the shut eyes of sleepers,
Wandering and confused, lost to myself, ill-assorted, contradictory,
Pausing, gazing, bending, stopping.

How solemn they look there, stretch'd and still,
How quiet they breathe, the little children in their cradles.

The wretched features of ennuyés, the white features of corpses, the livid faces of
    drunkards, the sick-gray faces of onanists,
The gash'd bodies on battle-fields, the insane in their strong-door'd rooms, the sacred
    idiots, the newborn emerging from gates, and the dying emerging from gates,
The night pervades them and infolds them.　　　　　　　　　　　10

The married couple sleep calmly in their bed, he with his palm on the hip of the wife,
    and she with her palm on the hip of the husband,
The sisters sleep lovingly side by side in their bed,
The men sleep lovingly side by side in theirs,
And the mother sleeps with her little child carefully wrapt.

The blind sleep, and the deaf and dumb sleep,
The prisoner sleeps well in the prison, the runaway son sleeps,
The murderer that is to be hung next day, how does he sleep?
And the murder'd person, how does he sleep?

The female that loves unrequited sleeps,
And the male that loves unrequited sleeps,　　　　　　　　　　　20
The head of the money-maker that plotted all day sleeps,
And the enraged and treacherous dispositions, all, all sleep.

I stand in the dark with drooping eyes by the worst-suffering and the most restless,
I pass my hands soothingly to and fro a few inches from them,
The restless sink in their beds, they fitfully sleep.

Now I pierce the darkness, new beings appear,
The earth recedes from me into the night,
I saw that it was beautiful, and I see that what is not the earth is beautiful.

I go from bedside to bedside, I sleep close with the other sleepers, each in turn,
I dream in my dream all the dreams of the other dreamers,　　　　　30
And I become the other dreamers.

I am a dance—play up there! the fit is whirling me fast!

I am the ever-laughing—it is new moon and twilight,
I see the hiding of douceurs, I see nimble ghosts whichever way I look,
Cache and cache again deep in the ground and sea, and where it is neither ground
    nor sea.

Well do they do their jobs, those journeymen divine,
Only from me can they hide nothing, and would not if they could,
I reckon I am their boss and they make me a pet besides,
And surround me and lead me and run ahead when I walk,
To lift their cunning covers to signify me with stretch'd arms, and resume the way;
Onward we move, a gay gang of blackguards! with mirth-shouting music and wild-
    flapping pennants of joy!   41

I am the actor, the actress, the voter, the politician,
The emigrant and the exile, the criminal that stood in the box,
He who has been famous and he who shall be famous after to-day,
The stammerer, the well-form'd person, the wasted or feeble person.

I am she who adorn'd herself and folded her hair expectantly,
My truant lover has come, and it is dark.

Double yourself and receive me darkness,
Receive me and my lover too, he will not let me go without him.

I roll myself upon you as upon a bed, I resign myself to the dusk.   50

He whom I call answers me and takes the place of my lover,
He rises with me silently from the bed.

Darkness, you are gentler than my lover, his flesh was sweaty and panting,
I feel the hot moisture yet that he left me.

My hands are spread forth, I pass them in all directions,
I would sound up the shadowy shore to which you are journeying.

Be careful darkness! already, what was it touch'd me?
I thought my lover had gone, else darkness and he are one,
I hear the heart-beat, I follow, I fade away.

2

I descend my western course, my sinews are flaccid,   60
Perfume and youth course through me and I am their wake.

It is my face yellow and wrinkled instead of the old woman's,
I sit low in a straw-bottom chair and carefully darn my grandson's stockings.

It is I too, the sleepless widow looking out on the winter midnight,
I see the sparkles of starshine on the icy and pallid earth.

A shroud I see and I am the shroud, I wrap a body and lie in the coffin,
It is dark here under ground, it is not evil or pain here, it is blank here, for reasons.

(It seems to me that every thing in the light and air ought to be happy,
Whoever is not in his coffin and the dark grave let him know he has enough.)

3

I see a beautiful gigantic swimmer swimming naked through the eddies of the sea, 70
His brown hair lies close and even to his head, he strikes out with courageous arms,
    he urges himself with his legs,

I see his white body, I see his undaunted eyes,
I hate the swift-running eddies that would dash him head-foremost on the rocks.

What are you doing you ruffianly red-trickled waves?
Will you kill the courageous giant? will you kill him in the prime of his middle age?

Steady and long he struggles,
He is baffled, bang'd, bruised, he holds out while his strength holds out,
The slapping eddies are spotted with his blood, they bear him away, they roll him, swing him, turn him,
His beautiful body is borne in the circling eddies, it is continually bruis'd on rocks,
Swiftly and out of sight is borne the brave corpse.   80

4

I turn but do not extricate myself,
Confused, a past-reading, another, but with darkness yet.

The beach is cut by the razory ice-wind, the wreck-guns sound,
The tempest lulls, the moon comes floundering through the drifts.

I look where the ship helplessly heads end on, I hear the burst as she strikes, I hear the howls of dismay, they grow fainter and fainter.

I cannot aid with my wringing fingers,
I can but rush to the surf and let it drench me and freeze upon me.

I search with the crowd, not one of the company is wash'd to us alive,
In the morning I help pick up the dead and lay them in rows in a barn.

5

Now of the older war-days, the defeat at Brooklyn,   90
Washington stands inside the lines, he stands on the intrench'd hills amid a crowd of officers.
His face is cold and damp, he cannot repress the weeping drops,
He lifts the glass perpetually to his eyes, the color is blanch'd from his cheeks,
He sees the slaughter of the southern braves confided to him by their parents.

The same at last and at last when peace is declared,
He stands in the room of the old tavern, the well-belov'd soldiers all pass through,
The officers speechless and slow draw near in their turns,
The chief encircles their necks with his arm and kisses them on the cheek,
He kisses lightly the wet cheeks one after another, he shakes hands and bids good-by to the army.

6

Now what my mother told me one day as we sat at dinner together,   100
Of when she was a nearly grown girl living home with her parents on the old homestead.

A red squaw came one breakfast-time to the old homestead,
On her back she carried a bundle of rushes for rush-bottoming chairs,

Her hair, straight, shiny, coarse, black, profuse, half-envelop'd her face,
Her step was free and elastic, and her voice sounded exquisitely as she spoke.

My mother look'd in delight and amazement at the stranger,
She look'd at the beauty of her tall-borne face and full and pliant limbs,
The more she look'd upon her she loved her,
Never before had she seen such wonderful beauty and purity,
She made her sit on a bench by the jamb of the fireplace, she cook'd food for her,
She had no work to give her, but she gave her remembrance and fondness.   111

The red squaw staid all the forenoon, and toward the middle of the afternoon she
     went away,
O my mother was loth to have her go away,
All the week she thought of her, she watch'd for her many a month,
She remember'd her many a winter and many a summer,
But the red squaw never came nor was heard of there again.

7

A show of the summer softness—a contact of something unseen—an amour of the
     light and air,
I am jealous and overwhelm'd with friendliness,
And will go gallivant with the light and air myself.

O love and summer, you are in the dreams and in me,   120
Autumn and winter are in the dreams, the farmer goes with his thrift,
The droves and crops increase, the barns are well-fill'd.

Elements merge in the night, ships make tacks in the dreams,
The sailor sails, the exile returns home,
The fugitive returns unharm'd, the immigrant is back beyond months and years,
The poor Irishman lives in the simple house of his childhood with the well-known
     neighbors and faces,
They warmly welcome him, he is barefoot again, he forgets he is well off,
The Dutchman voyages home, and the Scotchman and Welchman voyage home,
     and the native of the Mediterranean voyages home,
To every port of England, France, Spain, enter well-filled ships,
The Swiss foots it toward his hills, the Prussian goes his way, the Hungarian his
     way, and the Pole his way,   130
The Swede returns, and the Dane and Norwegian return.

The homeward bound and the outward bound,
The beautiful lost swimmer, the ennuyé, the onanist, the female that loves unre-
     quited, the money-maker,
The actor and actress, those through with their parts and those waiting to com-
     mence,
The affectionate boy, the husband and wife, the voter, the nominee that is chosen
     and the nominee that has fail'd,
The great already known and the great any time after to-day,
The stammerer, the sick, the perfect-form'd, the homely,
The criminal that stood in the box, the judge that sat and sentenced him, the fluent
     lawyers, the jury, the audience,

The laugher and weeper, the dancer, the midnight widow, the red squaw,
The consumptive, the erysipalite, the idiot, he that is wrong'd,   140
The antipodes, and every one between this and them in the dark,
I swear they are averaged now—one is no better than the other,
The night and sleep have liken'd them and restored them.

I swear they are all beautiful,
Every one that sleeps is beautiful, every thing in the dim night is beautiful,
The wildest and bloodiest is over, and all is peace.

Peace is always beautiful,
The myth of heaven indicates peace and night.

The myth of heaven indicates the soul,
The soul is always beautiful, it appears more or it appears less, it comes or it lags
    behind,   150
It comes from its embower'd garden and looks pleasantly on itself and encloses the
    world,
Perfect and clean the genitals previously jetting, and perfect and clean the womb
    cohering,
The head well-grown proportion'd and plumb, and the bowels and joints propor-
    tion'd and plumb.

The soul is always beautiful,
The universe is duly in order, every thing is in its place,
What has arrived is in its place and what waits shall be in its place,
The twisted skull waits, the watery or rotten blood waits,
The child of the glutton or venerealee waits long, and the child of the drunkard waits
    long, and the drunkard himself waits long,
The sleepers that lived and died wait, the far advanced are to go on in their turns,
    and the far behind are to come on in their turns,
The diverse shall be no less diverse, but they shall flow and unite—they unite now.

8

The sleepers are very beautiful as they lie unclothed,   161
They flow hand in hand over the whole earth from east to west as they lie un-
    clothed;
The Asiatic and African are hand in hand, the European and American are hand
    in hand,
Learn'd and unlearn'd are hand in hand, and male and female are hand in hand,
The bare arm of the girl crosses the bare breast of her lover, they press close without
    lust, his lips press her neck,
The father holds his grown or ungrown son in his arms with measureless love, and
    the son holds the father in his arms with measureless love,
The white hair of the mother shines on the white wrist of the daughter,
The breath of the boy goes with the breath of the man, friend is inarm'd by friend,
The scholar kisses the teacher and the teacher kisses the scholar, the wrong'd is made
    right,   169
The call of the slave is one with the master's call, and the master salutes the slave,
The felon steps forth from the prison, the insane becomes sane, the suffering of sick
    persons is reliev'd.

The sweatings and fevers stop, the throat that was unsound is sound, the lungs of
    the consumptive are resumed, the poor distress'd head is free,
The joints of the rheumatic move as smoothly as ever, and smoother than ever,   170
Stiflings and passages open, the paralysed become supple,
The swell'd and convuls'd and congested awake to themselves in condition,
They pass the invigoration of the night and the chemistry of the night, and awake.

I too pass from the night,
I stay a while away O night, but I return to you again and love you.

Why should I be afraid to trust myself to you?
I am not afraid, I have been well brought forward by you,   180
I love the rich running day, but I do not desert her in whom I lay so long,
I know not how I came of you, and I know not where I go with you, but I know
    I came well and shall go well.

I will stop only a time with the night, and rise betimes,
I will duly pass the day O my mother and duly return to you.

So Long!

To conclude, I announce what comes after me.

I remember I said before my leaves sprang at all,
I would raise my voice jocund and strong with reference to consummations.

When America does what was promis'd,
When through these States walk a hundred millions of superb persons,
When the rest part away for superb persons and contribute to them,
When breeds of the most perfect mothers denote America,
Then to me and mine our due fruition.

I have press'd through in my own right,
I have sung the body and the soul, war and peace have I sung, and the songs of life
    and death,   10
And the songs of birth, and shown that there are many births.
I have offer'd my style to every one, I have journey'd with confident step;
While my pleasure is yet at the full I whisper *So long!*
And take the young woman's hand and the young man's hand for the last time.

I announce natural persons to arise,
I announce justice triumphant,
I announce uncompromising liberty and equality,
I announce the justification of candor and the justification of pride.

I announce that the identity of these States is a single identity only,
I announce the Union more and more compact, indissoluble,   20
I announce splendors and majesties to make all the previous politics of the earth
    insignificant.

I announce adhesiveness, I say it shall be limitless, unloosen'd,
I say you shall yet find the friend you were looking for.

I announce a man or woman coming, perhaps you are the one, (*So long!*)
I announce the great individual, fluid as Nature, chaste, affectionate, compassionate, fully arm'd.

I announce a life that shall be copious, vehement, spiritual, bold,
I announce an end that shall lightly and joyfully meet its translation.

I announce myriads of youths, beautiful, gigantic, sweet-blooded,
I announce a race of splendid and savage old men.

O thicker and faster—(*So long!*)   30
O crowding too close upon me,
I foresee too much, it means more than I thought,
It appears to me I am dying.

Hasten throat and sound your last,
Salute me—salute the days once more. Peal the old cry once more.

Screaming electric, the atmosphere using,
At random glancing, each as I notice absorbing,
Swiftly on, but a little while alighting,
Curious envelop'd messages delivering,
Sparkles hot, seed ethereal down in the dirt dropping,   40
Myself unknowing, my commission obeying, to question it never daring,
To ages and ages, yet the growth of the seed leaving,
To troops out of the war arising, they the tasks I have set promulging,
To women certain whispers of myself bequeathing, their affection me more clearly explaining,
To young men my problems offering—no dallier I—I the muscle of their brains trying,
So I pass, a little time vocal, visible, contrary,
Afterward a melodious echo, passionately bent for, (death making me really undying,)
The best of me then when no longer visible, for toward that I have been incessantly preparing.

What is there more, that I lag and pause and crouch extended with unshut mouth?
Is there a single final farewell?   50

My songs cease, I abandon them,
From behind the screen where I hid I advance personally solely to you.

Camerado, this is no book,
Who touches this touches a man,
(Is it night? are we here together alone?)
It is I you hold and who holds you,
I spring from the pages into your arms—decease calls me forth.

O how your fingers drowse me,
Your breath falls around me like dew, your pulse lulls the tympans of my ears,
I feel immerged from head to foot,   60
Delicious, enough.

Enough O deed impromptu and secret,
Enough O gliding present—enough O summ'd-up past.

Dear friend whoever you are take this kiss,
I give it especially to you, do not forget me,
I feel like one who has done work for the day to retire awhile,
I receive now again of my many translations, from my avataras ascending, while
    others doubtless await me,
An unknown sphere more real than I dream'd, more direct, darts awakening rays
    about me, *So long!*
Remember my words, I may again return,
I love you, I depart from materials,   70
I am as one disembodied, triumphant, dead.

When Lilacs Last in the Dooryard Bloom'd

1

When lilacs last in the dooryard bloom'd,
And the great star early droop'd in the western sky in the night,
I mourn'd, and yet shall mourn with ever-returning spring.

Ever-returning spring, trinity sure to me you bring,
Lilac blooming perennial and drooping star in the west,
And thought of him I love.

2

O powerful western fallen star!
O shades of night—O moody, tearful night!
O great star disappear'd—O the black murk that hides the star!
O cruel hands that hold me powerless—O helpless soul of me!   10
O harsh surrounding cloud that will not free my soul.

3

In the dooryard fronting an old farm-house near the white-wash'd palings,
Stands the lilac-bush tall-growing with heart-shaped leaves of rich green,
With many a pointed blossom rising delicate, with the perfume strong I love,
With every leaf a miracle—and from this bush in the dooryard,
With delicate-color'd blossoms and heart-shaped leaves of rich green,
A sprig with its flower I break.

4

In the swamp in secluded recesses,
A shy and hidden bird is warbling a song.

Solitary the thrush,   20
The hermit withdrawn to himself, avoiding the settlements,
Sings by himself a song.

Song of the bleeding throat,
Death's outlet song of life, (for well dear brother I know,
If thou wast not granted to sing thou would'st surely die.)

5

Over the breast of the spring, the land, amid cities,
Amid lanes and through old woods, where lately the violets peep'd from the ground,
  spotting the gray debris,
Amid the grass in the fields each side of the lanes, passing the endless grass,
Passing the yellow-spear'd wheat, every grain from its shroud in the dark-brown fields
  uprisen,
Passing the apple-tree blows of white and pink in the orchards,   30
Carrying a corpse to where it shall rest in the grave,
Night and day journeys a coffin.

6

Coffin that passes through lanes and streets,
Through day and night with the great cloud darkening the land,
With the pomp of the inloop'd flags with the cities draped in black,
With the show of the States themselves as of crape-veil'd women standing,
With processions long and winding and the flambeaus of the night,
With the countless torches lit, with the silent sea of faces and the unbared heads,
With the waiting depot, the arriving coffin, and the sombre faces,
With dirges through the night, with the thousand voices rising strong and solemn,   40
With all the mournful voices of the dirges pour'd around the coffin,
The dim-lit churches and the shuddering organs—where amid these you journey,
With the tolling tolling bells' perpetual clang,
Here, coffin that slowly passes,
I give you my sprig of lilac.

7

(Nor for you, for one alone,
Blossoms and branches green to coffins all I bring,
For fresh as the morning, thus would I chant a song for you O sane and sacred death.

All over bouquets of roses,
O death, I cover you over with roses and early lilies,   50
But mostly and now the lilac that blooms the first,
Copious I break, I break the sprigs from the bushes,
With loaded arms I come, pouring for you,
For you and the coffins all of you O death.)

8

O western orb sailing the heaven,
Now I know what you must have meant as a month since I walk'd,
As I walk'd in silence the transparent shadowy night,
As I saw you had something to tell as you bent to me night after night,
As you droop'd from the sky low down as if to my side, (while the other stars all
  look'd on,)
As we wander'd together the solemn night, (for something I know not what kept me
  from sleep,)   60
As the night advanced, and I saw on the rim of the west how full you were of woe,
As I stood on the rising ground in the breeze in the cool transparent night,

As I watch'd where you pass'd and was lost in the netherward black of the night,
As my soul in its trouble dissatisfied sank, as where you sad orb,
Concluded, dropt in the night, and was gone.

9

Sing on there in the swamp,
O singer bashful and tender, I hear your notes, I hear your call,
I hear, I come presently, I understand you,
But a moment I linger, for the lustrous star has detain'd me,
The star my departing comrade holds and detains me.   70

10

O how shall I warble myself for the dead one there I loved?
And how shall I deck my song for the large sweet soul that has gone?
And what shall my perfume be for the grave of him I love?

Sea-winds blown from east and west,
Blown from the Eastern sea and blown from the Western sea, till there on the prairies
    meeting,
These and with these and the breath of my chant,
I'll perfume the grave of him I love.

11

O what shall I hang on the chamber walls?
And what shall the pictures be that I hang on the walls,
To adorn the burial-house of him I love?   80

Pictures of growing spring and farms and homes,
With the Fourth-month eve at sundown, and the gray smoke lucid and bright,
With floods of the yellow gold of the gorgeous, indolent, sinking sun, burning, ex-
    panding the air,
With the fresh sweet herbage under foot, and the pale green leaves of the trees
    prolific,
In the distance the flowing glaze, the breast of the river, with a wind-dapple here and
    there,
With ranging hills on the banks, with many a line against the sky, and shadows,
And the city at hand with dwellings so dense, and stacks of chimneys,
And all the scenes of life and the workshops, and the workmen homeward returning.

12

Lo, body and soul—this land,
My own Manhattan with spires, and the sparkling and hurrying tides, and the
    ships,   90
The varied and ample land, the South and the North in the light, Ohio's shores and
    flashing Missouri,
And ever the far-spreading prairies cover'd with grass and corn.

Lo, the most excellent sun so calm and haughty,
The violet and purple morn with just-felt breezes,
The gentle soft-born measureless light,
The miracle spreading bathing all, the fulfill'd noon,

The coming eve delicious, the welcome night and the stars,
Over my cities shining all, enveloping man and land.

13

Sing on, sing on you gray-brown bird,
Sing from the swamps, the recesses, pour your chant from the bushes,   100
Limitless out of the dusk, out of the cedars and pines.

Sing on dearest brother, warble your reedy song,
Loud human song, with voice of uttermost woe.

O liquid and free and tender!
O wild and loose to my soul—O wondrous singer!
You only I hear—yet the star holds me, (but will soon depart,)
Yet the lilac with mastering odor holds me.

14

Now while I sat in the day and look'd forth,
In the close of the day with its light and the fields of spring, and the farmers prepar-
    ing their crops,
In the large unconscious scenery of my land with its lakes and forests,   110
In the heavenly aerial beauty, (after the perturb'd winds and the storms,)
Under the arching heavens of the afternoon swift passing, and the voices of children
    and women,
The many-moving sea-tides, and I saw the ships how they sail'd,
And the summer approaching with richness, and the fields all busy with labor,
And the infinite separate houses, how they all went on, each with its meals and minu-
    tia of daily usages,
And the streets how their throbbings throbb'd, and the cities pent—lo, then and there,
Falling upon them all and among them all, enveloping me with the rest,
Appear'd the cloud, appear'd the long black trail,
And I knew death, its thought, and the sacred knowledge of death.

Then with the knowledge of death as walking one side of me,   120
And the thought of death close-walking the other side of me,
And I in the middle as with companions, and as holding the hands of companions,
I fled forth to the hiding receiving night that talks not,
Down to the shores of the water, the path by the swamp in the dimness,
To the solemn shadowy cedars and ghostly pines so still.

And the singer so shy to the rest receiv'd me,
The gray-brown bird I know receiv'd us comrades three,
And he sang the carol of death, and a verse for him I love.

From deep secluded recesses,
From the fragrant cedars and the ghostly pines so still,   130
Came the carol of the bird.

And the charm of the carol rapt me,
As I held as if by their hands my comrades in the night,
And the voice of my spirit tallied the song of the bird.

Come lovely and soothing death,
Undulate round the world, serenely arriving, arriving,

In the day, in the night, to all, to each,
Sooner or later delicate death.

Prais'd be the fathomless universe,
For life and joy, and for objects and knowledge curious,   140
And for love, sweet love—but praise! praise! praise!
For the sure-enwinding arms of cool-enfolding death.

Dark mother always gliding near with soft feet,
Have none chanted for thee a chant of fullest welcome?
Then I chant it for thee, I glorify thee above all,
I bring thee a song that when thou must indeed come, come unfalteringly.

Approach strong deliveress,
When it is so, when thou hast taken them I joyously sing the dead,
Lost in the loving floating ocean of thee,
Laved in the flood of thy bliss O death.   150

From me to thee glad serenades,
Dances for thee I propose saluting thee, adornments and feastings for thee,
And the sights of the open landscape and the high-spread sky are fitting,
And life and the fields, and the huge and thoughtful night.

The night in silence under many a star,
The ocean shore and the husky whispering wave whose voice I know,
And the soul turning to thee O vast and well-veil'd death,
And the body gratefully nestling close to thee.

Over the tree-tops I float thee a song,
Over the rising and sinking waves, over the myriad fields and the prairies wide,   160
Over the dense-pack'd cities all and the teeming wharves and ways,
I float this carol with joy, with joy to thee O death.

15

To the tally of my soul,
Loud and strong kept up the gray-brown bird,
With pure deliberate notes spreading filling the night.

Loud in the pines and cedars dim,
Clear in the freshness moist and the swamp-perfume,
And I with my comrades there in the night.

While my sight that was bound in my eyes unclosed,
As to long panoramas of visions.   170

And I saw askant the armies,
I saw as in noiseless dreams hundreds of battle-flags,
Borne through the smoke of the battles and pierc'd with missiles I saw them,
And carried hither and yon through the smoke, and torn and bloody,
And at last but a few shreds left on the staffs, (and all in silence,)
And the staffs all splinter'd and broken.

I saw battle-corpses, myriads of them,
And the white skeletons of young men, I saw them,
I saw the debris and debris of all the slain soldiers of the war,

But I saw they were not as was thought,
They themselves were fully at rest, they suffer'd not,
The living remain'd and suffer'd, the mother suffer'd,
And the wife and the child and the musing comrade suffer'd,
And the armies that remain'd suffer'd.

16

Passing the visions, passing the night,
Passing, unloosing the hold of my comrades' hands,
Passing the song of the hermit bird and the tallying song of my soul,
Victorious song, death's outlet song, yet varying ever-altering song,
As low and wailing, yet clear the notes, rising and falling, flooding the night,
Sadly sinking and fainting, as warning and warning, and yet again bursting with joy,

Covering the earth and filling the spread of the heaven,
As that powerful psalm in the night I heard from recesses,
Passing, I leave thee lilac with heart-shaped leaves,
I leave thee there in the door-yard, blooming, returning with spring.

I cease from my song for thee,
From my gaze on thee in the west, fronting the west, communing with thee,
O comrade lustrous with silver face in the night.

Yet each to keep and all, retrievements out of the night,
The song, the wondrous chant of the gray-brown bird,
And the tallying chant, the echo arous'd in my soul,

With the lustrous and drooping star with the countenance full of woe,
With the holders holding my hand nearing the call of the bird,
Comrades mine and I in the midst, and their memory ever to keep, for the dead I loved so well,
For the sweetest, wisest soul of all my days and lands—and this for his dear sake,
Lilac and star and bird twined with the chant of my soul,
There in the fragrant pines and the cedars dusk and dim.

Cavalry Crossing a Ford

A line in long array where they wind betwixt green islands,
They take a serpentine course, their arms flash in the sun—hark to the musical clank,
Behold the silvery river, in it the splashing horses loitering stop to drink,
Behold the brown-faced men, each group, each person a picture, the negligent rest on the saddles,
Some emerge on the opposite bank, others are just entering the ford—while,
Scarlet and blue and snowy white,
The guidon flags flutter gayly in the wind.

Bivouac on a Mountain Side

I see before me now a traveling army halting,
Below a fertile valley spread, with barns and the orchards of summer,

Behind, the terraced sides of a mountain, abrupt, in places rising high,
Broken, with rocks, with clinging cedars, with tall shapes dingily seen,
The numerous camp-fires scatter'd near and far, some away up on the mountain,
The shadowy forms of men and horses, looming, large-sized, flickering,
And over all the sky—the sky! far, far out of reach, studded, breaking out, the eternal
    stars.

The Last Invocation

At the last, tenderly,
From the walls of the powerful fortress'd house,
From the clasp of the knitted locks, from the keep of the well-closed doors,
Let me be wafted.

Let me glide noiselessly forth;
With the key of softness unlock the locks—with a whisper,
Set ope the doors O soul.

Tenderly—be not impatient,
(Strong is your hold O mortal flesh,
Strong is your hold O love.)   10

Ethiopia Saluting the Colors

Who are you dusky woman, so ancient hardly human,
With your woolly-white and turban'd head, and bare bony feet?
Why rising by the roadside here, do you the colors greet?

('Tis while our army lines Carolina's sands and pines,
Forth from thy hovel door thou Ethiopia com'st to me,
As under doughty Sherman I march toward the sea.)

Me master years a hundred since from my parents sunder'd,
A little child, they caught me as the savage beast is caught,
Then hither me across the sea the cruel slaver brought.

No further does she say, but lingering all the day,   10
Her high-borne turban'd head she wags, and rolls her darkling eye,
And courtesies to the regiments, the guidons moving by.

What is it fateful woman, so blear, hardly human?
Why wag your head with turban bound yellow, red and green?
Are the things so strange and marvelous you see or have seen?

Joy, Shipmate, Joy!

Joy, shipmate, joy!
(Pleas'd to my soul at death I cry,)

Our life is closed, our life begins,
The long, long anchorage we leave,
The ship is clear at last, she leaps!
She swiftly courses from the shore,
Joy, shipmate, joy!

To the Man-of-War Bird

Thou who hast slept all night upon the storm,
Waking renew'd on thy prodigious pinions,
(Burst the wild storm? above it thou ascended'st,
And rested on the sky, thy slave that cradled thee,)
Now a blue point, far, far in heaven floating,
As to the light emerging here on deck I watch thee,
(Myself a speck, a point on the world's floating vast.)

Far, far at sea,
After the night's fierce drifts have strewn the shore with wrecks,
With re-appearing day as now so happy and serene,   10
The rosy and elastic dawn, the flashing sun,
The limpid spread of air cerulean,
Thou also re-appearest.

Thou born to match the gale, (thou art all wings,)
To cope with heaven and earth and sea and hurricane,
Thou ship of air that never furl'st thy sails,
Days, even weeks untired and onward, through spaces, realms gyrating,
At dusk that look'st on Senegal, at morn America,
That sport'st amid the lightning-flash and thunder-cloud,
In them, in thy experiences, had'st thou my soul,   20
What joys! what joys were thine!

Italian Music in Dakota

"THE SEVENTEENTH—THE FINEST REGIMENTAL BAND I EVER HEARD."

Through the soft evening air enwinding all,
Rocks, woods, fort, cannon, pacing sentries, endless wilds,
In dulcet streams, in flutes' and cornets' notes,
Electric, pensive, turbulent, artificial,
(Yet strangely fitting even here, meanings unknown before,
Subtler than ever, more harmony, as if born here, related here,
Not to the city's fresco'd rooms, not to the audience of the opera house,
Sounds, echoes, wandering strains, as really here at home,
Sonnambula's innocent love, trios with *Norma's* anguish,
And thy ecstatic chorus *Poliuto*);   10
Ray'd in the limpid yellow slanting sundown,
Music, Italian music in Dakota.

While Nature, sovereign of this gnarl'd realm,
Lurking in hidden barbaric grim recesses,
Acknowledging rapport however far remov'd,
(As some old root or soil of earth its lastborn flower or fruit,)
Listens well pleas'd.

Herman Melville

✳ 1819–1891

The March into Virginia

JULY *1861*

Did all the lets and bars appear
   To every just or larger end,
Whence should come the trust and cheer?
   Youth must its ignorant impulse lend—
Age finds place in the rear.
   All wars are boyish, and are fought by
      boys,
The champions and enthusiasts of the
     state:
   Turbid ardours and vain joys
     Not barrenly abate—
   Stimulants to the power mature,   10
     Preparatives of fate.

Who here forecasteth the event?
What heart but spurns at precedent
And warnings of the wise,
Contemned foreclosures of surprise?
The banners play, the bugles call,
The air is blue and prodigal.
   No berrying party, pleasure-wooed,
No picnic party in the May,
Ever went less loth than they   20
   Into that leafy neighborhood.
In Bacchic glee they file toward Fate,
Moloch's uninitiate;
Expectancy, and glad surmise
Of battle's unknown mysteries.
All they feel is this: 'tis glory,
A rapture sharp, though transitory,
Yet lasting in belaurelled story.
So they gaily go to fight,

Chatting left and laughing right.   30
But some who this blithe mood present,
   As on its lightsome files they fare,
Shall die experienced ere three days are
     spent—
Perish, enlightened by the volleyed
     glare;
Or shame survive, and like to adamant,
   The throe of Second Manassas share.

Misgivings

When ocean-clouds over inland hills
   Sweep storming in late autumn
     brown,
And horror the sodden valley fills,
   And the spire falls crashing in the
     town,
I muse upon my country's ills—
The tempest bursting from the waste
   of Time
On the world's fairest hope linked with
   man's foulest crime.

Nature's dark side is heeded now—
   (Ah! optimist-cheer disheartened
     flown)—
A child may read the moody brow   10
   Of yon black mountain lone.
With shouts the torrents down the
     gorges go,
And storms are formed behind the
     storm we feel:
The hemlock shakes in the rafter, the
     oak in the driving keel.

The Maldive Shark

About the Shark, phlegmatical one,
Pale sot of the Maldive sea,
The sleek little pilot-fish, azure and slim,
How alert in attendance be.
From his saw-pit of mouth, from his char-
    nel of maw
They have nothing of harm to dread,
But liquidly glide on his ghastly flank
Or before his Gorgonian head;
Or lurk in the port of serrated teeth
In white triple tiers of glittering gates,
And there find a haven when peril's
    abroad,   11
An asylum in jaws of the Fates!
They are friends; and friendly they guide
    him to prey,
Yet never partake of the treat—
Eyes and brains to the dotard lethargic
    and dull,
Pale ravener of horrible meat.

The Berg

A DREAM

I saw a ship of martial build
(Her standards set, her brave apparel
    on)
Directed as by madness mere
Against a stolid iceberg steer,
Nor budge it, though the infatuate ship
    went down.
The impact made huge ice-cubes fall
Sullen, in tons that crashed the deck;
But that one avalanche was all—
No other movement save the foundering
    wreck.

Along the spurs of ridges pale,   10
Not any slenderest shaft and frail,
A prism over glass-green gorges lone,
Toppled; nor lace of traceries fine,
Nor pendant drops in grot or mine
Were jarred, when the stunned ship went
    down.

Nor sole the gulls in cloud that wheeled
Circling one snow-flanked peak afar,

But nearer fowl the floes that skimmed
And crystal beaches, felt no jar.
No thrill transmitted stirred the lock   20
Of jack-straw needle-ice at base;
Towers undermined by waves—the block
Atilt impending—kept their place.
Seals, dozing sleek on sliddery ledges
Slipt never, when by loftier edges
Through very inertia overthrown,
The impetuous ship in bafflement went
    down.

Hard Berg (methought), so cold, so vast,
With mortal damps self-overcast;
Exhaling still thy dankish breath—   30
Adrift dissolving, bound for death;
Though lumpish thou, a lumbering one—
A lumbering lubbard, loitering slow,
Impingers rue thee and go down,
Sounding thy precipice below,
Nor stir the slimy slug that sprawls
Along thy dead indifference of walls.

Bayard Taylor

✳ 1825–1878

Kilimandjaro

1

Hail to thee, monarch of African moun-
    tains,
Remote, inaccessible, silent, and lone,—
Who, from the heart of the tropical fer-
    vors,
Liftest to heaven thine alien snows,
Feeding forever the fountains that make
    thee
Father of Nile and Creator of Egypt.

2

The years of the world are engraved on
    thy forehead;

Time's morning blushed red on the first-
fallen snows;
Yet, lost in the wilderness, nameless, un-
noted,
Of Man unbeholden, thou wert not till
now.   10
Knowledge alone is the being of Nature,
Giving a soul to her manifold features,
Lighting through paths of the primitive
darkness
The footsteps of Truth and the vision of
Song.
Knowledge has born thee anew to Crea-
tion,
And long-baffled Time at thy baptism re-
joices.
Take, then, a name, and be filled with
existence,
Yea, be exultant in sovereign glory,
While from the hand of the wandering
poet
Drops the first garland of song at thy
feet.   20

3

Floating alone, on the flood of thy mak-
ing,
Through Africa's mystery, silence, and
fire,
Lo! in my palm, like the Eastern en-
chanter,
I dip from the waters a magical mirror,
And thou art revealed to my purified
vision.
I see thee, supreme in the midst of thy
co-mates,
Standing alone 'twixt the Earth and the
Heavens,
Heir of the Sunset and Herald of Morn.
Zone above zone, to thy shoulders of
granite,
The climates of Earth are displayed, as
an index,   30
Giving the scope of the Book of Crea-
tion.
There, in the gorges that widen, descend-
ing
From cloud and from cold into summer
eternal,

Gather the threads of the ice-gendered
fountains,—
Gather to riotous torrents of crystal,
And, giving each shelvy recess where
they dally
The blooms of the North and its ever-
green turfage,
Leap to the land of the lion and lotus!
There, in the wondering airs of the
Tropics
Shivers the Aspen, still dreaming of cold:
There stretches the Oak, from the loftiest
ledges,   41
His arms to the far-away lands of his
brothers,
And the Pine-tree looks down on his
rival, the Palm.

4

Bathed in the tenderest purple of dis-
tance,
Tinted and shadowed by pencils of air,
Thy battlements hang o'er the slopes and
the forests,
Seats of the Gods in the limitless ether,
Looking sublimely aloft and afar.
Above them, like folds of imperial er-
mine,
Sparkle the snow-fields that furrow thy
forehead,—   50
Desolate realms, inaccessible, silent,
Chasms and caverns where Day is a
stranger,
Garners where storeth his treasures the
Thunder,
The Lightning his falchion, his arrows
the Hail!

5

Sovereign Mountain, thy brothers give
welcome:
They, the baptized and the crownèd of
ages,
Watch-towers of Continents, altars of
Earth,
Welcome thee now to their mighty as-
sembly.
Mont Blanc, in the roar of his mad ava-
lanches,

Hails thy accession; superb Orizaba,   60
Belted with beech and ensandalled with
   palm;
Chimborazo, the lord of the regions of
   noonday,—
Mingle their sounds in magnificent chorus
With greeting august from the Pillars of
   Heaven,
Who, in the urns of the Indian Ganges
Filter the snows of their sacred do-
   minions,
Unmarked with a footprint, unseen but of
   God.

6

Lo! unto each is the seal of his lordship,
Nor questioned the right that his majesty
   giveth:
Each in his lawful supremacy forces   70
Worship and reverence, wonder and joy.
Absolute all, yet in dignity varied,
None has a claim to the honors of story,
Or the superior splendors of song.
Greater than thou, in thy mystery man-
   tled,—
Thou, the sole monarch of African moun-
   tains,
Father of Nile and Creator of Egypt.

Bedouin Song

From the Desert I come to thee
   On a stallion shod with fire;
And the winds are left behind
   In the speed of my desire.
Under thy window I stand,
   And the midnight hears my cry:
I love thee, I love but thee,
   With a love that shall not die
     Till the sun grows cold,
     And the stars are old,   10
     And the leaves of the Judgment
     Book unfold!

Look from thy window and see
   My passion and my pain;
I lie on the sands below,
   And I faint in thy disdain.

Let the night-winds touch thy brow
   With the heat of my burning sigh,
And melt thee to hear the vow
   Of a love that shall not die   20
     Till the sun grows cold,
     And the stars are old,
     And the leaves of the Judgment
     Book unfold!

My steps are nightly driven,
   By the fever in my breast,
To hear from thy lattice breathed
   The word that shall give me rest.
Open the door of thy heart
   And open thy chamber door,   30
And my kisses shall teach thy lips
   The love that shall fade no more
     Till the sun grows cold,
     And the stars are old,
     And the leaves of the Judgment
     Book unfold!

Henry Timrod

✳ 1828–1867

I Know Not Why, but All This Weary Day

I know not why, but all this weary day,
Suggested by no definite grief or pain,
Sad fancies have been flitting through my
   brain;
Now it has been a vessel losing way,
Rounding a stormy headland; now a gray
Dull waste of clouds above a wintry
   main;
And then, a banner, drooping in the rain,
And meadows beaten into bloody clay.
Strolling at random with this shadowy
   woe
At heart, I chanced to wander hither! Lo!
A league of desolate marsh-land, with its
   lush,   11
Hot grasses in a noisome, tide-left bed,

And faint, warm airs that rustle in the
hush,
Like whispers round the body of the
dead.

Most Men Know Love but as a Part of Life

Most men know love but as a part of life;
They hide it in some corner of the breast,
Even from themselves; and only when
they rest
In the brief pauses of that daily strife,
Wherewith the world might else be not
so rife,
They draw it forth (as one draws forth a
toy
To soothe some ardent, kiss-exacting
boy)
And hold it up to sister, child, or wife.
Ah me! why may not love and life be
one?
Why walk we thus alone, when by our
side,   10
Love, like a visible God, might be our
guide?
How would the marts grow noble! and
the street,
Worn like a dungeon floor by weary feet,
Seem then a golden court-way of the Sun!

Charleston

Calm as that second summer which pre-
cedes
The first fall of the snow,
In the broad sunlight of heroic deeds
The City bides the foe.

As yet, behind their ramparts stern and
proud,
Her bolted thunders sleep—
Dark Sumter like a battlemented cloud
Looms o'er the solemn deep.

No Calpe frowns from lofty cliff or scar
To guard the holy strand;   10
But Moultrie holds in leash her dogs of
war
Above the level sand.

And down the dunes a thousand guns lie
couched
Unseen beside the flood,
Like tigers in some Orient jungle
crouched,
That wait and watch for blood.

Meanwhile, through streets still echoing
with trade,
Walk grave and thoughtful men
Whose hands may one day wield the pa-
triot's blade
As lightly as the pen.   20

And maidens with such eyes as would
grow dim
Over a bleeding hound
Seem each one to have caught the
strength of him
Whose sword she sadly bound.

Thus girt without and garrisoned at
home,
Day patient following day,
Old Charleston looks from roof and spire
and dome
Across her tranquil bay.

Ships through a hundred foes, from
Saxon lands
And spicy Indian ports   30
Bring Saxon steel and iron to her hands
And Summer to her courts.

But still, along yon dim Atlantic line
The only hostile smoke
Creeps like a harmless mist above the
brine
From some frail, floating oak.

Shall the Spring dawn, and she, still clad
in smiles
And with an unscathed brow,
Rest in the strong arms of her palm-
crowned isles
As fair and free as now?   40

We know not: in the temple of the Fates
    God has inscribed her doom;
And, all untroubled in her faith, she waits
    The triumph or the tomb.

The Unknown Dead

The rain is plashing on my sill,
But all the winds of Heaven are still;
And so it falls with that dull sound
Which thrills us in the church-yard
    ground,
When the first spadeful drops like lead
Upon the coffin of the dead.
Beyond my streaming window-pane,
I cannot see the neighboring vane,
Yet from its old familiar tower
The bell comes, muffled, through the
    shower.   10
What strange and unsuspected link
Of feeling touched, has made me think—
While with a vacant soul and eye
I watch that gray and stony sky—
Of nameless graves on battle-plains
Washed by a single winter's rains,
Where, some beneath Virginian hills,
And some by green Atlantic rills,
Some by the waters of the West,
A myriad unknown heroes rest.   20
Ah! not the chiefs, who, dying, see
Their flags in front of victory,
Or, at their life-blood's noble cost
Pay for a battle nobly lost,
Claim from their monumental beds
The bitterest tears a nation sheds.
Beneath yon lonely mound—the spot
By all save some fond few forgot—
Like the true martyrs of the fight
Which strikes for freedom and for right.
Of them, their patriot zeal and pride,   31
The lofty faith that with them died,
No grateful page shall farther tell
Than that so many bravely fell;
And we can only dimly guess
What worlds of all this world's distress,
What utter woe, despair, and dearth,

Their fate has brought to many a hearth.
Just such a sky as this should weep
Above them, always, where they sleep;
Yet, haply, at this very hour,   41
Their graves are like a lover's bower;
And Nature's self, with eyes unwet,
Oblivious of the crimson debt
To which she owes her April grace,
Laughs gayly o'er their burial-place.

At Magnolia Cemetery

Sleep sweetly in your humble graves,
    Sleep, martyrs of a fallen cause;
Though yet no marble column craves
    The pilgrim here to pause.

In seeds of laurel in the earth
    The blossom of your fame is blown,
And somewhere, waiting for its birth,
    The shaft is in the stone!

Meanwhile, behalf the tardy years
    Which keep in trust your storied
        tombs,   10
Behold! your sisters bring their tears,
    And these memorial blooms.

Small tributes! but your shades will smile
    More proudly on these wreaths today,
Than when some cannon-molded pile
    Shall overlook this bay.

Stoop, angels, hither from the skies!
    There is no holier spot of ground
Than where defeated valor lies,
    By mourning beauty crowned.   20

Emily Dickinson
✳ 1830–1886

67

Success is counted sweetest
By those who ne'er succeed.

To comprehend a nectar
Requires sorest need.

Not one of all the purple Host
Who took the Flag today
Can tell the definition
So clear of Victory

As he defeated—dying—
On whose forbidden ear   10
The distant strains of triumph
Burst agonized and clear!

76

Exultation is the going
Of an inland soul to sea,
Past the houses—past the headlands—
Into deep Eternity—

Bred as we, among the mountains,
Can the sailor understand
The divine intoxication
Of the first league out from land?

89

Some things that fly there be—
Birds—Hours—the Bumblebee—
Of these no Elegy.

Some things that stay there be—
Grief—Hills—Eternity—
Nor this behooveth me.

There are that resting, rise.
Can I expound the skies?
How still the Riddle lies!

126

To fight aloud, is very brave—
But *gallanter*, I know
Who charge within the bosom
The Cavalry of Wo—

Who win, and nations do not see—
Who fall—and none observe—
Whose dying eyes, no Country
Regards with patriot love—

We trust, in plumed procession
For such, the Angels go—   10
Rank after Rank, with even feet—
And Uniforms of Snow.

189

It's such a little thing to weep—
So short a thing to sigh—
And yet—by Trades—the size of *these*
We men and women die!

210

The thought beneath so slight a film—
Is more distinctly seen—
As laces just reveal the surge—
Or Mists—the Appenine—

214

I taste a liquor never brewed—
From Tankards scooped in Pearl—
Not all the Frankfort Berries
Yield such an Alcohol!

Inebriate of Air—am I—
And Debauchee of Dew—
Reeling—thro endless summer days—
From inns of Molten Blue—

When "Landlords" turn the drunken Bee
Out of the Foxglove's door—   10
When Butterflies—renounce their
         "drams"—
I shall but drink the more!

Till Seraphs swing their snowy Hats—
And Saints—to windows run—
To see the little Tippler
From Manzanilla come!

249

Wild Nights—Wild Nights!
Were I with thee
Wild Nights should be
Our luxury!

Futile—the Winds—
To a Heart in port—
Done with the Compass—
Done with the Chart!

Rowing in Eden—
Ah, the Sea!   10
Might I but moor—Tonight—
In Thee!

254

"Hope" is the thing with feathers—
That perches in the soul—
And sings the tune without the words—
And never stops—at all—

And sweetest—in the Gale—is heard—
And sore must be the storm—
That could abash the little Bird
That kept so many warm—

I've heard it in the chillest land—
And on the strangest Sea—   10
Yet, never, in Extremity,
It asked a crumb—of Me.

258

There's a certain Slant of light,
Winter Afternoons—
That oppresses, like the Heft
Of Cathedral Tunes—

Heavenly Hurt, it gives us—
We can find no scar,
But internal difference,
Where the Meanings, are—

None may teach it—Any—
'Tis the Seal Despair—   10
An imperial affliction
Sent us of the Air—

When it comes, the Landscape listens—
Shadows—hold their breath—
When it goes, 'tis like the Distance
On the look of Death—

265

Where Ships of Purple—gently toss—
On Seas of Daffodil—
Fantastic Sailors—mingle—
And then—the Wharf is still!

303

The Soul selects her own Society—
Then—shuts the Door—
To her divine Majority—
Present no more—

Unmoved—she notes the Chariots—
    pausing—
At her low Gate—
Unmoved—an Emperor be kneeling
Upon her Mat—

I've known her—from an ample nation—
Choose One—   10
Then—close the Valves of her atten-
    tion—
Like Stone—

609

I Years had been from Home
And now before the Door
I dared not enter, lest a Face
I never saw before

Stare stolid into mine
And ask my Business there—

"My Business but a Life I left
Was such remaining there?"

I leaned upon the Awe—
I lingered with Before—   10
The Second like an Ocean rolled
And broke against my ear—

I laughed a crumbling Laugh
That I could fear a Door
Who Consternation compassed
And never winced before.

I fitted to the Latch
My Hand, with trembling care
Lest back the awful Door should spring
And leave me in the Floor—   20

Then moved my Fingers off
As cautiously as Glass
And held my ears, and like a Thief
Fled gasping from the House—

632

The Brain—is wider than the Sky—
For—put them side by side—
The one the other will contain
With ease—and You—beside—

The Brain is deeper than the sea—
For—hold them—Blue to Blue—
The one the other will absorb—
As Sponges—Buckets—do—

The Brain is just the weight of God—
For—Heft them—Pound for Pound—
And they will differ—if they do—   11
As Syllable from Sound—

640

I cannot live with You—
It would be Life—
And Life is over there—
Behind the Shelf

The Sexton keeps the Key to—
Putting up

Our Life—His Porcelain—
Like a Cup—

Discarded of the Housewife—
Quaint—or Broke—   10
A newer Sevres pleases—
Old Ones crack—

I could not die—with You—
For One must wait
To shut the Other's Gaze down—
You—could not—

And I—Could I stand by
And see You—freeze—
Without my Right of Frost—
Death's privilege?   20

Nor could I rise—with You—
Because Your Face
Would put out Jesus'—
That New Grace

Glow plain—and foreign
On my homesick Eye—
Except that You than He
Shone closer by—

They'd judge Us—How—
For You—served Heaven—You know,
Or sought to—   31
I could not—

Because You saturated Sight—
And I had no more Eyes
For sordid excellence
As Paradise

And were You lost, I would be—
Though My Name
Rang loudest
On the Heavenly fame—   40

And were You—saved—
And I—condemned to be
Where You were not—
That self—were Hell to Me—

So We must meet apart
You there—I—here—
With just the Door ajar
That Oceans are—and Prayer—
And that White Sustenance—
Despair—   50

701

A Thought went up my mind today—
That I have had before—
But did not finish—some way back—
I could not fix the Year—

Nor where it went—nor why it came
The second time to me—
Nor definitely, what it was—
Have I the Art to say—

But somewhere—in my Soul—I know—
I've met the Thing before—   10
It just reminded me—'twas all—
And came my way no more—

712

Because I could not stop for Death—
He kindly stopped for me—
The Carriage held but just Ourselves—
And Immortality.

We slowly drove—He knew no haste
And I had put away
My labor and my leisure too,
For His Civility—

We passed the School, where Children strove
At Recess—in the Ring—   10
We passed the Fields of Gazing Grain—
We passed the Setting Sun—

Or rather—He passed Us—
The Dews drew quivering and chill—
For only Gossamer, my Gown—
My Tippet—only Tulle—

We paused before a House that seemed
A Swelling of the Ground—
The Roof was scarcely visible—
The Cornice—in the Ground—   20

Since then—'tis Centuries—and yet
Feels shorter than the Day
I first surmised the Horses' Heads
Were toward Eternity—

739

I many times thought Peace had come
When Peace was far away—
As Wrecked Men—deem they sight the
    Land—
At Centre of the Sea—

And struggle slacker—but to prove
As hopelessly as I—
How many the fictitious Shores—
Or any Harbor be—

1100

The last Night that She lived
It was a Common Night
Except the Dying—this to Us
Made Nature different

We noticed smallest things—
Things overlooked before
By this great light upon our Minds
Italicized—as 'twere.

As We went out and in
Between Her final Room   10
And Rooms where Those to be alive
Tomorrow were, a Blame

That Others could exist
While She must finish quite
A Jealousy for Her arose
So nearly infinite—

We waited while She passed—
It was a narrow time—
Too jostled were Our Souls to speak
At length the notice came.   20

She mentioned, and forgot—
Then lightly as a Reed
Bent to the Water, struggled scarce—
Consented, and was dead—

And We—We placed the Hair—
And drew the Head erect—
And then an awful leisure was
Belief to regulate—

1176

We never know how high we are
Till we are asked to rise
And then if we are true to plan
Our statures touch the skies—

The Heroism we recite
Would be a normal thing
Did not ourselves the Cubits warp
For fear to be a King—

1207

He preached upon "Breadth" till it ar-
    gued him narrow—
The Broad are too broad to define
And of "Truth" until it proclaimed him a
    Liar—
The Truth never flaunted a Sign—

Simplicity fled from his counterfeit pres-
    ence
As Gold the Pyrites would shun—
What confusion would cover the innocent
    Jesus
To meet so enabled a Man!

1463

A Route of Evanescence
With a revolving Wheel—
A Resonance of Emerald—
A Rush of Cochineal—
And every Blossom on the Bush
Adjusts its tumbled Head—
The mail from Tunis, probably,
An easy Morning's Ride—

1510

How happy is the little Stone
That rambles in the Road alone,

And doesn't care about Careers
And Exigencies never fears—
Whose Coat of elemental Brown
A passing Universe put on,
And independent as the Sun
Associates or glows alone,
Fulfilling absolute Decree
In casual simplicity—   10

Sidney Lanier
❋ 1842–1881

Song of the Chattahoochee

Out of the hills of Habersham,
    Down the valleys of Hall,
I hurry amain to reach the plain,
Run the rapid and leap the fall,
Split at the rock and together again,
Accept my bed, or narrow or wide,
And flee from folly on every side
With a lover's pain to attain the plain
        Far from the hills of Habersham,
        Far from the valleys of Hall.   10

All down the hills of Habersham,
    All through the valleys of Hall,
The rushes cried *Abide, abide,*
The willful waterweeds held me thrall,
The laving laurel turned my tide,
The ferns and the fondling grass said
    Stay,
The dewberry dipped for to work delay,
And the little reeds sighed *Abide, abide,*
    Here in the hills of Habersham,
    Here in the valleys of Hall.   20

High o'er the hills of Habersham,
    Veiling the valleys of Hall,
The hickory told me manifold
Fair tales of shade, the poplar tall
Wrought me her shadowy self to hold,
The chestnut, the oak, the walnut, the
    pine,

Overleaning, with flickering meaning and
    sign,
Said, *Pass not, so cold, these manifold*
    Deep shades of the hills of Haber-
      sham,   29
    These glades in the valleys of Hall.

And oft in the hills of Habersham,
And oft in the valleys of Hall,
The white quartz shone, and the smooth
    brook-stone
Did bar me of passage with friendly
    brawl,
And many a luminous jewel lone
—Crystals clear or a-cloud with mist,
Ruby, garnet and amethyst—
Made lures with the lights of streaming
    stone
    In the clefts of the hills of Haber-
      sham,   39
    In the beds of the valleys of Hall.

But oh, not the hills of Habersham,
And oh, not the valleys of Hall
Avail: I am fain for to water the plain.
Downward the voices of Duty call—
Downward, to toil and be mixed with the
    main,
The dry fields burn, and the mills are to
    turn,
And a myriad flowers mortally yearn,
And the lordly main from beyond the
    plain   48
    Calls o'er the hills of Habersham,
    Calls through the valleys of Hall.

The Stirrup-Cup

Death, thou'rt a cordial old and rare:
Look how compounded, with what care!
Time got his wrinkles reaping thee
Sweet herbs from all antiquity.

David to thy distillage went,
Keats, and Gotama excellent,
Omar Khayyàm, and Chaucer bright,
And Shakespeare for a king-delight.

These were to sweeten thee with song;
The blood of heroes made thee strong.
What heroes! Ah, for shame, for shame!
The worthiest died without a name.   12

Then, Time, let not a drop be spilt:
Hand me the cup whene'er thou wilt;
'Tis thy rich stirrup-cup to me;
I'll drink it down right smilingly.

From the Flats

What heartache—ne'er a hill!
Inexorable, vapid, vague and chill
The drear sand-levels drain my spirit low.
With one poor word they tell me all they
    know;
Whereat their stupid tongues, to tease my
    pain,
Do draw it o'er again and o'er again.
They hurt my heart with griefs I cannot
    name:
    Always the same, the same.

Nature hath no surprise,
No ambuscade of beauty 'gainst mine
    eyes   10
From brake or lurking dell or deep defile;
No humors, frolic forms—this mile, that
    mile;
No rich reserves or happy-valley hopes
Beyond the bend of roads, the distant
    slopes.
Her fancy fails, her wild is all run tame:
    Ever the same, the same.

Oh might I through these tears
But glimpse some hill my Georgia high
    uprears,
Where white the quartz and pink the
    pebble shine,
The hickory heavenward strives, the
    muscadine   20
Swings o'er the slope, the oak's far-falling
    shade
Darkens the dogwood in the bottom-
    glade,
And down the hollow from a ferny nook
    Bright leaps a living brook!

The Crystal

At midnight, death's and truth's unlock-
ing-time,
When far within the spirit's hearing rolls
The great soft rumble of the course of
things—
A bulk of silence in a mask of sound—
When darkness clears our vision that by
day
Is sun-blind, and the soul's a ravening
owl
For truth and flitteth here and there
about
Low-lying woody tracts of time, and oft
Is minded for to sit upon a bough,
Dry-dead and sharp, of some long-
stricken tree   10
And muse in that gaunt place—'twas
then my heart,
Deep in the meditative dark, cried out:
  "Ye companies of governor-spirits
grave,
Bards, and old bringers-down of flaming
news
From steep-walled heavens, holy malcon-
tents,
Sweet seers, and stellar visionaries, all
That brood about the skies of poesy,
Full bright ye shine, insuperable stars;
Yet, if a man look hard upon you, none
With total luster blazeth, no, not one   20
But hath some heinous freckle of the flesh
Upon his shining cheek, not one but
winks
His ray, opaqued with intermittent mist
Of defect; yea, you masters all must ask
Some sweet forgiveness, which we leap to
give,
We lovers of you, heavenly-glad to meet
Your largesse so with love, and interplight
Your geniuses with our mortalities.

  Thus unto thee, O sweetest Shake-
speare sole,
A hundred hurts a day I do forgive   30
('Tis little, but, enchantment! 'tis for
thee):

Small curious quibble; Juliet's prurient
pun
In the poor, pale face of Romeo's fancied
death;
Cold rant of Richard; Henry's fustian roar
Which frights away that sleep he invo-
cates;
Wronged Valentine's unnatural haste to
yield;
Too-silly shifts of maids that mask as men
In faint disguises that could ne'er dis-
guise—
Viola, Julia, Portia, Rosalind;
Fatigues most drear, and needless over-
tax   40
Of speech obscure that had as lief be
plain;
Last I forgive (with more delight, be-
cause
'Tis more to do) the labored-lewd dis-
course
That e'en thy young invention's youngest
heir
Besmirched the world with.

                Father Homer! thee,
Thee also I forgive thy sandy wastes
Of prose and catalogue, thy drear ha-
rangues
That tease the patience of the centuries;
Thy sleazy scrap of story—but a rogue's
Rape of a light-o'-love—too soiled a patch
To broider with the gods.   51

                Thee, Socrates,
Thou dear and very strong one, I forgive
Thy year-worn cloak, thine iron strin-
gencies
That were but dandy upside-down, thy
words
Of truth that, mildlier spoke had mainlier
wrought.

So, Buddha, beautiful! I pardon thee
That all the All thou hadst for needy man
Was Nothing, and thy Best of being was
But not to be.

                Worn Dante, I forgive
The implacable hates that in thy horrid
hells   60

Or burn or freeze thy fellows, never
  loosed
By death, nor time, nor love.

                        And I forgive
Thee, Milton, those thy comic-dreadful
  wars
Where, armed with gross and inconclu-
  sive steel,
Immortals smite immortals mortalwise
And fill all heaven with folly.

                        Also thee,
Brave Aeschylus, thee I forgive, for that
Thine eye, by bare bright justice basil-
  isked,
Turned not, nor ever learned to look
  where Love
Stands shining.

          So, unto thee, Lucretius mine   70
(For oh! what heart hath loved thee like
  to this
That's now complaining?), freely I for-
  give
Thy logic poor, thine error rich, thine
  earth
Whose graves eat souls and all.

                        Yea, all you hearts
Of beauty, and sweet righteous lovers
  large:
Aurelius fine, oft superfine; mild Saint
à Kempis, overmild; Epictetus,
Whiles low in thought, still with old
  slavery tinct;
Rapt Behmen, rapt too far; high Sweden-
  borg,
O'ertoppling; Langley, that with but a
  touch   80
Of art hadst sung Piers Plowman to the
  top
Of English songs, whereof 'tis dearest
  now
And most adorable; Caedmon, in the
  morn
A-calling angels with the cow-herd's call
That late brought up the cattle; Emerson,
Most wise, that yet, in finding Wisdom,
  lost

Thy Self, sometimes; tense Keats, with
  angel's nerves
Where men's were better; Tennyson,
  largest voice
Since Milton, yet some register of wit
Wanting;—all, all, I pardon, ere 'tis
  asked,   90
Your more or less, your little mole that
  marks
You brother and your kinship seals to
  man.

  But Thee, but Thee, O sovereign Seer
    of time,
But Thee, O poet's Poet, Wisdom's
    Tongue,
But Thee, O man's best Man, O love's
    best Love,
O perfect life in perfect labor writ,
O all men's Comrade, Servant, King, or
    Priest,—
What *if* or *yet*, what mole, what flaw,
    what lapse,
What least defect or shadow of defect,
What rumor tattled by an enemy,   100
Of inference loose, what lack of grace,
Even in torture's grasp, or sleep's, or
    death's—
Oh, what amiss may I forgive in Thee,
Jesus, good Paragon, thou Crystal
    Christ?"

A Ballad of Trees and
The Master

Into the woods my Master went,
Clean forspent, forspent.
Into the woods my Master came,
Forspent with love and shame.
But the olives they were not blind to Him,
The little gray leaves were kind to Him:
The thorn-tree had a mind to Him
When into the woods He came.

Out of the woods my Master went,
And he was well content.   10
Out of the woods my Master came,

Content with death and shame.
When Death and Shame would woo Him
last,
From under the trees they drew Him last:
'Twas on a tree they slew Him—last
When out of the woods He came.

John Banister Tabb

✳ 1845–1909

Nekros

DURING MY FATHER'S LAST ILLNESS

Lo! all thy glory gone!
God's masterpiece undone!
The last created and the first to fall;
The noblest, frailest, godliest of all.

Death seems the conqueror now,
And yet his victor thou;
The fatal shaft, its venom quenched in
thee,
A mortal raised to immortality.

Child of the humble sod,
Wed with the breath of God,   10
Descend! for with the lowest thou must
lie—
Arise! thou hast inherited the sky.

Keats

THOU MOST ADORABLE OF POETS

Upon thy tomb 'tis graven, "Here lies one
Whose name is writ in water." Could
there be
A flight of fancy fitlier feigned for thee,
A fairer motto for her favorite son?
For, as the wave, thy varying numbers
run—
Now crested proud in tidal majesty,

Now tranquil as the twilight reverie
Of some dim lake the white moon looks
upon
While teems the world with silence. Even
there,   9
In each protean rainbow-tint that stains
The breathing canvas of the atmosphere,
We read an exhalation of thy strains.
Thus on the scroll of nature everywhere
Thy name, a deathless syllable, remains.

Shakespeare's Mourners

I saw the grave of Shakespeare in a
dream,
And round about it grouped a wondrous
throng,
His own majestic mourners, who belong
Forever to the Stage of Life, and seem
The rivals of reality. Supreme
Stood Hamlet, as erewhile the graves
among,
Mantled in thought; and sad Ophelia
sung
The same swan-dirge she chanted in the
stream.
Othello, dark in destiny's eclipse,   9
Laid on the tomb a lily. Near him wept
Dejected Constance. Fair Cordelia's lips
Moved prayerfully the while her father
slept,
And each and all, inspired of vital breath,
Kept vigil o'er the sacred spoils of death.

To a Photograph

O tender shade!
Lone captive of enamoured light,
That from an angel visage bright
A glance betrayed.

Dost thou not sigh
To wander from thy prison-place?
To seek again the vanished face,
Or else, to die?

A shadow like thee,
Dim Eidolon—a dream disproved—   10
A memory of light removed,
    Behold in me!

Father Damien

O God, the cleanest offering
    Of tainted earth below,
Unblushing to Thy feet we bring—
    "*A leper white as snow!*"

At Lanier's Grave

I stand beside a comrade tree
That guards the spot where thou art laid;
For since thy light is lost to me
    I loiter in the shade.
I lean upon the rugged stone
As on the breast from whence I came,
To learn 'tis not my heart alone
    That bears thy sacred name.

The Lake

OUR QUONDAM LAKE—WRITTEN ONE
SATURDAY AFTERNOON WHILE
KEEPING FIVE O'CLOCK STUDY.

I am a lonely woodland lake;
    The trees that round me grow,
The glimpse of heaven above me, make
    The sum of all I know.

The mirror of their dreams to be
    Alike in shade and shine,
To clasp in love's captivity,
    And keep them one—is mine.

Evolution

Out of the dusk a shadow
    Then a spark;

Out of the cloud a silence,
    Then a lark;
Out of the heart a rapture,
    Then a pain;
Out of the dead, cold ashes,
    Life again.

The Precipice

Above the unfathomed deep
Of Death we move in sleep,
And who among us knows
How near the brink he goes?

The Old Pastor

How long, O Lord, to wait
Beside this open gate?
My sheep with many a lamb
Have entered, and I am
Alone, and it is late.

Edgar Lee Masters
✱ 1868–1950

Fiddler Jones

The earth keeps some vibration going
There in your heart, and that is you.
And if the people find you can fiddle,
Why, fiddle you must, for all your life.
What do you see, a harvest of clover?
Or a meadow to walk through to the
    river?
The wind's in the corn; you rub your
    hands
For beeves hereafter ready for market;
Or else you hear the rustle of skirts
Like the girls when dancing at Little
    Grove.   10

To Cooney Potter a pillar of dust
Or whirling leaves meant ruinous drouth;
They looked to me like Red-Head Sammy
Stepping it off, to 'Toor-a-Loor.'
How could I till my forty acres
Not to speak of getting more,
With a medley of horns, bassoons and
    piccolos
Stirred in my brain by crows and robins
And the creek of a wind-mill—only
    these?
And I never started to plow in my
    life   20
That some one did not stop in the road
And take me away to a dance or picnic.
I ended up with forty acres;
I ended up with a broken fiddle—
And a broken laugh, and a thousand
    memories,
And not a single regret.

The Village Atheist

Ye young debaters over the doctrine
Of the soul's immortality,
I who lie here was the village atheist,
Talkative, contentious, versed in the
    arguments
Of the infidels.
But through a long sickness
Coughing myself to death
I read the *Upanishads* and the poetry of
    Jesus.
And they lighted a torch of hope and in-
    tuition
And desire which the Shadow,   10
Leading me swiftly through the caverns
    of darkness,
Could not extinguish.
Listen to me, ye who live in the senses
And think through the senses only:
Immortality is not a gift,
Immortality is an achievement;
And only those who strive mightily
Shall possess it.

Carl Hamblin

The press of the Spoon River *Clarion* was
    wrecked,
And I was tarred and feathered,
For publishing this on the day the An-
    archists were hanged in Chicago:
"I saw a beautiful woman with bandaged
    eyes
Standing on the steps of a marble temple.
Great multitudes passed in front of her,
Lifting their faces to her imploringly.
In her left hand she held a sword.
She was brandishing the sword,
Sometimes striking a child, again a la-
    borer,   10
Again a slinking woman, again a lunatic.
In her right hand she held a scale;
Into the scale pieces of gold were tossed
By those who dodged the strokes of the
    sword.
A man in a black gown read from a
    manuscript:
'She is no respecter of persons.'
Then a youth wearing a red cap
Leaped to her side and snatched away
    the bandage.
And lo, the lashes had been eaten away
From the oozy eye-lids;   20
The eye-balls were seared with a milky
    mucus;
The madness of a dying soul
Was written on her face—
But the multitude saw why she wore the
    bandage."

Anne Rutledge

Out of me unworthy and unknown
The vibrations of deathless music;
"With malice toward none, with charity
    for all."
Out of me the forgiveness of millions to-
    ward millions,
And the beneficent face of a nation

Shining with justice and truth.
I am Anne Rutledge who sleep beneath
    these weeds,
Beloved in life of Abraham Lincoln,
Wedded to him, not through union,
But through separation.   10
Bloom forever, O Republic,
From the dust of my bosom!

The Hill

Where are Elmer, Herman, Bert, Tom
    and Charley,
The weak of will, the strong of arm, the
    clown, the boozer, the fighter?
All, all, are sleeping on the hill.

One passed in a fever,
One was burned in a mine,
One was killed in a brawl,
One died in a jail,
One fell from a bridge toiling for chil-
    dren and wife—
All, all are sleeping, sleeping, sleeping on
    the hill.

Where are Ella, Kate, Mag, Lizzie and
    Edith,   10
The tender heart, the simple soul, the
    loud, the proud, the happy one?—
All, all, are sleeping on the hill.

One died in shameful child-birth,
One of a thwarted love,
One at the hands of a brute in a brothel,
One of a broken pride, in the search for
    heart's desire,
One after life in far-away London and
    Paris
Was brought to her little space by Ella
    and Kate and Mag—
All, all are sleeping, sleeping, sleeping on
    the hill.

Where are Uncle Isaac and Aunt Emily,
And old Towny Kincaid and Sevigne
    Houghton,   21
And Major Walker who had talked

With venerable men of the revolution?—
All, all, are sleeping on the hill.

They brought them dead sons from the
    war,
And daughters whom life had crushed,
And their children fatherless, crying—
All, all are sleeping, sleeping, sleeping on
    the hill.

Where is Old Fiddler Jones
Who played with life all his ninety years,
Braving the sleet with bared breast,   31
Drinking, rioting, thinking neither of wife
    nor kin,
Nor gold, nor love, nor heaven?
Lo! he babbles of the fish-frys of long
    ago,
Of the horse-races of long ago at Clary's
    Grove,
Of what Abe Lincoln said
One time at Springfield.

Henry C. Calhoun

I reached the highest place in Spoon
    River,
But through what bitterness of spirit!
The face of my father, sitting speechless,
Childlike, watching his canaries,
And looking at the court-house window
Of the county judge's room,
And his admonitions to me to seek
My own in life, and punish Spoon River
To avenge the wrong the people did him,
Filled me with furious energy   10
To seek for wealth and seek for power.
But what did he do but send me along
The path that leads to the grove of the
    Furies?
I followed the path and I tell you this:
On the way to the grove you'll pass the
    Fates,
Shadow-eyed, bent over their weaving.
Stop for a moment, and if you see
The thread of revenge leap out of the
    shuttle,
Then quickly snatch from Atropos

The shears and cut it, lest your sons,   20
And the children of them and their children
Wear the envenomed robe.

Edwin Arlington Robinson

❋ 1869–1935

Luke Havergal

Go to the western gate, Luke Havergal,
There where the vines cling crimson on
    the wall,
And in the twilight wait for what will
    come.
The leaves will whisper there of her, and
    some,
Like flying words, will strike you as they
    fall;
But go, and if you listen she will call.
Go to the western gate, Luke Havergal—
Luke Havergal.

No, there is not a dawn in eastern skies
To rift the fiery night that's in your eyes;
But there, where western glooms are
    gathering,   11
The dark will end the dark, if anything:
God slays Himself with every leaf that
    flies,
And hell is more than half of paradise.
No, there is not a dawn in eastern skies—
In eastern skies.

Out of a grave I come to tell you this,
Out of a grave I come to quench the kiss
That flames upon your forehead with a
    glow
That blinds you to the way that you must
    go.   20
Yes, there is yet one way to where she is,
Bitter, but one that faith may never miss.

Out of a grave I come to tell you this—
To tell you this.

There is the western gate, Luke Haver-
    gal,
There are the crimson leaves upon the
    wall.
Go, for the winds are tearing them
    away,—
Nor think to riddle the dead words they
    say,
Nor any more to feel them as they fall;
But go, and if you trust her she will call.
There is the western gate, Luke Haver-
    gal—   31
Luke Havergal.

The Master *

A flying word from here and there
Had sown the name at which we sneered,
But soon the name was everywhere,
To be reviled and then revered:
A presence to be loved and feared,
We cannot hide it, or deny
That we, the gentlemen who jeered,
May be forgotten by and by.

He came when days were perilous
And hearts of men were sore beguiled;
And having made his note of us,   11
He pondered and was reconciled.
Was ever master yet so mild
As he, and so untamable?
We doubted, even when he smiled,
Not knowing what he knew so well.

He knew the undeceiving fate
Would shame us whom he served un-
    sought;
He knew that he must wince and wait—
The jest of those for whom he fought;
He knew devoutly what he thought   21
Of us and of our ridicule;
He knew that we must all be taught
Like little children in a school.

* Supposed to have been written not long
after the Civil War.

We gave a glamour to the task
That he encountered and saw through,
But little of us did he ask,
And little did we ever do.
And what appears if we review
The season when we railed and chaffed?
It is the face of one who knew   31
That we were learning while we laughed.

The face that in our vision feels
Again the venom that we flung,
Transfigured to the world reveals
The vigilance to which we clung.
Shrewd, hallowed, harassed, and among
The mysteries that are untold,
The face we see was never young
Nor could it wholly have been old.   40

For he, to whom we had applied
Our shopman's test of age and worth,
Was elemental when he died,
As he was ancient at his birth:
The saddest among kings of earth,
Bowed with a galling crown, this man
Met rancor with a cryptic mirth,
Laconic—and Olympian.

The love, the grandeur, and the fame
Are bounded by the world alone;   50
The calm, the smouldering, and the flame
Of awful patience were his own:
With him they are forever flown
Past all our found self-shadowings,
Wherewith we cumber the Unknown
As with inept, Icarian wings.

For we were not as other men:
'Twas ours to soar and his to see;
But we are coming down again,
And we shall come down pleasantly;   60
Nor shall we longer disagree
On what it is to be sublime,
But flourish in our perigee
And have one Titan at a time.

Richard Cory

Whenever Richard Cory went down
        town,

We people on the pavement looked at
        him:
He was a gentleman from sole to crown,
Clean favored, and imperially slim.

And he was always quietly arrayed,
And he was always human when he
        talked;
But still he fluttered pulses when he said,
"Good-morning," and he glittered when
        he walked.

And he was rich—yes, richer than a
        king—
And admirably schooled in every grace:
In fine, we thought that he was every-
        thing   11
To make us wish that we were in his
        place.

So on we worked, and waited for the
        light,
And went without the meat, and cursed
        the bread;
And Richard Cory, one calm summer
        night,
Went home and put a bullet through his
        head.

Cliff Klingenhagen

Cliff Klingenhagen had me in to dine
With him one day; and after soup and
        meat,
And all the other things there were to
        eat,
Cliff took two glasses and filled one with
        wine
And one with wormwood. Then, without
        a sign
For me to choose at all, he took the
        draught
Of bitterness himself, and lightly quaffed
It off, and said the other one was mine.
And when I asked him what the deuce
        he meant
By doing that, he only looked at me   10

And grinned, and said it was a way of
  his.
And though I know the fellow, I have
  spent   ·
Long time a-wondering when I shall be
As happy as Cliff Klingenhagen is.

Reuben Bright

Because he was a butcher and thereby
Did earn an honest living (and did right)
I would not have you think that Reuben
  Bright
Was any more a brute than you or I;
For when they told him that his wife
  must die,
He stared at them, and shook with grief
  and fright,
And cried like a great baby half that
  night,
And made the women cry to see him cry.

And after she was dead, and he had paid
The singers and the sexton and the rest,
He packed a lot of things that she had
  made   11
Most mournfully away in an old chest
Of hers, and put some chopped-up cedar
  boughs
In with them, and tore down the slaugh-
  ter-house.

How Annandale Went Out

"They called it Annandale—and I was
  there
To flourish, to find words, and to attend:
Liar, physician, hypocrite, and friend,
I watched him; and the sight was not so
  fair
As one or two that I have seen else-
  where:
An apparatus not for me to mend—
A wreck, with hell between him and the
  end,
Remained of Annandale; and I was there.

"I knew the ruin as I knew the man;
So put the two together, if you can,   10
Remembering the worst you know of me.
Now view yourself as I was, on the
  spot—
With a slight kind of engine. Do you see?
Like this . . . You wouldn't hang me?
  I thought not."

Mr. Flood's Party

Old Eben Flood, climbing alone one
  night
Over the hill between the town below
And the forsaken upland hermitage
That held as much as he should ever
  know
On earth again of home, paused warily.
The road was his with not a native near;
And Eben, having leisure, said aloud;
For no man else in Tilbury Town to hear:

"Well, Mr. Flood, we have the harvest
  moon
Again, and we may not have many
  more;   10
The bird is on the wing, the poet says,
And you and I have said it here before.
Drink to the bird." He raised up to the
  light
The jug that he had gone so far to fill,
And answered huskily: "Well, Mr. Flood,
Since you propose it, I believe I will."

Alone, as if enduring to the end
A valiant armor of scarred hopes out-
  worn,
He stood there in the middle of the road
Like Roland's ghost winding a silent
  horn.   20
Below him, in the town among the trees,
Where friends of other days had honored
  him,
A phantom salutation of the dead
Rang thinly till old Eben's eyes were dim.

Then, as a mother lays her sleeping child
Down tenderly, fearing it may awake,
He set the jug down slowly at his feet

With trembling care, knowing that most
  things break;
And only when assured that on firm
  earth
It stood, as the uncertain lives of men
Assuredly did not, he paced away,   31
And with his hand extended paused
  again:

"Well, Mr. Flood, we have not met like
  this
In a long time; and many a change has
  come
To both of us, I fear, since last it was
We had a drop together. Welcome
  home!"
Convivially returning with himself,
Again he raised the jug up to the light;
And with an acquiescent quaver said:
"Well, Mr. Flood, if you insist, I might.

"Only a very little, Mr. Flood—   41
For auld lang syne. No more, sir; that
  will do."
So, for the time, apparently it did,
And Eben evidently thought so too;
For soon amid the silver loneliness
Of night he lifted up his voice and sang,
Secure, with only two moons listening,
Until the whole harmonious landscape
  rang—

"For auld lang syne." The weary throat
  gave out,
The last word wavered; and the song
  being done,   50
He raised again the jug regretfully
And shook his head, and was again alone.
There was not much that was ahead of
  him,
And there was nothing in the town be-
  low—
Where strangers would have shut the
  many doors
That many friends had opened long ago.

Walt Whitman

The master-songs are ended, and the man
That sang them is a name. And so is God

A name; and so is love, and life, and
  death,
And everything. But we, who are too
  blind
To read what we have written, or what
  faith
Has written for us, do not understand:
We only blink, and wonder.

Last night it was the song that was the
  man,
But now it is the man that is the song.   9
We do not hear him very much to-day:
His piercing and eternal cadence rings
Too pure for us—too powerfully pure,
Too lovingly triumphant, and too large;
But there are some that hear him, and
  they know
That he shall sing to-morrow for all men,
And that all time shall listen.

The master-songs are ended? Rather say
No songs are ended that are ever sung,
And that no names are dead names.
  When we write
Men's letters on proud marble or on sand,
We write them there forever.   21

The Mill

The miller's wife had waited long,
  The tea was cold, the fire was dead;
And there might yet be nothing wrong
  In how he went and what he said:
"There are no millers any more,"
  Was all that she had heard him say;
And he had lingered at the door
  So long that it seemed yesterday.

Sick with a fear that had no form
  She knew that she was there at last;
And in the mill there was a warm   11
  And mealy fragrance of the past.
What else there was would only seem
  To say again what he had meant;
And what was hanging from a beam
  Would not have heeded where she
    went.

And if she thought it followed her,
  She may have reasoned in the dark

That one way of the few there were
    Would hide her and would leave no
      mark: 20
Black water, smooth above the weir
    Like starry velvet in the night,
Though ruffled once, would soon appear
    The same as ever to the sight.

New England

Here where the wind is always north-
    north-east
And children learn to walk on frozen
    toes,
Wonder begets an envy of all those
Who boil elsewhere with such a lyric
    yeast
Of love that you will hear them at a feast
Where demons would appeal for some
    repose,
Still clamoring where the chalice over-
    flows
And crying wildest who have drunk the
    least.

Passion is here a soilure of the wits,
We're told, and Love a cross for them to
    bear;   10
Joy shivers in the corner where she knits
And Conscience always has the rocking-
    chair,
Cheerful as when she tortured into fits
The first cat that was ever killed by Care.

Stephen Crane
✳ 1871–1900

I Stood upon a High Place

I stood upon a high place,
And saw, below, many devils
Running, leaping,
And carousing in sin.

One looked up, grinning,
And said, "Comrade! Brother!"

A Man Saw a Ball of Gold in the Sky

A man saw a ball of gold in the sky;
He climbed for it,
And eventually he achieved it—
It was clay.

Now this is the strange part:
When the man went to the earth
And looked again,
Lo, there was the ball of gold.
Now this is the strange part:
It was a ball of gold.   10
Ay, by the heavens, it was a ball of gold.

It Was Wrong to Do This, Said the Angel

"It was wrong to do this," said the angel.
"You should live like a flower,
Holding malice like a puppy,
Waging war like a lambkin."

"Not so," quoth the man
Who had no fear of spirits;
"It is only wrong for angels
Who can live like flowers,
Holding malice like the puppies,
Waging war like the lambkins."   10

I Explain

I explain the silvered passing of a ship at
    night,
The sweep of each sad lost wave,
The dwindling boom of the steel thing's
    striving,
The little cry of a man to a man,
A shadow falling across the grayer night,
And the sinking of the small star;

Then the waste, the far waste of waters,
And the soft lashing of black waves
For long and in loneliness.

Remember, thou, O ship of love,   10
Thou leavest a far waste of waters,
And the soft lashing of black waves
For long and in loneliness.

The Black Riders

Black riders came from the sea.
There was clang and clang of spear and
    shield,
And clash and clash of hoof and heel,
Wild shouts and the wave of hair
In the rush upon the wind:
Thus the ride of sin.

The Blades of Grass

In Heaven,
Some little blades of grass
Stood before God.
"What did you do?"
Then all save one of the little blades
Began eagerly to relate
The merits of their lives.
This one stayed a small way behind,
Ashamed.
Presently, God said,   10
"And what did you do?"
The little blade answered, "Oh, my Lord,
Memory is bitter to me,
For, if I did good deeds,
I know not of them."
Then God, in all his splendor,
Arose from his throne.
"Oh, best little blade of grass!" he said.

A Newspaper

A newspaper is a collection of half-
    injustices
Which, bawled by boys from mile to
    mile,
Spreads its curious opinion
To a million merciful and sneering men,
While families cuddle the joys of the fire-
    side
When spurred by tale of dire love agony.
A newspaper is a court
Where everyone is kindly and unfairly
    tried
By a squalor of honest men.

A newspaper is a market   10
Where wisdom sells its freedom
And melons are crowned by the crowd.
A newspaper is a game
Where his error scores the player victory
While another's skill wins death.
A newspaper is a symbol;
It is fetless life's chronicle,
A collection of loud tales
Concentrating eternal stupidities,
That in remote ages lived unhaltered,
Roaming through a fenceless world.   21

The Peaks

In the night
Gray, heavy clouds muffled the valleys,
And the peaks looked toward God alone.
    "O Master, that movest the wind
        with a finger,
    Humble, idle, futile peaks are we.
    Grant that we may run swiftly
        across the world
    To huddle in worship at Thy feet."

In the morning
A noise of men at work came the clear
    blue miles,
And the little black cities were apparent.
    "O Master, that knowest the mean-
        ing of raindrops,   11
    Humble, idle, futile peaks are we.
    Give voice to us, we pray, O Lord,
    That we may sing Thy goodness to
        the sun."

In the evening
The far valleys were sprinkled with tiny
    lights.
  "O Master,
    Thou that knowest the value of
    kings and birds,
    Thou hast made us humble, idle,
    futile peaks.
    Thou only needest eternal patience;
    We bow to Thy wisdom, O Lord—
    Humble, idle, futile peaks."   22

In the night
Gray, heavy clouds muffled the valleys,
And the peaks looked toward God alone.

A Slant of Sun

A slant of sun on dull brown walls,
A forgotten sky of bashful blue.

Toward God a mighty hymn,
A song of collisions and cries,
Rumbling wheels, hoof-beats, bells,
Welcomes, farewells, love-calls, final
    moans,
Voices of joy, idiocy, warning, despair,
The unknown appeals of brutes,
The chanting of flowers,
The screams of cut trees,   10
The senseless babble of hens and wise
    men—
A cluttered incoherency that says at the
    stars:
"O God, save us!"

Robert Frost

✳ 1874–

Mending Wall

Something there is that doesn't love a
    wall,

That sends the frozen-ground-swell un-
    der it,
And spills the upper boulders in the sun;
And makes gaps even two can pass
    abreast.
The work of hunters is another thing:
I have come after them and made repair
Where they have left not one stone on a
    stone,
But they would have the rabbit out of
    hiding,
To please the yelping dogs. The gaps I
    mean,
No one has seen them made or heard
    them made,   10
But at spring mending-time we find them
    there.
I let my neighbor know beyond the hill;
And on a day we meet to walk the line
And set the wall between us once again.
We keep the wall between us as we go.
To each the boulders that have fallen to
    each.
And some are loaves and some so nearly
    balls
We have to use a spell to make them
    balance:
"Stay where you are until our backs are
    turned!"
We wear our fingers rough with handling
    them.   20
Oh, just another kind of outdoor game,
One on a side. It comes to little more:
There where it is we do not need the
    wall:
He is all pine and I am apple orchard.
My apple trees will never get across
And eat the cones under his pines, I tell
    him.
He only says, "Good fences make good
    neighbors."
Spring is the mischief in me, and I won-
    der
If I could put a notion in his head:
"*Why* do they make good neighbors?
    Isn't it   30
Where there are cows? But here there are
    no cows.
Before I built a wall I'd ask to know

What I was walling in or walling out,
And to whom I was like to give offense.
Something there is that doesn't love a
wall,
That wants it down!" I could say "elves"
to him,
But it's not elves exactly, and I'd rather
He said it for himself. I see him there,
Bringing a stone grasped firmly by the
top
In each hand, like an old-stone savage
armed.   40
He moves in darkness, as it seems to me,
Not of woods only and the shade of trees.
He will not go behind his father's saying,
And he likes having thought of it so well
He says again, "Good fences make good
neighbors."

The Wood-Pile

Out walking in the frozen swamp one
gray day,
I paused and said, 'I will turn back from
here.
No, I will go on farther—and we shall
see.'
The hard snow held me, save where now
and then
One foot went through. The view was all
in lines
Straight up and down of tall slim trees
Too much alike to mark or name a place
by
So as to say for certain I was here
Or somewhere else: I was just far from
home.
A small bird flew before me. He was care-
ful   10
To put a tree between us when he
lighted,
And say no word to tell me who he was
Who was so foolish as to think what *he*
thought.
He thought that I was after him for a
feather—
The white one in his tail; like one who
takes

Everything said as personal to himself.
One flight out sideways would have un-
deceived him.
And then there was a pile of wood for
which
I forgot him and let his little fear
Carry him off the way I might have
gone,   20
Without so much as wishing him good-
night.
He went behind it to make his last stand.
It was a cord of maple, cut and split
And piled—and measured, four by four
by eight.
And not another like it could I see.
No runner tracks in this year's snow
looped near it.
And it was older sure than this year's cut-
ting,
Or even last year's or the year's before.
The wood was grey and the bark warp-
ing off it
And the pile somewhat sunken. Clematis
Had wound strings round and round it
like a bundle.   31
What held it though on one side was a
tree
Still growing, and on one a stake and
prop,
These latter about to fall. I thought that
only
Someone who lived in turning to fresh
tasks
Could so forget his handiwork on which
He spent himself, the labour of his ax,
And leave it there far from a useful fire-
place
To warm the frozen swamp as best it
could
With the slow smokeless burning of de-
cay.   40

After Apple-Picking

My long two-pointed ladder's sticking
through a tree
Toward heaven still,
And there's a barrel that I didn't fill

Beside it, and there may be two or three
Apples I didn't pick upon some bough.
But I am done with apple-picking now.
Essence of winter sleep is on the night,
The scent of apples: I am drowsing off.
I cannot rub the strangeness from my
    sight
I got from looking through a pane of
    glass   10
I skimmed this morning from the drink-
    ing trough
And held against the world of hoary
    grass.
It melted, and I let it fall and break.
But I was well
Upon my way to sleep before it fell,
And I could tell
What form my dreaming was about to
    take.
Magnified apples appear and disappear,
Stem end and blossom end,   19
And every fleck of russet showing clear.
My instep arch not only keeps the ache,
It keeps the pressure of a ladder-round.
I feel the ladder sway as the boughs
    bend.
And I keep hearing from the cellar bin
The rumbling sound
Of load on load of apples coming in.

For I have had too much
Of apple-picking: I am overtired
Of the great harvest I myself desired.
There were ten thousand thousand fruit
    to touch,   30
Cherish in hand, lift down, and not let
    fall.
For all
That struck the earth,
No matter if not bruised or spiked with
    stubble,
Went surely to the cider-apple heap
As of no worth.
One can see what will trouble
This sleep of mine, whatever sleep it is.
Were he not gone,
The woodchuck could say whether it's
    like his   40
Long sleep, as I describe its coming on,
Or just some human sleep.

The Witch of Coös

I staid the night for shelter at a farm
Behind the mountain, with a mother and
    son,
Two old-believers. They did all the talk-
    ing.

MOTHER. Folks think a witch who has
    familiar spirits
She could call up to pass a winter eve-
    ning,
But won't, should be burned at the stake
    or something.
Summoning spirits isn't "Button, button,
Who's got the button," I would have
    them know.

SON. Mother can make a common table
    rear
And kick with two legs like an army
    mule.   10

MOTHER. And when I've done it, what
    good have I done?
Rather than tip a table for you, let me
Tell you what Ralle the Sioux Control
    once told me.
He said the dead had souls, but when I
    asked him
How could that be—I thought the dead
    were souls,
He broke my trance. Don't that make you
    suspicious
That there's something the dead are
    keeping back?
Yes, there's something the dead are keep-
    ing back.

SON. You wouldn't want to tell him what
    we have
Up attic, mother?   20

MOTHER. Bones—a skeleton.

SON. But the headboard of mother's bed
    is pushed
Against the attic door: the door is nailed.
It's harmless. Mother hears it in the night
Halting perplexed behind the barrier

Of door and headboard. Where it wants
   to get
Is back into the cellar where it came
   from.

MOTHER. We'll never let them, will we,
   son! We'll never!

SON. It left the cellar forty years ago
And carried itself like a pile of dishes   30
Up one flight from the cellar to the
   kitchen,
Another from the kitchen to the bed-
   room,
Another from the bedroom to the attic,
Right past both father and mother, and
   neither stopped it.
Father had gone upstairs; mother was
   downstairs.
I was a baby: I don't know where I was.

MOTHER. The only fault my husband
   found with me—
I went to sleep before I went to bed,
Especially in winter when the bed
Might just as well be ice and the clothes
   snow.   40
The night the bones came up the cellar-
   stairs
Toffile had gone to bed alone and left
   me,
But left an open door to cool the room
   off
So as to sort of turn me out of it.
I was just coming to myself enough
To wonder where the cold was coming
   from,
When I heard Toffile upstairs in the bed-
   room
And thought I heard him downstairs in
   the cellar.
The board we had laid down to walk
   dry-shod on
When there was water in the cellar in
   spring   50
Struck the hard cellar bottom. And then
   someone
Began the stairs, two footsteps for each
   step,
The way a man with one leg and a
   crutch,

Or a little child, comes up. It wasn't
   Toffile:
It wasn't anyone who could be there.
The bulkhead double-doors were double-
   locked
And swollen tight and buried under
   snow.
The cellar windows were banked up with
   sawdust
And swollen tight and buried under
   snow.
It was the bones. I knew them—and good
   reason.   60
My first impulse was to get to the knob
And hold the door. But the bones didn't
   try
The door; they halted helpless on the
   landing,
Waiting for things to happen in their
   favor.
The faintest restless rustling ran all
   through them.
I never could have done the thing I did
If the wish hadn't been too strong in me
To see how they were mounted for this
   walk.
I had a vision of them put together
Not like a man, but like a chandelier.
So suddenly I flung the door wide on
   him.   71
A moment he stood balancing with emo-
   tion,
And all but lost himself. (A tongue of fire
Flashed out and licked along his upper
   teeth.
Smoke rolled inside the sockets of his
   eyes.)
Then he came at me with one hand out-
   stretched,
The way he did in life once; but this time
I struck the hand off brittle on the floor,
And fell back from him on the floor my-
   self.
The finger-pieces slid in all directions.
(Where did I see one of those pieces
   lately?   81
Hand me my button-box—it must be
   there.)
I sat up on the floor and shouted,
   "Toffile,

It's coming up to you." It had its choice
Of the door to the cellar or the hall.
It took the hall door for the novelty,
And set off briskly for so slow a thing,
Still going every which way in the joints,
though,
So that it looked like lightning or a scrib-
ble,
From the slap I had just now given its
hand.   90
I listened till it almost climbed the stairs
From the hall to the only finished bed-
room,
Before I got up to do anything;
Then ran and shouted, "Shut the bed-
room door,
Toffile, for my sake!" "Company?" he
said,
"Don't make me get up; I'm too warm in
bed."
So lying forward weakly on the handrail
I pushed myself upstairs, and in the light
(The kitchen had been dark) I had to
own
I could see nothing. "Toffile, I don't see
it.   100
It's with us in the room though. It's the
bones."
"What bones?" "The cellar bones—out of
the grave."
That made him throw his bare legs out
of bed
And sit up by me and take hold of me.
I wanted to put out the light and see
If I could see it, or else mow the room,
With our arms at the level of our knees,
And bring the chalk-pile down. "I'll tell
you what—
It's looking for another door to try.
The uncommonly deep snow has made
him think   110
Of his old song, *The Wild Colonial Boy*,
He always used to sing along the tote-
road.
He's after an open door to get out-doors.
Let's trap him with an open door up at-
tic."
Toffile agreed to that, and sure enough,
Almost the moment he was given an
opening,

The steps began to climb the attic stairs.
I heard them. Toffile didn't seem to hear
them.
"Quick!" I slammed to the door and held
the knob.
"Toffile, get nails." I made him nail the
door shut   120
And push the headboard of the bed
against it.
Then we asked was there anything
Up attic that we'd ever want again.
The attic was less to us than the cellar.
If the bones liked the attic, let them have
it.
Let them stay in the attic. When they
sometimes
Come down the stairs at night and stand
perplexed
Behind the door and headboard of the
bed,
Brushing their chalky skull with chalky
fingers,
With sounds like the dry rattling of a
shutter,   130
That's what I sit up in the dark to say—
To no one any more since Toffile died.
Let them stay in the attic since they went
there.
I promised Toffile to be cruel to them
For helping them be cruel once to him.

SON. We think they had a grave down in
the cellar.

MOTHER. We know they had a grave
down in the cellar.

SON. We never could find out whose
bones they were.

MOTHER. Yes, we could too, son. Tell the
truth for once
They were a man's his father killed for
me.   140
I mean a man he killed instead of me.
The least I could do was to help dig their
grave.
We were about it one night in the cellar.
Son knows the story: but 'twas not for
him
To tell the truth, suppose the time had
come.

Son looks surprised to see me end a lie
We'd kept all these years between our-
selves
So as to have it ready for outsiders.
But tonight I don't care enough to lie—
I don't remember why I ever cared.   150
Toffile, if he were here, I don't believe
Could tell you why he ever cared him-
self . . .

She hadn't found the finger-bone she
wanted
Among the buttons poured out in her lap.
I verified the name next morning: Toffile.
The rural letter-box said Toffile Lajway.

The Tuft of Flowers

I went to turn the grass once after one
Who mowed it in the dew before the sun.

The dew was gone that made his blade
so keen
Before I came to view the leveled scene.

I looked for him behind an isle of trees;
I listened for his whetstone on the breeze.

But he had gone his way, the grass all
mown,
And I must be, as he had been,—alone,

"As all must be," I said within my heart,
"Whether they work together or apart."

But as I said it, swift there passed me
by   11
On noiseless wing a bewildered butterfly,

Seeking with memories grown dim o'er
night
Some resting flower of yesterday's de-
light.

And once I marked his flight go round
and round,
As where some flower lay withering on
the ground.

And then he flew as far as eye could see,
And then on tremulous wing came back
to me.

I thought of questions that have no reply,
And would have turned to toss the grass
to dry;   20

But he turned first, and led my eye to
look
At a tall tuft of flowers beside a brook,

A leaping tongue of bloom the scythe
had spared
Beside a reedy brook the scythe had
bared.

The mower in the dew had loved them
thus,
By leaving them to flourish, not for us,

Nor yet to draw one thought of ours to
him,
But from sheer morning gladness at the
brim.   30

The butterfly and I had lit upon,
Nevertheless, a message from the dawn,

That made me hear the wakening birds
around,
And hear his long scythe whispering to
the ground,

And feel a spirit kindred to my own;
So that henceforth I worked no more
alone;

But glad with him, I worked as with his
aid,
And weary, sought at noon with him the
shade;

And dreaming, as it were, held brotherly
speech
With one whose thought I had not hoped
to reach.   40

"Men work together," I told him from
the heart,
"Whether they work together or apart."

Stopping by Woods on a
Snowy Evening

Whose woods these are I think I know.
His house is in the village though;

He will not see me stopping here
To watch his woods fill up with snow.

My little horse must think it queer
To stop without a farmhouse near
Between the woods and frozen lake
The darkest evening of the year.

He gives his harness bells a shake
To ask if there is some mistake.   10
The only other sound's the sweep
Of easy wind and downy flake.

The woods are lovely, dark and deep.
But I have promises to keep,
And miles to go before I sleep,
And miles to go before I sleep.

The Onset

Always the same, when on a fated night
At last the gathered snow lets down as
    white
As may be in dark woods, and with a
    song
It shall not make again all winter long
Of hissing on the yet uncovered ground,
I almost stumble looking up and round,
As one who overtaken by the end
Gives up his errand, and lets death de-
    scend
Upon him where he is, with nothing done
To evil, no important triumph won,   10
More than if life had never been begun.

Yet all the precedent is on my side:
I know that winter death has never tried
The earth but it has failed: the snow may
    heap
In long storms an undrifted four feet
    deep
As measured against maple, birch and
    oak,
It cannot check the peeper's silver croak;
And I shall see the snow all go down
    hill
In water of a slender April rill
That flashes tail through last year's
    withered brake   20

And dead weeds, like a disappearing
    snake.
Nothing will be left white but here a
    birch,
And there a clump of houses with a
    church.

West-running Brook

"Fred, where is north?"

      "North? North is there, my love.
The brook runs west."

      "West-running Brook then call it."
(West-running Brook men call it to this
    day.)
"What does it think it's doing running
    west
When all the other country brooks flow
    east
To reach the ocean? It must be the brook
Can trust itself to go by contraries
The way I can with you—and you with
    me—
Because we're—we're—I don't know
    what we are.
What are we?"

      "Young or new?"

      "We must be something.
We've said we two. Let's change that to
    we three.   11
As you and I are married to each other,
We'll both be married to the brook. We'll
    build
Our bridge across it, and the bridge shall
    be
Our arm thrown over it asleep beside it.
Look, look, it's waving to us with a wave
To let us know it hears me."

      "Why, my dear,
That wave's been standing off this jut of
    shore—"
(The black stream, catching on a sunken
    rock,
Flung backward on itself in one white
    wave,   20

And the white water rode the black for-
ever,
Not gaining but not losing, like a bird
White feathers from the struggle of
whose breast
Flecked the dark stream and flecked the
darker pool
Below the point, and were at last driven
wrinkled
In a white scarf against the far shore
alders.)
"That wave's been standing off this jut of
shore
Ever since rivers, I was going to say,
Were made in heaven. It wasn't waved
to us."

"It wasn't, yet it was. If not to you   30
It was to me—in an annunciation."

"Oh, if you take it off to lady-land,
As't were the country of the Amazons
We men must see you to the confines of
And leave you there, ourselves forbid to
enter,—
It is your brook! I have no more to say."

"Yes, you have, too. Go on. You thought
of something."

"Speaking of contraries, see how the
brook
In that white wave runs counter to itself.
It is from that in water we were from
Long, long before we were from any
creature.   41
Here we, in our impatience of the steps,
Get back to the beginning of beginnings,
The stream of everything that runs away.
Some say existence like a Pirouot
And Pirouette, forever in one place,
Stands still and dances, but it runs away,
It seriously, sadly, runs away
To fill the abyss' void with emptiness.
It flows beside us in this water brook,
But it flows over us. It flows between
us   51
To separate us for a panic moment.
It flows between us, over us, and *with* us.
And it is time, strength, tone, light, life,
and love—

And even substance lapsing unsubstan-
tial;
The universal cataract of death
That spends to nothingness—and unre-
sisted,
Save by some strange resistance in itself,
Not just a swerving, but a throwing back,
As if regret were in it and were sacred.
It has this throwing backward on it-
self   61
So that the fall of most of it is always
Raising a little, sending up a little.
Our life runs down in sending up the
clock.
The brook runs down in sending up our
life.
The sun runs down in sending up the
brook.
And there is something sending up the
sun.
It is this backward motion toward the
source,
Against the stream, that most we see our-
selves in,
The tribute of the current to the source.
It is from this in nature we are from.   71
It is most us."

          "Today will be the day
You said so."

              "No, today will be the day
You said the brook was called West-
running Brook."

"Today will be the day of what we both
said."

Acquainted with the Night

I have been one acquainted with the
night.
I have walked out in rain—and back in
rain.
I have outwalked the furthest city light.

I have looked down the saddest city lane.
I have passed by the watchman on his
beat

And dropped my eyes, unwilling to ex-
plain.

I have stood still and stopped the sound
of feet
When far away an interrupted cry
Came over houses from another street,

But not to call me back or say good-
bye;   10
And further still at an unearthly height,
One luminary clock against the sky

Proclaimed the time was neither wrong
nor right.
I have been one acquainted with the
night.

Provide, Provide

The witch that came (the withered hag)
To wash the steps with pail and rag,
Was once the beauty Abishag,

The picture pride of Hollywood.
Too many fall from great and good
For you to doubt the likelihood.

Die early and avoid the fate.
Or if predestined to die late,
Make up your mind to die in state.

Make the whole stock exchange your
own!   10
If need be occupy a throne,
Where nobody can call *you* crone.

Some have relied on what they knew;
Others on being simply true.
What worked for them might work for
you.

No memory of having starred
Atones for later disregard,
Or keeps the end from being hard.

Better to go down dignified
With boughten friendship at your side
Than none at all. Provide, provide!   21

The Gift Outright

The land was ours before we were the
land's.
She was our land more than a hundred
years
Before we were her people. She was ours
In Massachusetts, in Virginia,
But we were England's, still colonials,
Possessing what we still were unpos-
sessed by,
Possessed by what we now no more pos-
sessed.
Something we were withholding made us
weak
Until we found out that it was ourselves
We were withholding from our land of
living,   10
And forthwith found salvation in sur-
render.
Such as we were we gave ourselves out-
right
(The deed of gift was many deeds of
war)
To the land vaguely realizing westward,
But still unstoried, artless, unenhanced,
Such as she was, such as she would be-
come.

Neither Out Far nor In Deep

The people along the sand
All turn and look one way.
They turn their back on the land.
They look at the sea all day.

As long as it takes to pass
A ship keeps raising its hull;
The wetter ground like glass
Reflects a standing gull.

The land may vary more;
But wherever the truth may be—   10
The water comes ashore,
And the people look at the sea.

They cannot look out far.
They cannot look in deep.

But when was that ever a bar
To any watch they keep?

Departmental

An ant on the tablecloth
Ran into a dormant moth
Of many times his size.
He showed not the least surprise.
His business wasn't with such.
He gave it scarcely a touch,
And was off on his duty run.
Yet if he encountered one
Of the hive's enquiry squad
Whose work is to find out God   10
And the nature of time and space,
He would put him onto the case.
Ants are a curious race;
One crossing with hurried tread
The body of one of their dead
Isn't given a moment's arrest—
Seems not even impressed.
But he no doubt reports to any
With whom he crosses antennae,
And they no doubt report   20
To the higher up at court.
Then word goes forth in Formic:
"Death's come to Jerry McCormic,
Our selfless forager Jerry.
With the special Janizary
Whose office it is to bury
The dead of the commissary
Go bring him home to his people.
Lay him in state on a sepal.
Wrap him for shroud in a petal.   30
Embalm him with ichor of nettle.
This is the word of your Queen."
And presently on the scene
Appears a solemn mortician;
And taking formal position
With feelers calmly atwiddle,
Seizes the dead by the middle,
And heaving him high in air,
Carries him out of there.
No one stands round to stare.   40
It is nobody else's affair.

It couldn't be called ungentle.
But how thoroughly departmental.

The Bear

The bear puts both arms around the tree
   above her
And draws it down as if it were a lover
And its choke cherries lips to kiss good-
   by,
Then lets it snap back upright in the sky.
Her next step rocks a boulder on the wall
(She's making her cross-country in the
   fall).
Her great weight creaks the barbed-wire   10
   in its staples
As she flings over and off down through
   the maples,
Leaving on one wire tooth a lock of hair.
Such is the uncaged progress of the bear.
The world has room to make a bear feel
   free;   11
The universe seems cramped to you and
   me.
Man acts more like the poor bear in a   20
   cage
That all day fights a nervous inward rage,
His mood rejecting all his mind suggests.
He paces back and forth and never rests
The toe-nail click and shuffle of his feet,
The telescope at one end of his beat,
And at the other end the microscope,
Two instruments of nearly equal hope,
And in conjunction giving quite a spread.
Or if he rests from scientific tread,   22
'Tis only to sit back and sway his head   30
Through ninety odd degrees of arc, it
   seems,
Between two metaphysical extremes.
He sits back on his fundamental butt
With lifted snout and eyes (if any) shut,
(He almost looks religious but he's not),
And back and forth he sways from cheek
   to cheek,
At one extreme agreeing with one Greek,   40
At the other agreeing with another Greek

Which may be thought, but only so to
    speak.   32
A baggy figure, equally pathetic
When sedentary and when peripatetic.

The Lovely Shall Be Choosers

The Voice said, "Hurl her down!"

The Voices, "How far down?"

"Seven levels of the world."

"How much time have we?"

"Take twenty years.
She *would* refuse love safe with wealth
    and honor!
The lovely shall be choosers, shall they?
Then let them choose!"

"Then we shall let her choose?"

"Yes, let her choose.
Take up the task beyond her choosing."

Invisible hands crowded on her shoulder
In readiness to weigh upon her.   12
But she stood straight still,
In broad round ear-rings, gold and jet
    with pearls
And broad round suchlike brooch,
Her cheeks high colored,
Proud and the pride of friends.

The Voice asked, "You can let her
    choose?"

"Yes, we can let her and still triumph."

"Do it by joys, and leave her always
    blameless.   21
Be her first joy her wedding,
That though a wedding,
Is yet—well something they know, he
    and she.
And after that her next joy
That though she grieves, her grief is
    secret:
Those friends know nothing of her grief
    to make it shameful.

Her third joy that though now they can-
    not help but know,
They move in pleasure too far off
To think much or much care.   30
Give her a child at either knee for fourth
    joy
To tell once and once only, for them
    never to forget,
How once she walked in brightness,
And make them see it in the winter fire-
    light.
But give her friends for then she dare not
    tell
For their foregone incredulousness.
And be her next joy this:
Her never having deigned to tell them.
Make her among the humblest even
Seem to them less than they are.   40
Hopeless of being known for what she
    has been,
Failing of being loved for what she is,
Give her the comfort for her sixth of
    knowing
She fails from strangeness to a way of life
She came to from too high too late to
    learn.
Then send some *one* with eyes to see
And wonder at her where she is,
And words to wonder in her hearing how
    she came there,
But without time to linger for her story.
Be her last joy her heart's going out to
    this one   50
So that she almost speaks.
You know them—seven in all."

"Trust us," the Voices said.

A Considerable Speck

(MICROSCOPIC)

A speck that would have been beneath
    my sight
On any but a paper sheet so white
Set off across what I had written there.
And I had idly poised my pen in air

To stop it with a period of ink
When something strange about it made
    me think.
This was no dust speck by my breathing
    blown,
But unmistakably a living mite
With inclinations it could call its own.
It paused as with suspicion of my pen,
And then came racing wildly on again
To where my manuscript was not yet
    dry;   12
Then paused again and either drank or
    smelt—
With loathing, for again it turned to fly.
Plainly with an intelligence I dealt.
It seemed too tiny to have room for feet,
Yet must have had a set of them com-
    plete

To express how much it didn't want to
    die.
It ran with terror and with cunning crept.
It faltered: I could see it hesitate;   20
Then in the middle of the open sheet
Cower down in desperation to accept
Whatever I accorded it of fate.
I have none of the tenderer-than-thou
Collectivistic regimenting love
With which the modern world is being
    swept.
But this poor microscopic item now!
Since it was nothing I knew evil of
I let it lie there till I hope it slept.
I have a mind myself and recognize   30
Mind when I meet with it in any guise.
No one can know how glad I am to find
On any sheet the least display of mind.

Carl Sandburg

✳ 1878—

Gone

Everybody loved Chick Lorimer in our town.
            Far off
        Everybody loved her.
So we all love a wild girl keeping a hold
        On a dream she wants.
Nobody knows now where Chick Lorimer went.
Nobody knows why she packed her trunk . . . a few old things
And is gone,
            Gone with her little chin
            Thrust ahead of her   10
            And her soft hair blowing careless
            From under a wide hat,
Dancer, singer, a laughing passionate lover.

Were there ten men or a hundred hunting Chick?
Were there five men or fifty with aching hearts?
        Everybody loved Chick Lorimer.
            Nobody knows where she's gone.

A Fence

Now the stone house on the lake front is finished and the workmen are beginning the
  fence.
The palings are made of iron bars with steel points that can stab the life out of any
  man who falls on them.
As a fence, it is a masterpiece, and will shut off the rabble and all vagabonds and
  hungry men and all wandering children looking for a place to play.
Passing through the bars and over the steel points will go nothing except Death and
  the Rain and To-morrow.

Cool Tombs

When Abraham Lincoln was shoveled into the tombs, he forgot the copperheads and
  the assassin . . . in the dust, in the cool tombs.
And Ulysses Grant lost all thought of con men and Wall Street, cash and collateral
  turned ashes . . . in the dust, in the cool tombs.
Pocahontas' body, lovely as a poplar, sweet as a red haw in November or a pawpaw
  in May, did she wonder? does she remember? . . . in the dust, in the cool
  tombs?
Take any streetful of people buying clothes and groceries, cheering a hero or throw-
  ing confetti and blowing tin horns . . . tell me if the lovers are losers . . . tell
  me if any get more than the lovers . . . in the dust . . . in the cool tombs.

Limited

I am riding on a limited express, one of the crack trains of the nation.
Hurtling across the prairie into blue haze and dark air go fifteen all-steel coaches
  holding a thousand people.
(All the coaches shall be scrap and rust and all the men and women laughing in the
  diners and sleepers shall pass to ashes.)
I ask a man in the smoker where he is going and he answers: "Omaha."

Bricklayer Love

I thought of killing myself because I am only a bricklayer and you a woman who
  loves the man who runs a drug store.
I don't care like I used to; I lay bricks straighter than I used to and I sing slower
  handling the trowel afternoons.
When the sun is in my eyes and the ladders are shaky and the mortar boards go
  wrong, I think of you.

Wallace Stevens

✳ 1879–1955

Sunday Morning

Complacencies of the peignoir, and late
Coffee and oranges in a sunny chair,
And the green freedom of a cockatoo
Upon a rug mingle to dissipate
The holy hush of ancient sacrifice.
She dreams a little, and she feels the dark
Encroachment of that old catastrophe,
As a calm darkens among water-lights.
The pungent oranges and bright, green
    wings
Seem things in some procession of the
    dead,   10
Winding across wide water, without
    sound.
The day is like wide water, without
    sound,
Stilled for the passing of her dreaming
    feet
Over the seas, to silent Palestine,
Dominion of the blood and sepulchre.

Why should she give her bounty to the
    dead?
What is divinity if it can come
Only in silent shadows and in dreams?
Shall she not find in comforts of the sun,
In pungent fruit and bright, green wings,
    or else   20
In any balm or beauty of the earth,
Things to be cherished like the thought
    of heaven?
Divinity must live within herself:
Passions of rain, or moods in falling
    snow;
Grievings in loneliness, or unsubdued
Elations when the forest blooms; gusty
Emotions on wet roads on autumn nights;
All pleasures and all pains, remembering
The bough of summer and the winter
    branch.

These are the measures destined for her
    soul.   30
Jove in the clouds had his inhuman birth.
No mother suckled him, no sweet land
    gave
Large-mannered motions to his mythy
    mind.
He moved among us, as a muttering king,
Magnificent, would move among his
    hinds,
Until our blood, commingling, virginal,
With heaven, brought such requital to
    desire
The very hinds discerned it, in a star.
Shall our blood fail? Or shall it come to
    be
The blood of paradise? And shall the
    earth   40
Seem all of paradise that we shall know?
The sky will be much friendlier then than
    now,
A part of labor and a part of pain,
And next in glory to enduring love,
Not this dividing and indifferent blue.

She says, "I am content when wakened
    birds,
Before they fly, test the reality
Of misty fields, by their sweet question-
    ings;
But when the birds are gone, and their
    warm fields
Return no more, where, then, is para-
    dise?"   50
There is not any haunt of prophecy,
Nor any old chimera of the grave,
Neither the golden underground, nor isle
Melodious, where spirits gat them home,
Nor visionary south, nor cloudy palm
Remote on heaven's hill, that has endured
As April's green endures; or will endure
Like her remembrance of awakened
    birds,
Or her desire for June and evening,
    tipped
By the consummation of the swallow's
    wings.   60

She says, "But in contentment I still feel
The need of some imperishable bliss."

Death is the mother of beauty; hence from her,
Alone, shall come fulfilment to our dreams
And our desires. Although she strews the leaves
Of sure obliteration on our paths,
The path sick sorrow took, the many paths
Where triumph rang its brassy phrase, or love
Whispered a little out of tenderness,
She makes the willow shiver in the sun
For maidens who were wont to sit and gaze   71
Upon the grass, relinquished to their feet.
She causes boys to pile new plums and pears
On disregarded plate. The maidens taste
And stray impassioned in the littering leaves.

Is there no change of death in paradise?
Does ripe fruit never fall? Or do the boughs
Hang always heavy in that perfect sky,
Unchanging, yet so like our perishing earth,
With rivers like our own that seek for seas   80
They never find, the same receding shores
That never touch with inarticulate pang?
Why set the pear upon those river-banks
Or spice the shores with odors of the plum?
Alas, that they should wear our colors there,
The silken weavings of our afternoons,
And pick the strings of our insipid lutes!
Death is the mother of beauty, mystical,
Within whose burning bosom we devise
Our earthly mothers waiting, sleeplessly.

Supple and turbulent, a ring of men   91
Shall chant in orgy on a summer morn
Their boisterous devotion to the sun,
Not as a god, but as a god might be,
Naked among them, like a savage source.

Their chant shall be a chant of paradise,
Out of their blood, returning to the sky;
And in their chant shall enter, voice by voice,
The windy lake wherein their lord delights,
The trees, like serafim, and echoing hills,
That choir among themselves long afterward.   101
They shall know well the heavenly fellowship
Of men that perish and of summer morn.
And whence they came and whither they shall go
The dew upon their feet shall manifest.

She hears, upon that water without sound,
A voice that cries, "The tomb in Palestine
Is not the porch of spirits lingering.
It is the grave of Jesus, where He lay."
We live in an old chaos of the sun,   110
Or old dependency of day and night,
Or island solitude, unsponsored, free,
Of that wide water, inescapable.
Deer walk upon our mountains, and the quail
Whistle about us their spontaneous cries;
Sweet berries ripen in the wilderness;
And, in the isolation of the sky,
At evening, casual flocks of pigeons make
Ambiguous undulations as they sink,
Downward to darkness, on extended wings.   120

Disillusionment of Ten O'Clock

The houses are haunted
By white night-gowns.
None are green,
Or purple with green rings,
Or green with yellow rings,
Or yellow with blue rings.
None of them are strange,
With socks of lace
And beaded ceintures.
People are not going   10
To dream of baboons and periwinkles,

Only, here and there, an old sailor,
Drunk and asleep in his boots,
Catches tigers
In red weather.

The Emperor of Ice-Cream

Call the roller of big cigars,
The muscular one, and bid him whip
In kitchen cups concupiscent curds.
Let the wenches dawdle in such dress
As they are used to wear, and let the boys
Bring flowers in last month's newspapers.
Let be be finale of seem.
The only emperor is the emperor of ice-
cream.

Take from the dresser of deal,   9
Lacking the three glass knobs, that sheet
On which she embroidered fantails once
And spread it so as to cover her face.
If her horny feet protrude, they come
To show how cold she is, and dumb.
Let the lamp affix its beam.
The only emperor is the emperor of ice-
cream.

The Idea of Order in Key West

She sang beyond the genius of the sea.
The water never formed to mind or voice,
Like a body wholly body, fluttering
Its empty sleeves; and yet its mimic mo-
tion
Made constant cry, caused constantly a
cry,
That was not ours although we under-
stood,
Inhuman, of the veritable ocean.

The sea was not a mask. No more was
she.
The song and water were not medleyed
sound,

Even if what she sang was what she
heard,   10
Since what she sang she uttered word by
word.
It may be that in all her phrases stirred
The grinding water and the gasping
wind;
But it was she and not the sea we heard.

For she was the maker of the song she
sang.
The ever-hooded, tragic-gestured sea
Was merely a place by which she walked
to sing.
Whose spirit is this? we said, because we
knew
It was the spirit that we sought and knew
That we should ask this often as she
sang.   20

If it was only the dark voice of the sea
That rose, or even colored by many
waves;
If it was only the outer voice of sky
And cloud, of the sunken coral water-
walled,
However clear, it would have been deep
air,
The heaving speech of air, a summer
sound
Repeated in a summer without end
And sound alone. But it was more than
that,
More even than her voice, and ours,
among
The meaningless plungings of water and
the wind,   30
Theatrical distances, bronze shadows
heaped
On high horizons, mountainous atmos-
pheres
Of sky and sea.

                    It was her voice that made
The sky acutest at its vanishing.
She measured to the hour its solitude.
She was the single artificer of the world
In which she sang. And when she sang,
the sea,

Whatever self it had, became the self
That was her song, for she was maker.
    Then we,
As we beheld her striding there alone,
Knew that there never was a world for
    her   41
Except that one she sang and, singing,
    made.

Ramon Fernandez, tell me, if you know,
Why, when the singing ended and we
    turned
Toward the town, tell why the glassy
    lights,
The lights in the fishing boats at anchor
    there,
As the night descended, tilting in the air,
Mastered the night and portioned out the
    sea,
Fixing emblazoned zones and fiery poles,
Arranging, deepening, enchanting night.

Oh! Blessed rage for order, pale Ra-
    mon,   51
The maker's rage to order words of the
    sea,
Words of the fragrant portals, dimly-
    starred,
And of ourselves and of our origins,
In ghostlier demarcations, keener sounds.

Mozart, 1935

Poet, be seated at the piano.
Play the present, its hoo-hoo-hoo,
Its shoo-shoo-shoo, its ric-a-nic,
Its envious cachinnation.

If they throw stones upon the roof
While you practice arpeggios,
It is because they carry down the stairs
A body in rags.
Be seated at the piano.

That lucid souvenir of the past,   10
The divertimento;
That airy dream of the future,

The unclouded concerto . . .
The snow is falling.
Strike the piercing chord.

Be thou the voice,
Not you. Be thou, be thou
The voice of angry fear,
The voice of this besieging pain.

Be thou that wintry sound   20
As of the great wind howling,
By which sorrow is released,
Dismissed, absolved
In a starry placating.

We may return to Mozart.
He was young, and we, we are old.
The snow is falling
And the streets are full of cries.
Be seated, thou.

Of Modern Poetry

The poem of the mind in the act of find-
    ing
What will suffice. It has not always had
To find: the scene was set; it repeated
    what
Was in the script.
              Then the theatre was changed
To something else. Its past was a sou-
    venir.
It has to be living, to learn the speech of
    the place.
It has to face the men of the time and to
    meet
The women of the time. It has to think
    about war
And it has to find what will suffice. It has
To construct a new stage. It has to be on
    that stage
And, like an insatiable actor, slowly and
With meditation, speak words that in the
    ear,
In the delicatest ear of the mind, repeat,
Exactly, that which it wants to hear, at
    the sound

Of which, an invisible audience listens,
Not to the play, but to itself, expressed
In an emotion as of two people, as of two
Emotions becoming one. The actor is
A metaphysician in the dark, twanging
An instrument, twanging a wiry string
    that gives   20
Sounds passing through sudden right-
    nesses, wholly
Containing the mind, below which it can-
    not descend,
Beyond which it has no will to rise.
                              It must
Be the finding of a satisfaction, and may
Be of a man skating, a woman dancing, a
    woman
Combing. The poem of the act of the
    mind.

No Possum, No Sop, No Taters

He is not here, the old sun,
As absent as if we were asleep.

The field is frozen. The leaves are dry.
Bad is final in this light.

In this bleak air the broken stalks
Have arms without hands. They have
    trunks

Without legs or, for that, without heads.
They have heads in which a captive cry

Is merely the moving of a tongue.
Snow sparkles like eyesight falling to
    earth,   10

Like seeing fallen brightly away.
The leaves hop, scraping on the ground.

It is deep January. The sky is hard.
The stalks are firmly rooted in ice.

It is in this solitude, a syllable,
Out of these gawky flitterings,

Intones its single emptiness,
The savagest hollow of winter-sound.

It is here, in this bad, that we reach
The last purity of the knowledge of
    good.   20

The crow looks rusty as he rises up.
Bright is the malice in his eye . . .

One joins him there for company,
But at a distance, in another tree.

The Poems of Our Climate

1

Clear water in a brilliant bowl,
Pink and white carnations. The light
In the room more like a snowy air,
Reflecting snow. A newly-fallen snow
At the end of winter when afternoons re-
    turn.
Pink and white carnations—one desires
So much more than that. The day itself
Is simplified: a bowl of white,
Cold, a cold porcelain, low and round,
With nothing more than the carnations
    there.   10

2

Say even that this complete simplicity
Stripped one of all one's torments, con-
    cealed
The evilly compounded, vital I
And made it fresh in a world of white,
A world of clear water, brilliant-edged,
Still one would want more, one would
    need more,
More than a world of white and snowy
    scents.

3

There would still remain the never-
    resting mind,
So that one would want to escape, come
    back
To what had been so long composed.   20
The imperfect is our paradise.
Note that, in this bitterness, delight,
Since the imperfect is so hot in us,
Lies in flawed words and stubborn
    sounds.

Vachel Lindsay
✳ 1879–1931

The Congo

A STUDY OF THE NEGRO RACE

1. Their Basic Savagery

Fat black bucks in a wine-barrel room,
Barrel-house kings, with feet unstable,
Sagged and reeled and pounded on the table,
Pounded on the table,
Beat an empty barrel with the handle of a broom,
Hard as they were able,
Boom, boom, BOOM.
With a silk umbrella and the handle of a broom,
Boomlay, boomlay, boomlay, BOOM.
THEN I had religion, THEN I had a vision.
I could not turn from their revel in derision.
THEN I SAW THE CONGO, CREEPING THROUGH THE BLACK,
CUTTING THROUGH THE FOREST WITH A GOLDEN TRACK.
Then along that riverbank
A thousand miles
Tattooed cannibals danced in files;
Then I heard the boom of the blood-lust song
And a thigh-bone beating on a tin-pan gong.
And "BLOOD" screamed the whistles and the fifes of the warriors,
"BLOOD" screamed the skull-faced, lean witch-doctors,
"Whirl ye the deadly voo-doo rattle,
Harry the uplands,
Steal all the cattle,
Rattle-rattle, rattle-rattle,
Bing.
Boomlay, boomlay, boomlay, BOOM,"
A roaring epic, rag-time tune
From the mouth of the Congo
To the Mountains of the Moon.
Death is an Elephant,
Torch-eyed and horrible,
Foam-flanked and terrible.
BOOM, steal the pygmies,
BOOM, kill the Arabs,

*A deep roll-
ing bass.*

10

*More
deliberate.
Solemnly
chanted.*

*A rapidly
piling climax
of speed and
racket.*

20

*With a
philosophic
pause.*

30   *Shrilly and
with a
heavily ac-
cented metre*

BOOM, kill the white men,

HOO, HOO, HOO.

Listen to the yell of Leopold's ghost

Burning in Hell for his hand-maimed host.

Hear how the demons chuckle and yell

Cutting his hands off, down in Hell.   40

Listen to the creepy proclamation,

Blown through the lairs of the forest-nation,

Blown past the white-ants' hill of clay,

Blown past the marsh where the butterflies play:

"Be careful what you do,

Or Mumbo-Jumbo, God of the Congo,

And all of the other

Gods of the Congo,

Mumbo-Jumbo will hoo-doo you,

Mumbo-Jumbo will hoo-doo you,   50

Mumbo-Jumbo will hoo-doo you."

Like the wind in the chimney.

All the "o" sounds very golden. Heavy accents very heavy. Light accents very light. Last line whispered.

2. *Their Irrepressible High Spirits*

Wild crap-shooters with a whoop and a call

Danced the juba in their gambling hall

And laughed fit to kill, and shook the town,

And guyed the policemen and laughed them down

With a boomlay, boomlay, boomlay, BOOM.

THEN I SAW THE CONGO, CREEPING THROUGH THE BLACK,

CUTTING THROUGH THE FOREST WITH A GOLDEN TRACK.

A negro fairyland swung into view,

A minstrel river   60

Where dreams come true.

The ebony palace soared on high

Through the blossoming trees to the evening sky.

The inlaid porches and casements shone

With gold and ivory and elephant-bone.

And the black crowd laughed till their sides were sore

At the baboon butler in the agate door,

And the well-known tunes of the parrot band

That trilled on the bushes of that magic land.

A troupe of skull-faced witch-men came   70

Through the agate doorway in suits of flame,

Yea, long-tailed coats with a gold-leaf crust

And hats that were covered with diamond-dust.

And the crowd in the court gave a whoop and a call

And danced the juba from wall to wall.

But the witch-men suddenly stilled the throng

With a stern cold glare, and a stern old song:—

"Mumbo-Jumbo will hoo-doo you." . . .

Just then from the doorway, as fat as shotes,

Came the cake-walk princes in their long red coats,   80

Canes with a brilliant lacquer shine,

Rather shrill and high

Read exactly as in first section.

Lay emphasis on the delicate ideas. Keep as light-footed as possible.

With pomposity

With a great deliberation and ghostliness

With overwhelming assurance, good cheer, and pomp

And tall silk hats that were red as wine.
And they pranced with their butterfly partners there,
Coal-black maidens with pearls in their hair,
Knee-skirts trimmed with the jassamine sweet,
And bells on their ankles and little black-feet.
And the couples railed at the chant and the frown
Of the witch-men lean, and laughed them down.
(Oh, rare was the revel, and well worth while
That made those glowering witch-men smile.)
The cake-walk royalty then began
To walk for a cake that was tall as a man
To the tune of "Boomlay, boomlay, BOOM,"
While the witch-men laughed, with a sinister air,
And sang with the scalawags prancing there:—
"Walk with care, walk with care,
Or Mumbo-Jumbo, God of the Congo,
And all of the other Gods of the Congo,
Mumbo-Jumbo will hoo-doo you.
Beware, beware, walk with care,
Boomlay, boomlay, boomlay, boom.
Boomlay, boomlay, boomlay, boom.
Boomlay, boomlay, boomlay, boom.
Boomlay, boomlay, boomlay,
BOOM."
(Oh, rare was the revel, and well worth while
That made those glowering witch-men smile.)

3. The Hope of Their Religion

A good old negro in the slums of the town
Preached at a sister for her velvet gown.
Howled at a brother for his low-down ways,
His prowling, guzzling, sneak-thief days.
Beat on the Bible till he wore it out
Starting the jubilee revival shout.
And some had visions, as they stood on chairs,
And sang of Jacob, and the golden stairs,
And they all repented, a thousand strong,
From their stupor and savagery and sin and wrong,
And slammed with their hymn books till they shook the room
With "Glory, glory, glory,"
And "Boom, boom, BOOM."
THEN I SAW THE CONGO, CREEPING THROUGH THE BLACK,
CUTTING THROUGH THE JUNGLE WITH A GOLDEN TRACK.
And the gray sky opened like a new-rent veil
And showed the Apostles with their coats of mail.
In bright white steel they were seated round
And their fire-eyes watched where the Congo wound.
And the twelve Apostles, from their thrones on high,

With growing speed and sharply marked dance-rhythm

90

With a touch of negro dialect, and as rapidly as possible toward the end.

100

Slow philosophic calm.

Heavy bass. With a literal imitation of camp-meeting racket, and trance.

110

120

Exactly as in the first section. Begin with terror and power, end with joy.

Thrilled all the forest with their heavenly cry:—
"Mumbo-Jumbo will die in the jungle;
Never again will he hoo-doo you,   130
Never again will he hoo-doo you."
Then along that river, a thousand miles,
The vine-snared trees fell down in files.
Pioneer angels cleared the way
For a Congo paradise, for babes at play,
For sacred capitals, for temples clean.
Gone were the skull-faced witch-men lean.
There, where the wild-ghost-gods had wailed
A million boats of the angels sailed
With oars of silver, and prows of blue   140
And silken pennants that the sun shone through.
'Twas a land transfigured, 'twas a new creation.
Oh, a singing wind swept the negro nation
And on through the backwoods clearing flew:—
"Mumbo-Jumbo is dead in the jungle.
Never again will he hoo-doo you.
Never again will he hoo-doo you."

Redeemed were the forests, the beasts and the men,
And only the vulture dared again
By the far, lone mountains of the moon   150
To cry, in the silence, the Congo tune:—
"Mumbo-Jumbo will hoo-doo you.
Mumbo-Jumbo will hoo-doo you,
Mumbo . . . Jumbo . . . will . . . hoo-doo . . . you."

Margin notes:

Sung to the tune of "Hark, ten thousand harps and voices."

With growing deliberation and joy.

In a rather high key— as delicately as possible.

To the tune of "Hark, ten thousand harps and voices."

Dying down into a penetrating terrified whisper.

The Eagle That Is Forgotten

JOHN P. ALTGELD—BORN DECEMBER 30, 1847, DIED MARCH 12, 1902

Sleep softly . . . eagle forgotten . . . under the stone.
Time has its way with you there, and the clay has its own.
"We have buried him now," thought your foes, and in secret rejoiced.
They made a brave show of their mourning, their hatred unvoiced.
They had snarled at you, barked at you, foamed at you day after day.
Now you were ended. They praised you, . . . and laid you away.

The others that mourned you in silence and terror and truth,
The widow bereft of her crust, and the boy without youth,
The mocked and scorned and the wounded, the lame and the poor
That should have remembered forever, . . . remember no more.   10

Where are those lovers of yours, on what name do they call
The lost, that in armies wept over your funeral pall?
They call on the names of a hundred high-valiant ones;
A hundred white eagles have risen the sons of your sons;

The zeal in their wings is a zeal that your dreaming began,
The valor that wore out your soul in the service of man.
Sleep softly, . . . eagle forgotten, . . . under the stone,
Time has its way with you there, and the clay has its own.
Sleep on, O brave-hearted, O wise man, that kindled the flame—
To live in mankind is far more than to live in a name,   20
To live in mankind, far, far, more . . . than to live in a name.

William Carlos Williams

✳ 1883—

Tract

I will teach you my townspeople
how to perform a funeral—
for you have it over a troop
of artists—
unless one should scour the world—
you have the ground sense necessary.

See! the hearse leads.
I begin with a design for a hearse.
For Christ's sake not black—
nor white either—and not polished!   10
Let it be weathered—like a farm
        wagon—
with gilt wheels (this could be
applied fresh at small expense)
or no wheels at all:
a rough dray to drag over the ground.

Knock the glass out!
My God—glass, my townspeople!
For what purpose? Is it for the dead
to look out or for us to see
how well he is housed or to see   20
the flowers or the lack of them—
or what?
To keep the rain and the snow from him?
He will have a heavier rain soon:
pebbles and dirt and what not.
Let there be no glass—
and no upholstery! phew!
and no little brass rollers

and small easy wheels on the bottom—
my townspeople what are you thinking
        of!   30

A rough plain hearse then
with gilt wheels and no top at all.
On this the coffin lies
by its own weight.

                    No wreaths please—
especially no hot-house flowers.
Some common memento is better,
something he prized and is known by:
his old clothes—a few books perhaps—
God knows what! You realize   40
how we are about these things,
my townspeople—
something will be found—anything—
even flowers if he had come to that.
So much for the hearse.

For heaven's sake though see to the
        driver!
Take off the silk hat! In fact
that's no place at all for him
up there unceremoniously
dragging our friend out to his own dig-
        nity!   50
Bring him down—bring him down!
Low and inconspicuous! I'd not have him
        ride
on the wagon at all—damn him—
the undertaker's understrapper!
Let him hold the reins

and walk at the side
and inconspicuously too!

Then briefly as to yourselves:
Walk behind—as they do in France,
seventh class, or if you ride   60
Hell take curtains! Go with some show
of inconvenience; sit openly—
to the weather as to grief.
Or do you think you can shut grief in?
What—from us? We who have perhaps
nothing to lose? Share with us
share with us—it will be money
in your pockets.
                    Go now
I think you are ready.

The Dance

In Breughel's great picture, The Kermess,
the dancers go round, they go round and
around, the squeal and the blare and the
tweedle of bagpipes, a bugle and fiddles
tipping their bellies (round as the thick-
sided glasses whose wash they impound)
their hips and their bellies off balance
to turn them. Kicking and rolling about
the Fair Grounds, swinging their butts,
        those
shanks must be sound to bear up under
        such   10
rollicking measures, prance as they dance
in Breughel's great picture, The Kermess.

Classic Scene

A power-house
in the shape of
a red brick chair
90 feet high

on the seat of which
sit the figures
of two metal
stacks—aluminum—

commanding an area
of squalid shacks   10

side by side—
from one of which

buff smoke
streams while under
a grey sky
the other remains

passive today—

The Botticellian Trees

The alphabet of
the trees

is fading in the
song of the leaves

the crossing
bars of the thin

letters that spelled
winter

and the cold
have been illumined   10

with
pointed green

by the rain and sun—
The strict simple

principles of
straight branches

are being modified
by pinched out

ifs of color, devout
conditions   20

the smiles of love—

        . . .

until the stript
sentences

move as a woman's
limbs under cloth

and praise from secrecy
with hot ardor

love's ascendancy
in summer—

In summer the song   30
sings itself

above the muffled words—

Like falling leaves, like fruit, before your
   shot.

2

The autumn frosts will lie upon the grass
Like bloom on grapes of purple-brown
   and gold.
The misted early mornings will be cold;
The little puddles will be roofed with
   glass.
The sun, which burns from copper into
   brass,
Melts these at noon, and makes the boys
   unfold
Their knitted mufflers; full as they can
   hold,
Fat pockets dribble chestnuts as they
   pass.

Peaches grow wild, and pigs can live in
   clover;
A barrel of salted herrings lasts a year;
The spring begins before the winter's
   over.   11
By February you may find the skins
Of garter snakes and water moccasins
Dwindled and harsh, dead-white and
   cloudy-clear.

3

When April pours the colours of a shell
Upon the hills, when every little creek
Is shot with silver from the Chesapeake
In shoals new-minted by the ocean swell,
When strawberries go begging, and the
   sleek
Blue plums lie open to the blackbird's
   beak,
We shall live well—we shall live very
   well.

The months between the cherries and the
   peaches
Are brimming cornucopias which spill
Fruits red and purple, sombre-bloomed
   and black;   10
Then, down rich fields and frosty river
   beaches
We'll trample bright persimmons, while
   you kill

This Is Just to Say

I have eaten
the plums
that were in
the icebox

and which
you were probably
saving
for breakfast.

Forgive me
they were delicious   10
so sweet
and so cold

Elinor Wylie

❋ 1885–1928

Wild Peaches

1

When the world turns completely upside
   down
You say we'll emigrate to the Eastern
   Shore
Aboard a river-boat from Baltimore;
We'll live among wild peach trees, miles
   from town,
You'll wear a coonskin cap, and I a gown
Homespun, dyed butternut's dark gold
   colour.
Lost, like your lotus-eating ancestor,
We'll swim in milk and honey till we
   drown.

The winter will be short, the summer
   long,
The autumn amber-hued, sunny and hot,
Tasting of cider and of scuppernong;   11
All seasons sweet, but autumn best of all.
The squirrels in their silver fur will fall

Bronze partridge, speckled quail, and canvasback.

4

Down to the Puritan marrow of my bones
There's something in this richness that I hate.
I love the look, austere, immaculate,
Of landscapes drawn in pearly monotones.
There's something in my very blood that owns
Bare hills, cold silver on a sky of slate,
A thread of water, churned to milky spate
Streaming through slanted pastures fenced with stones.

I love those skies, thin blue or snowy gray,
Those fields sparse-planted, rendering meagre sheaves;   10
That spring, briefer than apple-blossom's breath,
Summer, so much too beautiful to stay,
Swift autumn, like a bonfire of leaves,
And sleepy winter, like the sleep of death.

Ezra Pound

✳ 1885—

Sestina: Altaforte

Loquitur: *En* Bertrans de Born.
Dante Alighieri put this man in hell
for that he was a stirrer up of strife.
Eccovi! Judge ye!
Have I dug him up again?
The scene is at his castle, Altaforte.
"Papiols" is his jongleur.
"The Leopard," the device of Richard Coeur de Lion.

Damn it all! all this our South stinks peace.

You whoreson dog, Papiols, come! Let's to music!
I have no life save when the swords clash.
But ah! when I see the standards gold, vair, purple, opposing
And the broad fields beneath them turn crimson,
Then howl I my heart nigh mad with rejoicing.

In hot summer have I great rejoicing
When the tempest kills the earth's foul peace,
And the lightnings from black heav'n flash crimson,
And the fierce thunders roar me their music   10
And the winds shriek through the clouds mad, opposing,
And through all the riven skies God's swords clash.

Hell grant soon we hear again the swords clash!
And the shrill neighs of destriers in battle rejoicing,
Spiked breast to spiked breast opposing!
Better one hour's stour than a year's peace
With fat boards, bawds, wine and frail music!
Bah! there's no wine like the blood's crimson!

And I love to see the sun rise blood-crimson.
And I watch his spears through the dark clash   20
And it fills all my heart with rejoicing
And pries wide my mouth with fast music
When I see him so scorn and defy peace,
His lone might 'gainst all darkness opposing.

The man who fears war and squats opposing
My words for stour, hath no blood of crimson.
But is fit only to rot in womanish peace
For from where worth's won and the swords clash

For the death of such sluts I go rejoicing;
Yea, I fill all the air with my music.   30

Papiols, Papiols, to the music!
There's no sound like to swords swords
    opposing,
No cry like the battle's rejoicing
When our elbows and swords drip the
    crimson
And our charges 'gainst "The Leopard's"
    rush clash.
May God damn for ever all who cry
    "Peace!"

And let the music of the swords make
    them crimson!
Hell grant soon we hear again the swords
    clash!
Hell blot black for alway the thought
    "Peace!"

The River-Merchant's Wife: A Letter

While my hair was still cut straight across
    my forehead
I played about the front gate, pulling
    flowers.
You came by on bamboo stilts, playing
    horse,
You walked about my seat, playing with
    blue plums.
And we went on living in the village of
    Chokan:
Two small people, without dislike or
    suspicion.

At fourteen I married My Lord you.
I never laughed, being bashful.
Lowering my head, I looked at the wall.
Called to, a thousand times, I never
    looked back.   10

At fifteen I stopped scowling,
I desired my dust to be mingled with
    yours
Forever and forever and forever.
Why should I climb the look out?

At sixteen you departed,
You went into far Ku-to-yen, by the river
    of swirling eddies,
And you have been gone five months.
The monkeys make sorrowful noise over-
    head.

You dragged your feet when you went
    out.
By the gate now, the moss is grown, the
    different mosses,   20
Too deep to clear them away!
The leaves fall early this autumn, in wind.
The paired butterflies are already yellow
    with August
Over the grass in the West garden;
They hurt me. I grow older.
If you are coming down through the nar-
    rows of the river Kiang,
Please let me know beforehand,
And I will come out to meet you
            As far as Cho-fu-sa.

The Seafarer

FROM THE ANGLO-SAXON

May I for my own self song's truth
    reckon,
Journey's jargon, how I in harsh days
Hardship endured oft.
Bitter breast-cares have I abided,
Known on my keel many a care's hold,
And dire sea-surge, and there I oft spent
Narrow nightwatch nigh the ship's head
While she tossed close to cliffs. Coldly
    afflicted,
My feet were by frost benumbed.
Chill its chains are; chafing sighs   10
Hew my heart round and hunger begot
Mere-weary mood. Lest man know not
That he on dry land loveliest liveth,
List how I, care-wretched, on ice-cold
    sea,
Weathered the winter, wretched outcast
Deprived of my kinsmen;
Hung with hard ice-flakes, where hail-
    scur flew,

There I heard naught save the harsh sea
And ice-cold wave, at whiles the swan
    cries,   19
Did for my games the gannet's clamour,
Sea-fowls' loudness was for me laughter,
The mews' singing all my mead-drink.
Storms, on the stone-cliffs beaten, fell on
    the stern
In icy feathers; full oft the eagle
    screamed
With spray on his pinion.
                       Not any protector
May make merry man faring needy.
This he little believes, who aye in win-
    some life
Abides 'mid burghers some heavy busi-
    ness,
Wealthy and wine-flushed, how I weary
    oft
Must bide above brine.   30
Neareth nightshade, snoweth from north,
Frost froze the land, hail fell on earth
    then,
Corn of the coldest. Nathless there knock-
    eth now
The heart's thought that I on high
    streams
The salt-wavy tumult traverse alone.
Moaneth alway my mind's lust
That I fare forth, that I afar hence
Seek out a foreign fastness.
For this there's no mood-lofty man over
    earth's midst,
Not though he be given his good, but will
    have in his youth greed;   40
Nor his deed to the daring, nor his kind
    to the faithful
But shall have his sorrow for sea-fare
Whatever his lord will.
He hath not heart for harping, nor in
    ring-having
Nor winsomeness to wife, nor world's de-
    light
Nor any whit else save the wave's slash,
Yet longing comes upon him to fare forth
    on the water.
Bosque taketh blossom, cometh beauty of
    berries,

Fields to fairness, land fares brisker,
All this admonisheth man eager of mood,
The heart turns to travel so that he then
    thinks   51
On flood-ways to be far departing.
Cuckoo calleth with gloomy crying,
He singeth summerward, bodeth sorrow,
The bitter heart's blood. Burgher knows
    not—
He the prosperous man—what some per-
    form
Where wandering them widest draweth.
So that but now my heart burst from my
    breastlock,
My mood 'mid the mere-flood,
Over the whale's acre, would wander
    wide.   60
On earth's shelter cometh oft to me,
Eager and ready, the crying lone-flyer,
Whets for the whale-path the heart irre-
    sistibly,
O'er tracks of ocean; seeing that anyhow
My lord deems to me this dead life
On loan and on land, I believe not
That any earth-weal eternal standeth
Save there be somewhat calamitous
That, ere a man's tide go, turn it to twain.
Disease or oldness or sword-hate   70
Beats out the breath from doom-gripped
    body.
And for this, every earl whatever, for
    those speaking after—
Laud of the living, boasteth some last
    word,
That he will work ere he pass onward,
Frame on the fair earth 'gainst foes his
    malice,
Daring ado, . . .
So that all men shall honour him after
And his laud beyond them remain 'mid
    the English,
Aye, for ever, a lasting life's-blast,
Delight 'mid the doughty.
                 Days little durable,
And all arrogance of earthen riches,   81
There come now no kings nor Caesars
Nor gold-giving lords like those gone.
Howe'er in mirth most magnified,

Whoe'er lived in life most lordliest,
Drear all this excellence, delights un-
    durable!
Waneth the watch, but the world hold-
    eth.
Tomb hideth trouble. The blade is layed
    low.
Earthly glory ageth and seareth.
No man at all going the earth's gait,   90
But age fares against him, his face paleth,
Grey-haired he groaneth, knows gone
    companions,
Lordly men, are to earth o'ergiven,
Nor may he then the flesh-cover, whose
    life ceaseth,
Nor eat the sweet nor feel the sorry,
Nor stir hand nor think in mid heart,
And though he strew the grave with gold,
His born bothers, their buried bodies
Be an unlikely treasure hoard.

The Rest

O helpless few in my country,
O remnant enslaved!

Artists broken against her,
A-stray, lost in the villages,
Mistrusted, spoken-against,

Lovers of beauty, starved,
Thwarted with systems,
Helpless against the control;

You who can not wear yourselves out
By persisting to successes,   10
You who can only speak,
Who can not steel yourselves into re-
    iteration;

You of the finer sense,
Broken against false knowledge,
You who can know at first hand,
Hated, shut in, mistrusted:

Take thought:
I have weathered the storm,
I have beaten out my exile.

In a Station of the Metro

The apparition of these faces in the
    crowd;
Petals on a wet, black bough.

John Gould Fletcher
✳ 1886–1950

Elegy on an Empty Skyscraper

1

Against the wall of this sky,
Leaden pall threaded with cardboard
    boxes, the pale light of the towers
Flickers unearthly still,
Long leaden streets between them:
Against the wall of this sky, the cream-
    white faces
Of stone blocks bound in glittering steel
    gleam high;
Jut to the sky, and break
Packed huddled ranks of clouds and roofs
    apart
Thrusting their own horizon yet a little
    higher.

Beauty is spread   10
Here over hollow voids; beneath these
    walls,
Clamor of traffic slides through corridors,
Long elevator-shafts shoot mountainously
    downwards.
Steel on the surface repels
This drizzling daylight; through the inner
    core
Vertical darkness spreads,
Extends its empire upwards,
Forces the tower to tremble with dull
    sound.

Noise of wheels tuned to wheels
Driving the darkness skyward,   20
Forcing the human darkness that should hide
The earth in fruitfulness, still bleakly upward;
In a stark affirmation,
Stone flanged to steel here to repel the daylight;
Void affirmation, since the sky goes higher
And men drift past, unseeing,
Bowed deeper by the weight of locked-in stone:—

Balancing bodies against the heat that holds
Its swift course vertically downwards;
Dragging their heavy feet into its molten pavements,   30
Swaying their shrinking flesh against its reverberant walls;
Noise of wheels tuned to wheels,
Bewildered by the men that move amid them;
While still the tower lurches
Upwards with its long shadow,
Flight of white-ripples four-square on the sky.—

Here in this drift against the wall of sky,
Steel arms that lift,
Tackle that rattles,
Torches that sputter,   40
Chattering hammers that shake the empty brain,
The roar and the mutter
Of the swift elevated train;
And the ships at the dockside,
The pencilled lines of the bridges,
The dull green carpet of park,
The wide grey floor of the bay—
Is all this living to-day?
The fuming and looping line of the surly river to westward,
Stained by the sunset to red—   50
Is all this living or dead?
Dead are the twinkling lights and the sombre reflections

Of the earth-dwellers stretched heavenwards here from below?
Who is there living to know?
Only the wide hollow offices, the corridors empty of light,
Tier after tier going downwards here into the night.

2

Thick pencil of shadow stretched across the street,
If I could lift
Your weight and make you write;
Or if at night   60
I could make move that fixed and arrogant light
That stands there emptily glaring to repeat,
In higher guise, the street-lamp's signal-flight;
What against all the words that we repeat
In vain to-day,
What is the one word I would make you say?

"Here where once stared in dumb hope to the sky
Man by his naked blaze, and saw smoke take away
In folds of undulating grey
His prayer, not knowing walls however high: 70
Here wall on wall is heaped, steel thread to thread
Is riveted to extend the ever-dead:
Vain flight of shadow where the chasms cry."

Is this the word, or is some other thing
That which I seek? The sky gives no reply;
Will man grow wise and grow another wing
As powerful as the one that set on high
This thing?
I do not know:
But slow the darkness gathers; echoes bring   80
Only the wild cries of mechanic woe.

3

Could I but strip you down,
Tear steel from steel in long peeled
strips, and break
The interlocking blocks of cream-white
stone,
Send them like autumn leaves swift spin-
ning down,
Or level, near and far,
This city, spread about you greening
fields,
Leave you alone, all empty as you are,
Gleaming-nerved flower that no grass re-
veals,
Either I'd do: 90
But it is vain within your walls to go,
To feel in your dead heart the beat and
strain
Of hopes grown panic-smitten, to and fro
Millions of meaningless lights,
When all about you is the soundless
night's.

There is wide space between
Man's topmast and his keel, and in it
death
Comes without sign or sound or stir of
breath.
No one shall fill that room, or take his
place
In it, as stowaway or come-aboard;   100
Nor shall the meagre window-blind be
lowered,
Nor shall the dark be levelled by a face.

Robinson Jeffers

✳ 1887—

To the Stone-Cutters

Stone-cutters fighting time with marble,
you foredefeated
Challengers of oblivion

Eat cynical earnings, knowing rock splits,
records fall down,
The square-limbed Roman letters
Scale in the thaws, wear in the rain. The
poet as well
Builds his monument mockingly;
For man will be blotted out, the blithe
earth die, the brave sun
Die blind, his heart blackening:
Yet stones have stood for a thousand
years, and pained thoughts found
The honey peace in old poems.   10

Apology for Bad Dreams

1

In the purple light, heavy with redwood,
the slopes drop seaward,
Headlong convexities of forest, drawn in
together to the steep ravine. Below,
on the sea-cliff,
A lonely clearing; a little field of corn by
the streamside; a roof under spared
trees. Then the ocean
Like a great stone someone has cut to a
sharp edge and polished to shining.
Beyond it, the fountain
And furnace of incredible light flowing
up from the sunk sun. In the little
clearing a woman
Is punishing a horse; she had tied the
halter to a sapling at the edge of the
wood, but when the great whip
Clung to the flanks the creature kicked so
hard she feared he would snap the
halter; she called from the house
The young man her son; who fetched a
chain tie-rope, they working to-
gether
Noosed the small rusty links round the
horse's tongue
And tied him by the swollen tongue to
the tree.   10
Seen from this height they are shrunk to
insect size.
Out of all human relation. You cannot
distinguish

The blood dripping from where the chain
is fastened,
The beast shuddering; but the thrust
neck and the legs
Far apart. You can see the whip fall on
the flanks . . .
The gesture of the arm. You cannot see
the face of the woman.
The enormous light beats up out of the
west across the cloud-bars of the
trade-wind. The ocean
Darkens, the high clouds brighten, the
hills darken together. Unbridled and
unbelievable beauty
Covers the evening world . . . not cov-
ers, grows apparent out of it, as
Venus down there grows out
From the lit sky. What said the prophet?
"I create good: and I create evil: I
am the Lord."   20

2

This coast crying out for tragedy like all
beautiful places,
(The quiet ones ask for quieter suffering:
but here the granite cliff the gaunt
cypresses crown
Demands what victim? The dykes of red
lava and black what Titan? The
hills like pointed flames
Beyond Soberanes, the terrible peaks of
the bare hills under the sun, what
immolation?)
This coast crying out for tragedy like all
beautiful places: and like the pas-
sionate spirit of humanity
Pain for its bread: God's, many victims',
the painful deaths, the horrible
transfigurements: I said in my heart,
"Better invent than suffer: imagine vic-
tims
Lest your own flesh be chosen the
agonist, or you
Martyr some creature to the beauty of
the place." And I said,
"Burn sacrifices once a year to magic   30
Horror away from the house, this little
house here

You have built over the ocean with your
own hands
Beside the standing boulders: for what
are we,
The beast that walks upright, with speak-
ing lips
And little hair, to think we should always
be fed,
Sheltered, intact, and self-controlled? We
sooner more liable
Than the other animals. Pain and terror,
the insanities of desire; not accidents
but essential,
And crowd up from the core:" I imagined
victims for those wolves, I made
them phantoms to follow,
They have hunted the phantoms and
missed the house. It is not good to
forget over what gulfs the spirit
Of the beauty of humanity, the petal of a
lost flower blown seaward by the
night-wind, floats to its quietness.

3

Boulders blunted like an old bear's teeth
break up from the headland; below
them   41
All the soil is thick with shells, the tide-
rock feasts of a dead people.
Here the granite flanks are scarred with
ancient fire, the ghosts of the tribe
Crouch in the nights beside the ghost of
a fire, they try to remember the sun-
light,
Light has died out of their skies. These
have paid something for the future
Luck of the country, while we living keep
old griefs in memory: though God's
Envy is not a likely fountain of ruin, to
forget evils calls down
Sudden reminders from the cloud: re-
membered deaths be our redeemers;
Imagined victims our salvation: white as
the half moon at midnight
Someone flamelike passed me, saying, "I
am Tamar Cauldwell, I have my de-
sire,"   50
Then the voice of the sea returned, when

she had gone by, the stars to their towers.

. . . Beautiful country burn again, Point Pinos down to the Sur Rivers

Burn as before with bitter wonders, land and ocean and the Carmel water.

4

He brays humanity in a mortar to bring the savor

From the bruised root: a man having bad dreams, who invents victims, is only the ape of that God.

He washes it out with tears and many waters, calcines it with fire in the red crucible,

Deforms it, makes it horrible to itself: the spirit flies out and stands naked, he sees the spirit,

He takes it in the naked ecstasy; it breaks in his hand, the atom is broken, the power that massed it

Cries to the power that moves the stars, "I have come home to myself, behold me.

I bruised myself in the flint mortar and burnt me   60

In the red shell, I tortured myself, I flew forth,

Stood naked of myself and broke me in fragments,

And here am I moving the stars that are me."

I have seen these ways of God: I know of no reason

For fire and change and torture and the old returnings.

He being sufficient might be still. I think they admit no reason; they are the ways of my love.

Unmeasured power, incredible passion, enormous craft: no thought apparent but burns darkly

Smothered with its own smoke in the human brain-vault: no thought outside: a certain measure in phenomena:

The fountains of the boiling stars, the

flowers on the foreland, the ever-returning roses of dawn.

Shine, Perishing Republic

While this America settles in the mould of its vulgarity, heavily thickening to empire,

And protest, only a bubble in the molten mass, pops and sighs out, and the mass hardens,

I sadly smiling remember that the flower fades to make fruit, the fruit rots to make earth.

Out of the mother; and through the spring exultances, ripeness and decadence; and home to the mother.

You making haste haste on decay: not blameworthy; life is good, be it stubbornly long or suddenly

A mortal splendor: meteors are not needed less than mountains: shine, perishing republic.

But for my children, I would have them keep their distance from the thickening center; corruption

Never has been compulsory, when the cities lie at the monster's feet there are left the mountains.

And boys, be in nothing so moderate as in love of man, a clever servant, insufferable master.

There is the trap that catches noblest spirits, that caught—they say—God, when he walked on earth.   10

Hurt Hawks

1

The broken pillar of the wing jags from the clotted shoulder,

The wing trails like a banner in defeat,
No more to use the sky forever but live
    with famine
And pain a few days: cat nor coyote
Will shorten the week of waiting for
    death, there is game without talons.
He stands under the oak-bush and waits
The lame feet of salvation; at night he
    remembers freedom
And flies in a dream, the dawns ruin it.
He is strong and pain is worse to the
    strong, incapacity is worse.
The curs of the day come and torment
    him   10
At distance, no one but death the re-
    deemer will humble that head,
The intrepid readiness, the terrible eyes.
The wild God of the world is sometimes
    merciful to those
That ask mercy, not often to the arrogant.
You do not know him, you communal
    people, or you have forgotten him;
Intemperate and savage, the hawk re-
    members him;
Beautiful and wild, the hawks, and men
    that are dying, remember him.

      2

I'd sooner, except the penalties, kill a
    man than a hawk; but the great red-
    tail
Had nothing left but unable misery
From the bone too shattered for mend-
    ing, the wing that trailed under his
    talons when he moved.   20
We had fed him six weeks, I gave him
    freedom,
He wandered over the foreland hill and
    returned in the evening, asking for
    death,
Not like a beggar, still eyed with the old
Implacable arrogance. I gave him the
    lead gift in the twilight. What fell
    was relaxed,
Owl-downy, soft feminine feathers; but
    what
Soared: the fierce rush: the night-herons
    by the flooded river cried fear at its
    rising

Before it was quite unsheathed from
    reality.

Marianne Moore
✳ 1887—

Poetry

I, too, dislike it: there are things that are
    important beyond all this fiddle.
    Reading it, however, with a perfect
        contempt for it, one discovers in
    it after all, a place for the genuine.
        Hands that can grasp, eyes
        that can dilate, hair that can rise
            if it must, these things are impor-
    tant not because a

high-sounding interpretation can be put
        upon them but because they are
    useful. When they become so deriva-
        tive as to become unintelligible,
        the same thing may be said for all of
        us, that we
        do not admire what   10
        we cannot understand: the bat
            holding on upside down or in
            quest of something to

eat, elephants pushing, a wild horse tak-
        ing a roll, a tireless wolf under
    a tree, the immovable critic twitching
        his skin like a horse that feels
        a flea, the base-
    ball fan, the statistician—
        nor is it valid
            to discriminate against "business
            documents and

school-books"; all these phenomena are
        important. One must make a
        distinction
    however: when dragged into promi-
        nence by half poets, the result
        is not poetry,

nor till the poets among us can be 20
"literalists of
the imagination"—above
insolence and triviality and can
present

for inspection, imaginary gardens with
real toads in them, shall we
have
it. In the meantime, if you demand on
the one hand,
the raw material of poetry in
all its rawness and
that which is on the other hand
genuine, then you are interested
in poetry.

What Are Years?

What is our innocence,
what is our guilt? All are
naked, none is safe. And whence
is courage: the unanswered question,
the resolute doubt,—
dumbly calling, deafly listening—that
in misfortune, even death,
encourages others
and in its defeat, stirs

the soul to be strong? He 10
sees deep and is glad, who
accedes to mortality
and in his imprisonment, rises
upon himself as
the sea in a chasm, struggling to be
free and unable to be,
in its surrendering
finds its continuing.

So he who strongly feels,
behaves. The very bird, 20
grown taller as he sings, steels
his form straight up. Though he is cap-
tive,
his mighty singing
says, satisfaction is a lowly
thing, how pure a thing is joy.
This is mortality,
this is eternity.

John Crowe Ransom
✳ 1888—

Bells for John Whiteside's Daughter

There was such speed in her little body,
And such lightness in her footfall,
It is no wonder that her brown study
Astonishes us all.

Her wars were bruited in our high win-
dow.
We looked among orchard trees and be-
yond,
Where she took arms against her shadow,
Or harried unto the pond

The lazy geese, like a snow cloud
Dripping their snow on the green grass,
Tricking and stopping, sleepy and proud,
Who cried in goose, Alas, 12

For the tireless heart within the little
Lady with rod that made them rise
From their noon apple-dreams, and scut-
tle
Goose-fashion under the skies!

But now go the bells, and we are ready;
In one house we are sternly stopped
To say we are vexed at her brown study,
Lying so primly propped. 20

Philomela

Procne, Philomela, and Itylus,
Your names are liquid, your improbable
tale
Is recited in the classic numbers of the
nightingale.
Ah, but our numbers are not felicitous,
It goes not liquidly for us.

Perched on a Roman ilex, and duly
  apostrophized,
The nightingale descanted unto Ovid;
She has even appeared to the Teutons,
  the swilled and gravid;
At Fontainebleau it may be the bird was
  gallicized;
Never was she baptized.   10

To England came Philomela with her
  pain,
Fleeing the hawk her husband; queru-
  lous ghost,
She wanders when he sits heavy on his
  roost,
Utters herself in the original again,
The untranslatable refrain.

Not to these shores she came! this other
  Thrace,
Environ barbarous to the royal Attic;
How could her delicate dirge run demo-
  cratic,
Delivered in a cloudless boundless public
  place
To an inordinate race?   20

I pernoctated with the Oxford students
  once,
And in the quadrangles, in the cloisters,
  on the Cher,
Precociously knocked at antique doors
  ajar,
Fatuously touched the hems of the
  hierophants,
Sick of my dissonance.

I went out to Bagley Wood, I climbed
  the hill;
Even the moon had slanted off in a twin-
  kling,
I heard the sepulchral owl and a few
  bells tinkling,
There was no more villainous day to un-
  fulfil,
The diuturnity was still.   30

Up from the darkest wood where Philo-
  mela sat,
Her fairy numbers issued. What then
  ailed me?

My ears are called capacious but they
  failed me,
Her classics registered a little flat!
I rose, and venomously spat.

Philomela, Philomela, lover of song,
I am in despair if we may make us
  worthy,
A bantering breed sophistical and
  swarthy;
Unto more beautiful, persistently more
  young,
Thy fabulous provinces belong.

The Equilibrists

Full of her long white arms and milky
  skin
He had a thousand times remembered
  sin.
Alone in the press of people traveled he,
Minding her jacinth, and myrrh, and
  ivory.

Mouth he remembered: the quaint orifice
From which came heat that flamed upon
  the kiss,
Till cold words came down spiral from
  the head,
Grey doves from the officious tower ill-
  sped.

Body: it was a white field ready for love,
On her body's field, with the gaunt tower
  above,   10
The lilies grew, beseeching him to take,
If he would pluck and wear them, bruise
  and break.

Eyes talking: Never mind the cruel
  words,
Embrace my flowers, but not embrace
  the swords.
But what they said, the doves came
  straightway flying
And unsaid: Honor, Honor, they came
  crying.

Importunate her doves. Too pure, too
  wise,

Clambering on his shoulder, saying, Arise,
Leave me now, and never let us meet,
Eternal distance now command thy feet.

Predicament indeed, which thus dis-
    covers   21
Honor among thieves, Honor between
    lovers.
O such a little word is Honor, they feel!
But the grey word is between them cold
    as steel.

At length I saw these lovers fully were
    come
Into their torture of equilibrium;
Dreadfully had forsworn each other, and
    yet
They were bound each to each, and they
    did not forget.

And rigid as two painful stars, and
    twirled
About the clustered night their prison
    world,   30
They burned with fierce love always to
    come near,
But Honor beat them back and kept them
    clear.

Ah, the strict lovers, they are ruined now!
I cried in anger. But with puddled brow
Devising for those gibbeted and brave
Came I descanting: Man, what would
    you have?

For spin your period out, and draw your
    breath,
A kinder saeculum begins with Death.
Would you ascend to Heaven and bodi-
    less dwell?
Or take your bodies honorless to Hell?

In Heaven you have heard no marriage
    is,   41
No white flesh tinder to your lecheries,
Your male and female tissue sweetly
    shaped
Sublimed away, and furious blood es-
    caped.

Great lovers lie in Hell, the stubborn ones
Infatuate of the flesh upon the bones;

Stuprate they rend each other when they
    kiss,
The pieces kiss again, no end to this.

But still I watched them spinning, or-
    bited nice.
Their flames were not more radiant than
    their ice.   50
I dug in the quiet earth and wrought the
    tomb
And made these lines to memorize their
    doom:—

Epitaph

Equilibrists lie here; stranger, tread light;
Close, but untouching in each other's
    sight;
Mouldered the lips and ashy the tall
    skull,
Let them lie perilous and beautiful.

Janet Waking

Beautifully Janet slept
Till it was deeply morning. She woke
    then
And thought about her dainty-feathered
    hen,
To see how it had kept.

One kiss she gave her mother.
Only a small one gave she to her daddy
Who would have kissed each curl of his
    shining baby;
No kiss at all for her brother.

"Old Chucky, old Chucky!" she cried,
Running across the world upon the grass
To Chucky's house, and listening. But
    alas,   11
Her Chucky had died.

It was a transmogrifying bee
Came droning down on Chucky's old
    bald head
And sat and put the poison. It scarcely
    bled,
But how exceedingly

And purply did the knot
Swell with the venom and communicate

Its rigor! Now the poor comb stood up
    straight
But Chucky did not.   20

So there was Janet
Kneeling on the wet grass, crying her
    brown hen
(Translated far beyond the daughters of
    men)
To rise and walk upon it.

And weeping fast as she had breath
Janet implored us, "Wake her from her
    sleep!"
And would not be instructed in how
    deep
Was the forgetful kingdom of death.

Blue Girls

Twirling your blue skirts, traveling the
    sward
Under the towers of your seminary,
Go listen to your teachers old and con-
    trary
Without believing a word.

Tie the white fillets then about your lus-
    trous hair
And think no more of what will come to
    pass
Than bluebirds that go walking on the
    grass
And chattering on the air.

Practice your beauty, blue girls, before it
    fail;
And I will cry with my loud lips and
    publish   10
Beauty which all our power shall never
    establish,
It is so frail.

For I could tell you a story which is true:
I know a lady with a terrible tongue,
Blear eyes fallen from blue,
All her perfections tarnished—yet it is
    not long
Since she was lovelier than any of you.

T. S. Eliot

❋ 1888—

Preludes

1

The winter evening settles down
With smells of steaks in passageways.
Six o'clock.
The burnt-out ends of smoky days.
And now a gusty shower wraps
The grimy scraps
Of withered leaves about your feet
And newspapers from vacant lots;
The showers beat
On broken blinds and chimney-pots,   10
And at the corner of the street
A lonely cab-horse steams and stamps.
And then the lighting of the lamps.

2

The morning comes to consciousness
Of faint stale smells of beer
From the sawdust-trampled street
With all its muddy feet that press
To early coffee-stands.
With the other masquerades
That time resumes,   20
One thinks of all the hands
That are raising dingy shades
In a thousand furnished rooms.

3

You tossed a blanket from the bed,
You lay upon your back, and waited;
You dozed, and watched the night re-
    vealing
The thousand sordid images
Of which your soul was constituted;
They flickered against the ceiling.
And when all the world came back   30
And the light crept up between the shut-
    ters

And you heard the sparrows in the gut-
    ters,
You had such a vision of the street
As the street hardly understands;
Sitting along the bed's edge, where
You curled the papers from your hair,
Or clasped the yellow soles of feet
In the palms of both soiled hands.

4

His soul stretched tight across the skies
That fade behind a city block,   40
Or trampled by insistent feet
At four and five and six o'clock;
And short square fingers stuffing pipes,
And evening newspapers, and eyes
Assured of certain certainties,
The conscience of a blackened street
Impatient to assume the world.

I am moved by fancies that are curled
Around these images, and cling:
The notion of some infinitely gentle   50
Infinitely suffering thing.

Wipe your hand across your mouth, and
    laugh;
The worlds revolve like ancient women
Gathering fuel in vacant lots.

Rhapsody on a Windy Night

Twelve o'clock.
Along the reaches of the street
Held in a lunar synthesis,
Whispering lunar incantations
Dissolve the floors of memory
And all its clear relations
Its diversions and precisions,
Every street lamp that I pass
Beats like a fatalistic drum,
And through the spaces of the dark   10
Midnight shakes the memory
As a madman shakes a dead geranium.

Half-past one,
The street lamps sputtered,
The street lamp muttered,

The street lamp said, "Regard that
    woman
Who hesitates toward you in the light of
    the door
Which opens on her like a grin.
You see the border of her dress
Is torn and stained with sand,   20
And you see the corner of her eye
Twists like a crooked pin."

The memory throws up high and dry
A crowd of twisted things;
A twisted branch upon the beach
Eaten smooth, and polished
As if the world gave up
The secret of its skeleton,
Stiff and white.
A broken spring in a factory yard,   30
Rust that clings to the form that the
    strength has left
Hard and curled and ready to snap.

Half-past two,
The street-lamp said,
"Remark the cat which flattens itself in
    the gutter,
Slips out its tongue
And devours a morsel of rancid butter."
So the hand of the child, automatic,
Slipped out and pocketed a toy that was
    running along the quay.
I could see nothing behind that child's
    eye.   40
I have seen eyes in the street
Trying to peer through lighted shutters,
And a crab one afternoon in a pool,
An old crab with barnacles on his back,
Gripped the end of a stick which I held
    him.

Half-past three,
The lamp sputtered,
The lamp muttered in the dark.
The lamp hummed:
"Regard the moon,   **50**
La lune ne garde aucune rancune,
She winks a feeble eye,
She smiles into corners.
She smooths the hair of the grass.
The moon has lost her memory.

A washed-out smallpox cracks her face,
Her hand twists a paper rose,
That smells of dust and eau de Cologne,
She is alone
With all the old nocturnal smells   60
That cross and cross across her brain."
The reminiscence comes
Of sunless dry geraniums
And dust in crevices,
Smells of chestnuts in the streets,
And female smells in shuttered rooms,
And cigarettes in corridors
And cocktail smells in bars.

The lamp said,
"Four o'clock,   70
Here is the number on the door.
Memory!
You have the key,
The little lamp spreads a ring on the
     stair.
Mount.
The bed is open; the tooth-brush hangs
     on the wall,
Put your shoes at the door, sleep, prepare
     for life."

The last twist of the knife.

Journey of the Magi

"A cold coming we had of it,
Just the worst time of the year
For a journey, and such a long journey:
The ways deep and the weather sharp,
The very dead of winter."
And the camels galled, sore-footed, re-
     fractory,
Lying down in the melting snow.
There were times we regretted
The summer palaces on slopes, the ter-
     races,
And the silken girls bringing sherbet.   10
Then the camel men cursing and grum-
     bling
And running away, and wanting their
     liquor and women,

And the night fires going out, and the
     lack of shelters,
And the cities hostile and the towns un-
     friendly
And the villages dirty and charging high
     prices:
A hard time we had of it.
At the end we preferred to travel all
     night,
Sleeping in snatches,
With the voices singing in our ears, say-
     ing
This was all folly.   20

Then at dawn we came down to a tem-
     perate valley,
Wet, below the snow line, smelling of
     vegetation;
With a running stream and a water-mill
     beating the darkness,
And three trees on the low sky,
And an old white horse galloped away in
     the meadow.
Then we came to a tavern with vine-
     leaves over the lintel,
Six hands at an open door dicing for
     pieces of silver,
And feet kicking the empty wine-skins.
But there was no information, and so we
     continued
And arrived at evening, not a moment too
     soon   30
Finding the place; it was (you may say)
     satisfactory.

All this was a long time ago, I remember,
And I would do it again, but set down
This set down
This: were we led all that way for
Birth or Death? There was a Birth, cer-
     tainly,
We had evidence and no doubt. I had
     seen birth and death,
But had thought they were different; this
     Birth was
Hard and bitter agony for us, like Death,
     our death.
We returned to our places, these King-
     doms,   40

But no longer at ease here, in the old dispensation,
With an alien people clutching their gods.
I should be glad of another death.

Marina

Quis hic locus, quae regio, quae mundi plaga?

What seas what shores what grey rocks and what islands
What water lapping the bow
And scent of pine and the woodthrush singing through the fog
What images return
O my daughter.

Those who sharpen the tooth of the dog, meaning
Death
Those who glitter with the glory of the hummingbird, meaning
Death
Those who sit in the style of contentment, meaning   10
Death
Those who suffer the ecstasy of animals, meaning
Death

Are become unsubstantial, reduced by a wind,
A breath of pine, and the woodsong fog
By this grace dissolved in place

What is this face, less clear and clearer
The pulse in the arm, less strong and stronger—
Given or lent? more distant than stars and nearer than the eye

Whispers and small laughter between leaves and hurrying feet   20
Under sleep, where all the waters meet.

Bowsprit cracked with ice and paint cracked with heat.

I made this, I have forgotten
And remember.
The rigging weak and the canvas rotten
Between one June and another September.
Made this unknowing, half conscious, unknown, my own.
The garboard strake leaks, the seams need caulking.
This form, this face, this life
Living to live in a world of time beyond me; let me   30
Resign my life for this life, my speech for that unspoken,
The awakened, lips parted, the hope, the new ships.

What seas what shores what granite islands towards my timbers
And woodthrush calling through the fog
My daughter.

Conrad Aiken

✳ 1889—

Morning Song of Senlin

It is morning, Senlin says, and in the morning
When the light drips through the shutters like the dew,
I arise, I face the sunrise,
And do the things my fathers learned to do.
Stars in the purple dusk above the rooftops
Pale in a saffron mist and seem to die,
And I myself on a swiftly tilting planet
Stand before a glass and tie my tie.

Vine leaves tap my window,
Dew-drops sing to the garden stones,   10
The robin chirps in the chinaberry tree
Repeating three clear tones.

It is morning. I stand by the mirror
And tie my tie once more.
While waves far off in a pale rose twilight
Crash on a white sand shore.
I stand by a mirror and comb my hair:
How small and white my face!—
The green earth tilts through a sphere of
    air
And bathes in a flame of space.   20
There are houses hanging above the stars
And stars hung under a sea . . .
And a sun far off in a shell of silence
Dapples my walls for me . . .

It is morning, Senlin says, and in the
    morning
Should I not pause in the light to remem-
    ber god?
Upright and firm I stand on a star un-
    stable,
He is immense and lonely as a cloud.
I will dedicate this moment before my
    mirror
To him alone, for him I will comb my
    hair.   30
Accept these humble offerings, cloud of
    silence!
I will think of you as I descend the stair.

Vine leaves tap my window,
The snail-track shines on the stones,
Dew-drops flash from the chinaberry tree
Repeating two clear tones.

It is morning, I awake from a bed of si-
    lence,
Shining I rise from the starless waters of
    sleep.
The walls are about me still as in the
    evening,
I am the same, and the same name still I
    keep.   40

The earth revolves with me, yet makes no
    motion,
The stars pale silently in a coral sky.
In a whistling void I stand before my
    mirror,
Unconcerned, and tie my tie.

There are horses neighing on far-off hills
Tossing their long white manes,

And mountains flash in the rose-white
    dusk,
Their shoulders black with rains . . .
It is morning. I stand by the mirror
And surprise my soul once more;   50
The blue air rushes above my ceiling,
There are suns beneath my floor . . .

. . . It is morning, Senlin says, I ascend
    from darkness
And depart on the winds of space for I
    know not where,
My watch is wound, a key is in my
    pocket,
And the sky is darkened as I descend the
    stair.
There are shadows across the windows,
    clouds in heaven,
And a god among the stars; and I will go
Thinking of him as I might think of day-
    break
And humming a tune I know . . .   60

Vine-leaves tap at the window,
Dew-drops sing to the garden stones,
The robin chirps in the chinaberry tree
Repeating three clear tones.

Edna St. Vincent Millay

✳ 1892–1950

First Fig

My candle burns at both ends;
    It will not last the night;
But ah, my foes, and oh, my friends—
    It gives a lovely light!

Second Fig

Safe upon the solid rock the ugly houses
    stand:
Come and see my shining palace built
    upon the sand!

From *Epitaph for the Race of Man*

1

Before this coiling planet shall be cold,
Long, long before the music of the Lyre,
Like the faint roar of distant breakers
  rolled
On reefs unseen, when wind and flood
  conspire
To drive the ship inshore—long, long, I
  say,
Before this ominous humming hits the
  ear,
Earth will have come upon a stiller day,
Man and his engines be no longer here.
High on his naked rock the mountain
  sheep
Will stand alone against the final sky,   10
Drinking a wind of danger new and deep,
Staring on Vega with a piercing eye,
And gather up his slender hooves and
  leap
From crag to crag down Chaos, and so go
  by.

2

When Death was young and bleaching
  bones were few,
A moving hill against the risen day
The dinosaur at morning made his way,
And dropped his dung upon the blazing
  dew;
Trees with no name that now are agate
  grew
Lushly beside him in the steamy clay;
He woke and hungered, rose and stalked
  his prey,
And slept contented, in a world he knew.
In punctual season, with the race in
  mind,
His consort held aside her heavy tail,   10
And took the seed; and heard the seed
  confined

Roar in her womb; and made a nest to
  hold
A hatched-out conqueror . . . but to no
  avail:
The veined and fertile eggs are long since
  cold.

4

O Earth, unhappy planet born to die,
Might I your scribe and your confessor
  be,
What wonders must you not relate to me
Of Man, who when his destiny was high
Strode like the sun into the middle sky
And shone an hour, and who so bright as
  he,
And like the sun went down into the sea,
Leaving no spark to be remembered by.
But no; you have not learned in all these
  years
To tell the leopard and the newt apart;
Man, with his singular laughter, his droll
  tears,   11
His engines and his conscience and his
  art,
Made but a simple sound upon your ears:
The patient beating of the animal heart.

Archibald MacLeish

✳ 1892—

Ars Poetica

A poem should be palpable and mute
As a globed fruit

Dumb
As old medallions to the thumb

Silent as the sleeve-worn stone
Of casement ledges where the moss has
  grown—

A poem should be wordless
As the flight of birds

A poem should be motionless in time
As the moon climbs   10

Leaving, as the moon releases
Twig by twig the night-entangled trees,

Leaving, as the moon behind the winter
    leaves,
Memory by memory the mind—

A poem should be motionless in time
As the moon climbs

A poem should be equal to:
Not true

For all the history of grief
An empty doorway and a maple leaf   20

For love
The leaning grasses and two lights above
    the sea—

A poem should not mean
But be.

The Too-Late Born

We too, we too, descending once again
The hills of our own land, we too have
    heard
Far off—Ah, que ce cor a longue
    haleine—
The horn of Roland in the passages of
    Spain,
The first, the second blast, the failing
    third,
And with the third turned back and
    climbed once more
The steep road southward, and heard
    faint the sound
Of swords, of horses, the disastrous war,
And crossed the dark defile at last, and
    found
At Roncevaux upon the darkening plain
The dead against the dead and on the
    silent ground   11
The silent slain—

Empire Builders

The Museum Attendant:

This is *The Making of America in Five
    Panels:*

This is Mister Harriman making America:
Mister-Harriman-is-buying-the-Union-Pa-
    cific-at-Seventy:
The Santa Fe is shining on his hair:

This is Commodore Vanderbilt making
    America:
Mister-Vanderbilt-is-eliminating-the-
    short-interest-in-Hudson:
Observe the carving on the rocking chair:

This is J. P. Morgan making America:
(The Tennessee Coal is behind to the left
    of the Steel Company:)   9
Those in mauve are braces he is wearing:

This is Mister Mellon making America:
Mister-Mellon-represented-as-a-
    symbolical-figure-in-aluminum-
Strewing-bank-stocks-on-a-burnished-
    stair:

This is Bruce is the Barton making Amer-
    ica:
Mister-Barton-is-selling-us-Doctor's-
    Deliciousest-Dentifrice:
This is he in beige with the canary:

You have just beheld the Makers making
    America:
This is *The Making of America in Five
    Panels:*
America lies to the west-southwest of the
    Switch-Tower:
There is nothing to see of America but
    land: 20

*The Original Document
    under the Panel Paint:*

"To Thos. Jefferson Esq. his obd't serv't
M. Lewis: captain detached:

                              Sir:

Having in mind your repeated commands
    in this matter:

And the worst half of it done and the
streams mapped:

And we here on the back of this beach
beholding the
Other ocean—two years gone and the
cold

Breaking with rain for the third spring
since St. Louis:
The crows at the fishbones on the frozen
dunes:

The first cranes going over from south
north: 30
And the river down by a mark of the pole
since the morning:

And time near to return, and a ship
(Spanish)
Lying in for the salmon: and fearing
chance or the

Drought or the Sioux should deprive you
of these discoveries—
Therefore we send by sea in this writing:

Above the
Platte there were long plains and a clay
country:
Rim of the sky far off: grass under it:

Dung for the cook fires by the sulphur
licks:
After that there were low hills and the
sycamores:

And we poled up by the Great Bend in
the skiffs: 40
The honey bees left us after the Osage
River:

The wind was west in the evenings and
no dew and the
Morning Star larger and whiter than
usual—

The winter rattling in the brittle haws:
The second year there was sage and the
quail calling:

All that valley is good land by the river:
Three thousand miles and the clay cliffs
and

Rue and beargrass by the water banks
And many birds and the brant going over
and tracks of

Bear elk wolves marten: the buffalo   50
Numberless so that the cloud of their dust
covers them:

The antelope fording the fall creeks: and
the mountains and
Grazing lands and the meadow lands and
the ground

Sweet and open and well-drained:
                        We advise you to
Settle troops at the forks and to issue
licenses:

Many men will have living on these
lands:
There is wealth in the earth for them and
the wood standing

And the wild birds on the water where
they sleep.
There is stone in the hills for the towns of
a great people . . ."

You have just beheld the Makers making
America: 60

They screwed her scrawny and gaunt
with their seven-year panics:
They bought her back on their mortgages
old-whore-cheap:
They fattened their bonds at her breasts
till the thin blood ran from them:

Men have forgotten how full clear and
deep
The Yellowstone moved on the gravel and
grass grew
When the land lay waiting for her west-
ward people!

Brave New World

But you, Thomas Jefferson,
You could not lie so still,
You could not bear the weight of stone
On the quiet hill,

You could not keep your green grown
    peace
Nor hold your folded hand
If you could see your new world now,
Your new sweet land.

There was a time, Tom Jefferson,
When freedom made free men.   10
The new found earth and the new freed
    mind
Were brothers then.

There was a time when tyrants feared
The new world of the free.
Now freedom is afraid and shrieks
At tyranny.

Words have not changed their sense so
    soon
Nor tyranny grown new.
The truths you held, Tom Jefferson,
Will still hold true.   20

What's changed is freedom in this age.
What great men dared to choose
Small men now dare neither win
Nor lose.

You, Thomas Jefferson,
You could not lie so still,
You could not bear the weight of stone
On your green hill,

You could not hold your angry tongue
If you could see how bold   30
The old stale bitter world plays new—
And the new world old.

You, Andrew Marvel

And here face down beneath the sun
And here upon earth's noonward height
To feel the always coming on
The always rising of the night:

To feel creep up the curving east
The earthy chill of dusk and slow
Upon those under lands the vast
And ever climbing shadow grow

And strange at Ecbatan the trees
Take leaf by leaf the evening strange   10
The flooding dark about their knees
The mountains over Persia change

And now at Kermanshah the gate
Dark empty and the withered grass
And through the twilight now the late
Few travelers in the westward pass

And Baghdad darken and the bridge
Across the silent river gone
And through Arabia the edge
Of evening widen and steal on   20

And deepen on Palmyra's street
The wheel rut in the ruined stone
And Lebanon fade out and Crete
High through the clouds and overblown

And over Sicily the air
Still flashing with the landward gulls
And loom and slowly disappear
The sails above the shadowy hulls

And Spain go under and the shore
Of Africa the gilded sand   30
And evening vanish and no more
The low pale light across that land:

Nor now the long light on the sea

And here face downward in the sun
To feel how swift how secretly
The shadow of the night comes on . . .

E. E. Cummings

✳ 1894—

I Sing of Olaf

i sing of Olaf glad and big
whose warmest heart recoiled at war:
a conscientious object-or

his well-belovéd colonel (trig
westpointer most succinctly bred)

took erring Olaf soon in hand;
but—though an host of overjoyed
noncoms (first knocking on the head
him) do through icy waters roll
that helplessness which others stroke   10
with brushes recently employed
anent this muddy toiletbowl,
while kindred intellects evoke
allegiance per blunt instruments—
Olaf (being to all intents
a corpse and wanting any rag
upon what God unto him gave)
responds, without getting annoyed
"I will not kiss your f.ing flag"

straightway the silver bird looked grave
(departing hurriedly to shave)   21

but—though all kinds of officers
(a yearning nation's blueeyed pride)
their passive prey did kick and curse
until for wear their clarion
voices and boots were much the worse,
and egged the firstclassprivates on
his rectum wickedly to tease
by means of skilfully applied
bayonets roasted hot with heat—   30
Olaf (upon what were once knees)
does almost ceaselessly repeat
"there is some s. I will not eat"

our president, being of which
assertions duly notified
threw the yellowsonofabitch
into a dungeon, where he died

Christ (of His mercy infinite)
i pray to see; and Olaf, too

preponderatingly because   40
unless statistics lie he was
more brave than me: more blond than
    you.

Poem, or Beauty Hurts Mr. Vinal

take it from me kiddo
believe me
my country, 'tis of

you, land of the Cluett
Shirt Boston Garter and Spearmint
Girl With The Wrigley Eyes(of you
land of the Arrow Ide
and Earl &
Wilson
Collars)of you i   10
sing: land of Abraham Lincoln and
    Lydia E. Pinkham,
land above all of Just Add Hot Water
    And Serve–
from every B. V. D.

let freedom ring

amen. i do however protest, anent the un
-spontaneous and otherwise scented
    merde which
greets one(Everywhere Why)as divine
    poesy per
that and this radically defunct periodical.
    i would
suggest that certain ideas gestures
rhymes, like Gilette Razor Blades   20
having been used and reused
to the mystical moment of dullness em-
    phatically are
Not To Be Resharpened. (Case in point

if we are to believe these gently O
    sweetly
melancholy trillers amid the thrillers
these crepuscular violinists among my
    and your
skyscrapers–Helen & Cleopatra were Just
    Too Lovely,
The Snail's On The Thorn enter Morn
    and God's
In His andsoforth

do you get me?)according   30
to such supposedly indigenous
throstles Art is O World O Life
a formula: example, Turn Your Shirttails
    Into
Drawers and If It Isn't An Eastman It
    Isn't A
Kodak therefore my friends let
us now sing each and all fortissimo A–
mer
i

ca, I
love,   40
You.   And there's a
hund-red-mil-lion-oth-ers, like
all of you successfully if
delicately gelded (or spaded)
gentlemen(and ladies)–pretty

littleliverpill-
hearted-Nojolneeding-There's-A-Reason
americans(who tensetendoned and with
upward vacant eyes, painfully
perpetually   crouched,   quivering,   upon
     the   50
sternly allotted sandpile
–how silently
emit a tiny violetflavoured nuisance:
     Odor?

ono.
comes out like a ribbon lies flat on the
     brush

Pity This Busy Monster,
Manunkind

pity this busy monster,manunkind,

not.   Progress is a comfortable disease:
your victim(death and life safely be-
     yond)

plays with the bigness of his littleness
—electrons deify one razorblade
into a mountainrange;lenses extend

unwish through curving wherewhen till
     unwish
returns on its unself.
                         A world of made
is not a world of born—pity poor flesh

and trees,poor stars and stones,but never
     this   10
fine specimen of hypermagical

ultraomnipotence.   We doctors know

a hopeless case if—listen:there's a hell
of a good universe next door;let's go

A Salesman Is an It
That Stinks Excuse

a salesman is an it that stinks Excuse

Me whether it's president of the you were
     say
or a jennelman name misder finger isn't
important whether it's millions of other
     punks
or just a handful absolutely doesn't
matter and whether it's in lonjewray

or shrouds is immaterial it stinks

a salesman is an it that stinks to please

but whether to please itself or someone
     else
makes no more difference than if it sells
hate condoms education snakeoil vac   11
uumcleaners terror strawberries democ
ra(caveat emptor)cy superfluous hair

or Think We've Met subhuman rights Be-
     fore

Next to of Course God

"next to of course god america i
love you land of the pilgrims' and so forth
     oh
say can you see by the dawn's early my
country 'tis of centuries come and go
and are no more what of it we should
     worry
in every language even deafanddumb
thy sons acclaim your glorious name by
     gorry
by jingo by gee by gosh by gum
why talk of beauty what could be more
     beaut-
iful than these heroic happy dead   10
who rushed like lions to the roaring
     slaughter

they did not stop to think they died in-
stead
then shall the voice of liberty be mute?"

He spoke. And drank rapidly a glass
of water

The Way to Hump a Cow

the way to hump a cow is not
to get yourself a stool
but draw a line around the spot
and call it beautifool

to multiply because and why
dividing thens by nows
and adding and (i understand)
is hows to hump a cows

the way to hump a cow is not
to elevate your tool   10
but drop a penny in the slot
and bellow like a bool

to lay a wreath from ancient greath
on insulated brows
(while tossing boms at uncle toms)
is hows to hump a cows

the way to hump a cow is not
to push and then to pull
but practicing the art of swot
to preach the golden rull   20

to vote for me (all decent mem
and wonens will allows
which if they don't to hell with them)
is hows to hump a cows

My Father Moved through Dooms of Love

my father moved through dooms of love
through sames of am through haves of
    give,
singing each morning out of each night
my father moved through depths of
    height

this motionless forgetful where
turned at his glance to shining here;
that if (so timid air is firm)
under his eyes would stir and squirm

newly as from unburied which
floats the first who, his april touch   10
drove sleeping selves to swarm their fates
woke dreamers to their ghostly roots

and should some why completely weep
my father's fingers brought her sleep:
vainly no smallest voice might cry
for he could feel the mountains grow.

Lifting the valleys of the sea
my father moved through griefs of joy;
praising a forehead called the moon
singing desire into begin   20

joy was his song and joy so pure
a heart of star by him could steer
and pure so now and now so yes
the wrists of twilight would rejoice

keen as midsummer's keen beyond
conceiving mind of sun will stand,
so strictly (over utmost him
so hugely) stood my father's dream

his flesh was flesh his blood was blood:
no hungry man but wished him food;   30
no cripple wouldn't creep one mile
uphill to only see him smile.

Scorning the pomp of must and shall
my father moved through dooms of feel;
his anger was as right as rain
his pity was as green as grain

septembering arms of year extend
less humbly wealth to foe and friend
than he to foolish and to wise
offered immeasurable is   40

proudly and (by octobering flame
beckoned) as earth will downward climb,
so naked for immortal work
his shoulders marched against the dark

his sorrow was as true as bread:
no liar looked him in the head;
if every friend became his foe
he'd laugh and build a world with snow.

My father moved through theys of we,
singing each new leaf out of each
   tree   50
(and every child was sure that spring
danced when she heard my father sing)

then let men kill which cannot share,
let blood and flesh be mud and mire,
scheming imagine, passion willed,
freedom a drug that's bought and sold

giving to steal and cruel kind,
a heart to fear, to doubt a mind,
to differ a disease of same,
conform the pinnacle of am   60

though dull were all we taste as bright,
bitter all utterly things sweet,
maggoty minus and dumb death
all we inherit, all bequeath

and nothing quite so least as truth
—i say though hate were why men
   breathe—
because my father lived his soul
love is the whole and more than all

Stephen Vincent Benét

❋ 1898–1943

American Names

I have fallen in love with American
   names,
The sharp names that never get fat,
The snakeskin-titles of mining-claims,
The plumed war-bonnet of Medicine Hat,
Tucson and Deadwood and Lost Mule
   Flat.

Seine and Piave are silver spoons,
But the spoonbowl-metal is thin and
   worn,
There are English counties like hunting-
   tunes

Played on the keys of the postboy's horn,
But I will remember where I was born.

I will remember Carquinez Straits,   11
Little French Lick and Lundy's Lane,
The Yankee ships and the Yankee dates
And the bullet-towns of Calamity Jane.
I will remember Skunktown Plain.

I will fall in love with a Salem tree
And a rawhide quirt from Santa Cruz,
I will get me a bottle of Boston sea
And a blue-gum nigger to sing me blues.
I am tired of loving a foreign muse.   20

Rue des Martyrs and Bleeding-Heart-
   Yard,
Senlis, Pisa, and Blindman's Oast,
It is a magic ghost you guard
But I am sick for a newer ghost,
Harrisburg, Spartanburg, Painted Post.

Henry and John were never so,
And Henry and John were always right?
Granted, but when it was time to go
And the tea and the laurels had stood all
   night,
Did they never watch for Nantucket
   Light?   30

I shall not rest quiet in Montparnasse.
I shall not lie easy at Winchelsea.
You may bury my body in Sussex grass,
You may bury my tongue at Champmédy.
I shall not be there. I shall rise and pass.
Bury my heart at Wounded Knee.

From *John Brown's Body*

THE SONG OF THE BREATH

I heard the song of the breath
Go up from city and country,
The even breath of the sick,
The dry cough in the throat
Of the man with the death-sweat on him,
We breathe but do not hear.

The harsh gasp of the runner,
The long sigh of power

Heaving the weight aloft,
The grey breath of the old. 10
Men at the end of strength
With their lungs turned lead and fire,
Panting like thirsty dogs;
A child's breath, blowing a flame.

The breath that is the voice,
The silver, the woodwinds speaking,
The dear voice of your lover,
The hard voice of your foe,
And the vast breath of wind,
Mysterious over mountains, 20
Caught in pines like a bird
Or filling all hammered heaven.

I heard the song of breath,
Like a great strand of music,
Blown between void and void,
Uncorporal as the light.
The breath of nations asleep,
And the piled hills they sleep in,
The word that never was flesh
And yet is nothing but life. 30

What are you, bodiless sibyl,
Unseen except as the frost-cloud
Puffed from a silver mouth
When the hard winter's cold?
We cannot live without breath,
And yet we breathe without knowledge,
And the vast strand of sound
Goes on, eternally sighing,
Without dimension or space,
Without beginning or end. 40

I heard the song of breath
And lost it in all sharp voices,
Even my own voice lost
Like a thread in that huge strand,
Lost like a skein of air,
And with it, continents lost
In the great throat of Death.
I trembled, asking in vain,
Whence come you, whither art gone?
The continents flow and melt 50
Like wax in the naked candle,
Burnt by the wick of time—
Where is the breath of the Chaldees,
The dark, Minoan breath?
I said to myself in hate,

Hearing that mighty rushing,
Though you raise a new Adam up
And blow fresh fire in his visage,
He has only a loan of air,
And gets but a breathing-space. 60
But then I was quieted.

I heard the song of breath,
The gulf hollow with voices,
Fused into one slow voice
That never paused or was faint.
Man, breathing his life,
And with him all life breathing,
The young horse and the snake,
Beetle, lion and dove,
Solemn harps of the fir, 70
Trumpets of sea and whirlwind
And the vast, tiny grass
Blown by a breath and speaking.
I heard these things. I heard
The multitudinous river.
When I came back to my life,
My voice was numb in my ears,
I wondered that I still breathed.

Hart Crane
❈ 1899–1932

From THE BRIDGE

Praise for an Urn

IN MEMORIAM: ERNEST NELSON

It was a kind and northern face
That mingled in such exile guise
The everlasting eyes of Pierrot
And, of Gargantua, the laughter.

His thoughts, delivered to me
From the white coverlet and pillow,
I see now, were inheritances—
Delicate riders of the storm.

The slant moon on the slanting hill
Once moved us toward presentiments

Of what the dead keep, living still,   11
And such assessments of the soul

As, perched in the crematory lobby,
The insistent clock commented on,
Touching as well upon our praise
Of glories proper to the time.

Still, having in mind gold hair,
I cannot see that broken brow
And miss the dry sound of bees
Stretching across a lucid space.   20

Scatter these well-meant idioms
Into the smoky spring that fills
The suburbs, where they will be lost.
They are no trophies of the sun.

The Hurricane

Lo, Lord, Thou ridest!
Lord, Lord, Thy swifting heart

Naught stayeth, naught now bideth
But's smithereened apart!

Ay! Scripture flee'th stone!
Milk-bright, Thy chisel wind

Rescindeth flesh from bone
To quivering whittlings thinned—

Swept—whistling straw! Battered,
Lord, e'en boulders now out-leap   10

Rock sockets, levin-lathered!
Nor, Lord, may worm out-deep

Thy drum's gambade, its plunge abscond!
Lord God, while summits crashing

Whip sea-kelp screaming on blond
Sky-seethe, high heaven dashing—

Thou ridest to the door, Lord!
Thou bidest wall nor floor, Lord!

The Broken Tower

The bell-rope that gathers God at dawn
Dispatches me as though I dropped
    down the knell

Of a spent day—to wander the cathedral
    lawn
From pit to crucifix, feet chill on steps
    from hell.

Have you not heard, have you not seen
    that corps
Of shadows in the tower, whose shoul-
    ders sway
Antiphonal carillons launched before
The stars are caught and hived in the
    sun's ray?

The bells, I say, the bells break down
    their tower;
And swing I know not where. Their
    tongues engrave   10
Membrane through marrow, my long-
    scattered score
Of broken intervals . . . And I, their
    sexton slave!

Oval encyclicals in canyons heaping
The impasse high with choir. Banked
    voices slain!
Pagodas, campaniles with reveilles out-
    leaping—
O terraced echoes prostrate on the
    plain! . . .

And so it was I entered the broken world
To trace the visionary company of love,
    its voice
An instant in the wind (I know not
    whither hurled)
But not for long to hold each desperate
    choice.   20

My word I poured. But was it cognate,
    scored
Of that tribunal monarch of the air
Whose thigh embronzes earth, strikes
    crystal Word
In wounds pledged once to hope—cleft
    to despair?

The steep encroachments of my blood
    left me
No answer (could blood hold such a lofty
    tower
As flings the question true?)—or is it she

Whose   sweet   mortality   stirs   latent
  power?—

And through whose pulse I hear, count-
  ing the strokes
My veins recall and add, revived and
  sure   30
The angelus of wars my chest evokes:
What I hold healed, original now, and
  pure . . .

And builds, within, a tower that is not
  stone
(Not stone can jacket heaven)—but slip
Of pebbles—visible wings of silence
  sown
In azure circles, widening as they dip

The matrix of the heart, lift down the eye
That shrines the quiet lake and swells a
  tower . . .
The commodious, tall decorum of that
  sky
Unseals her earth, and lifts love in its
  shower.   40

Proem: To Brooklyn Bridge

How many dawns, chill from his rippling
  rest
The seagull's wings shall dip and pivot
  him,
Shedding white rings of tumult, building
  high
Over the chained bay waters Liberty—

Then, with inviolate curve, forsake our
  eyes
As apparitional as sails that cross
Some page of figures to be filed away;
—Till elevators drop us from our
  day . . .

I think of cinemas, panoramic sleights
With multitudes bent toward some flash-
  ing scene   10
Never disclosed, but hastened to again,
Foretold to other eyes on the same
  screen;

And Thee, across the harbor, silver-paced
As though the sun took step of thee, yet
  left
Some motion ever unspent in thy
  stride,—
Implicitly thy freedom staying thee!

Out of some subway scuttle, cell or loft
A bedlamite speeds to thy parapets,
Tilting there momently, shrill shirt bal-
  looning,
A jest falls from the speechless caravan.

Down Wall, from girder into street noon
  leaks,   21
A rip-tooth of the sky's acetylene;
All afternoon the cloud-flown derricks
  turn . . .
Thy cables breathe the North Atlantic
  still.

And obscure as that heaven of the Jews,
Thy guerdon . . . Accolade thou dost
  bestow
Of anonymity time cannot raise:
Vibrant reprieve and pardon thou dost
  show.

O harp and altar, of the fury fused,
(How could mere toil align thy choiring
  strings!)   30
Terrific threshold of the prophet's pledge,
Prayer of pariah, and the lover's cry,—

Again the traffic lights that skim thy swift
Unfractioned idiom, immaculate sigh of
  stars,
Beading thy path—condense eternity:
And we have seen night lifted in thine
  arms.

Under thy shadow by the piers I waited;
Only in darkness is thy shadow clear.
The City's fiery parcels all undone,
Already snow submerges an iron
  year . . .   40

O Sleepless as the river under thee,
Vaulting the sea, the prairies' dreaming
  sod,
Unto us lowliest sometime sweep, de-
  scend
And of the curveship lend a myth to God.

The Harbor Dawn

Insistently through sleep—a tide of voices—
They meet you listening midway in your dream,
The long, tired sounds, fog-insulated noises:
Gongs in white surplices, beshrouded wails,
Far strum of fog horns . . . signals dispersed in veils.

*400 years and
more . . . or is
it from the
soundless
shore of sleep
that time*

And then a truck will lumber past the wharves
As winch engines begin throbbing on some deck;
Or a drunken stevedore's howl and thud below
Comes echoing alley-upward through dim snow.

And if they take your sleep away sometimes   10
They give it back again. Soft sleeves of sound
Attend the darkling harbor, the pillowed bay;
Somewhere out there in blankness steam

Spills into steam, and wanders, washed away
—Flurried by keen fifings, eddied
Among distant chiming buoys—adrift. The sky,
Cool feathery fold, suspends, distills
This wavering slumber. . . . Slowly—
Immemorially the window, the half-covered chair,
Ask nothing but this sheath of pallid air.   20

*recalls you to
your love,
there in a
waking dream
to merge your
seed*

And you beside me, blessèd now while sirens
Sing to us, stealthily weave us into day—
Serenely now, before day claims our eyes
Your cool arms murmurously about me lay.
While myriad snowy hands are clustering at the panes—

> *yours hands within my hands are deeds;*
> *my tongue upon your throat—singing*
> *arms close; eyes wide, undoubtful*
> > *dark*
> > > *drink the dawn—*   30
> *a forest shudders in your hair!*

—with whom?

The window goes blond slowly. Frostily clears.
From Cyclopean towers across Manhattan waters
—Two—three bright window-eyes aglitter, disk
The sun, released—aloft with cold gulls hither.
The fog leans one last moment on the sill.
Under the mistletoe of dreams, a star—
As though to join us at some distant hill—
Turns in the waking west and goes to sleep.

*Who is the
woman with
us in the
dawn? . . .
whose is the
flesh our feet
have moved
upon?*

Van Winkle

Macadam, gun-gray as the tunny's belt,
Leaps from Far Rockaway to Golden
Gate:
Listen! the miles a hurdy-gurdy grinds—
Down gold arpeggios mile on mile un-
winds.

Times earlier, when you hurried off to
school,
—It is the same hour though a later
day—
You walked with Pizarro in a copybook,
And Cortes rode up, reining tautly in—
Firmly as coffee grips the taste,—and
away!

There was Priscilla's cheek close in the
wind,   10
And Captain Smith, all beard and cer-
tainty,
And Rip Van Winkle, bowing by the
way,—
"Is this Sleepy Hollow, friend—?" And
he—

And Rip forgot the office hours,
              and he forgot the pay;
Van Winkle sweeps a tenement
              down town on Avenue A,—

The grind-organ says . . . Remember,
remember
The cinder pile at the end of the back-
yard
Where we stoned the family of young
Garter snakes under . . . And the mono-
planes   21
We launched—with paper wings and
twisted
Rubber bands. . . . Recall—
              the rapid tongues
That flittered from under the ash heap
day
After day whenever your stick discovered
Some sunning inch of unsuspecting
fiber—

It flashed back at your thrust, as clean as
fire.

And Rip was slowly made aware
     that he, Van Winckle, was not here
Nor there. He woke and swore he'd seen
     Broadway a Catskill daisy chain in
     May—   31

So memory, that strikes a rhyme out of a
box,
Or splits a random smell of flowers
through glass—
Is it the whip stripped from the lilac tree
One day in spring my father took to me,
Or is it the Sabbatical, unconscious smile
My mother almost brought me once from
church
And once only, as I recall—?

It flickered through the snow screen,
blindly   40
It forsook her at the doorway; it was gone
Before I had left the window. It
Did not return with the kiss in the hall.

Macadam, gun-gray as the tunny's belt,
Leaps from Far Rockaway to Golden
Gate . . .
Keep hold of that nickel for car-change,
Rip,—
Have you got your paper—?
And hurry along, Van Winkle—it's get-
ting late!

The River

Stick your patent name on a signboard
brother—all   over—going   west—young
man
Tintex—Japalac—Certain-teed   Overalls
ads
and lands sakes! under the new playbill
ripped
in the guaranteed corner—see Bert Wil-
liams what?
Minstrels when you steal a chicken just
save me the wing, for if it isn't
Erie it ain't for miles around a

Mazda—and the telegraphic night com-
   ing on Thomas

a Ediford—and whistling down the
   tracks   10
a headlight rushing with the sound—can
   you
imagine—while an EXPRESS makes time
   like
SCIENCE—COMMERCE and the HOLYGHOST
RADIO ROARS IN EVERY HOME WE HAVE
   THE NORTHPOLE
WALLSTREET AND VIRGINBIRTH WITHOUT
   STONES OR
WIRES OR EVEN RUNning brooks connect-
   ing ears
and no more sermons windows flashing
   roar
Breathtaking—as you like it . . . eh?

            So the 20th Century—so
whizzed the Limited—roared by and left
three men, still hungry on the tracks,
   ploddingly   21
watching the tail lights wizen and con-
   verge,
slipping gimleted and neatly out of sight.
The last bear, shot drinking in the Dako-
   tas,
Loped under wires that span the moun-
   tain stream.
Keen instruments, strung to a vast pre-
   cision
Bind town to town and dream to ticking
   dream.
But some men take their liquor slow—
   and count—
Though they'll confess no rosary nor
   clue—
The river's minute by the far brook's
   year.   30
Under a world of whistles, wires and
   steam
Caboose-like they go ruminating through
Ohio, Indiana—blind baggage—
To Cheyenne tagging . . . Maybe Kala-
   mazoo.

Time's renderings, time's blendings they
   construe

As final reckonings of fire and snow;
Strange bird-wit, like the elemental gist
Of unwalled winds they offer, singing
   low
My Old Kentucky Home and *Casey
   Jones*,
Some Sunny Day. I heard a road-gang
   chanting so.   40
And afterwards, who had a colt's eyes—
   one said,
"Jesus! Oh I remember watermelon
   days!" And sped
High in a cloud of merriment, recalled
"—And when my Aunt Sally Simpson
   smiled," he drawled—
"It was almost Louisiana, long ago."

"There's no place like Booneville though,
   Buddy,"
One said, excising a last burr from his
   vest,
"—For early trouting." Then peering in
   the can,
"—But I kept on the tracks." Possessed,
   resigned,
He trod the fire down pensively and
   grinned,   50
Spreading dry shingles of a beard. . . .

                           Behind
My father's cannery works I used to see
Rail-squatters ranged in nomad raillery,
The ancient men—wifeless or runaway
Hobo-trekkers that forever search
An empire wilderness of freight and rails.
Each seemed a child, like me, on a loose
   perch,
Holding to childhood like some termless
   play.
John, Jake, or Charley, hopping the slow
   freight   60
—Memphis to Tallahassee—riding the
   rods,
Blind fists of nothing, humpty-dumpty
   clods.

Yet they touch something like a key per-
   haps.
From pole to pole across the hills, the
   states

—They know a body under the wide
rain;
Youngsters with eyes like fjords, old rep-
robates
With racetrack jargon,—dotting immen-
sity
They lurk across her, knowing her yonder
breast
Snow-silvered, sumac-stained or smoky
blue,
Is past the valley-sleepers, south or west.
—As I have trod the rumorous midnights,
too.   71

And past the circuit of the lamp's thin
flame
(O Nights that brought me to her body
bare!)
Have dreamed beyond the print that
bound her name.
Trains sounding the long blizzards out—I
heard
Wail into distances I knew were hers.
Papooses crying on the wind's long
mane
Screamed redskin dynasties that fled the
brain,
—Dead echoes! But I knew her body
there,
Time like a serpent down her shoulder
dark,   80
And space, an eaglet's wing, laid on her
hair.

Under the Ozarks, domed by Iron Moun-
tain,
The old gods of the rain lie wrapped in
pools
Where eyeless fish curvet a sunken foun-
tain
And re-descend with corn from querulous
crows.
Such pilferings make up their timeless
eatage,
Propitiate them for their timber torn
By iron, iron—always the iron dealt
cleavage!
They doze now, below axe and powder
horn.

And Pullman breakfasters glide glisten-
ing steel   90
From tunnel into field—iron strides the
dew—
Straddles the hill, a dance of wheel on
wheel.
You have a half-hour's wait at Siskiyou,
Or stay the night and take the next train
through.
Southward, near Cairo passing, you can
see
The Ohio merging,—borne down Ten-
nessee;
And if it's summer and the sun's in dusk
Maybe the breeze will lift the River's
musk
—As though the waters breathed that
you might know
*Memphis Johnny, Steamboat Bill, Mis-
souri Joe.*   100
Oh, lean from the window, if the train
slows down,
As though you touched hands with some
ancient clown,
—A little while gaze absently below
And hum *Deep River* with them while
they go.

Yes, turn again and sniff once more—look
see,
O Sheriff, Brakeman and Authority—
Hitch up your pants and crunch another
quid,
For you, too, feed the River timelessly.
And few evade full measure of their fate;
Always they smile out eerily what they
seem.   110
I could believe he joked at heaven's
gate—
Dan Midland—jolted from the cold
brake-beam.

Down, down—born pioneers in time's
despite,
Grimed tributaries to an ancient flow—
They win no frontier by their wayward
plight,
But drift in stillness, as from Jordan's
brow.

You will not hear it as the sea; even
    stone
Is not more hushed by gravity . . . But
    slow,
As loth to take more tribute—sliding
    prone
Like one whose eyes were buried long
    ago   120

The River, spreading, flows—and spends
    your dream.
What are you, lost within this tideless
    spell?
You are your father's father, and the
    stream—
A liquid theme that floating niggers swell.

Damp tonnage and alluvial march of
    days—
Nights turbid, vascular with silted shale
And roots surrendered down of moraine
    clays:
The Mississippi drinks the farthest dale.

O quarrying passion, undertowed sun-
    light!
The basalt surface drags a jungle grace
Ochreous and lynx-barred in lengthening
    might;   131
Patience! and you shall reach the biding
    place!

Over De Soto's bones the freighted floors
Throb past the City storied of three
    thrones.
Down two more turns the Mississippi
    pours
(Anon tall ironsides up from salt la-
    goons)

And flows within itself, heaps itself free.
All fades but one thin skyline 'round
    . . . Ahead
No embrace opens but the stinging sea;
The River lifts itself from its long bed,

Poised wholly on its dream, a mustard
    glow,   141
Tortured with history, its one will—flow!
—The Passion spreads in wide tongues,
    chocked and slow,
Meeting the Gulf, hosannas silently be-
    low.

National Winter Garden

Outspoken buttocks in pink beads
Invite the necessary cloudy clinch
Of bandy eyes. . . . No extra mufflings
    here:
The world's one flagrant, sweating cinch.

And while legs waken salads in the brain
You pick your blonde out neatly through
    the smoke.
Always you wait for someone else though,
    always—
(Then rush the nearest exit through the
    smoke).

Always and last, before the final ring
When all the fireworks blare, begins   10
A tom-tom scrimmage with a somewhere
    violin,
Some cheapest echo of them all—begins.

And shall we call her whiter than the
    snow?
Sprayed first with ruby, then with emer-
    ald sheen—
Least tearful and least glad (who knows
    her smile?)
A caught slide shows her sandstone grew
    between.

Her eyes exist in swivellings of her teats,
Pearls whip her thighs, a drench of whirl-
    ing strands.
Her silly snake rings begin to mount, sur-
    mount
Each other—turquoise fakes on tinselled
    hands.   20

We wait that writhing pool, her pearls
    collapsed,
—All but her belly buried in the floor;
And the lewd trounce of a final muted
    beat!
We flee her spasm through a fleshless
    door. . . .

Yet, to the empty trapeze of your flesh,
O Magdalene, each comes back to die
    alone.
Then you, the burlesque of our lust—and
    faith,

Lugs us back lifeward—bone by infant
bone.

The Tunnel

To Find the Western path
Right thr' the Gates of Wrath.

BLAKE

Performances, assortments, résumés—
Up Times Square to Colombus Circle
lights
Channel the congresses, nightly sessions,
Refractions of the thousand theatres,
faces—
Mysterious   kitchens . . . You   shall
search them all.
Some day by heart you'll learn each
famous sight
And watch the curtain lift in hell's de-
spite;
You'll find the garden in the third act
dead,
Finger your knees—and wish yourself in
bed
With tabloid crime-sheets perched in
easy sight.   10

Then let you reach your hat
and go.
As usual, let you—also
walking down—exclaim
to twelve upward leaving
a subscription praise
for what time slays.

Or can't you quite make up your mind to
ride;
A walk is better underneath the L a
brisk
Ten blocks or so before? But you find
yourself   20
Preparing penguin flexions of the arms,—
As usual you will meet the scuttle yawn:
The subway yawns the quickest promise
home.

Be minimum, then, to swim the hiving
swarms
Out of the Square, the Circle burning
bright—

Avoid the glass doors gyring at your
right,
Where boxed alone a second, eyes take
fright
—Quite unprepared rush naked back to
light:
And down beside the turnstile press the
coin
Into the slot. The gongs already rattle.

And so   31
of cities you bespeak
subways, rivered under streets
and rivers . . . In the car
the overtone of motion
underground, the monotone
of motion is the sound
of   other   faces,   also   under-
ground—

"Let's have a pencil Jimmy—living now
at Floral Park   40
Flatbush—on the Fourth of July—
like a pigeon's muddy dream—potatoes
to dig in the field—travlin the town—
too—
night after night—the Culver line—the
girls all shaping up—it used to be—"

Our tongues recant like beaten weather
vanes.
This answer lives like verdigris, like hair
Beyond extinction, surcease of the bone;
And repetition freezes—"What

"what do you want? getting weak on the
links?   50
fandaddle daddy don't ask for change—is
this
FOURTEENTH? it's half past six she said—
if
you don't like my gate why did you
swing on it, why *didja*
swing on it anyhow—"

And somehow anyhow swing—

The phonographs of hades in the brain
Are tunnels that re-wind themselves, and
love
A burnt match skating in a urinal—
Somewhere above Fourteenth TAKE THE
EXPRESS   60

To brush some new presentiment of
pain—

"But I want service in this office SERVICE
I said—after
the show she cried a little afterwards
but—"

Whose head is swinging from the swollen
strap?
Whose body smokes along the bitten rails,
Bursts from a smoldering bundle far be-
hind
In back forks of the chasms of the
brain,—
Puffs from a riven stump far out behind
In   interborough   fissures   of   the
mind . . . ?
And why do I often meet your visage
here,   70
Your eyes like agate lanterns—on and on
Below the toothpaste and the dandruff
ads?
—And did their riding eyes right through
your side,
And did their eyes like unwashed platters
ride?
And Death, aloft,—gigantically down
Probing through you—toward me, O
evermore!
And when they dragged your retching
flesh,
Your trembling hands that night through
Baltimore—
That last night on the ballot rounds, did
you
Shaking, did you deny the ticket, Poe?

For Gravesend Manor change at Cham-
bers Street.   81
The platform hurries along to a dead
stop.

The intent escalator lifts a serenade
Stilly
Of shoes, umbrellas, each eye attending
its shoe, then
Bolting outright somewhere above where
streets
Burst suddenly in rain . . . The gongs
recur:

Elbows and levers, guard and hissing
door.
Thunder is galvothermic here below . . .
The car
Wheels off. The train rounds, bending to
a scream,   90
Taking the final level for the dive
Under the river—
And somewhat emptier than before,
Demented, for a hitching second, humps;
then
Lets go. . . . Toward corners of the
floor
Newspapers wing, revolve and wing.
Blank windows gargle signals through the
roar.
And does the Daemon take you home,
also,
Wop washerwoman, with the bandaged
hair?
After the corridors are swept, the cuspi-
dors—   100
The gaunt sky-barracks cleanly now, and
bare,
O Genoese, do you bring mother eyes and
hands
Back home to children and to golden
hair?
Daemon, demurring and eventful yawn!
Whose hideous laughter is a bellows
mirth
—Or the muffled slaughter of a day in
birth—
O cruelly to inoculate the brinking dawn
With antennæ toward worlds that glow
and sink;—
To spoon us out more liquid than the dim
Locution of the eldest star, and pack 110
The conscience navelled in the plunging
wind,
Umbilical to call—and straightway die!

O caught like pennies beneath soot and
steam,
Kiss of our agony thou gatherest;
Condensed, thou takest all—shrill gan-
glia
Impassioned with some song we fail to
keep.
And yet, like Lazarus, to feel the slope,

The sod and billow breaking,—lifting ground,
—A sound of waters bending astride the sky
Unceasing with some Word that will not die . . . ! 120
A tugboat, wheezing wreaths of steam,
Lunged past, with one galvanic blare stove up the River.
I counted the echoes assembling, one after one,
Searching, thumbing the midnight on the piers.
Lights, coasting, left the oily tympanum of waters;
The blackness somewhere gouged glass on a sky.
And this thy harbor, O my City, I have driven under,
Tossed from the coil of ticking towers . . . Tomorrow,
And to be . . . Here by the River that is East—
Here at the waters' edge the hands drop memory; 130
Shadowless in that abyss they unaccounting lie.
How far away the star has pooled the sea—
Or shall the hands be drawn away, to die?

Kiss of our agony Thou gatherest,
                    O Hand of Fire
                              gatherest—

Allen Tate

✳ 1899—

The Mediterranean

Quem das finem, rex magne, dolorum?

Where we went in the boat was a long bay
A slingshot wide, walled in by towering stone—
Peaked margin of antiquity's delay,
And we went there out of time's monotone:

Where we went in the black hull no light moved
But a gull white-winged along the feckless wave,
The breeze, unseen but fierce as a body loved,
That boat drove onward like a willing slave:

Where we went in the small ship the seaweed
Parted and gave to us the murmuring shore 10
And we made feast and in our secret need
Devoured the very plates Aeneas bore:

Where derelict you see through the low twilight
The green coast that you, thunder-tossed, would win,
Drop sail, and hastening to drink all night
Eat dish and bowl—to take that sweet land in!

Where we feasted and caroused on the sandless
Pebbles, affecting our day of piracy,
What prophecy of eaten plates could landless
Wanderers fulfill by the ancient sea? 20

We for that time might taste the famous age
Eternal here yet hidden from our eyes
When lust of power undid its stuffless rage;
They, in a wineskin, bore earth's paradise.

Let us lie down once more by the breathing side
Of Ocean, where our live forefathers sleep
As if the Known Sea still were a month wide—
Atlantis howls but is no longer steep!

What country shall we conquer, what
  fair land
Unman our conquest and locate our
  blood?   30
We've cracked the hemispheres with
  careless hand!
Now, from the Gates of Hercules we flood

Westward, westward till the barbarous
  brine
Whelms us to the tired land where tassel-
  ing corn,
Fat beans, grapes sweeter than musca-
  dine
Rot on the vine: in that land were we
  born.

Last Days of Alice

Alice grown lazy, mammoth but not fat,
Declines upon her lost and twilight age;
Above in the dozing leaves the grinning
  cat
Quivers forever with his abstract rage:

Whatever light swayed on the perilous
  gate
Forever sways, nor will the arching grass,
Caught when the world clattered, undu-
  late
In the deep suspension of the looking-
  glass.

Bright Alice! always pondering to gloze
The spoiled cruelty she had meant to
  say   10
Gazes learnedly down her airy nose
At nothing, nothing thinking all the day.

Turned absent-minded by infinity
She cannot move unless her double move,
The All-Alice of the world's entity
Smashed in the anger of her hopeless
  love,

Love for herself who, as an earthly
  twain,
Pouted to join her two in a sweet one;
No more the second lips to kiss in vain

The first she broke, plunged through the
  glass alone—   20

Alone to the weight of impassivity,
Incest of spirit, theorem of desire,
Without will as chalky cliffs by the sea,
Empty as the bodiless flesh of fire:

All space, that heaven is a dayless night,
A nightless day driven by perfect lust
For vacancy, in which her bored eyesight
Stares at the drowsy cubes of human dust.

—We too back to the world shall never
  pass
Through the shattered door, a dumb
  shade-harried crowd   30
Being all infinite, function depth and
  mass
Without figure, a mathematical shroud

Hurled at the air—blesséd without sin!
O God of our flesh, return us to Your
  wrath,
Let us be evil could we enter in
Your grace, and falter on the stony path!

Sonnets at Christmas

1

This is the day His hour of life draws
  near,
Let me get ready from head to foot for it
Most handily with eyes to pick the year
For small feed to reward a feathered wit.
Some men would see it an epiphany
At ease, at food and drink, others at
  chase
Yet I, stung lassitude, with ecstasy
Unspent argue the season's difficult case

So: Man, dull critter of enormous head,
What would he look at in the coiling sky?
But I must kneel again unto the Dead
While Christmas bells of paper white and
  red,   12
Figured with boys and girls spilt from a
  sled,
Ring out the silence I am nourished by.

2

Ah, Christ, I love you rings to the wild
    sky
And I must think a little of the past:
When I was ten I told a stinking lie
That got a black boy whipped; but now
    at last
The going years, caught in an accurate
    glow,
Reverse like balls englished upon green
    baize—
Let them return, let the round trumpets
    blow
The ancient crackle of the Christ's deep
    gaze.

Deafened and blind, with senses yet un-
    found,
Am I, untutored to the after-wit   10
Of knowledge, knowing a nightmare has
    no sound;
Therefore with idle hands and head I sit
In late December before the fire's daze
Punished by crimes of which I would be
    quit.

Kenneth Fearing

✳ 1902—

Dirge

1-2-3 was the number he played but to-
    day the number came 3-2-1;
    bought his Carbide at 30 and it went
    to 29; had the favorite at Bowie
    but the track was slow—

O, executive type, would you like to drive
    a floating power, knee-action, silk-
    upholstered six? Wed a Holly-
    wood star? Shoot the course in
    58? Draw to the ace, king, jack?
    O, fellow with a will who won't take
    no, watch out for three cigarettes

on the same, single match; O,
    democratic voter born in August
    under Mars, beware of liquidated
    rails—

Denouement to denouement, he took a
    personal pride in the certain, cer-
    tain way he lived his own, private
    life,
    but nevertheless, they shut off his gas;
    nevertheless, the bank foreclosed;
    nevertheless, the landlord called;
    nevertheless, the radio broke,

And twelve o'clock arrived just once too
    often,
    just the same he wore one grey tweed
    suit, bought one straw hat, drank
    one straight Scotch, walked one
    short step, took one long look,
    drew one deep breath,
    just one too many,

And wow he died as wow he lived,   10
    going whop to the office and blooie
    home to sleep and biff got mar-
    ried and bam had children and
    oof got fired,
    zowie did he live and zowie did he die,

With who the hell are you at the corner
    of his casket, and where the hell
    we going on the right-hand silver
    knob, and who the hell cares
    walking second from the end with
    an American Beauty wreath from
    why the hell not,

Very much missed by the circulation staff
    of the New York Evening Post;
    deeply, deeply mourned by the
    B.M.T.,

Wham, Mr. Roosevelt; pow, Sears Roe-
    buck; awk, big dipper; bop, sum-
    mer rain;
    bong, Mr., bong, Mr., bong, Mr., bong.

SOS

It is posted in the clubrooms,
It is announced in the bright electric

lights on all the principal streets, it
is rumored, proclaimed, and radio'd
out to sea,
SOS, SOS,
That her hair is a dark cloud and her eyes
are deep blue;

Total strangers on the buses, at the
beaches, in the parks,
Argue and discuss, as though they really
knew,
Whether she prefers cork tips, likes a
sweet or dry sherry, takes lemon
with her tea,
SOS, SOS,

But they all agree that her hats, that her
gowns, that her slippers, that her
gloves, that her books, that her
flowers,
And her past, and her present, and her
future as stated in the cards, and as
written in the stars,   10

Are all about right,
And dead right and dead against the
law,

But her eyes are blue,
Blue for miles and miles and miles,
SOS, SOS,
Blue across the country and away across
the sea.

Richard Eberhart

✳ 1904—

The Groundhog

In June, amid the golden fields,
I saw a groundhog lying dead.
Dead lay he; my senses shook,
And mind outshot our naked frailty.
There lowly in the vigorous summer
His form began its senseless change,
And made my senses waver dim
Seeing nature ferocious in him.

Inspecting close his maggots' might
And seething cauldron of his being,   10
Half with loathing, half with a strange
love,
I poked him with an angry stick.
The fever arose, became a flame
And Vigour circumscribed the skies,
Immense energy in the sun,
And through my frame a sunless trem-
bling.
My stick had done nor good nor harm.
Then stood I silent in the day
Watching the object, as before;
And kept my reverence for knowledge
Trying for control, to be still,   21
To quell the passion of the blood;
Until I had bent down on my knees
Praying for joy in the sight of decay.
And so I left; and I returned
In Autumn strict of eye, to see
The sap gone out of the groundhog,
But the bony sodden hulk remained.
But the year had lost its meaning,
And in intellectual chains   30
I lost both love and loathing,
Mured up in the wall of wisdom.
Another summer took the fields again
Massive and burning, full of life,
But when I chanced upon the spot
There was only a little hair left,
And bones bleaching in the sunlight
Beautiful as architecture;
I watched them like a geometer,
And cut a walking stick from a birch.   40
It has been three years, now.
There is no sign of the groundhog.
I stood there in the whirling summer,
My hand capped a withered heart,
And thought of China and of Greece,
Of Alexander in his tent;
Of Montaigne in his tower,
Of Saint Theresa in her wild lament.

The Soul Longs to Return
Whence It Came

I drove up to the graveyard, which
Used to frighten me as a boy,

When I walked down the river past it,
And evening was coming on. I'd make
 sure
I came home from the woods early
 enough.
I drove in, I found to the place, I
Left the motor running. My eyes hurried,
To recognize the great oak tree
On the little slope, among the stones.
It was a high day, a crisp day,   10
The cleanest kind of Autumn day,
With brisk intoxicating air, a
Little wind that frisked, yet there was
Old age in the atmosphere, nostalgia,
The subtle heaviness of the Fall.
I stilled the motor. I walked a few paces;
It was good, the tree; the friendliness of
 it.
I touched it, I thought of the roots;
They would have pierced her seven
 years.
O all peoples! O mighty shadows!   20
My eyes opened along the avenue
Of tombstones, the common land of
 death.
Humiliation of all loves lost,
That might have had full meaning in any
Plot of ground, come, hear the silence,
See the quivering light. My mind worked
Almost imperceptibly, I
In the command, I the wilful ponderer.
I must have stood silent and thoughtful
There. A host of dry leaves   30
Danced on the ground in the wind.
They startled, they curved up from the
 ground,
There was a dry rustling, rattling.
The sun was motionless and brittle.
I felt the blood darken in my cheeks
And burn. Like running. My eyes
Telescoped on decay, I out of command.
Fear, tenderness, they seized me.
My eyes were hot, I dared not look
At the leaves. A pagan urge swept me.
Multitudes, O multitudes in one.   41
The urge of the earth, the titan
Wild and primitive lust, fused
On the ground of her grave.
I was a being of feeling alone.
I flung myself down on the earth

Full length on the great earth, full length,
I wept out the dark load of human love.
In pagan adoration I adored her.
I felt the actual earth of her.   50
Victor and victim of humility,
I closed in the wordless ecstasy
Of mystery: where there is no thought
But feeling lost in itself forever,
Profound, remote, immediate, and calm.
Frightened, I stood up, I looked about
Suspiciously, hurriedly (A rustling),
As if the sun, the air, the trees
Were human, might not understand.
I drew breath, it made a sound,   60
I stepped gingerly away. Then
The mind came like a fire, it
Tortured man, I thought of madness.
The mind will not accept the blood.
The sun and sky, the trees and grasses,
And the whispering leaves, took on
Their usual characters. I went away,
Slowly, tingling, elated, saying, saying
Mother, Great Being, O Source of Life
To whom in wisdom we return,   70
Accept this humble servant evermore.

The Fury of Aerial Bombardment

You would think the fury of aerial bom-
 bardment
Would rouse God to relent; the infinite
 spaces
Are still silent. He looks on shock-pried
 faces.
History, even, does not know what is
 meant.

You would feel that after so many cen-
 turies
God would give man to repent; yet he
 can kill
As Cain could, but with multitudinous
 will,
No farther advanced than in his ancient
 furies.

Was man made stupid to see his own
 stupidity?

Is God by definition indifferent, beyond
us all?   10
Is the eternal truth man's fighting soul
Wherein the Beast ravens in its own
avidity?

Of Van Wettering I speak, and Averill,
Names on a list, whose faces I do not re-
call
But they are gone to early death, who
late in school
Distinguished the belt feed lever from
the belt holding pawl.

Robert Penn Warren

 1905—

Original Sin: A Short Story

Nodding, its great head rattling like a
gourd,
And locks like seaweed strung on the
stinking stone,
The nightmare stumbles past, and you
have heard
It fumble your door before it whimpers
and is gone:
It acts like the old hound that used to
snuffle your door and moan.

You thought you had lost it when you left
Omaha,
For it seemed connected then with your
grandpa, who
Had a wen on his forehead and sat on the
veranda
To finger the precious protuberance, as
was his habit to do,
Which glinted in sun like rough garnet or
the rich old brain bulging through.

But you met it in Harvard Yard as the
historic steeple   11
Was confirming the midnight with its
hideous racket,

And you wondered how it had come, for
it stood so imbecile,
With empty hands, humble, and surely
nothing in pocket:
Riding the rods, perhaps—or grandpa's
will paid the ticket.

You were almost kindly then, in your first
homesickness,
As it tortured its stiff face to speak, but
scarcely mewed;
Since then you have outlived all your
homesickness,
But have met it in many another distem-
pered latitude:
Oh, nothing is lost, ever lost! at last you
understood.   20

But it never came in the quantum glare
of sun
To shame you before your friends, and
had nothing to do
With your public experience or private
reformation:
But it thought no bed too narrow—it
stood with lips askew
And shook its great head sadly like the
abstract Jew.

Never met you in the lyric arsenical
meadow
When children call and your heart goes
stone in the bosom;
At the orchard anguish never, nor ovoid
horror,
Which is furred like a peach or avid like
the delicious plum.
It takes no part in your classic prudence
or fondled axiom.   30

Not there when you exclaimed: "Hope is
betrayed by
Disastrous glory of sea-capes, sun-torment
of whitecaps
—There must be a new innocence for us
to be stayed by."
But there it stood, after all the timetables,
all the lamps,
In the crepuscular clutter of *always, al-
ways,* or *perhaps.*

You have moved often and rarely left an
    address,
And hear of the deaths of friends with a
    sly pleasure,
A sense of cleansing and hope, which
    blooms from distress;
But it has not died, it comes, its hand
    childish, unsure,
Clutching the bribe of chococlate or a
    toy you used to treasure.   40

It tries the lock; you hear, but simply
    drowse:
There is nothing remarkable in that
    sound at the door.
Later you hear it wander the dark house
Like a mother who rises at night to seek a
    childhood picture;
Or it goes to the backyard and stands like
    an old horse cold in the pasture.

Bearded Oaks

The oaks, how subtle and marine,
Bearded, and all the layered light
Above them swims; and thus the scene,
Recessed, awaits the positive night.

So, waiting, we in the grass now lie
Beneath the languorous tread of light:
The grasses, kelp-like, satisfy
The nameless motions of the air.

Upon the floor of light, and time,
Unmurmuring, of polyp made,   10
We rest; we are, as light withdraws,
Twin atolls on a shelf of shade.

Ages to our construction went,
Dim architecture, hour by hour:
And violence, forgot now, lent
The present stillness all its power.

The storm of noon above us rolled,
Of light the fury, furious gold,
The long drag troubling us, the depth:
Dark is unrocking, unrippling, still.   20

Passion and slaughter, ruth, decay
Descend, minutely whispering down,
Silted down swaying streams, to lay
Foundation for our voicelessness.

All our debate is voiceless here,
As all our rage, the rage of stone;
If hope is hopeless, then fearless fear,
And history is thus undone.

Our feet once wrought the hollow street
With echo when the lamps were dead
At windows, once our headlight glare
Disturbed the doe that, leaping, fled.   32

I do not love you less that now
The caged heart makes iron stroke,
Or less that all that light once gave
The graduate dark should now revoke.

We live in time so little time
And we learn all so painfully
That we may spare this hour's term
To practice for eternity.   40

Crime

Envy the mad killer who lies in the ditch
    and grieves,
Hearing the horns on the highway, and
    the tires scream:
He tries to remember, and tries, but he
    cannot seem
To remember what it was he buried
    under the leaves.

By the steamed lagoon, near the carnivor-
    ous orchid,
Pirates hide treasure and mark the place
    with a skull,
Then lose the map, and roar in pubs with
    a skinful,
In Devon or Barbados; but remember
    what they hid.

But what was it? But he is too tired to
    ask it.
An old woman mumbling her gums like
    incertitude?   10
The proud stranger who asked the match
    by the park wood,

Or the child who crossed the park every
day with the lunch-basket?

He cannot say, nor formulate the de-
licious
And smooth convolution of terror, like
whipped cream,
Nor the mouth, rounded and white for
the lyric scream
Which he never heard, though he still
tries, nodding and serious.

His treasure: for years down streets of
contempt and trouble,
Hugged under his coat, among sharp el-
bows and rows
Of eyes hieratic like foetuses in jars;
Or he nursed it unwitting, like a child
asleep with a bauble.   20

Happiness: what the heart wants. That is
its fond
Definition, and wants only the peace in
God's eye.
Our flame bends in that draft; and that is
why
He clutched at the object bright on the
bottom of the murky pond.

Peace, all he asked: past despair and past
the uncouth
Violation, he snatched at the fleeting
hem, though in error;
Nor gestured before the mind's sycophant
mirror,
Nor made the refusal and spat from the
secret side of his mouth.

Though a tree for you is a tree, and in the
long
Dark, no sibilant tumor inside your enor-
mous   30
Head, though no walls confer in the silent
house,
Nor the eyes of pictures protrude, like a
snail's, each on its prong,

Yet envy him, for what he buried is
buried
By the culvert there, till the boy with the
air-gun
In spring, at the violet, comes; nor is ever
known

To go on any vacations with him, lend
money, break bread.

And envy him, for though the seasons
stammer
Past pulse in the yellow throat of the
field-lark,
Still memory drips, a pipe in the cellar-
dark,
And in its hutch and hole, as when the
earth gets warmer,   40

The cold heart heaves like a toad, and
lifts its brow
With that bright jewel you have no use
for now;
While puzzled yet, despised with the
attic junk, the letter
Names over your name, and mourns
under the dry rafter.

Theodore Roethke

✻ 1908—

Dolor

I have known the inexorable sadness of
pencils,
Neat in their boxes, dolor of pad and
paper-weight,
All the misery of manila folders and
mucilage,
Desolation in immaculate public places,
Lonely reception room, lavatory, switch-
board,
The unalterable pathos of basin and
pitcher,
Ritual of multigraph, paper-clip, comma,
Endless duplication of lives and objects.
And I have seen dust from the walls of
institutions,
Finer than flour, alive, more dangerous
than silica,   10
Sift, almost invisible, through long after-
noons of tedium,

Dripping a fine film on nails and delicate eyebrows,
Glazing the pale hair, the duplicate gray standard faces.

My Papa's Waltz

The whiskey on your breath
Could make a small boy dizzy;
But I hung on like death:
Such waltzing was not easy.

We romped until the pans
Slid from the kitchen shelf;
My mother's countenance
Could not unfrown itself.

The hand that held my wrist
Was battered on one knuckle;   10
At every step you missed
My right ear scraped a buckle.

You beat time on my head
With a palm scraped hard by dirt,
Then waltzed me off to bed
Still clinging to your shirt.

Night Crow

When I saw that clumsy crow
Flap from a wasted tree,
A shape in the mind rose up:
Over the gulfs of dream
Flew a tremendous bird
Further and further away
Into a moonless black,
Deep in the brain, far back.

Elegy for Jane

MY STUDENT, THROWN BY A HORSE

I remember the neckcurls, limp and damp as tendrils;
And her quick look, a sidelong pickerel smile;

And how, once startled into talk, the light syllables leaped for her,
And she balanced in the delight of her thought,
A wren, happy, tail into the wind,
Her song trembling the twigs and small branches.
The shade sang with her;
The leaves, their whispers turned to kissing,
And the mould sang in the bleached valleys under the rose.

Oh, when she was sad, she cast herself down into such a pure depth,   10
Even a father could not find her:
Scraping her cheek against straw,
Stirring the clearest water.

My sparrow, you are not here,
Waiting like a fern, making a spiney shadow.
The sides of wet stones cannot console me,
Nor the moss, wound with the last light.

If only I could nudge you from this sleep,
My maimed darling, my skittery pigeon.
Over this damp grave I speak the words of my love: 20
I, with no rights in this matter,
Neither father nor lover.

The Dream

1

I met her as a blossom on a stem
Before she ever breathed, and in that dream
The mind remembers from a deeper sleep:
Eye learned from eye, cold lip from sensual lip.
My dream divided on a point of fire;
Light hardened on the water where we were;
A bird sang low; the moonlight sifted in;
The water rippled, and she rippled on.

2

She came toward me in the flowing air,
A shape of change, encircled by its fire.
I watched her there, between me and the
    moon;   11
The bushes and the stones danced on and
    on;
I touched her shadow when the light
    delayed;
I turned my face away, and yet she
    stayed.
A bird sang from the center of a tree;
She loved the wind because the wind
    loved me.

3

Love is not love until love's vulnerable.
She slowed to sigh, in that long interval.
A small bird flew in circles where we
    stood;
The deer came down, out of the dappled
    wood.   20
All who remember, doubt. Who calls that
    strange?
I tossed a stone, and listened to its
    plunge.
She knew the grammar of least motion,
    she
Lent me one virtue, and I live thereby.

4

She held her body steady in the wind;
Our shadows met, and slowly swung
    around;
She turned the field into a glittering sea;
I played in flame and water like a boy
And I swayed out beyond the white sea
    foam;
Like a wet log, I sang within a flame.   30
In that last while, eternity's confine,
I came to love, I came into my own.

The Shape of the Fire

1

What's this? A dish for fat lips.
Who says? A nameless stranger.

Is he a bird or a tree? Not every-
    one can tell.
Water recedes to the crying of spiders.
An old scow bumps over black rocks.
A cracked pod calls.
    Mother me out of here. What
        more will the bones allow?
    Will the sea give the wind suck?
        A toad folds into a stone.
    These flowers are all fangs. Com-
        fort me, fury,
    Wake me, witch, we'll do the
        dance of rotten sticks.   10
Shale loosens. Marl reaches into the field.
    Small birds pass over water.
Spirit, come near. This is only the edge
    of whiteness.
I can't laugh at a procession of dogs.
    In the hour of ripeness the tree is
        barren.
    The she-bear mopes under the
        hill.
    Mother, mother, stir from your
        cave of sorrow.
A low mouth laps water. Weeds, weeds,
    how I love you.
The arbor is cooler. Farewell, farewell,
    fond worm.
The warm comes without sound.

2

    Where's the eye?   20
    The eye's in the sty.
    The ear's not here
    Beneath the hair,
    When I took off my clothes
    To find a nose,
    There was only one shoe
    For the waltz of To,
    The pinch of Where.
Time for the flat-headed man. I recognize
    that listener,
Him with the platitudes and rubbery
    doughnuts,   30
Melting at the knees, a varicose horror.
Hello, hello. My nerves knew you, dear
    boy.
Have you come to unhinge my shadow?
Last night I slept in the pits of a tongue.

The silver fish ran in and out of my
  special bindings;
I grew tired of the ritual of names and
  the assistant keeper of the molluscs:
Up over a viaduct I came, to the snakes
  and sticks of another winter,
A two-legged dog hunting a new horizon
  of howls.
The wind sharpened itself on a rock;
A voice sang: 40

> Pleasure on ground
> Has no sound,
> Easily maddens
> The uneasy man.
>
> Who, careless, slips
> In coiling ooze
> Is trapped to the lips,
> Leaves more than shoes;
>
> Must pull off clothes
> To jerk like a frog   50
> On belly and nose
> From the sucking bog.

My meat eats me. Who waits at the gate?
Mother of quartz, your words writhe into
  my ear.
Renew the light, lewd whisper.

3

The wasp waits.
      The edge cannot eat the centre.
The grape glistens.
      The path tells little to the serpent.
An eye comes out of the wave.   60
      The journey from flesh is longest.
A rose sways least.
      The redeemer comes a dark way.

4

Morning-fair, follow me further back
Into that minnowy world of weeds and
  ditches,
When the herons floated high over the
  white houses,
And the little crabs slipped into silvery
  craters,
When the sun for me glinted the sides of
  a sand-grain,

And my intent stretched over the buds at
  their first trembling.
That air and shine: and the flicker's loud
  summer call;   70
The bearded boards in the stream and
  the all of apples;
The glad hen on the hill; and the trellis
  humming.
Death was not. I lived in a simple
  drowse:
Hands and hair moved through a dream
  of waking blossoms;
Rain sweetened the cave and the dove
  still called;
The flowers leaned on themselves, the
  flowers in hollows;
And love, love sang toward.

5

To have the whole air!—
The light, the full sun
Coming down on the flowerheads,   80
The tendrils turning slowly,
A slow snail-lifting, liquescent;
To be by the rose
Rising slowly out of its bed,
Still as a child in its first loneliness;
To see cyclamen veins become clearer in
  early sunlight,
And mist lifting, drifting out of the
  brown cat-tails;
To stare into the after-light, the glitter
  left on the lake's surface
When the sun has fallen behind a wooded
  island;
To follow the drops sliding from a lifted
  oar,   90
Held up, while the rower breathes, and
  the small boat drifts quietly shore-
  ward;
To know that light falls and fills, often
  without our knowing,
As an opaque vase fills to the brim from a
  quick pouring,
Fills and trembles at the edge yet does
  not flow over,
Still holding and feeding the stem of the
  contained flower.

Elizabeth Bishop

✳ 1911—

A Miracle for Breakfast

At six o'clock we were waiting for coffee,
waiting for coffee and the charitable
crumb
that was going to be served from a cer-
tain balcony,
—like kings of old, or like a miracle.
It was still dark. One foot of the sun
steadied itself on a ripple in the river.

The first ferry of the day had just crossed
the river.
It was so cold we hoped that the coffee
would be very hot, seeing that the sun
was not going to warm us; and that the
crumb   10
would be a loaf each, buttered, by a
miracle.
At seven a man stepped out on the bal-
cony.

He stood for a minute alone on the bal-
cony
looking over our heads toward the river.
A servant handed him the makings of a
miracle,
consisting of one lone cup of coffee
and one roll, which he proceeded to
crumb,
his head, so to speak, in the clouds—
along with the sun.

Was the man crazy? What under the sun
was he trying to do, up there on his bal-
cony!   20
Each man received one rather hard
crumb,
which some flicked scornfully into the
river,
and, in a cup, one drop of the coffee.
Some of us stood around, waiting for the
miracle.

I can tell what I saw next; it was not a
miracle.
A beautiful villa stood in the sun
and from its doors came the smell of hot
coffee.
In front, a baroque white plaster balcony
added by birds, who nest along the river,
—I saw it with one eye close to the
crumb—   30
and galleries and marble chambers. My
crumb
my mansion, made for me a miracle,
through ages, by insects, birds, and the
river
working the stone. Every day, in the sun,
at breakfast time I sit on my balcony
with my feet up, and drink gallons of
coffee.

We licked up the crumb and swallowed
the coffee.
A window across the river caught the sun
as if the miracle were working, on the
wrong balcony.

Wading at Wellfleet

In one of the Assyrian wars
a chariot first saw the light
that bore sharp blades around its wheels.

The chariot from Assyria
went rolling down mechanically
to take the warriors by the heels.

A thousand warriors in the sea
could not consider such a war
as that the sea itself contrives

but hasn't put in action yet.   10
This morning's glitterings reveal
the sea is "all a case of knives."

Lying so close, they catch the sun,
the spokes directed at the shin.
The chariot front is blue and great.

The war rests wholly with the waves:
they try revolving, but the wheels
give way, they will not bear the weight.

Florida

The state with the prettiest name,
The state that floats in brackish water,
held together by mangrove roots
that bear while living oysters in clusters,
and when dead strew white swamps with
    skeletons,
dotted as if bombarded, with green hum-
    mocks
like ancient cannon-balls sprouting grass.
The state full of long S-shaped birds, blue
    and white,
and unseen hysterical birds which rush
    up the scale
every time in a tantrum.   10
Tanagers embarrassed by their flashiness,
and pelicans whose delight it is to clown;
who coast for fun on the strong tidal cur-
    rents
in and out among the mangrove islands
and stand on the sand-bars drying their
    damp gold wings
on sun-lit evenings.
Enormous turtles, helpless and mild,
die and leave their barnacled shells on
    the beaches,
and their large white skulls with round
    eye-sockets
twice the size of a man's.   20
The palm trees clatter in the stiff breeze
like the bills of pelicans. The tropical rain
    comes down
to freshen the tide-looped strings of fad-
    ing shells:
Job's Tear, the Chinese Alphabet, the
    scarce Junonia,
parti-coloured pectins and Ladies' Ears,
arranged as on a gray rag of rotted calico,
the buried Indian Princess's skirt;
with these the monotonous, endless, sag-
    ging coast-line
is delicately ornamented.
Thirty or more buzzards are drifting
    down, down, down,   30
over something they have spotted in the
    swamp,

in circles like stirred up flakes of sediment
sinking through water.
Smoke from woods-fires filters fine blue
    solvents.
On stumps and dead trees the charring
    is like black velvet.
The mosquitoes
go hunting to the tune of their ferocious
    obbligatos.
After dark, the fire-flies map the heavens
    in the marsh
until the moon rises.
Cold white, not bright, the moonlight is
    coarse-meshed,   40
and the careless, corrupt state is all black
    specks
too far apart, and ugly whites; the poorest
post-card of itself.
After dark, the pools seem to have slipped
    away.
The alligator, who has five distinct calls:
friendliness, love, mating, war, and a
    warning,
whimpers and speaks in the throat
of the Indian Princess.

Karl Shapiro
✳ 1913—

Adam and Eve

1. The Sickness of Adam

In the beginning, at every step, he turned
As if by instinct to the East to praise
The nature of things. Now every path
    was learned
He lost the lifted, almost flower-like gaze

Of a temple dancer. He began to walk
Slowly, like one accustomed to be alone.
He found himself lost in the field of talk;
Thinking became a garden of its own.

In it were new things: words he had
    never said,

Beasts he had never seen and knew were
not   10
In the true garden, terrors, and tears shed
Under a tree by him, for some new
thought.

And the first anger. Once he flung a staff
At softly coupling sheep and struck the
ram.
It broke away. And God heard Adam
laugh
And for his laughter made the creature
lame.

And wanderlust. He stood upon the Wall
To search the unfinished countries lying
wide
And waste, where not a living thing could
crawl,
And yet he would descend, as if to hide.

His thought drew down the guardian at
the gate,   21
To whom man said, "What danger am I
in?"
And the angel, hurt in spirit, seemed to
hate
The wingless thing that worried after sin,

For it said nothing but marvelously un-
furled
Its wings and arched them shimmering
overhead,
Which must have been the signal from
the world
That the first season of our life was dead.

Adam fell down with labor in his bones,
And God approached him in the cool of
day   30
And said, "This sickness in your skeleton
Is longing. I will remove it from your
clay."

He said also, "I made you strike the
sheep."
It began to rain and God sat down beside
The sinking man. When he was fast
asleep
He wet his right hand deep in Adam's
side

And drew the graceful rib out of his
breast.
Far off, the latent streams began to flow
And birds flew out of Paradise to nest
On earth. Sadly the angel watched them
go.   40

2. The Recognition of Eve

Whatever it was she had so fiercely
fought
Had fled back to the sky, but still she lay
With arms outspread, awaiting its assault,
Staring up through the branches of the
tree,
The fig tree. Then she drew a shuddering
breath
And turned her head instinctively his
way.
She had fought birth as dying men fight
death.

Her sigh awakened him. He turned and
saw
A body swollen, as though formed of
fruits,
White as the flesh of fishes, soft and raw.
He hoped she was another of the brutes,
So he crawled over and looked into her
eyes,   52
The human wells that pool all absolutes.
It was like looking into double skies.

And when she spoke the first word (it
was *thou*)
He was terror-stricken, but she raised
her hand
And touched his wound where it was fad-
ing now,
For he must feel the place to understand.
Then he recalled the longing that had
torn
His side, and while he watched it whitely
mend,   60
He felt it stab him suddenly like a thorn.

He thought the woman had hurt him.
Was it she
Or the same sickness seeking to return;

Or was there any difference, the pain set
free
And she who seized him now as hard as
iron?
Her fingers bit his body. She looked old
And involuted, like the newly born.
He let her hurt him till she loosed her
hold.

Then she forgot him and she wearily
stood
And went in search of water through the
grove.   70
Adam could see her wandering through
the wood,
Studying her footsteps as her body wove
In light and out of light. She found a pool
And there he followed shyly to observe.
She was already turning beautiful.

3. The Kiss

The first kiss was with stumbling finger-
tips.
Their bodies grazed each other as if by
chance
And touched and untouched in a kind of
dance.
Second, they found out touching with
their lips.

Some obscure angel, pausing on his
course,   80
Shed such a brightness on the face of
Eve
That Adam in grief was ready to believe
He had lost her love. The third kiss was
by force.

Their lips formed foreign, unimagined
oaths
When speaking of the Tree of Guilt. So
wide
Their mouths, they drank each other from
inside.
A gland of honey burst within their
throats.

But something rustling hideously over-
head,
They jumped up from the fourth caress
and hid.

4. The Tree of Guilt

Why, on her way to the oracle of Love,
Did she not even glance up at the Tree
Of Life, that giant with the whitish cast
And glinting leaves and berries of dull
gray,   93
As though covered with mold? But who
would taste
The medicine of immortality,
And who would "be as God"? And in
what way?

So she came breathless to the lowlier one
And like a priestess of the cult she knelt,
Holding her breasts in token for a sign,
And prayed the spirit of the burdened
bough   100
That the great power of the tree be seen
And lift itself out of the Tree of Guilt
Where it had hidden in the leaves till
now.

Or did she know already? Had the pea-
cock
Rattling its quills, glancing its thousand
eyes
At her, the iridescence of the dove,
Stench of the he-goat, everything that
joins
Told her the mystery? It was not enough,
So from the tree the snake began to rise
And dropt its head and pointed at her
loins.   110

She fell and hid her face and still she saw
The spirit of the tree emerge and slip
Into the open sky until it stood
Straight as a standing-stone, and spilled
its seed.
And all the seed were serpents of the
good.
Again he seized the snake and from its
lip
It spat the venomous evil of the deed.

And it was over. But the woman lay
Stricken with what she knew, ripe in her
thought
Like a fresh apple fallen from the limb
And rotten, like a fruit that lies too long.

This way she rose, ripe-rotten in her
  prime   122
And spurned the cold thing coiled against
  her foot
And called her husband, in a kind of
  song.

5. The Confession

As on the first day her first word was
  thou.
He waited while she said, "Thou art the
  tree."
And while she said, almost accusingly,
Looking at nothing, "Thou art the fruit
  I took."
She seemed smaller by inches as she
  spoke,
And Adam wondering touched her hair
  and shook,   130
Half understanding. He answered softly,
  "How?"

And for the third time, in the third way,
  Eve:
"The tree that rises from the middle part
Of the garden." And almost tenderly,
  "Thou art
The Garden. *We.*" Then she was over-
  come,
And Adam coldly, lest he should suc-
  cumb
To pity, standing at the edge of doom,
Comforted her like one about to leave.

She sensed departure and she stood aside
Smiling and bitter. But he asked again,
"How did you eat? With what thing did
  you sin?"   141
And Eve with body slackened and un-
  couth,
"Under the tree I took the fruit of truth
From an angel. I ate it with my other
  mouth."
And saying so, she did not know she lied.

It was the man who suddenly released
From doubt, wept in the woman's heavy
  arms,
Those double serpents, subtly winding
  forms

That climb and drop about the manly
  boughs;
And dry with weeping, fiery and aroused,
Fell on her face to slake his terrible
  thirst   151
And bore her body earthward like a
  beast.

6. Shame

The hard blood falls back in the manly
  fount,
The soft door closes under Venus' mount,
The ovoid moon moves to the Garden's
  side
And dawn comes, but the lovers have not
  died.
They have not died but they have fallen
  apart
In sleep, like equal halves of the same
  heart.

How to teach shame? How to teach
  nakedness
To the already naked? How to express
Nudity? How to open innocent eyes 161
And separate the innocent from the wise?
And how to re-establish the guilty tree
In infinite gardens of humanity?

By marring the image, by the black de-
  vice
Of the goat-god, by the clown of Para-
  dise,
By fruits of cloth and by the navel's bud,
By itching tendrils and by strings of
  blood,
By ugliness, by the shadow of our fear,
By ridicule, by the fig-leaf patch of hair.

Whiter than tombs, whiter than whitest
  clay,   171
Exposed beneath the whitening eye of
  day,
They awoke and saw the covering that
  reveals.
They thought they were changing into
  animals.
Like animals they bellowed terrible cries
And clutched each other, hiding each
  other's eyes.

7. *Exile*

The one who gave the warning with his
  wings,
Still doubting them, held out the sword
  of flame
Against the Tree of Whiteness as they
  came
Angrily, slowly by, like exiled kings,   180

And watched them at the broken-open
  gate
Stare in the distance long and overlong,
And then, like peasants, pitiful and
  strong,
Take the first step toward earth and hesi-
  tate.

For Adam raised his head and called
  aloud,
"My Father, who has made the garden
  pall,
Giving me all things and then taking all,
Who with your opposite nature has en-
  dowed

Woman, give us your hand for our
  descent.
Needing us greatly, even in our disgrace,
Guide us, for gladly do we leave this
  place   191
For our own land and wished-for banish-
  ment."

But woman prayed, "Guide us to Para-
  dise."
Around them slunk the uneasy animals,
Strangely excited, uttering coughs and
  growls,
And bounded down into the wild abyss.

And overheard the last migrating birds,
Then empty sky. And when the two had
  gone
A slow half-dozen steps across the stone,
The angel came and stood among the
  shards   200

And called them, as though joyously, by
  name.
They turned in dark amazement and be-
  held

Eden ablaze with fires of red and gold,
The garden dressed for dying in cold
  flame,

And it was autumn, and the present
  world.

Delmore Schwartz

❋ 1913—

From *The Repetitive Heart*

10

A dog named Ego, the snowflakes as
  kisses
Fluttered, ran, came with me in Decem-
  ber,
Snuffing the chill air, changing, and halt-
  ing,
There where I walked toward seven
  o'clock,
Sniffed at some interests hidden and
  open,
Whirled, descending, and stood still, at-
  tentive,
Seeking their peace, the stranger, un-
  known,
With me, near me, kissed me, touched
  my wound,
My simple face, obsessed and pleasure
  bound.

"Not free, no liberty, rock that you
  carry,"   10
So spoke Ego in his cracked and harsh
  voice,
While snowflakes kissed me and satisfied
  minutes,
Falling from some place half believed
  and unknown,
"You will not be free, nor ever alone,"
So spoke Ego, "Mine is the kingdom,
Dynasty's bone: you will not be free,
Go, choose, run, you will not be alone."

"Come, come, come," sang the whirling
    snowflakes,
Evading the dog who barked at their
    smallness,
"Come!" sang the snowflakes, "Come
    here! and here!"   20
How soon at the sidewalk, melted, and
    done,
One kissed me, two kissed me! So many
    died!
While Ego barked at them, swallowed
    their touch,
Ran this way! And that way! While they
    slipped to the ground,
Leading him further and farther away,
While night collapsed amid the falling,
And left me no recourse, far from my
    home,
And left me no recourse, far from my
    home.

Starlight like Intuition
Pierced the Twelve

The starlight's intuitions pierced the
    twelve,
The brittle night sky sparkled like a tune
Tinkled and tapped out on the xylo-
    phone.
Empty and vain, a glittering dune, the
    moon
Arose too big, and, in the mood which
    ruled,
Seemed like a useless beauty in a pit;
And then one said, after he carefully
    spat:
"No matter what we do, he looks at it!

"I cannot see a child or find a girl
Beyond his smile which glows like that
    spring moon."   10
"—Nothing no more the same," the sec-
    ond said,
"Though all may be forgiven, never quite
    healed
The wound I bear as witness, standing
    by;

No ceremony surely appropriate,
Nor secret love, escape or sleep because
No matter what I do, he looks at it—"

"Now," said the third, "no thing will be
    the same:
I am as one who never shuts his eyes,
The sea and sky no more are marvelous,
And I no longer understand surprise!"
"Now," said the fourth, "nothing will be
    enough,
—I heard his voice accomplishing all
    wit:
No word can be unsaid, no deed with-
    drawn,
—No matter what is said, he measures
    it."

"Vision, imagination, hope or dream
Believed, denied, the scene we wished
    to see?
It does not matter in the least: for what
Is altered if it is not true? That we
Saw goodness, as it is—*this* is the awe
And the abyss which we will not forget,
His story now the skull which holds all
    thought: 31
No matter what I think, I think of it!"

"And I will never be what once I was,"
Said one for long as single as a knife,
"And we will never be as once we were;
We have died once, this is a second life."
"My mind is spilled in moral chaos," one
Righteous as Job exclaimed, "now infinite
Suspicion of my heart stems what I will,
—No matter what I choose, he stares at
    it!"   40

"I am as one native in summer places,
—Ten weeks' excitement paid for by the
    rich;
Debauched by that, and then all winter
    bored,"
The sixth declared, "his peak left us a
    ditch."
"He came to make this life more diffi-
    cult,"
The seventh said, "No one will ever fit

His measures' heights, all is inadequate:
No matter what we have, what good is
    it?"

"He gave forgiveness to us: what a gift!"
The eighth chimed in. "But now we
    know how much   50
Must be forgiven. But if forgiven, what?
The crime which was will be; and the
    least touch
Revives the memory: what is forgiveness
    worth?"
The ninth spoke thus: "Who now will
    ever sit
At ease in Zion at the Easter feast?
No matter what the place, he touches
    it!"

"And I will always stammer, since he
    spoke,"
One, who had been most eloquent, said,
    stammering,
"I looked too long at the sun; like too
    much light,
So too much of goodness is a boomerang,"
Laughed the eleventh of the troop. "I
    must   61
Try what he tried: I saw the infinite
Who walked the lake and raised the
    hopeless dead:
No matter what the feat, he first accom-
    plished it!"

So spoke the twelfth; and then the twelve
    in chorus:
"Unspeakable unnatural goodness is
Risen and shines, and never will ignore
    us;
He glows forever in all consciousness;
Forgiveness, love, and hope possess the
    pit,
And bring our endless guilt, like shadow's
    bars: 70
No matter what we do, he stares at it!
What pity then deny? what debt defer?
We know he looks at us like all the
    stars,
And we shall never be as once we were,
This life will never be what once it was!"

Randall Jarrell
✳ 1914—

Losses

It was not dying: everybody died.
It was not dying: we had died before
In the routine crashes—and our fields
Called up the papers, wrote home to our
    folks,
And the rates rose, all because of us.
We died on the wrong page of the alma-
    nac,
Scattered on mountains fifty miles away;
Diving on haystacks, fighting with a
    friend,
We blazed up on the lines we never saw.
We died like ants or pets or foreigners.
(When we left high school nothing else
    had died   11
For us to figure we had died like.)

In our new planes, with our new crews,
    we bombed
The ranges by the desert or the shore,
Fired at towed targets, waited for our
    scores—
And turned into replacements and woke
    up
One morning, over England, operational.
It wasn't different: but if we died
It was not an accident but a mistake
(But an easy one for anyone to make).
We read our mail and counted up our
    missions—   21
In bombers named for girls, we burned
The cities we had learned about in
    school—
Till our lives wore out; our bodies lay
    among
The people we had killed and never seen.
When we lasted long enough they gave
    us medals;
When we died they said, "Our casualties
    were low."

They said, "Here are the maps"; we
    burned the cities.

It was not dying—no, not ever dying;
But the night I died I dreamed that I was
    dead,   30
And the cities said to me: "Why are you
    dying?
We are satisfied if you are; but why did
    I die?"

The Angels at Hamburg

In caves emptied of their workers, turn-
    ing
From spent mines to the ruins of fac-
    tories,
The soul sleeps under the hive of earth.
Freed for an hour from its deadly dreams
Of Good and Evil, from the fiery judge
Who walks like an angel through the
    guilty state
The world sets up within the laboring
    breast,
It falls past Heaven into Paradise:
Here man spins his last Eden like a worm.

Here is Knowledge, the bombs tempt
    fruitlessly.   10
In the darkness under the fiery missions
That fail, and are renewed by every sea-
    son,
He is estranged from suffering, and will-
    ingly
Floats like a moon above the starving
    limbs
Oppressed with remembrance, tossed un-
    certainly
Under the angels' deadly paths—the
    strongest
Stammers, "My burden is more than I
    can bear."
He knows neither good, nor evil, nor the
    angels,
Nor their message: There is no justice,
    man, but death.
He watches the child and the cat and the
    soldier dying,   20

Not loving or hating their judges, who
    neither love nor hate;
In his heart Hamburg is no longer a city,
There is no more state.

The judges come to judge man in the
    night.
How bitterly they look on his desire!
Here at midnight there is no darkness,
At day no light.
The air is smoke and the earth ashes
Where he was fire;
He looks from his grave for life, and
    judgment   30
Rides over his city like a star.

The Orient Express

One looks from the train
Almost as one looked as a child. In the
    sunlight
What I see still seems to me plain,
I am safe; but at evening
As the lands darken, a questioning
Precariousness comes over everything.

Once after a day of rain
I lay longing to be cold; and after a while
I was cold again, and hunched shivering
Under the quilt's many colors, gray   10
With the dull ending of the winter day.
Outside me there were a few shapes
Of chairs and tables, things from a
    primer;
Outside the window
There were the chairs and tables of the
    world. . . .
I saw that the world
That had seemed to me the plain
Gray mask of all that was strange
Behind it—of all that *was*—was all.

But it is beyond belief.   20
One thinks, "Behind everything
An unforced joy, an unwilling
Sadness (a willing sadness, a forced joy)
Moves changelessly"; one looks from the
    train
And there is something, the same thing

Behind everything: all these little vil-
lages,
A passing woman, a field of grain,
The man who says good-bye to his
wife—
A path through a wood full of lives, and
the train
Passing, after all unchangeable   30
And not now ever to stop, like a heart—

It is like any other work of art.
It is and never can be changed.
Behind everything there is always
The unknown unwanted life.

John Berryman

✳ 1914—

From *Homage to*
Mistress Bradstreet

Born 1612 Anne Dudley, married at six-
teen Simon Bradstreet, a Cambridge
man, steward to the Countess of War-
wick and protégé of her father Thomas
Dudley secretary to the Earl of Lincoln.
Crossed in the *Arbella,* 1630, under
Governor Winthrop.

1

The Governor your husband lived so long
moved you not, restless, waiting for him?
Still,
You were a patient woman.—
I seem to see you pause here still:
Sylvester, Quarles, in moments odd you
pored
before a fire at, bright eyes on the Lord,
all the children still.
Simon, . . Simon will listen while you
read a Song.

2

Outside the New World winters in
grand dark

white air lashing high thro' the virgin
stands   10
foxes down foxholes sigh,
surely the English heart quails, stunned.
I doubt if Simon than this blast, that sea,
spares from his rigour for your poetry
more. We are on each other's hands
who care. Both of our worlds unhanded
us. Lie stark,

3

thy eyes look to me mild. Out of maize &
air
your body's made, and moves. I summon,
see,
from the centuries it.
I think you won't stay. How do we   20
linger, diminished, in our lovers' air,
implausibly visible, to whom, a year,
years, over interims; or not;
to a long stranger; or not; shimmer & dis-
appear.

4

Jaw-ript, rot with its wisdom, rending
then;
then not. When the mouth dies, who
misses you?
Your master never died,
Simon ah thirty years past you—
Pockmarkt & westward staring on a hag-
gard deck
it seems I find you, young. I come to
check,   30
I come to stay with you,
and the Governor, & Father, & Simon,
and the huddled men.

5

By the week we landed we were, most,
used up.
Strange ships across us, after a fortnight's
winds
unfavouring, frightened us;
bone-sad cold, sleet, scurvy; so were ill
many as one day we could have no ser-
mons;
broils, quelled; a fatherless child unken-
nelled, vermin

crowding & waiting; waiting.
And the day itself he leapt ashore young
   Henry Winthrop   40

6

(delivered from the waves; because he
   found
off their wigwams, sharp-eyed, a lone
   canoe
across a tidal river,
that water glittered fair & blue
& narrow, none of the other men could
   swim
and the plantation's prime theft up to
   him,
shouldered on a glad day
hard on the sumptuous feasting of
   thanksgiving) drowned.

7

How long with nothing in the ruinous
   heat,
clams & acorns stomaching, distinction
   perishing,   50
at which my heart rose,
with brackish water, we would sing.
When whispers knew the Governor's last
   bread
was browning in his oven, we were dis-
   courag'd.
The Lady Arbella dying—
dyings—at which my heart rose, but I
   did submit.

8

That beyond the Atlantic wound our
   woes enlarge
is hard, hard that starvation burnishes
   our fear,
but I do gloss for You.
Strangers & pilgrims fare we here,   60
declaring we seek a City. Shall we be
   deceived?
I know whom I have trusted, & whom I
   have believed,
and that he is able to
keep that I have committed to his
   charge.

9

Winter than summer worse, that first, like
   a file
on a quick, or the poison suck of a
   thrilled tooth;
and still we may unpack.
Wolves & storms among, uncouth
board-pieces, boxes, barrels vanish, grow
houses, rise. Moats that hop in sunlight
   slow   70
indoors, and I am Ruth
away: open my mouth, my eyes wet: I
   wóuld smile:

10

vellum I palm, and dream. Their forest
   dies
to greensward, privets, elms & towers,
   whence
a nightingale is throbbing.
Women sleep sound. I was happy once..
(Something keeps on not happening; I
   shrink?)
These minutes all their passions & powers
   sink
and I am not one chance
for an unknown cry or a flicker of un-
   known eyes.   80

11

Chapped souls ours, by the day Spring's
   strong winds swelled,
Jack's pulpits arched, more glad. The
   shawl I pinned
flaps like a shooting soul
might in such weather Heaven send.
Succumbing half, in spirit, to a salmon
   sash
I prod the nerveless novel succotash—
I must be disciplined,
in arms, against that one, and our dissi-
   dents, and myself.

12

Versing, I shroud among the dynasties;
quaternion on quaternion, tireless I
   phrase

anything past, dead, far,   91
sacred, for a barbarous place.
—To please your wintry father? all this
    bald
abstract didactic rime I read appalled
harassed for your fame
mistress neither of fiery nor velvet verse,
    on your knees

13

hopeful & shamefast, chaste, laborious,
    odd,
whom the sea tore.—The damned roar
    with loss,
so they hug & are mean
with themselves, and I cannot be thus.
Why then do I repine, sick, bad, to long
after what must not be? I lie wrong   102
once more. For at fourteen
I found my heart more carnal and sit-
    ting loose from God

14

vanity & the follies of youth took hold of
    me;
then the pox blasted, when the Lord re-
    turned.
That year for my sorry face
so-much-older Simon burned,
so Father smiled, with love. Their will be
    done.
He to me ill lingeringly, learning to shun
a bliss, a lightning blood   111
vouchsafed, what did seem life. I kissed
    his Mystery.

15

Drydust in God's eye the aquavivid skin
of Simon snoring lit with fountaining
    dawn
when my eyes unlid, sad.
John Cotton shines on Boston's sin—
I ám drawn, in pieties that seem
the weary drizzle of an unremembered
    dream.
Women have gone mad
at twenty-one. Ambition mines, atrocious,
    in.   120

16

Food endless, people few, all to be done.
As pippins roast, the question of the
    wolves
turns & turns.
Fangs of a wolf will keep, the neck
round of a child, that child brave. I re-
    member who
in meeting smiled & was punisht, and I
    know who
whispered & was stockt.
We lead a thoughtful life. But Boston's
    cage we shun.

17

The winters close, Springs open, no child
    stirs
under my withering heart, O seasoned
    heart   130
God grudged his aid.
All things else soil like a shirt.
Simon is much away. My executive stales.
The town came through for the cartway
    by the pales,
but my patience is short.
I revolt from, I am like, these savage for-
    esters

18

whose passionless dicker in the shade,
    whose glance
impassive & scant, belie their muderous
    cries
when quarry seems to show.
Again I must have been wrong, twice.
Unwell in a new way. Can that begin?
God brandishes. O love, O I love. Kin,
gather. My world is strange   143
and merciful, ingrown months, blessing a
    swelling trance.

19

So squeezed, wince you I scream? I love
    you & hate
off with you. Ages! *Useless.* Below my
    waist
he has me in Hell's vise.
Stalling. He let go. Come back: brace

me somewhere. No. No. Yes! everything
  down
hardens I press with a horrible joy down
my back cracks like a wrist   151
shame I am voiding oh behind it is too
  late

20

hide me forever I work thrust I must free
now I all muscles & bones concentrate
what is living from dying?
Simon I must leave you so untidy
Monster you are killing me Be sure
I'll have you later Women do endure
I can *can* no longer
and it passes the wretched trap whelming
  and I am me   160

21

drencht & powerful, I did it with my
  body!
One proud tug greens Heaven. Marvel-
  lous,
unforbidding Majesty.
Swell, imperious bells. I fly.
Mountainous, woman not breaks and will
  bend:
sways God nearby: anguish comes to an
  end.
Blossomed Sarah, and I
blossom. Is that thing alive? I hear a
  famisht howl.

John Ciardi

✳ 1916—

Mystic River

MEDFORD, MASSACHUSETTS

1

The dirty river by religious explorers
Named Mysticke and recorded forever
  into its future

Civilization of silt and sewerage, recovers
The first sweet moon of time tonight. A
  tremor
More thought than breeze, more exhala-
  tion than motion
Stirs the gold water totem, Snake of the
  Moon.

"A most pleasynge gentle and salubrious
  river
Wherein lieth no hindraunce of rock nor
  shoal
To the distresse of nauvigation, but ever
Aboundaunce of landynge and of fisherie,
  and withal   10
Distillynge so sweet an air through its
  course
Sith it runneth salt from the sea, fresh
  from the source

"And altereth daily through its greater
  length
Thus chaungynge and refreshynge the
  valleys breath,
That," wrote the Gods, "God grauntynge
  strength
We took up laundes, and here untill oure
  death
Shall be oure hearthes oure labour and
  oure joye."
But what the Gods will have they first
  destroy.

Still Mystic lights the wake of Gods—
  the moon
Dances on pollution, the fish are fled   20
Into a finer instinct of revulsion
Than Gods had. And the Gods are dead,
Their sloops and river rotted, and their
  bones
That scrubbed old conscience down like
  holystones

Powdered imperceptibly. Their land
Is an old land where nothing's planted
Beside the rollerdrome and hot dog
  stand—
Still Mystic lights the wake of Gods, still
  haunted
By the reversing moon. "Let me be
  clean,"

It cries and cries, but there are years be-
    tween.   30

2

And I have stoned and swum and sculled
    them all:
Naked behind the birches at the cove
Where Winthrop built a landing and a
    yawl
And tabloids found a famous corpse of
    love
Hacked small and parceled into butcher's
    paper,
Joe La Conti stumbled on an old pauper

Dying of epilepsy or DT's,
And I came running naked to watch the
    fit.
We had to dress to run for the police.
But did we run for help or the joy of
    it?   40
And who was dying at the sight of blood?
Weeks long we conjured its traces in the
    mud

And there was no trace. Later above the
    cat-tails
A house frame grew, and another, and
    then another.
Our naked bank bled broken tiles and
    nails.
We made a raft and watched the alewife
    smother.
But there our play drank fever, and Wil-
    lie Crosby
Went home from that dirty water and
    stayed to die.

3

So I know death is a dirty river
At the edge of history, through the mid-
    dle of towns,   50
At the backs of stores, and under the
    cantilever
Stations of bridges where the moon
    drowns
Pollution in its own illusion of light.
Oh rotten time, rot from my mind to-
    night!

Let me be lit to the bone in this one stir,
And where the Gods grew rich and posi-
    tive
From their ruinous landing, I'll attend
    disaster
Like night birds over a wake, dark and
    alive
Above the shuttered house, and, bound
    and free,
Wheel on the wing, find food in flight,
    and be   60

Captured by light, drawn down and
    down and down
By moonshine, streetlamps, windows,
    moving rays,
By all that shines in all the caved-in town
Where Mystic in the crazy moon outstays
The death of Gods, and makes a life of
    light
That breaks, but calls a million birds to
    flight.

Peter Viereck

✳ 1916—

The Day's No Rounder Than Its Angles Are

FOR ANYA

Mere dark is not so night-like as it seems.
The night's more silken than the dark by
    far.
So many dark things are not night at all:
The cupboard where the cakes and poi-
    sons are;
The coffin where old men get locked in
    dreams
Alive, and no one hears their knocks and
    screams;
Shadows; and lightlessness of curtain's
    fall.

The night is further than the dark is far.
The night is farness, farnesses that reel.
The day is nearness, nearnesses that jar.
The day's no rounder than its angles are.
But though its angles gash you with a
    wound   12
Invisible, each night is soft and round.

The night is softer than the dark is satin.
The night is softness, softnesses that heal
The many, many gashes where you bled.
The day is loudness, loudnesses that
    threaten;
An evil sexton-dwarf hides in your head.
Oh where escape his bells that peal and
    peal?   19

The night is stiller than the dark is dead.

Robert Lowell

✳ 1917—

Mr. Edwards and the Spider

I saw the spiders marching through the
    air,
Swimming from tree to tree that mil-
    dewed day
    In latter August when the hay
      Came creaking to the barn. But where
      The wind is westerly,
Where gnarled November makes the
    spiders fly
Into the apparitions of the sky,
They purpose nothing but their ease and
    die
Urgently beating east to sunrise and the
    sea;

What are we in the hands of the great
    God?   10
It was in vain you set up thorn and briar
    In battle array against the fire
      And treason crackling in your blood;
      For the wild thorns grow tame
And will do nothing to oppose the flame;
Your lacerations tell the losing game

You play against a sickness past your
    cure.
How will the hands be strong? How will
    the heart endure?

A very little thing, a little worm,
Or hourglass-blazoned spider, it is said,
    Can kill a tiger. Will the dead   21
    Hold up his mirror and affirm
      To the four winds the smell
And flash of his authority? It's well
If God who holds you to the pit of hell,
Much as one holds a spider, will destroy,
Baffle and dissipate your soul. As a small
    boy

On Windsor Marsh, I saw the spider die
When thrown into the bowels of fierce
    fire:
    There's no long struggle, no desire   30
    To get up on its feet and fly—
      It stretches out its feet
And dies. This is the sinner's last retreat;
Yes, and no strength exerted on the heat
Then sinews the abolished will, when
    sick
And full of burning, it will whistle on a
    brick.

But who can plumb the sinking of that
    soul?
Josiah Hawley, picture yourself cast
    Into a brick-kiln where the blast
      Fans your quick vitals to a coal—   40
      If measured by a glass,
How long would it seem burning! Let
    there pass
A minute, ten, ten trillion; but the blaze
Is infinite, eternal: this is death,
To die and know it. This is the Black
    Widow, death.

Where the Rainbow Ends

I saw the sky descending, black and
    white,
Not blue, on Boston where the winters
    wore
The skulls to jack-o'-lanterns on the
    slates,

And Hunger's skin-and-bone retrievers
tore
The chickadee and shrike. The thorn tree
waits
Its victim and tonight
The worms will eat the deadwood to the
foot
Of Ararat: the scythers, Time and Death,
Helmed locusts, move upon the tree of
breath;
The wild ingrated olive and the root   10

Are withered, and a winter drifts to
where
The Pepperpot, ironic rainbow, spans
Charles River and its scales of scorched-
earth miles
I saw my city in the Scales, the pans
Of judgment rising and descending. Piles
Of dead leaves char the air—
And I am a red arrow on this graph
Of Revelations. Every dove is sold.
The Chapel's sharp-shinned eagle shifts
its hold
On serpent-Time, the rainbow's epitaph.

In Boston serpents whistle at the cold.
The victim climbs the altar steps and
sings: 22
"Hosannah to the lion, lamb, and beast
Who fans the furnace-face of IS with
wings:
I breathe the ether of my marriage feast."
At the high altar, gold
And a fair cloth. I kneel and the wings
beat
My cheek. What can the dove of Jesus
give
You now but wisdom, exile? Stand and
live,
The dove has brought an olive branch to
eat.   30

The Drunken Fisherman

Wallowing in this bloody sty,
I cast for fish that pleased my eye
(Truly Jehovah's bow suspends
No pots of gold to weight its ends);
Only the blood-mouthed rainbow trout

Rose to my bait. They flopped about
My canvas creel until the moth
Corrupted its unstable cloth.

A calendar to tell the day;
A handkerchief to wave away   10
The gnats; a couch unstuffed with storm
Pouching a bottle in one arm;
A whiskey bottle full of worms;
And bedroom slacks: are these fit terms
To mete the worm whose molten rage
Boils in the belly of old age?

Once fishing was a rabbit's foot—
O wind blow cold, O wind blow hot,
Let suns stay in or suns step out:
Life danced a jig on the sperm-whale's
spout—   20
The fisher's fluent and obscene
Catches kept his conscience clean.
Children, the raging memory drools
Over the glory of past pools.

Now the hot river, ebbing, hauls
Its bloody waters into holes;
A grain of sand inside my shoe
Mimics the moon that might undo
Man and Creation too; remorse
Stinking, has puddled up its source;   30
Here tantrums thrash to a whale's rage.
This is the pot-hole of old age.

Is there no way to cast my hook
Out of this dynamited brook?
The Fisher's sons must cast about
When shallow waters peter out.
I will catch Christ with a greased worm,
And when the Prince of Darkness stalks
My bloodstream to its Stygian term . . .
On water the Man-Fisher walks.   40

Richard Wilbur

✳ 1921—

The Death of a Toad

A toad the power mower caught,
Chewed and clipped of a leg, with a hob-
bling hop has got

To the garden verge, and sanctuaried
him
Under the cineraria leaves, in the
shade
Of the ashen heartshaped leaves, in
a dim,
Low, and a final glade.

The rare original heartsblood goes,
Spends on the earthen hide, in the folds
and wizenings, flows
In the gutters of the banked and star-
ing eyes. He lies
As still as if he would return to stone,
And soundlessly attending, dies   11
Toward some deep monotone,

Toward misted and ebullient seas
And cooling shores, toward lost Am-
phibia's emperies.
Day dwindles, drowning, and at length
is gone
In the wide and antique eyes, which
still appear
To watch, across the castrate lawn,
The haggard daylight steer.

Juggler

A ball will bounce, but less and less. It's
not
A light-hearted thing, resents its own
resilience.
Falling is what it loves, and the earth
falls
So in our hearts from brilliance,
Settles and is forgot.
It takes a skyblue juggler with five red
balls

To shake our gravity up. Whee, in the air
The balls roll round, wheel on his wheel-
ing hands,
Learning the ways of lightness, alter to
spheres
Grazing his finger ends,   10
Cling to their courses there,
Swinging a small heaven about his ears.

But a heaven is easier made of nothing at
all
Than the earth regained, and still and sole
within
The spin of worlds, with a gesture sure
and noble
He reels that heaven in,
Landing it ball by ball,
And trades it all for a broom, a plate, a
table.

Oh, on his toe the table is turning, the
broom's
Balancing up on his nose, and the plate
whirls   20
On the tip of the broom! Damn, what a
show, we cry:
The boys stamp, and the girls
Shriek, and the drum booms
And all comes down, and he bows and
says goodbye.

If the juggler is tired now, if the broom
stands
In the dust again, if the table starts to
drop
Through the daily dark again, and
though the plate
Lies flat on the table top,
For him we batter our hands
Who has won for once over the world's
weight.   30

Allen Ginsberg
✳ 1926—

Howl

FOR CARL SOLOMON

1

I saw the best minds of my generation destroyed by madness, starving hysterical
naked,
dragging themselves through the negro streets at dawn looking for an angry fix,
angelheaded hipsters burning for the ancient heavenly connection to the starry dy-
namo in the machinery of night,
who poverty and tatters and hollow-eyed and high sat up smoking in the supernatural
darkness of cold-water flats floating across the tops of cities contemplating jazz,
who bared their brains to Heaven under the El and saw Mohammedan angels stag-
gering on tenement roofs illuminated,
who passed through universities with radiant cool eyes hallucinating Arkansas and
Blake-light tragedy among the scholars of war,
who were expelled from the academies for crazy & publishing obscene odes on the
windows of the skull,
who cowered in unshaven rooms in underwear, burning their money in wastebaskets
and listening to the Terror through the wall,
who got busted in their pubic beards returning through Laredo with a belt of mari-
juana for New York,
who ate fire in paint hotels or drank turpentine in Paradise Alley, death, or purga-
toried their torsos night after night   10
with dreams, with drugs, with waking nightmares, alcohol and cock and endless balls,
incomparable blind streets of shuddering cloud and lightning in the mind leaping
toward poles of Canada & Paterson, illuminating all the motionless world of Time
between,
Peyote solidities of halls, backyard green tree cemetery dawns, wine drunkenness over
the rooftops, storefront boroughs of teahead joyride neon blinking traffic light,
sun and moon and tree vibrations in the roaring winter dusks of Brooklyn, ashcan
rantings and kind king light of mind,
who chained themselves to subways for the endless ride from Battery to holy Bronx
on benzedrine until the noise of wheels and children brought them down shud-
dering mouth-wracked and battered bleak of brain all drained of brilliance in
the drear light of Zoo,
who sank all night in submarine light of Bickford's floated out and sat through the
stale beer afternoon in desolate Fugazzi's, listening to the crack of doom on the
hydrogen jukebox,

who talked continuously seventy hours from park to pad to bar to Bellevue to mu-
seum to the Brooklyn Bridge,

a lost battalion of platonic conversationalists jumping down the stoops off fire escapes
off windowsills off Empire State out of the moon,

yacketayakking screaming vomiting whispering facts and memories and anecdotes and
eyeball kicks and shocks of hospitals and jails and wars,

whole intellects disgorged in total recall for seven days and nights with brilliant eyes,
meat for the Synagogue cast on the pavement,

who vanished into nowhere Zen New Jersey leaving a trail of ambiguous picture post-
cards of Atlantic City Hall,   20

suffering Eastern sweats and Tangerian bone-grindings and migraines of China under
junk-withdrawal in Newark's bleak furnished room,

who wandered around and around at midnight in the railroad yard wondering where
to go, and went, leaving no broken hearts,

who lit cigarettes in boxcars boxcars boxcars racketing through snow toward lone-
some farms in grandfather night,

who studied Plotinus Poe St. John of the Cross telepathy and bop kaballa because the
cosmos instinctively vibrated at their feet in Kansas,

who loned it through the streets of Idaho seeking visionary indian angels who were
visionary indian angels,

who thought they were only mad when Baltimore gleamed in supernatural ecstasy,

who jumped in limousines with the Chinaman of Oklahoma on the impulse of winter
midnight streetlight smalltown rain,

who lounged hungry and lonesome through Houston seeking jazz or sex or soup, and
followed the brilliant Spaniard to converse about America and Eternity, a hope-
less task, and so took ship to Africa,

who disappeared into the volcanoes of Mexico leaving behind nothing but the shadow
of dungarees and the lava and ash of poetry scattered in fireplace Chicago,

who reappeared on the West Coast investigating the F.B.I. in beards and shorts with
big pacifist eyes sexy in their dark skin passing out incomprehensible leaflets,

who burned cigarette holes in their arms protesting the narcotic tobacco haze of
Capitalism,   31

who distributed Supercommunist pamphlets in Union Square weeping and undress-
ing while the sirens of Los Alamos wailed them down, and wailed down Wall,
and the Staten Island ferry also wailed,

who broke down crying in white gymnasiums naked and trembling before the ma-
chinery of other skeletons,

who bit detectives in the neck and shrieked with delight in policecars for committing
no crime but their own wild cooking pederasty and intoxication,

who howled on their knees in the subway and were dragged off the roof waving
genitals and manuscripts,

who let themselves be ...... in the ... by saintly motorcyclists, and screamed with
joy,

who blew and were blown by those human seraphim, the sailors, caresses of Atlantic
and Caribbean love,

who balled in the mornings in the evenings in rosegardens and the grass of public
parks and cemeteries scattering their semen freely to whomever come who may,

who hiccupped endlessly trying to giggle but wound up with a sob behind a partition in a Turkish Bath when the blonde & naked angel came to pierce them with a sword,

who lost their loveboys to the three old shrews of fate the one eyed shrew of the heterosexual dollar the one eyed shrew that winks out of the womb and the one eyed shrew that does nothing but sit on her ass and snip the intellectual golden threads of the craftsman's loom,   40

who copulated ecstatic and insatiate with a bottle of beer a sweetheart a package of cigarettes a candle and fell off the bed, and continued along the floor and down the hall and ended fainting on the wall with a vision of ultimate c... and come eluding the last gyzym of consciousness,

who sweetened the snatches of a million girls trembling in the sunset, and were red eyed in the morning but prepared to sweeten the snatch of the sunrise, flashing buttocks under barns and naked in the lake,

who went out whoring through Colorado in myriad stolen night-cars, N.C., secret hero of these poems, cocksman and Adonis of Denver—joy to the memory of his innumerable lays of girls in empty lots & diner backyards, moviehouses, rickety rows on mountaintops in caves or with gaunt waitresses in familiar roadside lonely petticoat upliftings & especially secret gas-station solipisisms of johns, & hometown alleys too,

who faded out in vast sordid movies, were shifted in dreams, woke on a sudden Manhattan, and picked themselves up out of basements hungover with heartless Tokay and horrors of Third Avenue iron dreams & stumbled to unemployment offices,

who walked all night with their shoes full of blood on the snowbank docks waiting for a door in the East River to open to a room full of steamheat and opium,

who created great suicidal dramas on the apartment cliff-banks of the Hudson under the wartime blue floodlight of the moon & their heads shall be crowned with laurel in oblivion,

who ate the lamb stew of the imagination or digested the crab at the muddy bottom of the rivers of Bowery,

who wept at the romance of the streets with their pushcarts full of onions and bad music,

who sat in boxes breathing in the darkness under the bridge, and rose up to build harpsichords in their lofts,

who coughed on the sixth floor of Harlem crowned with flame under the tubercular sky surrounded by orange crates of theology,   50

who scribbled all night rocking and rolling over lofty incantations which in the yellow morning were stanzas of gibberish,

who cooked rotten animals lung heart feet tail borsht & tortillas dreaming of the pure vegetable kingdom,

who plunged themselves under meat trucks looking for an egg,

who threw their watches off the roof to cast their ballot for Eternity outside of Time, & alarm clocks fell on their heads every day for the next decade,

who cut their wrists three times successively unsuccessfully, gave up and were forced to open antique stores where they thought they were growing old and cried,

who were burned alive in their innocent flannel suits on Madison Avenue amid blasts of leaden verse & the tanked-up clatter of the iron regiments of fashion & the nitroglycerine shrieks of the fairies of advertising & the mustard gas of sinister intelligent editors, or were run down by the drunken taxicabs of Absolute Reality,

who jumped off the Brooklyn Bridge this actually happened and walked away unknown and forgotten into the ghostly daze of Chinatown soup alleyways & firetrucks, not even one free beer,

who sang out of their windows in despair, fell out of the subway window, jumped in the filthy Passaic, leaped on negroes, cried all over the street, danced on broken wineglasses barefoot smashed phonograph records of nostalgic European 1930's German jazz finished the whiskey and threw up groaning into the bloody toilet, moans in their ears and the blast of colossal steamwhistles,

who barreled down the highways of the past journeying to each other's hotrod-Golgotha jail-solitude watch or Birmingham jazz incarnation,

who drove crosscountry seventytwo hours to find out if I had a vision or you had a vision or he had a vision to find out Eternity,

who journeyed to Denver, who died in Denver, who came back to Denver & waited in vain, who watched over Denver & brooded & loned in Denver and finally went away to find out the Time, & now Denver is lonely for her heroes,

who fell on their knees in hopeless cathedrals praying for each other's salvation and light and breasts, until the soul illuminated its hair for a second,

who crashed through their minds in jail waiting for impossible criminals with golden heads and the charm of reality in their hearts who sang sweet blues to Alcatraz,

who retired to Mexico to cultivate a habit, or Rocky Mount to tender Buddha or Tangiers to boys or Southern Pacific to the black locomotive or Harvard to Narcissus to Woodlawn to the daisychain or grave,

who demanded sanity trials accusing the radio of hypnotism & were left with their insanity & their hands & a hung jury,

who threw potato salad at CCNY lecturers on Dadaism and subsequently presented themselves on the granite steps of the madhouse with shaven heads and harlequin speech of suicide, demanding instantaneous lobotomy,

and who were given instead the concrete void of insulin metrasol electricity hydrotherapy psychotherapy occupational therapy pingpong & amnesia,

who in humorless protest overturned only one symbolic pingpong table, resting briefly in catatonia,

returning years later truly bald except for a wig of blood, and tears and fingers, to the visible madman doom of the wards of the madtowns of the East,

Pilgrim State's Rockland's and Greystone's foetid halls, bickering with the echoes of the soul, rocking and rolling in the midnight solitude-bench dolmen-realms of love, dream of life a nightmare, bodies turned to stone as heavy as the moon,

with mother finally ******, and the last fantastic book flung out of the tenement window, and the last door closed at 4 AM and the last telephone slammed at the wall in reply and the last furnished room emptied down to the last piece of mental furniture, a yellow paper rose twisted on a wire hanger in the closet, and even that imaginary, nothing but a hopeful little bit of hallucination—   71

ah, Carl, while you are not safe I am not safe, and now you're really in the total animal soup of time—

and who therefore ran through the icy streets obsessed with a sudden flash of the alchemy of the use of the ellipse the catalog the meter & the vibrating plane,

who dreamt and made incarnate gaps in Time & Space through images juxtaposed, and trapped the archangel of the soul between 2 visual images and joined the elemental verbs and set the noun and dash of consciousness together jumping with sensation of Pater Omnipotens Aeterna Deus

to recreate the syntax and measure of poor human prose and stand before you speechless and intelligent and shaking with shame, rejected yet confessing out the soul to conform to the rhythm of thought in his naked and endless head,

the madman bum and angel beat in Time, unknown, yet putting down here what might be left to say in time come after death,

and rose reincarnate in the ghostly clothes of jazz in the goldhorn shadow of the band and blew the suffering of America's naked mind for love into an eli eli lamma lamma sabacthani saxophone cry that shivered the cities down to the last radio

with the absolute heart of the poem of life butchered out of their own bodies good to eat a thousand years.

2

What sphinx of cement and aluminum bashed open their skulls and ate up their brains and imagination?

Moloch! Solitude! Filth! Ugliness! Ashcans and unobtainable dollars! Children screaming under the stairways! Boys sobbing in armies! Old men weeping in the parks!   80

Moloch! Moloch! Nightmare of Moloch! Moloch the loveless! Mental Moloch! Moloch the heavy judger of men!

Moloch the incomprehensible prison! Moloch the crossbone soulless jailhouse and Congress of sorrows! Moloch whose buildings are judgement! Moloch the vast stone of war! Moloch the stunned governments!

Moloch whose mind is pure machinery! Moloch whose blood is running money! Moloch whose fingers are ten armies! Moloch whose breast is a cannibal dynamo! Moloch whose ear is a smoking tomb!

Moloch whose eyes are a thousand blind windows! Moloch whose skyscrapers stand in the long streets like endless Jehovahs! Moloch whose factories dream and croak in the fog! Moloch whose smokestacks and antennae crown the cities!

Moloch whose love is endless oil and stone! Moloch whose soul is electricity and banks! Moloch whose poverty is the specter of genius! Moloch whose fate is a cloud of sexless hydrogen! Moloch whose name is the Mind!

Moloch in whom I sit lonely! Moloch in whom I dream Angels! Crazy in Moloch! C . . . sucker in Moloch! Lacklove and manless in Moloch!

Moloch who entered my soul early! Moloch in whom I am a consciousness without a body! Moloch who frightened me out of my natural ecstasy! Moloch whom I abandon! Wake up in Moloch! Light streaming out of the sky!

Moloch! Moloch! Robot apartments! invisible suburbs! skeleton treasuries! blind capitals! demonic industries! spectral nations! invincible madhouses! granite cocks! monstrous bombs!

They broke their backs lifting Moloch to Heaven! Pavements, trees, radios, tons! lifting the city to Heaven which exists and is everywhere about us!

Visions! omens! hallucinations! miracles! ecstasies! gone down the American river!

Dreams! adorations! illuminations! religions! the whole boatload of sensitive bullshit!

Breakthroughs! over the river! flips and crucifixions! gone down the flood! Highs! Epiphanies! Despairs! Ten years' animal screams and suicides! Minds! New loves! Mad generation! down on the rocks of Time!   92

Real holy laughter in the river! They saw it all! the wild eyes! the holy yells! They
   bade farewell! They jumped off the roof! to solitude! waving! carrying flowers!
   Down to the river! into the street!

   3

Carl Solomon! I'm with you in Rockland
        where you're madder than I am
I'm with you in Rockland
        where you must feel very strange
I'm with you in Rockland
        where you imitate the shade of my mother
I'm with you in Rockland
        where you've murdered your twelve secretaries
I'm with you in Rockland
        where you laugh at this invisible humor
I'm with you in Rockland
        where we are great writers on the same dreadful typewriter
I'm with you in Rockland
        where your condition has become serious and is reported on the radio   100
I'm with you in Rockland
        where the faculties of the skull no longer admit the worms of the senses
I'm with you in Rockland
        where you drink the tea of the breasts of the spinsters of Utica
I'm with you in Rockland
        where you pun on the bodies of your nurses the harpies of the Bronx
I'm with you in Rockland
        where you scream in a straightjacket that you're losing the game of the actual
        pingpong of the abyss
I'm with you in Rockland
        where you bang on the catatonic piano the soul is innocent and immortal it
        should never die ungodly in an armed madhouse
I'm with you in Rockland
        where fifty more shocks will never return your soul to its body again from its
        pilgrimage to a cross in the void
I'm with you in Rockland
        where you accuse your doctors of insanity and plot the Hebrew socialist revo-
        lution against the fascist national Golgotha
I'm with you in Rockland
        where you will split the heavens of Long Island and resurrect your living
        human Jesus from the superhuman tomb
I'm with you in Rockland
        where there are twentyfive-thousand mad comrades all together singing the
        final stanzas of the Internationale
I'm with you in Rockland
        where we hug and kiss the United States under our bedsheets the United
        States that coughs all night and won't let us sleep   110
I'm with you in Rockland
        where we wake up electrified out of the coma by our own souls' airplanes
        roaring over the roof they've come to drop angelic bombs the hospital illu-

minates itself   imaginary walls collapse   O skinny legions run outside   O starry-spangled shock of mercy the eternal war is here   O victory forget your underwear we're free

I'm with you in Rockland

in my dreams you walk dripping from a sea-journey on the highway across America in tears to the door of my cottage in the Western night

On Poetry and Poets

We may not have had an American style in poetry as the French, for example, measure such things. We have lacked until very lately a formed critical tradition in anything like the European sense. But we have produced by now a body of poetry of absorbing quality. If this poetry reveals violent contrasts and unresolved conflicts, it corresponds thereby to American life.

F. O. MATTHIESSEN

It is time . . . to regard American poetry as severely as we would regard Greek or Chinese or English poetry. For if American poetry is not yet great, it has at least reached that point at which one may say that it is mature. It has a history of nearly three hundred years. In sheer quantity, if one keeps in mind all the minor poets and poetasters of the eighteenth and nineteenth centuries, it is enormous: few people, unless we except librarians, can have any idea of it. And if we admit cheerfully enough that the first two-thirds of it is pretty barren, nevertheless one can also say with some assurance that it now comprises names of which no country need be ashamed, and it is beginning to wear the dignity that goes with a tradition.

CONRAD AIKEN

It is quite possible, and indeed necessary, to write of American literature in terms of its European, and especially its British sources. That was the way in which Longfellow viewed our literature, the way in which Howells seems to have felt

it could be best understood. It was the approach of teachers, critics, and historians in general until the 1920's. From the academic point of view, American literature was simply a hoped-for extension of the literature of the English-speaking peoples. And so it is; and such a history, as far as it goes, is entirely valid. Even the radical Walt Whitman insisted that in this new country we should absorb, not discard, our European past. We could not discard it, if we willed to do so. The progenitors of our literature are in a European and usually in an Anglo-Saxon past. Chaucer, Shakespeare, the folk ballads, the great religious literature of the English seventeenth century, are as deep in our ancestral strain as in the genealogy of modern British writing. The English eighteenth century, English romanticism, the English novel of character, and all later and vital English literature, have a family resemblance to ours, and a family influence, with which any other source for the American imagination outside our own terrain is by comparison weak indeed. A history of American literature exclusively in terms of democracy or the frontier is no less false than a history of American writing regarded as a colonial extension. There is a blending of elements in our culture which is inevitable in a newspaper editorial or in *John Brown's Body* or the *Song of Myself*.

From ROBERT E. SPILLER and OTHERS, *Literary History of the United States*

The Ushers, brother and sister, betrayed the Holy Ghost in themselves. They would love, love, love without resistance. They would love, they would merge, they would be one thing. So they dragged each other down into death. For the Holy Ghost says you must *not* be as one thing with another being. Each must abide by itself, and correspond only within certain limits. . . .

But Poe knew only love, love, love, intense vibrations and heightened consciousness. Drugs, women, self-destruction, but anyhow the prismatic ecstasy of heightened consciousness and sense of love, of flow. The human soul in him was beside itself. But it was not lost. He told us plainly how it was, so that we should know.

He was an adventurer into vaults and cellars and horrible underground passages of the human soul. He sounded the horror and the warning of his own doom.

Doomed he was. He died wanting more love, and love killed him. A ghastly disease, love. Poe telling us of his disease: trying even to make his disease fair and attractive. Even succeeding.

D. H. LAWRENCE

I am wondering if you might not profitably go to Lincoln for a greater understanding of Twain and Whitman. There is something—a quality there—common to the three men. In Lincoln it is perhaps more out in front of you.

I [have] a sense of three very honest boys brought suddenly to face the complex and intricate world. There is a stare in their eyes. They are puzzled and confused. You will be inclined to think Whitman the greater man perhaps. He came closer to understanding. He lacked Lincoln's very great honesty of soul.

Twain's way lies somewhere between the road taken by the other two men.

I am struck with the thought that I would like to have you believe that Twain's cheapness was not really a part of him. It was a thing out of the civiliza-

tion in which he lived that crept in and invaded him.

Lincoln let it creep in less, because he was less warm and human. He did not love and hate. In a simple solid way he stuck to abstract principles. . . .

Twain got more deeply into the complex matter of living. He was more like you and me, facing more nearly our kind of problems.

Here I am going to confess something to you. Whitman does not mean as much to me as do the other two. There is somewhere a pretense about him, even trickiness. When I was a boy and another boy caught me fairly—doing some second-rate thing—I was supposed to do what we called "acknowledge the corn."

Lincoln wouldn't have done the second-rate thing.

Twain would have and would have acknowledged the corn.

Whitman wouldn't have owned up.

Well there you are. I am putting Whitman below where he stands in my mind.

It is unfair. It springs from a growing desire I have to sell you Twain.

SHERWOOD ANDERSON

People who try to do new things, or even old things in a new way, are never popular. There is nothing revolutionary in the sentiment of the following as we read it now:

Come, Muse, migrate from Greece and Ionia,
Cross out please those immensely overpaid
    accounts,
That matter of Troy and Achilles' wrath . . .
Placard "Remove" and "To Let" on the rocks
    of your snowy Parnassus

—but imagine the feelings that must have been hurt by the language no less than the sentiment in Whitman's classic-fronted day!

Even so in our time the audience for poetry, necessarily limited at any time, has been jolted by some poets and inexcusably badgered by others, until one author complained that the act of publication was like dropping a rose petal in the Grand Canyon and waiting to hear the echo.

Let us admit at once that two characteristics of post-war [post 1918] verse have stood between the poets and a healthy audience: a philosophy of isolation and a private language.

The first of these began in France in the mid-nineteenth century when artists, as we observed, were expressing their revolt by retiring into some form of ideal dream-world of their own making. Great poets, intense but too isolated to contribute to the development of a tradition in accord with the new social and scientific facts, rose on the crest of the first symbolist tide. One of them, Rimbaud, carried his escape so far as to anticipate such a recent phenomenon as surrealism. The following passage from his most mature work is self-explanatory and prophetic:

One must be modern completely. . . . I loved meaningless door-tops, backgrounds, acrobats, back-cloths, sign-boards, popular prints, old-fashioned literature, church Latin, misspelled erotica, . . . I invented the color of the vowels! A black, E white, I red, O blue, U green, . . . I accustomed myself to simple hallucinations: I saw quite freely a mosque in place of a factory, a school of drums made by the angels, a drawing room at the bottom of a lake . . . I finished by finding the disorder of my sense sacred.

Poets who followed him, if they did not carry their burden to the same extremity, were content to develop some particular facet of the hard symbolist jewel.

SELDEN RODMAN

On modernist poetry: Very interesting language, a great emphasis on connotation, "texture"; extreme intensity, forced emotion—violence; a good deal of obscurity; emphasis on sensation, perceptual nuances; emphasis on details, on the part rather than the whole; experimental or novel qualities of some sort; a tendency toward disorganization—these are justified, generally, as the disorganization required to express a disorganized age, or alternatively, as newly discovered and more complex types of organization; . . . there is a good deal more of emphasis on the unconscious dream structure, the thoroughly subjective; the poet's attitudes are usually anti-scientific, anti-commonsense, anti-public—he is essentially removed.

RANDALL JARRELL

I wonder, indeed, if a high degree of difficulty is not an aspect of the modern poetic style, just as a peculiarly brilliant and aggressive clarity was a stylistic feature of the school of Pope. We know that by and large the school of Pope was sympathetic toward the society of its age and regarded itself as the champion of accepted values against dunces and outlaws; whereas contemporary poets are the heirs of the century-old tension between artists and society. Of course I do not mean that modern poets deliberately obscure their meaning in order to be rude to a world they cannot abide. It is not a question of individual poets and their motives, but of a general style, of which no single poet was the inventor and in which those who participate do so without necessarily having full awareness of its cultural implications. Indeed, so prevalent is the style today that poets with only a lesser grievance against the modern world . . . are only a little less difficult than Eliot or Rimbaud. And finally, the difficulty style is present in painting, in certain works of prose fiction, and in other contemporary arts.

F. W. DUPEE

The poets of today are still in what may be called the romantic situation . . . the result of that disintegration of orthodoxy that took place toward the end of the eighteenth century. During that century the standards of belief and taste, of which Augustan poetry was the expression, had begun to crumble. The consequence was that poets felt at sea in a way that the poets of previous ages had not done.

DAVID CECIL

In authentic poetry the total statement is identical with the poem itself. As it can find expression only through component statements that constitute the poem, it cannot be summarized without essential loss. The "scenario content" of the poem can be summarized, as in Lamb's *Tales* and in many a college syllabus, but the poetic statement is destroyed in translation. . . . My answer is that while no poetic statement can ever be translated or summarized into literal language adequately, there are cases in which a literal restatement can approximate the poetic original more nearly than in other cases, and that light can be thrown upon the nature of the poetic statement by comparing such approximations.

PHILIP WHEELWRIGHT

Let me put it this way: A poem works immediately upon us when we are ready for it. And it may require the mediation of a great deal of critical activity by ourselves before we are ready. And for the greater works we are never fully ready. That is why criticism is a never ending process.

ROBERT PENN WARREN

. . . people are exasperated by poetry which they do not understand, and contemptuous of poetry which they understand without effort.

T. S. ELIOT

When we read Kipling we can usually say, "That is just how I feel." Of course there is nothing "wrong" with that, but, when we read a great poet, we say, "I never realized before what I felt. From now on, thanks to this poem, I shall feel differently."

W. H. AUDEN

The pleasure is the pleasure of powers that create a truth that cannot be arrived at by the reason alone, a truth that the poet recognizes by sensation. The morality of the poet's radiant and productive atmosphere is the morality of the right sensation.

WALLACE STEVENS

I believe in an absolute rhythm, a rhythm, that is, in which poetry corresponds exactly to the emotion or shade of emotion to be expressed. A man's rhythm must be interpretive, it will be therefore, in the end, his own, uncounterfeiting, uncounterfeitable. . . . I think there is a "fluid" as well as a "solid" content, that some poems may have form as a tree has form, some as water poured into a vase.

EZRA POUND

The line will have the more charm for not being mechanically straight. We enjoy the straight crookedness of a good walking stick.

ROBERT FROST

Notes on the Poets

Conrad (Potter) Aiken (1889—)

Conrad Aiken was a member of the Harvard class of 1911 that included T. S. Eliot and Van Wyck Brooks. In the early nineteen-twenties he moved to England, where he lived for some years. His *Scepticisms* (1919) is a brilliant volume of critical essays, and he has also written distinguished novels and short stories. *Ushant: an Essay*, his autobiography, appeared in 1952, and *Collected Poems* in 1953. In 1930 he won the Pulitzer Prize for poetry and in 1956 he was given a Bollingen Award.

Stephen Vincent Benét (1898–1943)

Benét began to publish while still an undergraduate at Yale. He took a B.A. in 1919 and an M.A. in 1920, then did further study at the Sorbonne. He spent 1926 and 1927 on a Guggenheim Fellowship in France writing the long narrative poem *John Brown's Body*, which won a Pulitzer Prize in 1929. Benét spent most of his brief career investigating and writing about American themes. He wrote many short stories and, during the war, radio scripts. He was an intensely patriotic and idealistic man. There is a fine biographical and critical study of him by Charles Fenton. He won a second Pulitzer Prize in 1944.

John Berryman (1914—)

John Berryman was born in Oklahoma, attended Columbia University and Clare College, Cambridge. He has taught at a number of universities, and is now a member of the staff at the University of Minnesota. He published *Poems* (1942), *The Dispossessed* (1948) and *Homage to Mistress Anne Bradstreet* (1956). He is also the author of *Stephen Crane* (1950).

Elizabeth Bishop (1911—)

Miss Bishop was born in Worcester, Massachusetts, and graduated from Vassar. She has won many prizes and awards. Her early work shows the influence of Marianne Moore. She is the author of *North and South* (1946) and *A Cold Spring* (1955). She now lives in Rio de Janeiro, Brazil. In 1956 she won a Pulitzer Prize.

Anne Bradstreet (1612?–1672)

Anne Bradstreet was born in Northampton, England, about 1612. Her father, Thomas Dudley, was steward of the estates of the Earl of Lincoln. Thomas Dudley was a studious man, drawn toward Puritanism. In her poetry one can observe a tension or pull between the writings of the Puritans and the world, just beginning to fade when she was born, of Shakespeare and Ben Jonson. In 1628 she married Simon Bradstreet. Two years later, she and Bradstreet, and her father and his family sailed for America. Both Dudley and Bradstreet were eminent figures in the Massachusetts Bay Colony. Anne Bradstreet managed to write a good number of poems despite the hardships of early colonial life and of raising eight children. Her first book,

The Tenth Muse Lately Sprung Up in America appeared in 1650, and the second, *Several Poems Compiled with Great Variety of Wit and Learning,* after her death.

William Cullen Bryant (1794–1878)

Bryant, with the possible exception of Freneau, was the first American-born poetic genius. He lived as a boy in Cummington, Massachusetts, in the Berkshires. He spent one year at Williams College, but already he had read widely in his father's library. He practiced law and was also an important editor. Bryant was one of the great personalities of his era, a dynamic liberal, and a poet and critic who taught American poets how to assimilate the poetic theories of the English Romantic movement. *The Life and Works of William Cullen Bryant,* edited by Parke Godwin (1883–1884), is the standard collection of his writings.

John Ciardi (1916—)

John Ciardi is a poet, editor, and translator. He was born in Massachusetts. He has taught poetry in many American Universities including Rutgers, where he is now a professor. Mr. Ciardi is poetry editor of the *Saturday Review* and director of the Breadloaf Writers Conference.

Hart Crane (1899–1932)

Hart Crane's father was a candy manufacturer in Ohio, and he wanted his son to have a business career. But young Crane was determined to be a writer, and this led to a breach with his father. Before he finished high school he came to New York, where he became associated with many leading literary figures. He wrote for the *Seven Arts Magazine* and the *Little Review.* He published *White Buildings* in 1926, which established him as a poet's poet. *The Bridge,* his long mythopoeic poem about American history, appeared in 1930 and was widely acclaimed. Allen Tate has said, "Crane was the most original and powerful imagination that appeared in America in the nineteen-twenties." Crane committed suicide by jumping into the Gulf of Mexico from a steamer carrying him back to New York from Mexico. There is a fine biography of Crane by Philip Horton. Brom Weber has edited his letters.

Stephen Crane (1871–1900)

Crane wrote the novel *Maggie* when he was twenty and another novel, *The Red Badge of Courage,* when he was twenty-four. In 1895 he published his collected poems. These are sometimes said to owe a debt to Emily Dickinson and to augur the Imagist Movement of a generation later. Crane is far from being a great poet, but he was an important innovator. His main achievement was in fiction. John Berryman's *Stephen Crane* (1950) is a full-scale biography and critical study.

E. E. Cummings (1894—)

E. E. Cummings was born in Cambridge, Massachusetts, and took his B.A. and M.A. from Harvard. He served as an ambulance driver in France before the U.S. entered World War I. Through an error he was sent to a detention camp for three months. Out of this experience came his interesting prose work *The Enormous Room.* During the nineteen-twenties he lived both in Paris and the United States and won a reputation as a painter and an experimental poet. In 1931 he travelled through Russia and reported his journey in *Eimi* (1933). A series of lectures given at Harvard is entitled *i: six non-lectures*. His collected poems appear in *Poems 1923–1954* (1954). In 1958 Charles Norman published *The Magic-Maker: E. E. Cummings*.

Emily Dickinson *(1830–1886)*

Emily Dickinson's father was an eminent person in Amherst, Massachusetts, who served one term in the U.S. House of Representatives. Reputedly his was a sternly run household. Emily Dickinson spent very little time away from this house: a year at school in South Hadley and brief visits to Washington, Philadelphia, and Boston. There have been many speculations about her "love affairs," with Ben Newton, Reverend Charles Wadsworth, and even with an elderly judge. But very little is definitely known. She early became a recluse. Thomas Wentworth Higginson, a literary man, tried to improve her poems, but for the most part she kept her own counsel. She is undoubtedly a writer of genius. *Ancestors Brocades* by Millicent T. Bingham is a fascinating account of the squabbles that surrounded the publication of her various manuscripts. The definitive edition is *The Poems of Emily Dickinson* (1955), edited by T. H. Johnson. There are good critical studies by Allen Tate, Richard Chase, and Henry W. Wells.

Richard Eberhart *(1904—)*

Richard Eberhart was born in Austin, Minnesota, but has spent most of his adult life in the East. He received a B.A. from Dartmouth and an M.A. from Cambridge University. He taught English for almost ten years at St. Mark's School, Southborough, Massachusetts. After several years in the Navy he joined a Boston manufacturing firm. Among Eberhart's many volumes are *Reading the*

Spirit (1936), *Selected Poems* (1951), and *Greek Praises* (1957).

T. S. Eliot *(1888—)* Jan. 1965

T. S. Eliot was born in St. Louis, was educated at Harvard, the Sorbonne, and Oxford, and eventually became an English subject. His works include *Collected Poems 1909–1935, Old Possum's Book of Practical Cats, Four Quartets, Murder in in the Cathedral, The Family Reunion, The Cocktail Party, The Elder Statesman,* and *Selected Essays.* He was given the Nobel Prize for Literature in 1948. Eliot's "The Waste Land," published in the early nineteen-twenties, set the tone for much of the poetry and prose of the next thirty years. Many textbooks and literary histories have such headings as "The Waste Land Writers" or "The Waste Land Period." Eliot's criticism has been equally influential. Such terms as "the objective correlative" and "the fusion of thought and feeling" have been widely employed. In the recent past he has had considerable success as a playwright. Eliot's poetic practices, his criticism, and his social, political, and religious opinions have also been highly controversial. In the opinion of many American writers, including the editor of this anthology, Eliot's literary and esthetic influences have been more destructive to American poetry than any other single force. Leonard Unger's *T. S. Eliot: A Selected Critique* is a useful introduction to the criticism that has been devoted to Eliot's work.

Ralph Waldo Emerson *(1803–1882)*

Emerson's father was pastor of the First Unitarian Church in Boston. He died early, leaving a widow and five sons. But the boy Waldo was able to get through school and to attend Harvard College. In

1825 he entered the Harvard Divinity School, and later served as a Unitarian minister. But in 1832 he resigned from the ministry saying he could no longer accept certain church doctrines. In his "Divinity School Address" (1836) he said that he opposed fixed dogmas and conventions. Emerson enjoyed a very successful career as a lecturer, and he was associated with many of the eminent literary figures of his day. His prose publications were mostly collections of his lectures, *Essays* (1841) and *Essays: Second Series* (1844). He published his first volume of poems in 1847, a second in 1867, and *Selected Poems* in 1876. Emerson was among the first literary men to accept Whitman. There are a number of editions of Emerson's works and many critical studies. The biography by R. L. Rusk is a definitive one.

Kenneth Fearing (1902—)

Kenneth Fearing was born in Chicago and worked as a mill hand and journalist. His first book was published in 1929.

John Gould Fletcher (1886–1950)

Fletcher was born in Little Rock, Arkansas. He studied Greek and Latin with private tutors when he was a child. He left Harvard four months before graduation because his father had died and left him enough money to enable him to travel and to write. He lived in England from 1908 to 1933. He was primarily known for his association with the Imagists. His autobiography, *Life Is My Song*, appeared in 1937 and his *Selected Poems* in 1938 for which he won a Pulitzer Prize in 1939. During the latter years of his life Fletcher lived in Little Rock. He took his own life. Stanley Coffman's *Imagism* (1951) is a good discussion of Imagism

as a movement and of Fletcher's part in it.

Philip Freneau (1752–1832)

Freneau was born in New York of French Huguenot and Scottish parentage. At Princeton he became friends with James Madison and Hugh Henry Brackenridge, one of the first American novelists. Freneau was trained in the Neo-Classical tradition but his impulse, when he was not being polemical or satirical, was romantic sentiment. During the Revolution he wrote a number of patriotic poems, collected as *The Poems of Philip Freneau Written Chiefly During the Late War* (1786). After the war he was a political journalist and a supporter of Jefferson against Hamilton. He suffered financial reverses at various times and made his living as a sea captain, a farmer, and a tinker. In 1815 he published *A Collection of Poems Written Between the Year 1797 and the Present Time*. Freneau pointed in the direction of American literary independence.

Robert Frost (1874—) 1963

Frost was born in California. His father had left New Hampshire during the Civil War. He named his son Robert Lee, after General Robert E. Lee. The boy was eleven when the father died and his mother returned to Massachusetts to teach school. He and a girl named Elinor White were the joint valedictorians of their high school senior class, and three years after graduation they married. Frost attended Dartmouth briefly and Harvard for two years. He taught school and worked as a farmer. Hoping for the acceptance of his poetry, he took his family to England. In 1913 his *A Boy's Will* was hailed as a work of great importance. So too was *North of Boston* (1914). Frost returned to the United States and to a life-long chorus of critical acclaim. He has been given over forty honorary degrees and has won innumerable prizes, including Pulitzer Prizes in 1924, 1931, 1937, and 1943. *Fire and Ice* by Lawrance Thompson is an excellent critical introduction to his poetry.

Allen Ginsberg (1926—)

Allen Ginsberg was born in Newark, New Jersey. He graduated from Columbia University, and has held various jobs, including a stint in the merchant marine. He settled for a time in San Francisco, where he joined the Kenneth Rexroth group of poets. *Howl,* which was originally seized by the authorities as an "obscene" book, is generally regarded as the key poem of the Beat Generation.

Oliver Wendell Holmes (1809–1894)

Holmes had a very successful career as a physician, a professor of medicine, and Dean of the Harvard Medical School. Literature was his avocation. His first volume, *Poems,* was published in 1836, the year he took his medical degree at Harvard. By 1850 he had published several volumes and had a considerable reputation as the author of light verses. In 1857 he and other members of the Saturday Club founded *The Atlantic Monthly.* For the *Atlantic* he wrote his whimsical "table talk," which was later collected in several volumes. He also wrote novels. Holmes attacked the Boston "Brahmin" caste for its snobbishness, supported the right of women to attend medical schools, and supported necessary but unpopular changes in medical practices.

Randall Jarrell (1914—)

Randall Jarrell studied at Vanderbilt University under both John Crowe Ransom

and Robert Penn Warren. He took his B.A. and M.A. there, and has taught at the University of Texas, Kenyon College, and the Women's College, University of North Carolina. He served for several years in the Air Corps. For a short period he was acting literary editor of *The Nation.* He has written one novel, a satire on academic life, *Pictures from an Institution,* and a volume of criticism, *Poetry and the Age.* His poems have been collected in *Blood for a Stranger* (1942), *Little Friend, Little Friend* (1945), *Losses* (1948), and *Selected Poems* (1955).

Robinson Jeffers (1887—)

Jeffers was born in Pittsburgh, where his father was professor of Biblical languages and literature at Western Theological Seminary. He studied at the University of Pittsburgh, Occidental College, the University of Zurich, the University of Southern California, and the University of Washington. His interests included languages, medicine, and forestry. *Flagons and Apples,* his first book of poems, was published in 1904. A few years later a small legacy made it possible for him to give all of his time to writing. At Carmel, California, on a cliff overlooking the ocean, he built a stone house and tower. There, with his family, he has lived in seclusion for many years. In 1937 he was awarded a Book-of-the-Month Club Fellowship for distinguished work, and he inaugurated a series of readings at the Library of Congress. Among his best known works are *Roan Stallion, Tamar and Other Poems* (1925) and *Medea* (1946), a verse rendering of the play by Euripides.

Sidney Lanier (1842–1881)

Lanier was born in Macon, Georgia, and attended Oglethorpe University. He served in the Civil War. During the rest of his life he suffered from tuberculosis. His first book was a novel, *Tiger-Lilies* (1867). Lanier was a musician and tried to explore the relations between poetry and music. In 1879 he lectured at Johns Hopkins University on English literature and versification. His lectures on versification were published in 1880 as *The Science of English Verse*. He advocated a fluid verse form. Lanier was only forty when he died.

Vachel Lindsay (1879–1931)

Carl Sandburg and Edgar Lee Masters were among the first Midwesterners to contribute to the "New Poetry" movement. But Lindsay had published *General Booth Enters Heaven and Other Poems* in 1913 and *The Congo and Other Poems* in 1914, the latter a year before Masters' *Spoon River Anthology* and two years before Sandburg's *Chicago Poems*. Lindsay conceived of poetry as minstrelsy, or in his own phrase, "the higher vaudeville." He took rhythms from hymns, the circus, and from songs and games. He had given up preparation for the ministry and had attended art school in Chicago and later in New York. He was a popular lecturer and reader of his poetry. In 1931, for reasons that are not clear, he took his own life. *Selected Poems of Vachel Lindsay*, edited by H. Spencer in 1931, is a good introduction to his work.

Henry Wadsworth Longfellow (1807–1882)

Longfellow was enormously popular in his lifetime, but in the nineteen-twenties and nineteen-thirties there was a reaction against his more sentimental and didactic poems. There is, however, another side to Longfellow, and recent criticism has emphasized his remarkable powers of construction, his imagination, and his fundamental seriousness. Longfellow was born in Maine and attended Bowdoin College. After his graduation he taught foreign languages at Bowdoin. Later he held the Smith Professorship at Harvard. The one-volume *Complete Poetical Works* (1893) is still available. The standard biography was written by his brother, Samuel Longfellow. There is also an interesting study by Lawrance Thompson, *The Young Longfellow* (1938).

Robert (Trail Spence) Lowell (1917—)

Robert Lowell, the third member of the Lowell family to publish poetry, attended St. Mark's School and took his B.A. from Kenyon College in 1940. He spent five months in jail during World War II as a conscientious objector. *Land of Unlikeness* appeared in a limited edition in 1944. *Lord Weary's Castle* won the Pulitzer Prize for poetry in 1947. He has been Consultant in Poetry at the Library of Congress and has taught at the University of Iowa, the University of Cincinnati, and Emerson College. Recently he published his autobiography.

Archibald MacLeish (1892—)

Archibald MacLeish took his B.A. from Yale, and his LL.B. from Harvard. During World War I he served in France. He practiced law briefly after the war and then took his family to Paris in 1923. Much of his early work is in the expatriate tradition formulated by Pound and others. But in "American Letter" he announced his determination to return to the U.S. and to write about American themes. *Conquistador* (1932) won him a Pulitzer Prize. MacLeish's social consciousness is clearly evident in *New Found Land* (1930) and *Frescoes for*

Mr. Rockefeller's City (1933). MacLeish wrote a number of radio plays during the nineteen-thirties. In 1939 he was appointed Librarian of Congress, in 1944 he was made Assistant Secretary of State, and in 1946 he went to Paris as chairman of the American delegation to UNESCO. In 1953 he won another Pulitzer Prize for *Collected Poems*. At present he is Boylston Professor at Harvard. In 1959 his verse play *JB*, based on the Job story, was produced on Broadway.

Edgar Lee Masters (1869–1950)

Masters was raised in Petersburg and Lewistown, Illinois, the Spoon River Country about which he wrote. He left Knox College after one year, and was admitted to the bar in 1891. He practiced law successfully in Chicago for twenty-five years. *Spoon River Anthology* (1915) was his most popular book. He gave up the law in 1920 and moved to New York, where he wrote fiction, boys' stories, biographies and poetry. *Domesday Book* (1920), *The New Spoon River* (1924), *Selected Poems* (1925), and his autobiography *Across Spoon River* are among his better known books.

Herman Melville (1819–1891)

Melville was born into a substantial New York family, but his father suffered severe business setbacks shortly before his death. Melville went to sea when he was eighteen. When he married the daughter of a Boston chief justice he settled down to a career as a writer. His early novels were quite popular. In 1850 he bought a house near Pittsfield, Massachusetts, and it was there he became friendly with Hawthorne. *Moby-Dick*, his masterpiece, was not well received. He published three later volumes of fiction, but his reputation declined steadily. Several volumes of poems were published at his uncle's expense. He also published a long poem entitled *Clarel*, inspired by a visit to the Holy Land. In 1866 he became a customs inspector in New York, and in the same year published *Battle-Pieces*. At the time of his death Melville was almost wholly forgotten. But since his rediscovery in the nineteen-twenties, his reputation has risen steadily. Some of Melville's works are curious failures, but even in these books there is an air of great literary power. There is an essay on Melville as a poet in Robert Penn Warren's *Selected Essays*.

Edna St. Vincent Millay (1892–1950)

When she was twenty Edna Millay published "Renascence," a poem that immediately established her reputation. In 1917, the poem, somewhat revised, was used as the title poem of her first book. In 1920 *A Few Figs from Thistles* appeared, and led to her becoming the lyric voice of the "Jazz Age." She became identified with female emancipation. After her marriage in 1923 she lived quietly in the Berkshires. She wrote the libretto for the opera *The King's Henchman*. Among her best known books are *The Harp Weaver and Other Poems, The Buck in the Snow and Other Poems, Fatal Interview,* and *Conversation at Midnight.* During the Second World War she wrote many poems with patriotic and social themes. Although Miss Millay's reputation is no longer as high as it was in the nineteen-twenties and nineteen-thirties, a number of her lyrics are usually held to be of a high order. She won a Pulitzer Prize in 1923.

Marianne Moore (1887—)

Miss Moore was born in St. Louis, Missouri, and was educated at the Metzger

Institute, Carlisle, Pennsylvania, and at Bryn Mawr College. Her first American book *Observations* (1924) won the Dial Award. She became acting editor of the *Dial* in 1926 and remained with it until it ceased publication in 1929. After the publication of *Collected Poems* (1951) she was given a Bollingen Award and a Pulitzer Prize in 1952. Miss Moore has published critical essays and translated the fables of La Fontaine. She lives in Brooklyn.

Edgar Allan Poe (1809–1849)

Poe has become a symbol of the alienated writer. The son of itinerant actors, he was born in Boston. His father, David Poe, disappeared some months later, and Poe was left an orphan when his mother, Elizabeth Arden Poe, died on tour in Richmond, Virginia. John Allan took the child as his ward, but he and Poe got along poorly, and in the end Allan disowned him. Poe suffered from some deep insecurity, and despite his great abilities as an editor and a writer, misfortune dogged him all his life. His marriage to a childlike girl, his cousin Virginia Clemm, has caused many speculations of a psychological sort by critics and biographers. Poe is sometimes said to be the father of the American short story and the inventor of the story of detection. Poe has long fascinated European as well as American readers. There are interesting essays on Poe by D. H. Lawrence in *Studies in Classical American Literature*, by Allen Tate in *The Forlorn Demon*, and by Richard Wilbur in his Laurel edition of Poe.

Ezra Pound (1885—)

Ezra Pound was born in Hailey, Idaho. He attended the University of Pennsylvania and Hamilton College. In 1908 he went abroad. By 1912 he had written seven volumes of poetry and prose and established himself as a person of great originality. He championed many experimental writers. Both T. S. Eliot and Ernest Hemingway have acknowledged indebtedness to him. Pound's critical, and later his social and political, opinions have been uttered with fervor and vehemence, and a considerable portion of his writing is satiric. His most ambitious works are the *Cantos*. During World War II he broadcast propaganda from Italy. He was indicted by the U.S. government but not tried because he was found to be insane. He spent twelve years at St. Elizabeths Hospital in Washington. In 1958 the U.S. District Court dropped the charges against him and he was released. Many controversies have raged about Pound's theories and his poetry. T. S. Eliot has written introductions to Pound's *Selected Poems* and *Literary Essays*.

John Crowe Ransom (1888—)

John Crowe Ransom took his B.A. from Vanderbilt University in 1909, then spent three years as a Rhodes scholar at Oxford. He joined the English faculty at Vanderbilt and remained there, except for two years spent in the Army, until 1937. At Vanderbilt he helped establish *The Fugitive*, a "little magazine" to which Allen Tate, Robert Penn Warren, and other students of Ransom contributed. In 1938 he moved to Kenyon College, where he edited the *Kenyon Review* until his retirement in 1959. Ransom is sometimes credited with having sponsored and partly formulated the "New Criticism." In addition to several volumes of poetry he has published critical essays, *The World's Body* (1938) and *The New Criticism* (1941). The Summer, 1948, issue of *Sewanee Review* was devoted to articles about Ransom as poet, teacher, and critic.

Edwin Arlington Robinson (1869–1935)

Robinson was born in Maine, and one of his critics has said that all of his poetry is about the decay of the "Big House" people, those who had once been wealthy. He left Harvard when his father died. *The Torrent and the Night Before* (1896) won favorable critical attention. He worked for a time in New York City but was eventually able to support himself by writing. *The Man Against the Sky* (1916) established him firmly, and he won a Pulitzer Prize in 1922 for *Collected Poems*. He was to win it on two other occasions, for *The Man Who Died Twice* and *Tristram*. His Arthurian poems were very popular. Robinson was an extremely reticent man. There are biographies of him by Hermann Hagedorn and Emory Neff and there is a good critical study of his work by Yvor Winters.

Theodore Roethke (1908—)

Theodore Roethke was born in Saginaw, Michigan. He attended the University of Michigan and Harvard. He has taught at Lafayette College, Pennsylvania State College, Bennington College, and the University of Washington. He won the Pulitzer Prize for poetry in 1954. He is the author of *Open House* (1941), *The Lost Son and Other Poems* (1948), *Praise to the End* (1951), *The Waking, Poems 1933–1953* (1953), for which he won a Pulitzer Prize in 1954, and *Words for the Wind* (1958).

Carl Sandburg (1878—)

Carl Sandburg started to work at thirteen, and was at various times a dishwasher, bricklayer, barbershop porter, sign painter, and house painter. He served for six months in the Spanish-American War. He attended Lombard College for four years but left without a degree. He established himself as a journalist in Milwaukee and in Chicago. His first success with poetry was "Chicago," published in *Poetry* in 1914. During the nineteen-twenties he was one of the leading figures in the "Chicago Renaissance" and in the "New Poetry" movement. His six-volume life of Lincoln won a Pulitzer Prize in 1950. Sandburg has been a frequent public performer, usually with a guitar, of American ballads. In 1953 he published an autobiography, *Always the Young Strangers*. In 1951 he won another Pulitzer Prize for *Complete Poems*.

Delmore Schwartz (1913—)

Delmore Schwartz was born in Brooklyn. He took his B.A. from New York University in 1935 and studied at Columbia University, the University of Wisconsin, and Harvard. He received a Guggenheim Fellowship in 1939 and taught at Harvard from 1940 to 1947. He has contributed to many magazines, but has been most closely associated with *Partisan Review*. He has written fiction as well as poetry. His principal works are *In Dreams Begin Responsibilities* (1938), *Shenandoah* (1941), *The World is a Wedding* (1948), and *Vaudeville for a Princess* (1950).

Karl Shapiro (1913—)

Karl Shapiro was born in Baltimore. He attended the University of Virginia and Johns Hopkins University. *Person, Place and Thing* (1942) was published while he was en route with the first American troops going to Australia. *V-Letter and Other Poems* (1944) won a Pulitzer Prize. *Essay on Rime*, an extended verse commentary on modern poetry, was written in New Guinea and on Biak. Later books have been *Trial of a Poet, Poems, 1940–1953,* and *Poems of a Jew.* Shapiro was Consultant in Poetry at the Library of Congress, and later the editor of *Poetry.* For the past few years he has been professor of English at the University of Nebraska and editor of *The Prairie Schooner.*

Wallace Stevens (1879–1955)

Stevens, by profession a lawyer, spent most of his life working for the Hartford Accident and Indemnity Company. In 1934 he became vice president and continued in this office until his death in 1955. He was forty-four when he published *Harmonium* in 1923, a volume of exquisitely wrought poems. Twelve years went by before another volume appeared, but from 1935 to 1937 there were three, and thereafter he published with great regularity. His subject throughout his various volumes is the relationship between imagination and reality. He expounded his theories in prose in *The Necessary Angel* in 1951. He was the recipient of the Bollingen Award for poetry in 1949 and the Pulitzer Prize in 1955. There is a study of his poetry by W. V. O'Connor, *The Shaping Spirit: A Study of Wallace Stevens.*

John Banister Tabb (1845–1909)

John Banister Tabb was born in Baltimore, Maryland. He became a convert to Roman Catholicism. He went to Hawaii to join a leper colony as priest, and died of leprosy in 1909. He is buried in Richmond, Virginia.

Allen Tate (1899—)

Allen Tate was the classmate of Robert Penn Warren at Vanderbilt University and the student of John Crowe Ransom. After graduation he went to New York as a free-lance writer. His principal works are *Reactionary Essays on Poetry and Ideas* (1936), *Selected Poems* (1937), *Poems, 1922–47* (1949), and *The Forlorn Demon* (1953). Tate has held the Chair of Poetry at the Library of Congress, edited the *Sewanee Review,* worked for a New York publishing house, and taught at a number of universities. At present he is professor of English at the University of Minnesota.

Bayard Taylor (1825–1878)

Taylor was an extremely prolific writer of poetry and travel books, and he held diplomatic posts. His articles were syndicated in many newspapers, and he was a popular lecturer. His reputation has declined greatly, but he is a good representative of what Santayana called "the genteel tradition" in American philosophy and literature. There is an interesting comparison to be made between Taylor's treatment of the great African mountain Kilimanjaro and Hemingway's treatment of it.

Edward Taylor (1645?–1729)

At his death, the poems of Edward Taylor were deposited in the Yale library and lay there for over two hundred years before they were discovered and published. Taylor was born in Coventry, England, studied at Harvard, and spent a long career as a preacher in Westfield, a frontier village in Connecticut. His poems were written as acts of devotion. They are in a style that is sometimes called metaphysical and sometimes baroque. The poems have obvious affinities with much of the poetry written in England at the same period, especially that written by Richard Crashaw and

George Herbert. In 1939 Thomas H. Johnson published *The Poetical Works of Edward Taylor*.

Henry David Thoreau (1817–1862)

Thoreau lived and died in Concord, Massachusetts. He attended Harvard College, but except for giving a few lectures and doing some tutoring and teaching he followed no profession. He was a close friend of Emerson and a member of the Transcendental Club. He also contributed to *The Dial*, the magazine sponsored by the Club. He was a rebel in many respects. He refused to pay church taxes, and he refused to pay a poll tax, for which he was given a jail sentence. *A Week on the Concord and Merrimack Rivers* is a description of a canoe trip he took with his brother in 1839. He was an accurate, sympathetic, and witty reporter of nature. Most of Thoreau's poetry was written early. Some of the poems appeared in *The Dial* and others were incorporated into his prose works. The collected works of Thoreau are published in a Cambridge edition (1947), and there is an interesting biography by Joseph Wood Krutch.

Henry Timrod (1828–1867)

Only Poe among Southern writers born prior to the Civil War wrote with greater clarity than Timrod. The war gave him his most comprehensive and meaningful subject, but also hastened his death. Timrod had hoped to be a university professor, but poor health and financial difficulties forced him to leave the University of Georgia after one year. For a few months he served in the Confederate army, and for a brief period he was editor of the Columbia *South Carolinian*. He died in 1867 at the age of thirty-nine.

Jones Very (1813–1880)

Jones Very, born in Salem, Massachusetts, was a friend of Emerson, Channing, Hawthorne, and Bryant. Two volumes of his work, essays and poems, were published during his lifetime, one of them edited in part by Emerson. In 1886 a complete edition of his essays and poems was published. Yvor Winters, who wrote an excellent essay (*Maule's Curse*) on Very, speculates that the considerable amount of dead material in the volume caused the decline of his reputation. Critics like Winters have re-established Very as a poet of "impressive qualities" and remarkable verbal and rhythmical control.

Peter Viereck (1916—)

Peter Viereck was born in New York City and was educated at Harvard and Oxford. During World War II, he served in the African and Italian campaigns and taught at the American Army University in Florence. He is professor of history and literature at Mount Holyoke and is well known as a poet, critic, and historian. He won a Pulitzer Prize in 1949 for *Terror and Decorum*.

Robert Penn Warren (1905—)

Robert Penn Warren studied at Vanderbilt University and was a Rhodes scholar at Oxford. With Cleanth Brooks he edited *The Southern Review* at Louisiana State University. He later taught at the University of Minnesota and at Yale. Warren won distinction as a poet when he was in his early twenties, and his novel *All the King's Men* won a Pulitzer Prize in 1947 and brought him to national attention. He has since written other novels, a long poem, *Brother to*

Dragons, a collection of short poems, *Promises,* for which he won a Pulitzer Prize in 1958, several textbooks, and a collection of critical essays.

Walt Whitman (1819–1892)

Whitman was born on a farm on Long Island. As a boy he attended school for five years in Brooklyn. He began work as an office boy but was soon drawn toward printing shops and newspapers. Eventually he became editor of the Brooklyn *Eagle.* In 1848 he spent a few months in New Orleans. He returned to Brooklyn to edit the *Freeman.* He gave up newspaper work to write poetry. The first edition of *Leaves of Grass,* which he revised and reworked for the rest of his life, appeared in 1855. It was privately printed. The book did not receive much attention, but it caused Emerson to send Whitman this message: "I greet you at the beginning of a great career." In 1862 Whitman went to Washington and served as a war nurse. This experience led to *Drum Taps* (1865). Whitman lost one government job because *Leaves of Grass* was held to be unsavory, but he was given another in the Attorney General's office. He suffered a severe stroke in 1873 and thereafter lived with his brother George in Camden, New Jersey. In 1879 he journied west as far as Nevada. During the last decade of his life he had a considerable American reputation, and his books sold well enough to enable him to buy a small house in Camden. The 1892 edition of *Leaves of Grass,* signed on his deathbed, is commonly held to be the beginning of modern American poetry and one of the world's great books. Among the many interesting studies of Whitman are *The Solitary Singer* (1955) by G. W. Allen, *Leaves of Grass One Hundred Years After* (1955), edited by Milton Hindus, and James E. Miller's study of *Leaves of Grass.*

John Greenleaf Whittier (1807–1892)

Whittier is one of the New England "graybeard" poets whose reputations have declined in the twentieth century. He was born into a Quaker family that owned a farm on the Merrimac River, near the sea. From his family he took the moral earnestness of the Quaker tradition. A schoolmaster lent him the poetry of Robert Burns, and the influence of the Scottish poet is everywhere evident in Whittier's poetry. Both write about the common, everyday life of simple people, but Whittier's imagination was more genteel, and he lacked the quick-witted earthiness of Burns. During most of his adult life Whittier was a newspaper editor, and prior to the Civil War he was an ardent abolitionist. He published many volumes of poetry, but it was only after the publication of "Snow-Bound" in 1866 that he was widely acclaimed.

Richard Wilbur (1921—)

Richard Wilbur was born in New York and graduated from Amherst College in 1942. After service with the army during World War II, he took his M.A. at Harvard. At Harvard from 1947 to 1954 he was a Junior Fellow. He has had a Guggenheim Fellowship and was awarded the Prix de Rome of the American Academy of Arts and Letters in 1954. He teaches at Wesleyan University in Connecticut. Wilbur is the author of *The Beautiful Changes and Other Poems* (1947), *Ceremony and Other Poems* (1950), and *Things of This World* (1956) for which he won a Pulitzer Prize in 1957.

William Carlos Williams (1883—)

William Carlos Williams practiced medicine in Rutherford, New Jersey, until his retirement a few years ago. At the University of Pennsylvania, where he received his M.D. degree, he knew Ezra Pound, and the two have been friends ever since. He has written novels, short stories, and essays as well as many volumes of poetry. Dr. Williams has been preoccupied with American subjects and American rhythms. One of his prose works is entitled *In the American Grain.* His most widely acclaimed work is the long poem "Paterson." Dr. Williams published his autobiography in 1951.

Elinor Wylie (1885–1928)

Elinor Wylie, born Elinor Hoyt, spent her childhood near Philadelphia and in Washington, D.C. Married to Philip Hichborn, she eloped to Europe with Horace Wylie, whom she later married. In 1921 she published *Nets to Catch the Wind.* By 1924 she had published another volume and had married William Rose Benét. She also wrote fiction, employing a highly disciplined and ornate prose. Her *Collected Poems* was published in 1932 and her *Collected Prose* in 1933.

Suggested Critical Readings

An asterisk indicates that the book is available in a paperback edition.

ABBOTT, C. D., ed., *Poets at Work*. New York: Harcourt, Brace & Co., 1948. Essays by Auden, Stauffer, Shapiro, and Arnheim.

BAYLEY, JOHN, *The Romantic Survival*. London: Constable & Co., Ltd., 1957.

BLACKMUR, R. P., *The Double Agent*. New York: Arrow Editions, 1935.

————, *The Expense of Greatness*. New York: Arrow Editions, 1940.

*————, *Form and Value in Modern Poetry*. Anchor Books, Doubleday & Company, Inc.

————, *Language as Gesture*. London: George Allen & Unwin, Ltd., 1954.

*BOGAN, LOUISE, *Achievement in American Poetry*. Chicago: Henry Regnery Co., 1951. Paperback: Gateway Books, Henry Regnery Co.

————, *Selected Criticism*. New York: The Noonday Press, 1955.

BOWRA, C. M., *The Background of Modern Poetry*. London: Oxford University Press, 1946.

*————, *The Creative Experiment*. London: Macmillan & Co., Ltd., 1949. Paperback: Evergreen Books, Grove Press.

————, *The Heritage of Symbolism*. London: Macmillan & Co., Ltd., 1947.

BROOKS, CLEANTH, *Modern Poetry and the Tradition*. Chapel Hill: University of North Carolina Press, 1939.

*————, *The Well Wrought Urn*. New York: Reynal & Hitchcock, 1947. Paperback: Harvest Books, Harcourt, Brace & Co.

*BURKE, KENNETH, *Counterstatement*. New York: Harcourt, Brace & Co., 1931. Paperback: Phoenix Books, University of Chicago Press.

COFFMAN, S. K., *Imagism: A Chapter for the History of Modern Poetry*. Norman: University of Oklahoma Press, 1951.

DAICHES, DAVID, *Poetry and the Modern World*. Chicago: University of Chicago Press, 1940.

DEUTSCH, BABETTE, *Poetry in Our Time*. New York: Henry Holt & Co., Inc., 1952.

————, *This Modern Poetry*. New York: W. W. Norton & Co., Inc., 1935.

DREW, ELIZABETH, and SWEENY, J. L., *Directions in Modern Poetry*. New York: W. W. Norton & Co., Inc., 1940.

ELIOT, T. S., *On Poetry and Poets*. New York: Farrar, Straus & Cudahy, 1957.

————, *The Use of Poetry and the Use of Criticism*. Cambridge, Mass.: Harvard University Press, 1933.

*EMPSON, WILLIAM, *Seven Types of Ambiguity*. 2d ed.; New York: New Directions, 1947. Paperback: Meridian Books, Inc.

FEIDELSON, CHARLES, *Symbolism and American Literature*. Chicago: University of Chicago Press, 1953.

FRANKENBURG, LLOYD, *Pleasure Dome*. Boston: Houghton Mifflin Co., 1949.

GREGORY, HORACE, and ZATURENSKA, MARYA, *A History of American Poetry, 1900–1940*. New York: Harcourt, Brace & Co., 1946.

HULME, T. E., *Further Speculations*. Minneapolis: University of Minnesota Press, 1955.

257

HULME, T. E., *Speculations*. New York: Harcourt, Brace & Co., 1924.

*HYMAN, S. E., *The Armed Vision*. New York: Alfred A. Knopf, Inc., 1948. Paperback: Vintage Books, Alfred A. Knopf, Inc.

*JARRELL, RANDALL, *Poetry and the Age*. Vintage Books, Alfred A. Knopf, Inc.

KERMODE, FRANK, *Romantic Image*. London: Routledge & Kegan Paul, Ltd., 1957.

LANGBAUM, ROBERT, *The Poetry of Experience: The Dramatic Monologue in Modern Literary Tradition*. London: Chatto & Windus, 1957.

LEAVIS, F. R., *The Common Pursuit*. London: Chatto & Windus, 1952.

———, *New Bearings in English Poetry*. Rev. ed.; London: Chatto & Windus, 1932.

LOWELL, AMY, *Tendencies in Modern American Poetry*. New York: The Macmillan Co., 1917.

MATTHIESSEN, F. O., *American Renaissance*. New York: Oxford University Press, Inc., 1941.

MINER, EARL, *The Japanese Tradition in British and American Literature*. Princeton, N.J.: Princeton University Press, 1958.

MONROE, HARRIET, *A Poet's Life*. New York: The Macmillan Co., 1938.

MOORE, MARIANNE, *Predilections*. New York: The Viking Press, Inc., 1955.

O'CONNOR, WILLIAM VAN, *Sense and Sensibility in Modern Poetry*. Chicago: University of Chicago Press, 1948.

QUINN, SISTER M. B., *The Metamorphic Tradition in Modern Poetry*. New Brunswick, N.J.: Rutgers University Press, 1955.

RAIZISS, SONA, *The Metaphysical Passion: Seven Modern American Poets and the Seventeenth-Century Tradition*. Philadelphia: University of Pennsylvania Press, 1952.

RANSOM, JOHN CROWE, "The Poetry of 1900–1950." *Kenyon Review,* Vol. XIII (1951), pp. 445–57.

*RICHARDS, I. A., *Practical Criticism*. New York: Harcourt, Brace & Co., 1929. Paperback: Harvest Books, Harcourt, Brace & Co.

———, *Principles of Literary Criticism*. London: Kegan Paul, Trench, Trubner. 1926.

———, *Science and Poetry*. London: Kegan Paul, Trench, Trubner, 1935.

RIDING, LAURA, and GRAVES, ROBERT, *A Survey of Modernist Poetry*. New York: Doubleday, Doran & Co., Inc., 1928.

SHAPIRO, KARL, *Beyond Criticism*. Lincoln: University of Nebraska Press, 1953.

———, *English Prosody and Modern Poetry*. Baltimore: The Johns Hopkins Press, 1947.

SITWELL, EDITH, *Aspects of Modern Poetry*. London: Gerald Duckworth, 1934.

———, *Poetry and Criticism*. New York: Henry Holt & Co., Inc., 1926.

STAUFFER, DONALD, *The Nature of Poetry*. New York: W. W. Norton & Co., Inc., 1946.

*SYMONS, ARTHUR, *The Symbolist Movement in Literature*. New York: E. P. Dutton & Co., Inc., 1918. Paperback; Dutton Everyman Paperbacks, E. P. Dutton & Co., Inc.

*TATE, ALLEN, *The Man of Letters in the Modern World*. Meridian Books, Inc.

———, *On the Limits of Poetry*. New York: The Swallow Press, 1948.

———, *Reactionary Essays on Poetry and Ideas*. New York: Charles Scribner's Sons, 1936.

———, *Reason in Madness*. London: Putnam & Co., 1941.

TAUPIN, RENÉ, *L'influence du symbolisme français sur la poésie américaine (de 1910 à 1920)*. Paris: H. Campion, 1929.

WAGGONER, H. H., *The Heel of Elohim: Science and Values in Modern American Poetry*. Norman: University of Oklahoma Press, 1950.

WARREN, ROBERT PENN, *Selected Essays*. New York: Random House, 1959.

WILDER, A. N., *Modern Poetry and the Christian Tradition*. New York: Charles Scribner's Sons, 1952.

*WILSON, EDMUND, *Axel's Castle*. New York: Charles Scribner's Sons, 1931. Paperback: Charles Scribner's Sons.

*————, ed., *The Shock of Recognition*. New York: Doubleday & Co., Inc., 1942. Paperback: Universal Library, Grossett & Dunlap, Inc.

WINTERS, YVOR, *In Defense of Reason*. Denver: The Swallow Press and New York: William Morrow & Co., Inc., 1947.

————, *The Function of Criticism: Problems and Exercises*. Denver: Alan Swallow, 1957.

BIBLIOGRAPHIES

ARMS, GEORGE, AND KUNTZ, J. M., *Poetry Explication*. Denver: The Swallow Press, 1950.

LEARY, LEWIS, ed., *Articles on American Literature Appearing in Current Periodicals*. Durham, N.C.: Duke University Press, 1955.

MILLETT, F. B., *Contemporary American Authors*. New York: Harcourt, Brace & Co., 1944.

SPILLER, R. E., *et al.*, eds., *A Literary History of the United States*. New York: The Macmillan Co., 1948. Vol. III.

TATE, ALLEN, ed., *Sixty American Poets, 1896–1944*. Rev. ed.; Washington, D.C.: Library of Congress, 1954.

ZABEL, M. D., ed., *Literary Opinion in America*. Rev. ed.; New York: Harper & Brothers, 1951. Extensive bibliography.

Index of Poets

Biographical sketches of the poets, alphabetically arranged, may be found on pages 244–256.

Index of Titles